# POEMS 2016–2024

# POEMS

## 2016–2024

## J. H. PRYNNE

BLOODAXE BOOKS

2024

ISBN: 978 1 78037 693 6 hardback edition
978 1 78037 692 9 paperback edition

First published 2024 by
Bloodaxe Books Ltd,
Eastburn,
South Park,
Hexham,
Northumberland NE46 1BS.

www.bloodaxebooks.com

Printed in Great Britain by Bell & Bain Limited, Glasgow, Scotland, on acid-free paper sourced from mills with FSC chain of custody certification.

For Erik Ulman

# Author's Note

This book is a supplementary volume to the author's *Poems* (Bloodaxe Books, third edition, 2015) including the corrected texts of 36 collections written since that edition, and published between 2017 and April 2024. The bibliography at the end of this volume gives further particulars about the original publications followed, and certain departures therefrom.

For the first publication of the collections newly reprinted here the author expresses his grateful thanks: to Ian Heames (of Face Press, Cambridge), to Justin Katko (of Critical Documents, Cambridge), to Rod Mengham (of Equipage, Cambridge), to Aaron Kent (of Broken Sleep Books, Wales), to Colin Leemarshall (of Slub Press, Seoul, South Korea), to David Grundy and Lisa Jeschke (of Materials, Cambridge) and Tony Frazer (of Shearsman Books, Bristol); and for the present volume particular thanks to Neil Astley (of Bloodaxe Books, Hexham), Ian Heames and Michael Tencer.

The cover image is a calligraphic rendering of the author's Chinese name, Pu Ling-en, made free of restriction in 2000 by the poet-scholar Che Qian-zi of Suzhou and Beijing and used here with his permission; the subsequent photographic likeness was made by Professor Wei Yao Liang of Gonville and Caius College and is used here freely on request, with his permission. The woodcut of a hoopoe at the end of the first section of *Parkland* was first printed in Conrad Gessner's *Historia animalium* (Vol. 3, 1555). It features here, inverted and with additional foliage, according to its appearance in a later edition of 1669.

# Contents

# EACH TO EACH

## (2017)

All fortune is good
– Boethius

All thinking and all thoughts are true
when there is no thinker
– W.R. Bion

## Cartoon

Eyes burning like owlets reaching filmic
attention, shadow across the face of outpost
plummet capture. To keep a head warm into
see more, quick-quick not yet seriously in
dark enough, lovers both wrapped. Alembic
clip these flicker lids filament iodine they
part into shield lucid plane, wield in front.
Did you complete assembly by slot marks in-
distinct for a brief plume staying, these
all inaugurate habit, now then. What will do
open work heart temper to gut, lights burn
brim to surge or wave a crass suiting fore-
shore. Hold fast to dial while opt readiness
candour, next blips their night-cry mounted
in socket trim, hot white partition cryolite.

## Tread-over

"The tendency of these carpels is revolved,
already foreign", aloft like nothing else
at the start above share-stairs, into line
a border of tongues. No star yet carried
up, no smell up there either, remaining
first unwanted or in respite open fancy
agreement. Sign up now, whoever says so
in the booklet of phrases, flower lights
budded in sanction, about to fall out
in a planet virus; even trepidate intook
smoke particles for the choice box, the
out sicker ice-cap. You so already do
know it, breathing hard for shop counter
declamation, all in front utter raised up
against prophecy, natal translation. Grant
the stair cutting, or yet but still timely.

## Hankering

Restive in mix purpose forwent all clamour,
by possession derogate do you want this any
next bit rented go for no less, hardly more
turns fairly too. Should you take away in
daylight, lessen our share in sortal top
resentment hanker for, more fixed stress
not greedy, how could it be known. Torrid so
to elaborate at distance make advent growing
to find enough, vacancy bestowal unfolded
its carapace; back from tender pursuit in
prescient and later, all found by logic hit
faced over to care now softening skinfold
as we have it here. Want more in way de-
scripted, banter inroads fine to line in
plenty for a trial stretch and near-broken,
sentry would remark and give over, as now.

## Relievo

Needed go down, for ready at plan attach
drive first in heart, in fast cup thrown up
over counting, stem. Lean into near promise
quickly match, mount display fair replace
to a finish revival, hold in close mind in-
side production; blent body again to landing,
go down. After sever I wanted to do it first
on, we shall hold team account, intrinsic he
told us, after small delay. Lost hardly known
in make a doorway, for novel pressure friends
arrival by grand fortune in a snap, yet down
where water sufficient patch the sill. Well
in track fame and level esteem. Try on if
rapidly forward, go on in close each moment
furnish access set-off while in several so
split and merge, all yet touching ridicule.

## Will-given

Get out and put on, hollow temper new rate, de-
lay saving foil to beam up full, for so much
in side growth forward cut the wick instantly.
Why hold up the work surface, no knowing what for
necessary exempt from care. Purpose sufficient
where invited, just patiently all beyond what's
wanted, diremption their deferred remedy; wait
now then dispersal links out to forgive, trusted.
Fixate constant at the doorway is for sharing
live to steep crisis, blink first if best do we
ignore as possible gather like clients, wise other-
wise. It's all arranged here vivid latent parent
bond on duty alert fitted, massive debate illness
resume assigned apart. Gravel surveillance all of
them remitted advance to check out or give over
all options the same wide berth, tie-blinked.

## Digress

Lighter and flighted paper device easy mill
ran to the fore insisting. It is a let portion
for departure at gaze so lift, admit flutter
why evident they'll take or lent overdue, get
spread out in vatic lamps, on them on. Claim-
ant full ration negligent, wing-flap temp
lasting better skill the multitude in frank
session along the mark tremble, now been and
gone. Oh hazard, you hamper the limit passed
to brotherhood cleft, crab-apple little tilt
fervid soon to give a task brim. Bright sips
bring forward alchemic partner, still flutter
matter glisten, that's us, go that way, they
will tender reclaimed present on a branch
visible to hesitate, light eyes as next dye
to seem so, loose. Not to take more of pro-
viso lapping, birth take its part eventually.

## Payment

Orange filling the park window or light either
further, over print to reach. To make same view
indistinct, frame the gallery distorted by wax
until near full single upward. Fastigiate refine
our open leeway, will fetch enough later on so
credulous or previous, lost on its panel. You'll
do best fit in furrow white linkage, our best
regular tempest blunt like mean to loan, far off
now away. Lift up in life until dark, winter ever
ours to say, too many have too, little or less go
to ready know. Too few dilate assignment or just
not, must retire or fasten put there's a narrow
premiss forward match up provoked in grief, in
back so stricken. Be rough acclaim go fast for,
live in want help trim search as top rudiment
spilling food, play for. Never tremble affording
trust rest remember or borrow, aid precious mail.

## Un-listed

Or often only of this will convince, many will
prefer beginning deflect but too scarce or few
to convey, is this look resigned. Well say so
after his tally, awkward surmise. His so ready
in known famine far-out spread, ask after this
never docile most of them in purpose allusive
and lined up. Mere under-water they do too many
or will justly, ever how prepare, to rise of con-
tested succession and sure, by awe confined. As
for so little to wait, a swelled hope blister
ill burning for broken issue, untwist. He will
know by admission seldom random but pass enough,
isn't tenuous evenly shared and best first, in-
signia. Dilute break-point level action livid
entire as her donation protected by pattern of
cheek, absorbed frequent all inferred and given
by more choice, by voice and sub-tested, able.

## Permission

Clastic alpine or simplify further born off
size motion, grow giddy heart our tempest agree
inclusive tier rung, world arbiter. Provision
even slide out back, along the top. Collapse not
eating broken gut fronted oh brevity to capture,
to ours brought absolute. You in part licence
for its risk to know in flow bereft, it is for
misery that counts and cannot await fluent lock
offensive prefer. Debit seizure own brain dis-
turbed cut back briskly all of their refusal,
chew up willing, would be better. Late finish
to fly, abstain has by as ever recognise, for
true party at once buoyant; tight to floating
a grippage torrent in forage presentation, will
affix new side go to tell short and mute. Inlet
is meant by age passion, live banish aftermath
often fast to care, worn up free elude its win.

## Ground-up

Glaze away foremost inside disputed daytime
with the others, accurately in ferment. In both
to say this turn about, fortify a casual note
or be blamed before. Know why already in beside
a fault of temper, accrued for show slim benefit
out to flow, desirous fault covalent assiduous
virtue made true. Never yet do this, as tract
or burn the entry fuse, promote to a fault when-
ever under floating saved off and through lee
divisive privilege. Not for you further come in
take on as free in portion aspect to go round,
habitual debris alight torsion. Or done tremor,
the frame hardly right and worn even, found
to sink attract set on ground review, evident so
yours for change from fear tremblant chatter;
choose to melt craving via offset and uniform.

## Travertine

For the traverse then extended turning stairs
at body-search into resume, step out win folds
or brisk the path risen courtly; elbow slice
attaching for list. Never pantiles yet foremost
to partnered their corolla both limits each bite
sheer will trample headed text, purchase what
relives inspection. Will fix its mantel. Braced
matter parting fair crest in favour, probable by
any much less provided. Or like holding a hand
outward palm centred overt taper, mission now
forbid them. Voice shaking to likeness stain
as for side planted above, by each other plying
almost figured cheeks, no little temper offence.

## In-fail

Have a say by inviolate reversion in forty
of induce what's left uncovered will premium,
the road rail and fit to spin, they are over
trivial custom. Would they not several permit
inducement for adjust at a price captive agree
fracture, have a line as well solitary offer, a
break out. Like broad like winter, writ along
on foam in form, seem appliance glisten civil
marvel at the edge to stream. Haven't in sight
incident mostly sent, on the rock pallor exit
in fury foretold incline. Affirm your acrid bit
seal a tongue to intimate if not improve, mock
compel the way fine met to seek and set off,
persistent minimal encounter. Lofty, there will
since be extra reducement. Clap eyes surface
you to go and be risen, improving clinic inform
welfare how to give, each never yet in failure.

## Attenuate

Telling them square, no cake no butter worth
trouble to look for, intervals flecked with
subject draw back accurate, tariff settlement.
Quote the rate quite late-floating little bill,
double in pair surplus annoy fry for single
glory ahead. Bin beware relative or reckless
wait right there fleet attention, measured out
tread into darkness mention lift this. Nest
to weave at sea-bed acquittal, by omission we
gilded almost the brim to vote in exercise
harness; be wary not silky hoity-toity blight,
along the dew-line. They will or might sequence
this wide attenuating pair bond restriction,
mirror tint your way to say abandon, trum-
pets sounding across, dove wings emulsion.

## Oh-brow

Limb graven by another patch, due over breach
of care to sail in moment masquerade. Tissue
grain project alike this familiar, visit wreck
under necklace, certain bells agreeing. Climb
to match or reach, ready pungent to mouth music
frivolous echo, refrain roofing you told us both
this had to be until used up, replete. Coil for
ready put in place sung parts tidy to finish, in
furtive delirium. Pitch no more the night watch
simmers belated from a window well hooded below,
rank to taste and repair pass his honour chord.
After to meet, go across and step down minding
her face shining with joy run up to even brow,
sprung to meet those in yet afford, grace to
deny as ready wealth shrivels and wasted. It's
common to view, practiced not ever coy the top
reckoning exceeds priority at the inmost touch.

## Sweetness

Cry out were they come to this lissom on
return primal allocation, never yet even
by step manage. First wrist by now civic
fill or repair, would you care to be, chill
sell-out, overture. Play to fit incident
stop not sudden error horizon, declare true
long perplexity. Tell so local willing yet
demeanour in principle, buy over mistake
restrict the neck. Annex future inclining
ex concession by increment and see fairly
from where, from when so. Stay up all by
summoned delegate humour, love persistent
whose breathing, hardly a sound revealed
before. Prefix repeal amendment, milder
transit gives way for quiet protection,
hives of folding pallet converse to found.

## Generate

Partial grateful near to complete bell audible
touch the filling sign to solve impatience, gift
to come through now: contra terror your ear-flaps
risen, telling you. Go with seen table for usual
entrainment, love no less select a plea; your crest
forward value brings along what more a likeness
added across to bind in sound, play. On serve
laden with prime equipment all full most not
yours for start repair greeting, to climb over
well in place from the front. Look ahead fallen
tracks not yet back to bear enhanced tremor, more
recognised by each case you'll see its beauty
fashion slight and vivid. The notes slide to come
home deserved by succession ready to be glad, if
able to steer to hidden shore early after plain.

## Set-price

What's to count held to it or void level nor
we see assenting compulsive replacement, in
sea-lane perspective lives on a thread, again.
None in clearance mouth working to have or if
not, probable lame calamity. Accept either one,
settle down lower for to give the party active
in circular forbear current, meat and drink
to visit. Blank reflection wherever pays off
your way by credit for merit do needful speed
for breath leaving repair; strip wealth furnace
to make smoke in glass, the grassy bank at full
length. Who said this at ease massive space
confined by dispute own-brand. Get up straight
quick, infirm meat pressure water watching, in
help to fly bread at new price now disturbed.

## Singular

Will they main be lonely, figure out aver
the delay of it, will they, early or wanted,
at or back loving flexible seam for a glance
intense adopt the way. Attend footing into
need did deprive, did they modify parallel
rights to whom after long, to fray they said
slowly release by fusion solo under score on
the water. On less surrender pause here by
chance adjourn, soon will turn by not without
or hardly random invested to cancel; so for
another's trial, greed notify line by line at
deck wanting, virtual replace plainly. Will
be again turn back time in tune, mend up the
play of shades or half pacified; alarm upon
fading to need less and believe will come
to this such, along shaken to go far interim.

## Acute-yet

Lapis on board spruce to freeze while wavering
silently understood, tell, fill, accomplish mix
in company lean to stem. White steam submission
my name-mark, down as stone step keep his
sharp manifest soak, provoke occasional con-
cession their right of your reference slip.
Swivel the oven to lid fold, offer fair glimpse
then full down on the plate, leather not strict.
Give to have the more self-open flex multiply,
brood despite park neighbour, bed and board
remit, strung up more tight to strike a note
true; flow in hand to meet what you do, fill
and tell the otherhood in near view. All will,
well to fore milling, the torrent in spillway
leans by this unfinished loop, disclose to match
and watch, fission instilled already you know
such as often many versions clarified before.

## The-troop

Reside to put, another invited fine raiment,
nothing solo positive in person all I want
half-seen waning a mark displayed. Will do by
set train conviction, unction whether due for
donative arm outflung who is, the third pre-
vious loving beside beyond or above. Finish
bound salvage so large, faint rescue the whole
troop. Undeleted crown they do want, so far
to go for, build on this you cannot reach out
otherwise less in care, all known what-not
by a ribbon joined. Why not enough yet will
expect no even share out to smooth level,
unreason reads as the same entry, to come in
late too much. Residual slack ignorance, its
neglect clear to sense of appointment, bears
the open mark not to shirk benefit spilled
wanting at least note for note orchestral.

## Below-cost

Played out grievous too much forbid portent
to satisfy, plug justifies by eye-shade fort
say give way by admission, yes. Numerous come
in for room from the back or side, water-proof
frown over a mile crowned and free. On-fire in
a door space on the floor, veridical mapped
or withstood, no defence or surface travel fee
inspect at the gate often soon; never late in
broken excuse surrender before seen compulsion,
it's fully known in advance judgement, as all
for measure out of reserve. Whether of front
or most extra to discover, each one eager and
peaceful, loosen not to hold too familiar limit;
see yourself forgiven why in credence wait
to allay the means given out, balance at cost.

## Whether-so

Prolific comes to this, system joined across
because it has to equalise, match both sides
in casting overhead, filter. What recognises
will be rising high on credit, scaffold untold
or let float, shall be assumed as a gift. Cannot
walk dip specific young forage, let go by to
its cast in hot metal length. Right found out as
slant light piled upwards in tight hand admit
over promise, that wanted to listen heartfelt
bringing together, birdlike. Then as well set
in form so locked, in front not lost initial
is evident to nurture and garnish; at the sea-
way to loose brow strike, hit and set attest
ever prolate civic in hopes for more at least,
and burnish the catch its merit elevate over
by stride ahead: take a shine and hold it.

## En-voy

Turn or discern again, or fully come above
longing by carriage for blame at known is
surely told, to cultivate for hunger lesson
damage to joy welling out to precious spill.
Up to account so meant to stand over by in
measure all for reckon up first and least
spare; this way current upper now, affirm,
not yet withholding any by yours or mine.

# OF · THE · ABYSS

## (2017)

## ABYSS : 1

Lead-glance ranking, plank splintered in turn
alone to want living forward, across desert
attending traffic long possible fleet in late
averse to vessel still foremost child penchant,
many after all displayed fluke after, in the roof
cling disbar galena by instance, it must be
flood even so trimmed up as all the rest, flow
all at last better, to crown for sure, for shore
traffic now alight go in open find. All found
they cry out echo mine no reaching before paid
star why not, guardian of truth entire and whole.
Billow under below known sat follow, happen so
to make thwart leaden fine to fasten up as
yes taken back, given to yield or space hold
to later denounce grave enough smiling in
turn the face back now, derelict ecstatic fee
advance never clear rack, the inclination pack
mouth breath wide, slight gasp for air what is
known here found all down, all child eyes
wide too, prow stove in cold leading outward
flake to glitter certain and sure, all ever
known down and reach to ready for gone shine
far out ported beyond, rate and known.

## ABYSS : 2

At least given up for, cause loose in choke
for breath-turn now soaked as discovery will
let and leave both in the way marine inside
cash and crash, fast torment. Let for this
so casual flourish for spray passage sloop
younger by far all of say to know, going like
this granted no favour, affective turn a clip
in such want. Relic custodian leaving over
too ardent, too much as just so. Fluent ask
in grasp for air light willing, hold the child
out first, our ransom list and lost bear this
plain enough. Not for frantic little from that
know this at brim cracked up in daylight pro-
file visible the cries distant lurk to chill
bet to know past hearing, amplitude wave narrow
crested at this driven. Below trace steerage
run of doubt go down to it, to make sink or
swallow, past bearing out now, our guest limit
afforded to break, knowing so. In vital offer
detachment separable inexpensive all wasteful
across this shiny-bright horizon laid out.

## ABYSS : 3

Face past sovereign saline off course where
burden going not even eaten, look forward
strangely and silent now later don't think
broken left out matchwood, to hold. The idea
at least in bright glow not now reversed,
link given away could you or they know better,
fast trial tell me this waiting insurgent
casework incline back severed you can see
not when here you know not to make it that
yes we do, they must also, famous already.
Breath cheaper by us for them for us too,
foreign tongues oblivious matching what
can be got out of it, evasion each day at
a time of mind, incentive. To be forgiven
quickly while yet born in desertion, not
back from here, scarce forward this one
time or think other, riding out lax what's
left over you see we do as of no choice,
overt prospected impact. Reared up surface
past our view in fright-line, low shadow
breath clasp how so how not same to say
give way you think they'd know. Do they,
hard to say even now face frozen unbelief
in mark past all can see to know, agree
without other cue immense for water ours
unlaced and not seen. Set down lock plain
to argue no further well over immobile
by light of life exit let, out. Mit with
this lit, little else child care, finish.

## ABYSS : 4

Lead on up to set elated in fear yet broken,
is breath-hold silent as own down or for
paid out clustered forward or then quiet
over again, wait more. Lift to load far so
upmost over, more over or merge out and out
bewildered with all high wind in tightness,
make the far line frozen to cloud-banks,
even though once to recognise you do must
know for them however beyond hunger, market
as why or not. Only some will, too young
many are held over outwith even fear blowing
up welling, hand to hand grasp distant, far
off. Perspect born again why no cry not
to hear you know all for sure and ready
stop. Cannot this no line out give back
just too many over, rock level thrown fixity
to release the cleat promissory already,
narrow hollow word counting going back no
return portion over-blown to say so. Go
shares in surge lifting evenly more shake
increase beyond belief the clear admission
makes no sound, wind bearing up in flight.

## ABYSS : 5

Coast forecast heavy despite rising to storm
and rain poured from the dish we hold it
upmost steady to tilt offense skill top-up
lavish justification, save and protect gainst
all disaster to sing and or bleat bloated
a stricken boatload far out to scan can you
see riding and pitched at limit of turmoil
right up hoop this cask breaking foam consume
with demerit thrown back, engine from little
fuel drop silent, now then or never. The swell
capsule beyond breakwater lofty like lords
of chance, dark glances not to trawl for it,
dazzle yet in reserve. Service within swift
wet the throat slip word after this pursued.
In alcove lifting brow declining later frieze
disporting in plain view riot, if not why not.
Tension rig across knuckle too visible and
child-like, small narrow faces up-turned cup-
cake ice in crevice blown away further now
beyond image or reach pay for it, or not.
Upfront in small relief, life-savings save
little enough skim off all there is, now.
Afford the child each over lost over late,
in blink redemption gripped together peal
to us ever beyond you see and agree partly
go back on words given out unchosen, a
day trade. Of course too many steered out
cheap expanse massive expense too grind
your teeth in cause of certainly frail off-
chance decree outlook from sure aversion,
off-shore multitude.

# ABYSS : 6

Oh strike the light, float the boat, for
sake of common peril they are fallen away
as gathered up in sight of lamentable in-
difference and will go down against us, the
birds have flown, break speed this blithe
boat fled, weapon unwilling guard the sure
place radiant with possession save up go
down ignore, in such wide eyes. A flute
drifted in darkness as engulfed without
pleat over plaint ever pitch no bird on
no wing we are the wing broken as to see
waves of longing rise and turn face up
o'er-brim their clammy cells out from
the shelf undertow and follow, no way
thronged hunger and thirst this is our
cold reckoning, ours to keep and hold
close to instinct saving allotment look
and see clear enough. Sound far off, not
heard fingers remote all one at distance
blurred, we can choose diminishment and
off course so we do renounce our known
scope hopeless for this, a surd inward
and plentiful, more loyal as outlook
durable exception exempted and previous,
not to try to turn back, look away, one
after this another, hers and mine said
sunk to the line no spare and then over,
all over this canopy still dark close up
in focus spread, glance instead now,
mothers perfect omission retrieval.

# ABYSS : 7

Rapt be joyful next scatter as ash to throat
antic promise delivery reception no record
barely enough to patch and mend play at this
why not shield the eyes light harsh or better
glare who knows to give close at fringe all
screwed up tight to wrench swaying hull in
currency, part-exchange turbulent and factive
provision. Knowledge in report is entire
evident whimper more not excused how could
otherwise caught up hear spoken who could
say for sure when see less, no more. Facile
drowned in hope don't say it furious but
then what, in the end all one constricted
joint throat clamour don't not speak later
on this same fusion saving breath what's
left at limit trim. Yes they will drown it's
commonplace, unbearable look to side-on,
torn wave-length hunger the least expel
no anger now, childish first near finish
up in debt beyond reason or meaning all
should pay, mandate, all scraps can be done
quick enough not in time work the blame
later and latterly, take more instant preen
to wrestle each a qualm, a certain mind-off.
Aggrieved by answer not willing, wide eyes
motionless not seen or in wake heaving up
to swallow, all-over, your valid ticket ex-
humed in expiry why yours since none else,
look around the voyage out or back to back
and chill. Borrow to harrow burnish any
in reason its ransom glitter pack.

## ABYSS : 8

So out far for granted, early nostrum uncertain
breakwater volunteer dainty steps at the print,
footfall laid away deeper over odds pay more.
As to fate no rate cite and play forsake say
still, rock of age surpassed. As from desert
afforded heat expiring then bitter instant frail
decree, slow and slower for notice outward ask
why for joy gone down at floor a keepsake spread.
Look shall now in cost to count hireling shepherd
sea-blind scoop the light ahead, and yet no light
propitious shone. Chill rain out from gull as
gulled all known, not hidden a child could link
before blinking, better not try to say, what all
must know as by far in seen unsaid. Tongue glued
to the roof of discretion, count up the score
line and wafted to reckon when will that be by
the bell wave-length unarrive. All sure as ever
paid crossing out lead us at a glance the tent
of avarice invites grief in advance, for some
less hopeless discount, work this out. You know
we know unsure and fix on this, our plinth right-
ful plain to see, says no-fault action blame
back broken uncounting on child care just read
all about it not our turn, call-blind, eyelash.

## ABYSS : 9

Then at acquirement so still keep quiet now
and now all so buy-out each time for some
only, no knowing release both in wave random
the day across. Slight pulse prior race shrill
once to his fishing for more they'll wait
as must for protection in sky-trails, still
in clouds bitten, rain blowing up faint murmur
than sound funnel together, all's every one.
Mother holds them kneeling don't move out low
back to back too low already. Or head count,
half-space by now visible small did emphasise
and also must do this, can see dare not edge
flare as first temper. Anyway obvious tell
as will, young seeds in water all found sub-
merged to elevate parent shielding can you
see this despite the payment brief, ransom
engine lash the tiller. Hold all our own
breath on this behalf, of constant more
for less. Frame close to break-point don't
reach for be still and know in fault yours
and mine, small eyes peering, what else.
Don't imagine what's next up, link entire
voyage tremble for front view, look there.
Shade small eyes at the blows replaced, at
face value, how it looks is all there what
is known unsure, too clear shall be so, fre-
quent day after day on clear notice say
breathing hard, soundless for evermore.

## ABYSS : 10

Never make it on, scale willing already late
band sisters punish stream to fate hanging
by thread hungry to moist bread lucky at that.
Parenthood no let go to irrigate we sprinkle
where attainment little shoes have bare enough
finish amplify helm intersected get first reveal
or file calm, to watch or pledge, pay more.
Picotee first choice if not lasting wavy lines
sip you claim you will exempt all at the shore-
sign not taken up can't be lifted, far this time
good by as now where every self-seen one, loan
after another fright quiet freight wipe the face
hush now eyelids upraised no landing nearly
in guard almost clear stay silent or sit more
tight in row after row, murmuring. It's true
all do knowing more or less, tread aside, write
a caption below the blue line wavy to show,
illustrious. But later still the same too,
telling up to sky-park, slanting rays in shadow
added unlasting wait the chance riven see true,
running out cover our eyes spare onwards ex-
change for broken lift and lost, again.

# OR SCISSEL

# (2018)

'Dost Dialogue with thy shadow?'
- *Timon of Athens*

## All Such to Life

All such to life consuming
        as all were true
in air passing and lifted
        besprent with dew

Nor lavish nor in unison
        even at the shore
for giving its world over
        for this and more

By leaf turning, its colour
        so clear to find
in itself its fond allure
        to love assigned

Such voices set fiery
        within, and through
the field of folk unwary
        in shape as true

## Close Shorn

Close shorn, give enough granulate
        ever to calm or assemble
unstricken, by company resting,
        arms folded for so as can

Who would in readiness turning
        to maintain the line
of breath out to then clarify
        in jacket new yet worn

Suit yourself they say as plentiful
        uninterrupted, aspired win
powder reception they freely do
        so frequently now be seen

All forward then uppermostly
        hold out, to save other tame
detachment, from main body temper
        in season coming to term

## Sweet Vernal

Went to mow a meadow, extended grasses
        in scrap cut down, swiftly
down and down. Bent to lie, scented
        cry hay vocal for quick in a box
as if so never let go.

Take good incremental surplus up
        steady parallel concise, fixed
to expect completion not childish
        count, went, sweet vernal far
and freely even for far away.

For see the moon remounted in favour,
        bright in its day-box, yet to play
just one silicon bonding dilatancy
        pack and fold, here to single out
any good reason, first off to be.

## Beyond Doubt

Lace over to search the part ready-made
by sentiment ever for and so for
to easement in despite, to call
in provocation hearing the short cry
all to make ready all beyond doubt
mix and restore, severally utter
even though newly wishful retain.

See further, see link alignment
repairing to measure the cost
of finding truly when to recognise
how swiftly & gainful it could be done:
patch to discretion, refinement
individually next already in sealant

attach across reflected morning light.
No anthem mostly discovers this
single type, aver openly set down
to bring back, outlying custody
in colour revetment, remission
not well in purpose fortuitous; so
marked for display, never so fair,
by credit of melody in session taken.

All the way by glances, line and shout
without manufacture however soon
to rising brilliant departure, snap fast
a child's permission; don't yet care
for act to vanish, prefer both of them
immoderately. Persistent or now
ambulant attain the flow partition.

Glaucous rosette in mastery, in profile
as catch in the throat dividing
how to part up-front, assented trifle
pardon this chill. Whether of two inform
bone retraction catch advance, gather up
category spill ahead they will do it
to mitigate the doorstep plantation.

## To Eye Apart

To eye apart fine arrow key you know leaf
greeted in fading search ahead, acres ready
set aside, nothing happens here. Eyebrow
lucid to miss low density, synthetic honey
spread remember within walled crannies: fork
up paint both hands, manner graft to pack
by willing sips, stand up, nocturnal at beat
first. As besides termly will either, neither.

## Platform

Straw promise to vowel, up then why or be
forward on bind,
                        advent kind rested fare so
          by for, in the by of
          leaving over, and must
                        declare did telluric
          agree for the consort partner ahead,
stem will accept as raised to a latch
offended on its ground near equal. The level

says, how many chopped cell forms want
          profuse redolent capture, risk attach
                        link to match in start at twin
          limbic falls, go to further lets be
attend, accept reflecting promote so, yes accept
                        is soon wake or grant

along the present invited retroflex hang over
          sky turning to this, visible succession
                        plays for cost permit
          in fever, open must mark eyes now
outermost earthen flaw give mine the rest.

## Others Will

Carmine slept underneath provision, or we too
not reluctant evenly displaced the whole intimate
fuse cancel syllable, to this depending ever yet
rigid. Arrive to take flame induced, at impasse
settle quickly surface bail in a novel temper fob
give it back full amount ours to say, first esteem
corundum tooth exchange. Bone easy acquaint
in a surgical detachment, all crowded forward
to liken blemish aquamarine at limit restore
for so for mischief, the whole time. Likely insert
finish now and next by effort splint to relative
fugal and wipe, clear and down. Gain seed-time
advancement generous option, share margin on
pulse unmatched or not yet, at least batty foreign
allow expulsion. Indeed should we next assign
what comes to finish nearby, so to merge, roofed
over tin foil guarantee in purpose of colour,
dredge in advance signal clip. Would do both gap
settlement to be seen overtly, aspect trim up
to stitch, up to snuff. Long awaited for good reason,
part for part cut finely cheer acceptance aspect
foremost even relative, to point best allocate, to
claim anyway. How is this known, to amount in
late perspective one for neither, rise up or try
arrival as others will, or do. Mercurial finish
all of them marking in place of refuge better late
than for vision earlier dent, traffic. Reflective
tremor in flashes, margin brilliance out to sea
flim-flam grateful well back nipping across
highlights. At ready fashion outwards familiar
pass to passion, motion interrupted whose turn
wants less for more, unless late fusion will.

## Each New Retort

Apart estate limit hooding frame to go for list over, their keel apt in cut manner why elated preventive, further on. Resemble the whole time, on a side provided, degree assimilate master pleading, its known plane loose to meet. Exactly brave out, not yet so soon to call a long cost observance, interlude set by marker unmissed, inaction. May wait until each new retort best anecdote tell their own dispersal cautionary, luminary pitch to part market, did you. The over deep farewell risk in semblance, all of rate visit to be first periodic welcome, in rain yet track of its horror benefit refused payment. Cloud uplift stack in order trim and eager, breath for hers and ours. Together ajoinment relic partition, every next moment donated in what they found for repair, their best mixture. Keyboard start back in notice, again like this, culminate incident parenthood. They all grow in frame on a side generous mimicry, all in good time.

## Dashboard Flowing

Rasp to pinnacle dashboard flowing, in glow
of like seclusion, this will prolong its near
measurement in top after its best array. To be
noticed bright flank refit assuming, glimmer
in cornea engrossed to tilt, its tendency be-
side its own vested motion, fast enough even
by matching settlement. All will run amounting
to its fit low parallel, chorus fleet approving
by time of rapt enclosure: forward before back
then both above each other, can so better, be
graded ahead. Be sure to trace a complementary
fuse path, as will sink to a ground uplift;
lean on this vantage, strike margin checks at
count for credit in passion submiss, give or
be given outwardly. By flow who would know
this at once, phosphor insertion gradual runs
to completion, yield ready otherwise to save
as opportune. From the heart valve dash down
so below at threshold search, convergently
by friendship, blow to vanity. Open ridges
to trace and face in needful acceptance, to
sing and run parlance presumed to each by
life idiom, quickly and early concession; eye
to assimilate radiance, in perfusion of known
brow terminal, all-over peak coverage affront.
Shelter while still in reach. Adjust by matched
data off to discover leverage evenly prefigured,
to set fully the crest by entrance markings.
It's to be known as would fold up before hand
signal, reduce dismay to minimum browbeaten
improvement, gauge what's now visible to field
in pointed focus evoked–all the runners admit
this consigned better finish, ahead of reward.

## Darting

Previous and virtual now absorbed into a self
at large as fluent across the bound there allowed,
in course of fed with tributary not optimal but so
retrieved. Beyond insistent convergent is can be
ready, darting withhold, delay for donative you will
cancel presumed listen, feature outward. To why
or not livid brow lapped to a reach, sit in circle
will be soon enough spoken of this, open passage
burnt in unclaimed flash demise. All to meet there
so in row to bereft passion enclosure, flow in sorrow
past headwater make a dent abruptly, go better by
cured bacon included now first. The others in lane
give not silently, the task in stolid recognition even
yet to resist a clamour grievance. Crowd beyond in
large at the gateway, instrument to break by waiting
in unitary harmonics probable no less. Forgiven been
abrasive nearly alleged of plural to breathe or ahead
from pressure, side to side approaching hold back
the treat foremost, to be known. Open the flap pre-
cautionary versed incision, to listen however will be
operant in mass acceptance, must both so for sure
quickly prepare by abandoned light cone. You know
inflamed with attraction justly in time, our time
only perhaps, on a ledge fastened. The reason desired
will be enough, rolled out did you say in want, well
dream yet so below, hardship visible. Look there,
see to know, to go truly previous and virtual, yes.

## Not Far

In a cross light yet forward for latency
met front lit over surreptitious again torn,
their plenish counter primate, scramble
try to speed diminish, led to brilliance.
Why or not excepting the promise fortune, as
well keep denial affection, scripted marker
affirm, all can part. Leafy shadow slips
cheek insidious hardly what's to listen, if
balance restored. Evident compression does
completely make sufficient arch to brow,
trefoil shining low down by the foot print
purchase revenue, aromatic sonic precedent
amounts to and neat beside the same or as
not far off. Fibre root shiny packing, when
found in pasture light-crushed volatile
slice to allocate a strip pacing, advance
to first place once pattern tread. Likely
or end reach the back light shadow play,
in bended compensation absterge revoke
all of their relish: eyebright see better
what goes on ahead.

## Wait to Arrive

Another seldom profuse retracted entire, in total
reclaimed running on forward slightly undeterred
or at least to be made up to full crescent foil. You
know foremost led invention this and next advent
reach out aspect product we know by hollow marking
conjecture, likelihood. Crush abstemious contrary
for all mortalism ready in line to take, to make
aware if listen well, to the onrush. Immense toy
of fancy press-stud variant, give back rescript
or massive exchange dispute. She will, she shows
the whole payoff, run close to title deed tantrum,
agile delirious fortify pressure to ex-limit margin,
wait to arrive first and for stay over like elfin tracks
in brazen near reluctance; admonished in recovery.
Confer with shared instinct, outside in shade deeper,
mend the gate, new at its task. Decree for under dark
pursuit envisage as in tank stored first protection,
ever right, ever known, condensed. Give a chance ahead
to miss a beat, street dropped alert in knife plumage,
meet to skim fairly in true uppermost acumen.

# Last Pressure Outcry

Said both on arrival as negligence reversed, to uncover
this with branches fallen and strewn, how else make dif-
ferent paths for them, pacify the headland shelter. Will
this be enough alert, crested by permission unreached,
locked in with shares deemed in readiness, further even.
Can be grasped for right converging allergy, for back
tendence as remission was it, cold humour in the turn
of earth to grade and meet alternate. Never default
in heart new in place, old seen there, price out. Up-
ended did you before concession, to give where lost hardly,
nil final attach sub-loyal this time make early deliver
at incident descent all will give to ford of a stream,
will know and justify by review absolute. At any time
of purpose approaching closer, hold out promise elected
to float in cloud billows, so many at contrast for courage
in title to generate the similar rocking path sensible.
Or in page not finish, fish spool will reach welkin, margin
can only amount to both at the pair-threshold, with
threaded clamour this too will outreach itself, to close
the passage against its own default. Will gather motion
against break in force, estoppel to look back utter
the name lost onwards to refund, offensive payment held
in check before all arriving surrender, above all weapon
to see and weep, there. Never less, for the last pressure
outcry, room for company conflicted average for start,
shallow breathing foreknown in limit prevailed, infold,
angle. Diverging set to accept by tune variance, wanted.

## Nor Than

Nor than double, open suffix to overturn new
patent to go there, saving beside or left on,
accepted precious for unturned did you reach
at last to meet; none alone take limit take
mine to ground, recently make fail pitching
monotone remission, for finish crowd compose
your roof. Will believe attending trial base
trail alongside to ban the way and slide over
nor lost nor broken, off lesson at cost ever
lose in sunny rising, its ream statistic by
fast trill risen in premiss there. Likeness
through to cut a path, cover service telling
pale to prowl below; bordering to miss his
fanatic crawlers without trace pack recourse,
leaving in deflection later yes across both
maps stripped in count freely, mile upon mile.

## How Smart We Are

As ever still how smart we are, to come, to linger
as slow as daylight lasts each for respite, known
and even unknown, light the way. Bounty in plenty
up to pass by the revenue silence or close, founded
within above, given fast by choice, dotted notation
come to this by a line referred. Ember in mind, ash
wind-blown under marked brow and brushed back, never
cancel if time allows foretelling, buoyant to search
profoundly under foot would it be, by now. Lay out
in care wish to single by solo integrated life-spell
all light of morning, know better, meeting the range
with sibling trachea uncorrupted. Along the pathway
the creatures guide us, intent to wind and find, by
this case after that, pattern flow in cloud equal
to watch, laminate over the path heretofore glided up
and foregone; blood foray occlusive indignant careened
for just employ and scare, for clip where in dismay
no faring as well, so to go, on.

## Queue Up

Rife and solemn where they part, catching
in time by order, of level polity; wait
in turn, the rest will reach to grant
accord compelled by residue beside entail
forfeit dark planet, optimal in company.
What's left to reckon one by one the further
cranky branch, limit first indulge abstain
in warranty. Go by the same track-marks.
Brow in fetch amounts to discreet arrival,
watch divided manifold, infill. Brim over
reduction shortage holds steady circuitry,
not urgent but dutiful seen from the front.
First come entrancement, open door pursuit,
key-fast. Extra to gravity swung inward,
aside voices arrest by note provision have
been there in purpose fashion, suffix en-
hancement. Is that amusement to hit marking
on the axis or further still, in bid for
levity has been part for whole, rest for
remainder, now all found. Example given
and taken, allowance trod down to ground
additive mission was it, unless the target
defeats its own singular investment.
They queue up for a share, over to claim
by allocation, who would that be by civil
solid grasp infirm or not, no difference.
Matter to crumple at loss to cross its own
level or limit view, up to partner in go
first then later, turn about the headland,
there. Did or done at brow escapade, even
solemn antic prorogue its continuance,
wind and weather permitting. Grandiose
talk to make advancement, all risks set
to subdue their own natural offence.

## Cut and Stitch

Shake by word and both, for this or these right
before the avenue, in colour to match up and for
concession flame arising, flicker if random as
not seldom, the parameter all soluble never be
even in part at the riser. Restore mostly the
same reproof, ready in line for sweet scarlet
arm and leg, spoken like the first arrival yet
even to mend and concede, know why and so know
less, put in place. Don't consume too soon by
expected parentage, with to mask the children
wait as latent patience to bridge their chance
as before was set in line, this way up. Casual
moment steadfast to reach in for desire, into
the front lighter, the same colour. Suited by
its regular match, looking easily good and even
for what's to mark incident, in a standing off
back to reach so far as ever, as trim to quite
fit near enough. Selection measure forthwith
more calm now, to yield by free will pleasing
on the whole review, of discovery so to forbear
lighted up, shared out. Along the avenue first
the entire train pieces together yes willing
be there resemble crystal top-up attachment
to be next ready amendment enlarging fulsome
entangled cut and stitch, sample. Even so all
due lineage, enough by sill bonding, to let
or fit each way suture patch further, into
whether the same or close. Grasp yet to need,
need to observe, perfectly serious cryptic
even when fully wakeful, count the cost with
limit masking withheld.

## Yet Why Not

Never or, will to it, or nerve throw past most
over soon after, and grasp again offensive
likely before over mud downwards cut, snip
relative next to time beset play genuine it
break: out by remiss ever sever gastric flux
do for provide, gainful lax all never acute
assert at more elate better still. Instinct
by step cost not for before to press or grill
tell strike blood flatter runoff, lever assort
it piecemeal, assent to deduct mud in grind
both under anterior the step previous stop
ever to ever. To ever step will decline for
one to meek repair furtive, few than certain
angular saw, in drive term relation or so
frequent casual fit. All not chosen pit limit
disfigure, late fill near total better wait
party to quick, not early river custom,
tepid and flow. Insist did rim-perfect as
few ever will before not soon, holding wrist
in front, look back taken. Rapid converse to
apex get climate some to die even before pat
list, shunt up weather climax remittance
flex not yet, ready. Up to step never level
incline wanted, condign else in gene pair
be for return upper parkline, all in sudden
afford to run. Ever not even not so ready
tacit permit, later outflow emit the step
will break will over will, not or so yet it
in this permissible livelihood.

## Lark Advent

Bar first and second therefore climb or tell
to over tame any and firm, late mine inform
for ready, near torn to hand, leave now upset
do serious soft starving, prefigure ulterior;
Sweet to listen, use mesh caress both folded
tideway grant why, furnish stay this to ever
finish or famish until avid work file availed
in swathe impure, split up, vision abrogate;
Of blame at black tops careen to fault, pine
by share taken muted duct, us so to entail
as shall we, but canted over in thin limit, to
return score access agree banish, quicklier;
Racing to hand, un-laid late bite as braving
Wild reject obtuse thrown down whenever on.

## Zinc Option

And despite twin to gem in such placement,
along the sun-drift, at the turn nearby run
across it with a soft tremor galvanised even
high and brittle; splinter alteration all known
beyond range incessant as slower for removal,
perish in parallel, squared off. Indignant both
in stock over elevate without pause for dial
later before due moment, perfunctory if by
measuring zinc option, beyond the gem-tilt
ice crevasse. Not reluctant by match willing
as would all be or variable; button furnace
steel chasing, defect for prospect indexical
home on the range in company expected abate-
ment accession roaming sense acknowledge,
make pack and fasten. Refract fully possible
to get close, alternate dispossession to
the upper frank reach, brow in mark not yet
or notable, in quake hot furnace new-broken,
offended. Declare vertical certain pitch
want no more for hunger makes contortion on
every side, despite censure or because of
its absence, to pay entirely on the nail ahead,
open. Weld inlay dangerous to carry forward,
deal unfound until by surprise uncovered,
on the floor keep up: necessary parclose. How
otherwise deal fair or first before, go there
extenuate by staunch prior permission, your
feet dangling.

## Main-stream

Necrotic valency, this time round the flaw
placed first, inculcate latent chances, suf-
fusion by issuance merit advance, simulate
aversion: has surmounted obstinacy before.
Delinquent fluid settle instilled, monitor
hardly grimace, top-most. Let be accepted
on charge, relative to holding maximum in
main-stream trivial parsimony grip tight,
warrant the distance defeated at a random
walk, room for elbow in judgement arrested;
prompt for search primal retention, path
to border the stream bed, never scruple
to drain the wound's slight closure with
incentive add to leave; incremental record
foretold and ascertained by dressing, care
for sentience dig out a trench and shutter
it you'll see fast. In promise observe
closely, do what's true esteem all down
by provident attachment, fitting accom-
plished display. Treasure by treatment,
value-added resistant matching variation.
You do know what you find by revolving
trial, as waiting time rescinds the marks
that show deterrence, all the way. How you
know is not known, but so is so and ever
will remain.

## In a Plan

Over to put a single aperture, by its even
mark to be given, to attach all will clearly
be set and taken in good time. Afford another
you might, all the whole arrangement but for
either to go allegedly, probably around however
cannot ignore or depute, because that's turned
in a plan so warm, already. Stream and climb
as tap ah so gently, to a finger rise advancing
part to entrance, come to faster charm you know
sibilant fixture, fore-brain, assign safe brim.
Patchwork amends the colour chart you'd not
pause at this, be generous no finnick tappet
make to amount just rightly consonant would be
in line for arrival, for effort. Future in plant
up to the limit intone in permission fast to
say and say ready back tremulous, all over in-
cidental by guarantee please to be, session
unbounded to the doorway; push forward upper
slope both ways gather it indigent compression
cool to brow head-wave, back. Yet accepting
visible perforate adjust will all hear close to
a full assembly, stay at this reversal given out
enough to join up near to may and may, time
out of reach, to come in. At child care will all
in touch, over be not converged, ambulant
take it on perfect offer; neighbour division.

## Throat Notation

Fortunate orphic resentment gathers dust,
hesitant river get in line, coy singing buzz
larynx fault diffraction, close measurement.
You heard the same sounds, underneath attend
vanquish or stipple in a choice prepared, sur-
charge furious deep down heavy in waiting, in
footprint tracement, incision. Did you care
to find out how many if they were equivalent
in recess darkened clue member, resounding
to her cuff just our poor luck: each in watch
for the other, at cave mouth donate pining
sink to the mark pinchbeck illusion, incise
shade plummet descending by nectar guides;
throat notation late fabular discontent. Of
incessant here or thereafter tuning up so
to play so to hear, voiceover entreated for
her own sweet sake or due still approximate
tribute fire-play. All fuel counting up on
the river be open in streamy flow, wet stones
and the woman calling, for now our plaintiff
ask debate, returning echo fixative. Wind in
flow and know besides incline perpetual first
come first served by estimate subdued fission
and teeming, frankly to a careless fault, never
going back. Look up, you'll see beyond un-
certainly, inform loss adjusted.

## Entitlement

First ticket was known to him, holding up
in stub to match remedy, conduce entitlement
cast aside. Reprieve day by day pitching in,
curt lucid odium, before parody lays its mark.
Grip fast, journey to justify all spent out,
blood fusion segregate primal shortage, dabble
in wrath. Others will soon see what's missed,
without care, focussed ahead as soon as scan
returns. Bract detain addendum, try out a kick-
start vital pitch affray, dress antic wounds.
Crisis pushed down to nothing, foreseen parted
efflux incriminated far ahead, violent before
called to account. Throw out the whole folio
of greedy shots, his total abandoned chances
in tariff marking, pulse specific blockade
to beat back wasteful casualty. Reject the
promise exchange pedigree, thick saline in-
difference, however advanced.

## Keep Alive

Evident in repulse and concentric why
delay loop, fair bay shining, distorted
catchment each of them loose meander to
beckon foreign and line-up. Partnership
makes amends or excuses, how otherwise
colourant restores pensive agreement to
invoke unhurt recension by divisional
separate tenancy. They perturb the others
by sharp echoes, in scarf boastful drive
while fast fading presumed to announce
a patois assignment: accent-free. Alike
why in access reverberated, plentiful
earnest task fetched as per novel request,
notion to vision cohort fluorescence hers
to keep alive. Cloth squares yield their
rank order, give away a plain sequence
by meticulous activity; planning the steps
never too soon on a classic dorsal air
repayment. Part for whole, installation
holding sunlight in fetchwork inner decay
risen to it, first off, be in tune early
birdsong. Ruff up the trill as gleefully
augmented, will if she can in bel canto
attend blameless retrieval, outwardly calm.
Why would she not, by agreement fast in-
clined, not even scratched, rebate flung
off as omission breaks apart the shell
of fancy, quelled if needed.

## Overlay Sash

New assure azure perform out of the corner
active intaglio memorial, get in line and stay
put missive affront malachite, flake. Yet lit
streak presumptive knee joint not so often
pedal the team confers to save space all indeed
sensibly capped. Ethiopic pearl sumptuous vital
leader flexed cloud base, flicker critic adds
animus they stand and watch, greedy if else
crude batch from leisure resected and unmute.
Better be terrified instant dressed out in fear
partition lapse, will cut you out of play de-
vice reclaim, anticipate destruction before
its level share. Be first or nothing, calorific
overlay sash by spent delivery, expensive did
you instigate fixture. Did you want it, banal
measure desired like the others cooked up, in
new fissure under forfeit, is that consumed
alongside store deprivation, would you even
notice italic if leafage obscured debenture.
Want this alone with otherhood visible purchase,
coercive appointment wrist burn, coverlet
pricked up in fashion trinket.

## Chant Measure

Tamper-proof evangelist all of them why-ever not
mean ingrate, replete too, restriction metro division
hardly in avoidance, foot-print in levity. Livid
furnace, all smoke shored up arising come right
out patiently ground to scraps, in the mincer, turn
in full view at front, at most. A wave of dilute
resemblance will grant a pause before cause to be
ahead by waiting fraction, late to satisfy; right.
They do all know even if late proclaimed, ever
tardy passage of salt, moist crust or blinking
furtive ingression. Tear out the line markers, if
replaced for aggregate one by one, neural ply, out
to get back. Finish with flourish, wave overly
let them or most ring out wild, back incipit
where not already resumed. You can slantwise
see that all of them hitherto will rip the cover,
anger plot grist to beauty in the face. Pray up
violent by chant measure, foolish rotation merely
established and greedy. Are they for even so
placid, other shunt aside and refracted sink
down harmful if yet diminish now and then,
excess confabulate, outright and limpid shower.

## We Do

Alight get set to fasten and impugn knit temper
astonish; we allow finally like all the others,
their retracted storm to cloud over. Did you see
that or catch turbulence whirled upward, cream
horizontal luft where we contrive best impression
going on through. There are vacant steps at inter-
val, follow trifle spick and span, crass. Amaze
too, aggrandise bright frequency in pack grimoire,
finger and thumb catch as catch can, soon out to
plan better spin stud enticement actual. Lattice
tremors eagerly forward, ink rising with tube
in hand, slow down tempest within conspected
grievance at the blame in cautious subtraction;
alliance exceptional draft annoyance run-time,
ray tilts. Upper partial extra striking all off
memory lit up silhouette flex protection first
downpour in name only, care to pick one quickly,
stricken forehead under brim recognisance where
so in note, turning out not to belong here should
late intern culminate; we do. As level pathway
both more tilted and near under-water, trodden
in fancy alliance, inveigle what you almost
will not give away, insinuate. We shall confirm
and lean aslant streaming the brook's demeanour,
casually while there's time, or fate single, or
yet later invited and ever intrinsic, ever full.

## Follow Turmoil

Such fabric so torn, for tune by hazard chrome
in line feeling to part if not ready cavil time
watch, level shift cirrus reflected even when
soon whether practice longing to send, find, make
way by extreme aspersion. Better by next dis-
covered, open frame sedulous unlikely, cater for
other sentiment midst of life itself so early
waiting, waiting as will call to a sift-point
or now and then after, loyal. Brim at full regain,
follow turmoil or judgement, size enough capture
in scale. Take off the rest overnight vivid profile
disjunct and bright inflamed, it is known evenly
replaced, truly held. Could also be upper wrack
best in reach penitent by disclosed admission,
anticipate exact at birth. Darker trim first cut
away felt and tremble, many voices steeped there
in blue uprising, new cloud in its clue, search
entire forgiven unwilling but enough. By late proof
has birdlike review deployed, so flown to fledge
ambition, never too late within. Cordial bypass
rapture outwards in company select as verified,
presuming or yet by confirmation from parallel
inflicted, relented, sight self-made as brevet
ever find. Or this or that pretext set up in view
quickly, living colour first applied to like,
demonstrate, gather the threads once still bright
already and torn.

## The Way, Forward

Levy accept countenance over this near
hill promised will the breach make up
for missing parts, forward to slope,
steep under guard. Did esteem design in
grateful addition loose the remedies
on top, not sufficient unless right in
capture fortitude. For drastic delete
askew, offspring few cloud fringes, less
moisture crepitate main wrong. Admit
returning balance to claim alight at the
stand illusion, at once or last revision,
don't resist too soon. When in reflection
mirror fold finds its due place in scale,
all in nurture, a plain tale on the mend.
Notice will all of them down-hill, scent
of rain creeps inward, over the sill
arrested or wary. Procession amounts and
grounds, whether disturbance reaches
high up in fixed delay, for cover and
over limit summit, raise the stakes in
what's to be seen yet clearly still enough.
Beyond play of fracture, profession lift
concealment water flow and grow by match
of a wanted seam, release as can be open
to latch or weir. In new place love what's
added on, paramount attach loyal acknow-
ledgement. If beyond doubt, hand-fast
care for rising profile again temper not
to excuse eye fortune or its near double,
chance occasion benign for steep native
pertinency rapid into transit endowed
subsistence. The way, forward step-fast,
hand by clue in hand.

# OF BETTER SCRAP

# (2019)

Go to bed third, a golden bird
– Halliwell, 1844

They haue been at a great feast
of Language, and stoln the scraps
– *Loves Labours Lost*, 1598

1786 *Philos. Trans.* (Royal Soc.) 76 63
There are...persons who have denied the magnetism of purified nickel

*OED3* (2003)

1881 *Athenaeum* 27 Aug. 274/2
We do not believe in the jussive pluperfect subjunctive

*OED2* (1901)

## To Them

It is however for to love and other care
in the day of flight, each one of when
turn to look and long given, under fair
prodigy out hand by level share placement
there first before, certain advocate sign
lapwing ever flutter. Eye forward be proof
to find, pair leaning way gate of truth
to on hold attach deep shoulder vivid or
rick on wave, admit. Damper by warm lee
pensive, in view cherish for sake better
back exchange bright glow evince shadow
be steady beseem conviction if in both
reachment. Already where in turn over
gaze deflected already understood, in-
version of promise returning, mutual to
search as implicit fortunate in both
out of shade yes to steady assented, to
guarantee. The other way too, if across
to weft liminal, glance to favourite
anticipate loyal spread craving truly
outreach. In truth, again as there will
predict to soft entrancement, hold out
topmost praise filling, aware. As your
wish will of to both, awash and seem
in known held shore-line, rustle back
and over by turn of love sentence told.
Known it is, across forth pattern trust
relinquish to claim opportune glimpse,
fair brow loft carried, raised between
lift to them and them as for now most.

18th March 2019

## Lesser Fine Antidote

1

At the door yet so open, cage evenly enhanced porous
tip step let for infer traceable side to front blink
abstain and say refusal, grown impassive most further
to slit up the entrance exhaust near toy finishers

2

As air swept away stand readily vacant will converge,
on this. On which this too not so sink clemency
inflicted to know mean subdue randomise over ill
taken fringe still centre place value tin or none,

3

Not full even by half smoke lassitude without trim
profession, tell them. Drain out from the livid main
start, colours invited less each time run or gather
presented for gate, inside to willing slide, as to

4

Allocate undue dispersal. Each one fewer in feature
close to token shelf order minish furnish claim time,
a space park boiling instruct front to common plea
injury. Several lesser fine antidote taken back

5

For room more so unoccupied, right across ledge till
portal phantom birth yet truly sense wide and seen
pledge-work, easy to know steep path to ever ride.
Our path then upmost first of all tint better these

6

Views intrinsic by custom, linear through dense brim,
each depriving the other both removed more at each
succession, propense enough giving out new ground
in fee. Thus unobstructed the light flutter clears

7

Impartial, not holding on boldly, current apt, all
fresh and nourished. Or by such limit salve trampled
through the whole way first before next encroaching
permission, passage loaned for reflection so as polar

8

Full tractable come in, now for time ahead at term
benefit alert why ill resist more on more off; chill
trace enable or risible yet less incentive nor go
void delivery back to back final perfected storm.

## Merchant to Purchase

Merchant to purchase, not by hire but level off our anvil
sent stir planet office, surface enough fire handful nurse

Diffident principal, not lent abroad in words given, will
lift by indent or fraud braided innocent repentful shunt

Lacustrine optimal not ever little tiny success lack bet
to waver refine entire brine savour, benefit astute fate.

## Finding Where Joined

As why forward way will open across yet to be
astigmatic corrected mostly offence back shadow
to rise snuff whether spar fitting, layout often
dense and pitch. Forbear twins along a plane,
foil direction will meet compacted folio, folded
in waiting, block. As late intrusion, cryptic
basement step own place ascent to mark them all,
rift in horizon, sight to match close to finding
where joined, next after first. Trickle linear fill
nor soon exceeded, petrific watch fixture, sound
acclaimed for discovery; as who knowing whole for
to climb, other to track inured with a team in
pair, insert gravity metric. Now we all know and
must elevate, able ready utter within average risen
bitumen agreement, recognise lack inter remontant
and wafting, as must and visible. Party go allot
by observation nominal in and for, fitted twice
fast enough for stipulate in company according, as
foot after foot, by measure already trim outward
wanting to stay. Plumb lithic suffuse anticipate
colour margin gleaming inside order best links,
each raising the other flocculent tuft fittings.
Fold back agreed void, held by line tabs ever we
set to be just in better time readiment entire
or get a found start forward again merciful, now
of kind serrated the whole blade running tempered
in glim attached, go fast as all of them invited.
Limb crown reflecting its own interior sill lumen
for fond temporal occlusion, early before return
to gain sufferance brought into sight, remainder
as this why, forward, reason to raisin, magnify.

## At the Goose Window

Excavate foremost sluice broken to burn harsh or missive, addendum proclivic indignant all facing outward, recover at the goose window notification. Persistent they inflame sediment drypoint, volatile take what offers along the ridgeway, more than expected. Than which carried or copied, make a list provision, care more for a novel outcome; how could either follow or turn, uncertain. First to find, either off track verified in certainty written over. Evident in pencil or lost to sight furthermore. Superable last to fasten surface advocate one by one right where darkness substitutes profusion alight his deputy, abrupt drainage join in accentuate adjust stalk panicle in florets. Put crash to banish, both overhead intimate ant bother, found out credit formic to punish and by slit admonish, by active tenancy. You will, you will seen before as trap sprung torn, insipid decussation give them both insurgent back quickly, childlike in mind if never fortify.

## Upset Past Foreign

Most be or of for them, be in trust vertical allied from legerdemain approve silent, benefit filling aim in test fortress may or they, will intermit across illust far to lean exhume and plaintiff, outworn further scheme vigil or dove. Bear upward age river brushing forecast upset past foreign when add prime rivalry, when or where filled must better child, in air promise citadel to cross, overly last intention forage mafic ledge. Believe inverse argent honestly crush inflict squill aerated overtone departure, flowing daughters outer to measured average, if by less birth import willing. By massive narrational trental brow saving too, flake borrow evince dissent remiss also claimant, citric mast ahead. Even given lee, way beside, presume as sibling order errancy swollen sweet water refuge, milder further amused trifle utterance. Let be, of frame agency into go share restore non-trivial they or may, will averse of limit for when either known attented. Surrogate on arrival humerus advantage, clavis by interest, relations tribal here dwelt. With them prove this sought to set by missive point, rest gadabout in rise barrack win. Entire, single persuance quite attainder broken, requital first choice plan, if worth amended or then followed, for them again at fleet design coin. Since never yet aver, affined.

## Florid Largesse

Never or further play aslant go to fill relent
above box shining, not to close terminal switch
far ride along familiar road, as bent. Instigate
a fruit harvest mostly up front, leaf catchment,
by step forward evident already, pliant. Both
well waiting in outlook to simplify orange cloud-
base, tribute lain the pie crick obvious all in
line, chart ingress unlock. Ahead sent, slice,
cut level path dissented, finish, retinue bidden
sideway and pitch, to run severally hereby, deny
what's seen bicuspid narrow screen: blanket fold.
Avail head-wind or heart murmur frond grate, bite
trill adamant catch nail off colour? Not to blame,
insidious relineate profligate mixture, plenti-
ful ever both will, twice last cheek, astute;
viscous by all try lost tarte obligate, loaded
florid largesse as ungrateful, interminable.

## Accumulate in Fortune

Rash manicure amounts, hardly you should, lean soffit
over to sentiment matching, preview calorific smile
bow terrain rise to fieldwork, heavily put. Often did
insufficient morbid ratings as you do reckon, counter
far against plethoric surge prevention; mother first
urgently bar none invert or sanguine, leave out of
measure under loyal, uncertain. Under so much to will
be there at once deletion over seizure, float across
to make new fire pit heart antecedent perhaps furious
demur. Edge deterrence too, courage after. Betterment
providing you might, by now installed lock up corrode
gradual decline. Anyway you should even or so, glance
carbon charring incline to mission reduplicate, alter
what's traffic pushing on forward, against invidious
tidal counter-flow. Still loyal caught sight alleging
aggregate boundary marks beaten off for an early song,
protect uprisen accumulate in found fortune, besides.
All intact by countenance on these hills assembled, on
further swung and round openly reduced as to ember
catchment inclusion. Go your ways fictive proposal ban
nothing apartment, deployment, apex concision on offer
into quick safe reply. Claim return team spun arising
blood faction feudal strife dismiss before arrival,
ride in formation right touch: or here, all before.

## Inspect to Leap

Is flown bracken, quicken assertion mercenary enquire
and find out of question imminent list manipulate,
all of them at the skyline tangle. Index wait slowly
greet tiresome reputed lock accession, time now to
fend former and match plates first ready. A spark on
certain track, drawn to curtail livid property under
value trim sennet purpose, full sail in top session
indicate alert affect. Furnished base-point ready mix
along the horizon cirrus tremble contracted to narrow
mission, assure motive unsealed. Admit to this much
at least defended, instant blur understood for why
inform particular latitude revoked. Expect uppermost
friendship running through, space debit all contriving
as they say without measure in fancy or near folly
time neglected paradox. Known ready into all found
officious intimation perpetrating soon to declare.
Altitude attainment outlook cloudy, in shreds mostly,
assign. Even less inspect to leap, out of kilter fit
prescient allay first enjoining hazardous filtration
by notice, enough. Aspect filament bring fast to bear
or make way ingression bright gold raise intrinsic
decorate. Provide all for this too, allegiance lifted
at the window sash, nothing yet denied, at gallop.

## Dear Heart Unlikely

As ornate twill was for them all, share profound
but not victim in usual perpended across density
avian letterhead sisters wild rampaging; in noisy,
fulmination. Yet to concentrate was also a traffic
loss decision, laughter abounding advocate dividual
each separate come to pass, intone. Deep sloe ripen
lenient to a fault intrepid browncoal or yes front
to render fair and hunt back, for them. Why or say
when you know, better to use and arrange in future
now less strict too, did not and will not foot-fall
ignited to glow, red-shift oblate suffusion within
air tenancy. All of them already primed, belated
so soon to top out, sentinel give back impervious
pattern in portion contrite hearts, passive. Echo
fitter restrain them why not or before to imitate
crowding alongside, run to meet them their letter
terror-struck just in time flow, pallor indistinct,
late to bite in the frame manifest joy. Or yet now
further or tamper to relieve impressive canopy fold
into cover, spread. Limit known into most of them
after another one to relent prolific refreshment
dear heart unlikely so late on, into daylight glow
waiting still to play, onwards. Or to remonstrate
in attire borrowed for this, raiment in summerhood
core alight vestment filament instinctive. Prune
into clung shape bee swarm, even better for them
and/or for us, close-matching too.

## Separate Tackle Benefit

Insolvent tissue abundant affirming in design acid lithe topic excision, so few to bind consistent blink exacting parallel. Blue and white issuance involute, satisfy and fetch refined alabaster fluting, night tied photon agreement intuit. Bring out swift offset take manner to size up, fort. Error function for non-final sky to grave estimate by instant rule, vestige addition skip amazement, know the way. Insinuate at pivot force blend by colour shading, vapour trails approximate arm's length care more. Singular noted pitch, pine further, soon to find the others follow as late errant inquest, optional light to hand. Print fission median separate tackle benefit gather advance mass delivery. Let be, cause to slide, match slope in breath inheld transition elemental, maintain still be litter posted undulant to donate inflow persistent double admirable tee-marking. Clean rivalry organic tangent compensate pass for passion, foresight by prelusive intimate candour, at best. Bean now, be quick elide family party classical doubt permission instructed scot-free in theorbo fluency, incidental note for slope attended. All set let shine revision principal company new snow in summer shimmer talent accurate profusion its bed reclined, well it would. Minor precession sky harping overly prevalent be fluid lung tremble abiding behaviour, sonant fall arriving to meet what's said in surprise, supper tandem consume prodigal cliff, sit by the open tide.

## Dainty Fine Trill

Insist did they for real conceal missing in partnership not heard inflection what more after listen despite trial date vigil single teasing entice under or over. Gift in clove avail replace fanciful pressed hydration, sail lift gaining enforcement and sealed. Draft exacted instrument may or will, retrain in zeal detect surplus bail contest return portion yet mild, audit. Lamp tarragon inkling did for piecemeal revelation beasts address, surface inflict rectify mean insipid, dainty fine trill. Water inside lap rebuke diluted classify confection, assisted vain hardship avoidance liberated to scatter as seedheads will, resign ataraxy last about hold back. Shall they all share enter option filament to redden face-watch, beam closed ready as made back who knows restricted valuation they do, lift under pressure release. Inflame occupy no grain, none in same-day testify compression taming famish, performance all seen envy will modest certify, action band plowing pertinent tribune all they did; sing-song all at last.

## Top Silver Deliver

Eximious talent infringe the bill, tap-tap mend
or modify bred canteloupe nightly bird on brede
gullet orient sprinkle and dropping, on purpose
top silver deliver pannier floated. Not or to fit
even before latency what's in mind eventual sip
elute insolvency, gang-plank for milk repeating,
repent, reticent infarct hand to mouth intervene
marsupial slight cling scrape finally in venture
to vertical. To giddy remiss fiction buoy up debar
instant palarver optical, all farce investigated,
never enough throughout. Across the aqueduct made
here for love working, the troupe entire on-stair
print out on first foot epicure nasal to banish
patrimony donated. Because you both do know of
limit fence dissemble steady incline retention
to close drip after assertion advancing have more
trod effigy why tell the same. New marble instep
astrantia clip surmising domain mental proficient
action suppress what for, veinous implicated over
counterpart. Metal facings reveal their origin,
luminous partition at birth, at bird observant
provident no sky falter depriving its white muse
lift to stabilise. Full agreement incident, name
alternate marking more hope mere tremor affine
grasp future shadow on the road, now openly.

## Say Pieces Enjoined

Derelict amusement sylvan mascot together sent, cannot
need professional, allergic meant the same, seem nominal
was no dream off surplus alembic, finger. Dig deeper so
leave aside in slips for payment, refused, comical orbat
all bribes shore battery casuist; promise more often or
substitute bordering deterrent, rivet by rustle elastic
park kept by animus in warm hazel. Spread abroad or as
by rumour intimated, hold tight flew over, skein of left
birds not yet rancorous, benefit, ticket window gravity
given back prune abstention. Never too late to mend firm
autumn push, harmful without recipience brother arming
collision prone question sprit. Betoken what or now when
flood recovery, made a gash aghast transfusion by type
immediate crowding imitation, aloft excuse wet all over
front to side shared vital duct presence. Forage billet
is for or was, also possible furtive evidence grimpen
primacy voluble; say pieces enjoined to diffuse fit
angle full stand clean attire deign admitted, consume
on fire almost away. Viral outspread, spoilt medial
energy spilled over, face up to ready cut and grant
or by free effectual simulation russian triangulate.

## Liquid Persistence

Nod steady or nod too, indifferent assize curated, tell whole was for merge, intact to blend streams attended part amount, assent eye-light distinguish. Premiss for entrant filtration skim, talon will swoop horrid resect tin foliar minted. All will go so far, to ride and balance edit pronounce upper lip tap, at offer by now capitulate entire. Or prudent coinage, brave in flutter, rapidly as all would, choice sweeten, so far sparkle or not, time to verify leave behind litter party, iconic brew gibbous halogen, agonist. All found, no extra inflict afterthought nod pert adornment fly faster, slippage this for that, both willing prodigy, tower. Alleviate liquid persistence, go without fear or grief defence, far in advance told by them effortless, muff both ways. Best to trust them, confer ahead set omen proclaim, trammel culvert tied up to participate stoking the furnace for brightening. Ready to esteem them for magnified track object, given principal resource by leave to amplify; miss nothing, all in order renewed. Reason to margin align, founder's doorway visible tend identify, end display plentiful instant path in lane.

## Watch and Ward

Oak forage indifferent, for now or later immersed
profligate running up perfection, livery worn out
will wash, nebulous. A fringe trifling benefit my
own to advocate equality unfinished dry at first
attempt. Essential light pandemonium ever drives
up refer incline to pass where full, refuelled,
less few costly imitation likeness plausible these
days off. Aware door open floor creature, on level
passage wait to state entreat, victorious pungent
hyssop miniature comes well ahead, or blameless.
Galling in pigs lost reverend mental sty aspect,
out crowded taken hot wax, a dish limitless shared
in parkland, interspersed so fondly. All watchers
assume the post, eyes wide by enterprise, not yet
timid openly at gaze lifting fixity manners, most;
or see out flat promise cannot childhood version
measure up chill hat furniture, on guard at price
to stay put. Restricted movement channel, or rush
at display, forbear collective in plenty of room,
in cool wanting remission uproar assuaged. Watch
and ward for synthetic impetus heuristic levity,
discount mild gear attended companionable, new tax.
Foreign runaway eagerness, in forest shade full
for dry pigeon clutter pork fancy medicated alp
to the snowline, rise and shine at once by fall
lenient, adown. Clamber in mystery, top suited
parallel squeak watching intent, back turned not
to mind or demonstrate outboard particular cup.

## Deputed Head Start

Cursory gradients recoil by innervation, attract
artisan conjunction at warranty issue reflexed
and qualify infill, all stream affluent complain
in search of pliant modicum restored. So to know
best affording, incline to ascertain supple tag
rated alone, steep step to hold as found not so
hard to raise property residuum. Craft purpose
skill, sing out novel burden to purchase tenor
ascended crayon hatch, raise fury in hot swarm
of roaming bee stimulants. Elected silence into
wood veneer replacement, agree plain heated plume
ostensible like the others, seen for this under-
neath, leaf cover critical path anodyne up-end,
locum favourite deputed head start. In part ready
torn, aside to swim crab-wise delirium deflected,
in anecdote volume grateful all the same; treasure
found preferred intricate major tactic tooth-comb
deferential ruminant climb and till. Fresh soil
nor hot water craving, soften brow crush fast
majestic on forehead, hive roofing at a pitch
rural and voluble both ways. They will so pass
swiftly as day-mist, as moorland all to stream.

## To Tweet for Profit

Conciliate to enlarge will they, all sawn and trim,
off minimal whence blank retainer, hold fire and
stoop to pacify mitral corrosion designated with
stream alongside; spun insect or spilling also met
webbing harvest in proof, grated and principle at
less effort. Implicate bell tonic hamper the way
need and spread, formation. If or not pitted in
welcome tryout, heels in too, anterior. Condign
famous edge repeal makes for splutter and butter
haunting the shore in march past gently dip prior
swivel or tepid. What's to see is several brim
transfer adhesions for ripple boast to grandeur,
positive select presented arms as when they do.
Rectify each bent stick prepare the samovar teem
in tesserae pavement, laid down smooth as silk
to grin and bear, new dispersed across the field.
Panoptic debate accrues by fits and starts level
initially in marital pledge address, formulaic
ancestral tempest in slate parlance, that will go
to the far corner at once, dendrite. For them all.
Rain-sodden pour down treaty with them, active
by amount predicted sweetness, surge of green into
pleasantry ratified and held. Why so pale and wan
of temper, expecting play soon to impugn negative
replacement shelfwise, vote to soak distinct, eat
to tweet for profit, folderol. They will and must
bind up tightly, before new menace to intrude in
bright welter amended into point of nuisance.

## Daze Trophy Safeguard

Ketone monumental inflorescence for the door stop admixture reach and search blow up a storm gratify glimmer of new sense adjuvant avian in hinterland assessment grip starburst quadrant; over difference engine held abeyant be general part fraction at the window frame. Loop tail imitate flame other daze trophy safeguard, cretonne to tell and assist fissile charging, to hear close partition invade biscuit pair to share alike. Your intense ingot for munch most hot working, ribbon reminder ultra inhale degree elegant adjustment, get ahead too membrane taut pitch, too menu optic mail chosen file to mend. Track link memory rescue alpha hitch precision similar grist ready for daylight to add lumen for cone taper, bestow trace source outflow noise rebated; safe in promise offering, enjoin at proven estimated prentice temporary induction, hasten to increment and crystal test refractive glass consent in writing. Found on record, lit up from below to cast attic shadow, eavesdrop inside snow melting, steam pursuit cranny drainage own routine without risk. Diagram condiment refined acrid macerate and simmer by text provision worn broken of time disturbed, resist to flex tarnish quest for colour opening; patient treatment into symptom rampage tantrum out for dinner invoked plastic additive. Full ahead succeed in training panoramic rush dissembled, await we shall go with way to spare, feats of arms flourish and finish both affixed at the roof-line parapet. Most token ensemble produce delete revelatory our side on line by line, parget affirm in whether anecdote.

## Give Out and Finish

Adoptive interview watching the skyline, slow turning
and falling as cloud fictions, by settlement most ignored
there in darkness further on. Specific adamant indicate
pinfold assertion, will preference logical asset detour
onside custom, device to clarify speaking within range
give back, give up, overtax the bare outline deeply into
avoidance calculus. Nothing to win of this grasp, as to
declare promptly, franchise redemptive posture indrawn
at temperament milk titration, all the brothers assemble
foremost in profit amiss. Tell above what you know, will
fast logic joined to control gates, induce birth over-
turning parlando: quick patter. Agitate remedial redial,
relay in difference defer to judgement, are you agreed
to soft-touch experiment, up in front. Perverse levity
insufficient to prevented topic abrasion, tolerate mass
restore in first light, gleaming vivid sidelines modest
accent agreement to suit. To be fitted closely astonish
hearing emphatic dismay in relic energy left out; pit
numeral reckon, at last. Attentive indiscreetly, into
ready admission, opening slide to give out and finish
or furnish derision exceeded forensic aperture, invert
to reach appraisal, appetite. Unknown sunshine within
bright day, ray flicker for glimpse, for furtherhood.
You do know this much, inception completely noticed,
apparatus coronal jacket at nearest horizon zodiac
presumed in flight. Dauntless match filter orbital
craft invocated alloy, margin soup interfolding as
more often than not. Praise be, full voice upraised
in charge remitted to oracle semblance, hard-wired
aria endeavour box offer musical repertory entire.

## Familiar Left Hand

Frost at noon, singular and fragile assign rapier point
aftermath as well indent, splash out unaltered blighted
witty fleece, pull back into foremost perpended ground;
melt and sip deceptive as seen from otherwise platter in
servery flummery receipt life for pudding, lifted driver
fret by fury; swallow or narrow drift opaline in atoned
lost image tracework magnify several times over at new
second chance attraction. Roof over waft off nowish, awry
neighbour calling hollow as before, relief plan to settle
and yet amaze; convert for balcony over to stair in pair,
line to shout famous or famish; table laid for time out
familiar left hand, keyboard instruct. All do take this
open chance improve the hour, foreseen blink within lair
deterrent, steady daffy and humorous in critical outlay
cutting arrest crisp invalid, sung full justice extract
induce; pretty much visitor pathway atrium specific, in
terms defined inch primate division and uniform devoid
of dash and carry, like a chance for all to tremble or
approve. Watch out in range of eye-shadow trial if also
trivial in near crease, light as possible in lift to win
reckoning, conic rattan tied, obdurate yet nominate not
finished old treads level steppage don't cringe for nap
gruesome agreement cloud thickens up; early or late fume
dowel entreat the joiner's antiphon from time in fathom
near out of mind, loose mileage deflected into penalty
brisk reverse the feast of keys less aggrieved after
calm, mollified over water, or find the chance agreed.

## Draconian Held Tight

Insect winter ripening deeper relief surf evaluate trim
must prime examine avoid to cry out, under ill presume
famous. Sentence polity mischief, dapple in principle
collusion, oaten modify cautionary come on out to bear
as passer-by remark freeway equalise. Fill evident park
is populous by now, already stanchion upheld residual
epic probity, not far to train; our turn save to flee
or seek by option flown. All familiar by account tip
pruning, in household temper cold snap blush determine
popular proximate disclose, summon decision overturn
indifferent, either way regretful; serum max coin to
battery lay down saracen taste antigen, graze walking
in break of fire to bank, accident thrown fast forward
by impetuous saunter. Fossil pallor their plentiful
disposal, litmus skip front parlour, detested docile
brat-stop fungus wrist adjournment, however new and
rectified, compliant precursors. Trouble or life going
strong front chamber as in flush elusive discrepant
protocol, all the way known and placed up in virtue,
to dress well assumed, visible profile optimal laid
terrace magnitude, draconian held tight, to not split
sable decorate retrain. Break easy dear heart unequal
provision disclaimed if or when print acceptance,
deem to carry laminate and bring off, or wring out
wrist turn carp report to animate, envisaged tacit
mischief closure decrepit syntax fringe avenge burn
maroon rack dauntless, splash piteous or nauseous
income, as paint. Ultrasound both interpret mild
undercoat thoroughfare, under-done insouciant try
to inspect thorax speculate mission perfume nearly
deliberate, counterfeit: few defeat the open day.

## Deep Pure Rosin

Purse twice invaded prominent repine, rapturous ditch
come home by later payment bar to sight exaggerate whim
birdsong corner to manage rustic dawn clad peach down
mantle solemnise prism lentil, crackle or yet civil.
Arise: main entry brimful darkening scape hinterland,
guan guan, ospreys climb pretty massive, elbow well
pacified iterate who tells them when to pile mournful
or silvery; faint krill parapet illusion vain twelve
indulge panoply stave to sell nugget scale leafage
locate retaken entity isle at last light. Frustrate
capture win better with butt licence both side gadget
mingle and fitted, yeast holdfast surmount pacific
mask of rime, remit parade palinode too splendid via
account first rank in shade or least within elated.
Nightshade it was, a tropic bell to ring donation,
listen peal smoke in essence to go round, acerbic if
not polymer profit or unaccountable; distribute by
sad steps animate room to trespass and board, waning
current tantalise by sash degree rotation, pinion in
relief cold snap immolate sold invented, unwanted.
Will who, will when neater, later indulge weight loss
simplify and woven tailoring to borrow up and scrim,
arch digest motivate implausible. Care for cure rick
attracted to deep pure rosin, static addit outflow
more than most saw this too, crampon infixed fast
vent the pent implacable substitute, to implicate
dictum unsaid; private instilled account, why will
sitting tight authorise and track them, twin avocet.

## Circuit Where They Roam

Skip-jack to plentiful deeps, grey goose will wander
under the wrack within, plashy drops announcing cleft
deposit cloudier indigo, heavy to bear. Make head-
wave frown, or let fall tactful, brow to furrow assess
raisin fold overland from voice leave by leafy dell.
Bare in sky, price wet official, bank wheeling going
on by, eyes moist in full day ford and cloud yet in
stricken, too, ragged by risen clemency whether or not
by more apt review. Entrain hang branch resign, ensign
manner freshen, in breath amount upwards; permittance
intake dial up too, script mace intermit in host by
fire circuit where they roam, heart in darkness splay
out and pilfer arrant in sparkling nebular gateway.

Simmer also, pinch ice flakes caress and scatter, har-
bour entrance mobile to splash progress envisage sell
mortify, inveigh imply tremendous red quotient offer
deterrence waving sea-birds listen and find, outweigh.
Radical tune noted for mission frame, downpour press
seasonal macular antidote, so many all ready to alter
and design. Unfold ye clouds due with the morning dew,
tread further on; this, that, and so honest symmetry
incident prolong what all to know and promise, infuse
try stir vigilance, macerate assurance; untangle to
run, run to climb, abandon what won't debit immunity
or yield in time disjoint damage patch—eloquent as
lemon inhibition, evident propulsive seam's affray.

## Intruded Nullity

Dormant interest fallible remind lend also best extravagant
up and with enmesh, affix skin unfailing. Treatment reclaimed
from highest points, upper still, kept overturn magical in
cup fiery and bright, in want. How unreal to vow more curtal
fashion, implemented meal in bone, steam declare before egg
hot living tardy wane. Arise and go not yet but in bit, fin
gain ocean; rove to occupant alight quantum while day lasts
obvious vital and seething, back row soon seen clearance
explain tribulate: all of them. Discreet intruded nullity
to catch up welcome, phantom refer tread into powder gel, in
fixative, gazing unfrozen, ownership in remedy amazement ill
said. Grind division crossed fallow coppice to follow, lent
to watch in-close, size exhume remainder; pelt infiltrate
muzzle doxa rump and sound, always along the meadow drove.
That's how estimate, chronic delusion ready fit rebate par
tranquil exchange, plainly in series skill, until foremost
incessant bloom folded from involute; hidden the cheek, ban
under blameless scrutiny, as true. Gather in touch, fill
to care for and after, love rewound by staff and necklace,
all full to amplify lost in front of craft; seen in broad
light, improve tenor, alleviate onto the nigh sea shore.

## Not Too Late

Soever pulse made, bridle off grade spindle why
and so deep by course stave away of broken for as
by lesser tailor tacit nearby critic adamantine,
speed overhead when face to foot seen divergent
how told step-watch, on selzer marble dissolute
at floor demise. You for alum your sun anvil rock
washed gleaming, licit enlacement, calls whether
encroaching lucent modal or mounted aperture dim
ever how. Forbear also no stint limit, florin to
suffix partner which approve at gathering toil
profuse turf mimic. What they say, by early into
fate renewal better, right now, so far condone,
proclaimed frequency so much for activate fame
reserve; hold intended in a line apply or wheel
underset probable. All dire remit to snare fully
gain, said true, wave even cross; see to summon
what's arisen, sure for shore, horizon builded
here at a bound clearly. Why not this time bell
plentiful in view over, avian top-most furnish
crest benefit note undercurrent split at how so
presume matching. Or how annex also in reclaim
round eyebrow pitched supplant, lent to enlist
first before test along fluent doubt. Converge
like which said, enough net admission not too
late, to give away as of most the rest, or if.

## Harmonic Cuneiform

Saving brunt verifies knee patent, riding and turning
multiple stealth woven, unwieldy intrepid plumage so
relentful in flamboyant measure numinous, palace will
saturate with gravel lawful mannerist brave and free.
Tappet invite might ridgeway bent, edge suspicion ill
resign dint local enjoy defray salt bite assailant to
scent circulate refrangible; in pacify deputise whittle
upset, ruffle extempore by range control snippet onion
colonise frail too. How much random distraint stock
levy step forward volunteer atemper groan, fatuous and
alert retelling its score, gloss revealing in rainbow
muster they newly root to crevice and all hang down.
Packet ascript drainage plumage hold your breath now
faster, dab premise lionise, jump and shout york rose
retract by felt immersal; grope cupola, fever rutile
fascinate impression rare to read code, outlive them.
Why even so ahead of minutes granted, confirm what is
by phalange communicable, harmonic cuneiform irritable
disclaimer talisman antimony rail indurated with salt:
in triumph, shouting with glee. Moral final repressive
attribute mosaic advert satisfy, gadarene porkers well
enjoined to flee, with or without the same disguises.

## Gratin Pause Understate

Fervent carry two disarming credit over too, alarm dispossessed most film respire, neck perfect while join immanent candid and true. Nothing respond sale forcible invaluable, twin merge went incisive they will cry to train mended, coincident. This mash for limitation, initial pressure astringent qualified old aquamarine, bearing tincture alpine distribute all select offer to parry, to swim. You and we bid to not clash hurriedly, gratin pause understate, fill opal fickle disturbance provoking trifle bound cream: watch antonym. All of them, stack optic trim mountainous interfere, reflection gastric pervaded in drama outlined, give them back dissemble react length attempt; illusory title and tactic impression for passion ulterior but reduce plan, ascertain in nicety shaven the outer rim. Eagle central cram, wash out debris rough tenement afterwards within crowd distil; in water chasm minority instinctive our new loss, rete refract coverlet opportunist by transmission, fuming. Did tell, did find pole far out of mind to say clearly, bent light engorged prickle and smart nomenclature alibi all lit up fair to flare in all parts beseem; betray often grown, proportionate sulcus pacify. No-fault into decision party to motivate and infill, demeaning crisis turbulence anodyne faction or politic out-brave, double panorama agreement in full effort principle: principiate sulk temper, nullify tinge.

## Ingest by Patronage

Wolf to lamb, lamb to beetle, orchid nip unbeknown
filament texture pint of claret as once apportioned
to expectant hedge-folding chop; echo in pence demure
cadge in hose waste spite replacement buy plough sat
spare doff novice, undulate did fizz legation, face
to face notary versed in premium creature; at visor
cap in padded uniform, march askew in bonny rank into
step proposed to signet restored provision criminal
partner severe, jug petty base. Fermented sugar oil
wander up abstemious, furious and cavernous; motley
over blank cautious as would be desired along play
at start venerate, either to pursue or tuck lissom
portrait manacle. Ingest by patronage, cell abandon
the rest to wind-blow, buffet stir bandage, in lint
forecast move to smooth and speech domain; or give
away peter out tendentious, groom. Rational foil
committal fly out grove, by sickle chink preferment
is more than new often, queue for talon, child care
inevitable chide anomaly. Never blandish, mitre
flourish palpable invested, tame them into calmer
destiny approach from the front, tacit. Or game
wrest adherent seeding tray, flex tissue regrade
tramp indigenous, jussive polari monetary spill
notable, grit. By staff position fashion slippage,
instil and travel heavy package deft for left, off
target manifold launch; profound re-enter lively
civilian conciliar drop, else wit. All now to flow
integument, a spring orthodox trick of the light.

## Attending with Conscience

Assert bantam crucial processional untouched, even by
transient perceived figwort noyance clustered square
mince and flinch, vigil. Quote to float also, whistle
at close range consume parcel overture; lifted fossil
anger surpassed, through the side window per vanitas
overhood touch of greed. All knew, new for all pricket
racing through undergrowth felt intermittent drifting
by choice only, leaf-folding at night in due retinue.
With all the others best to nest bin ransom, the whole
gamut employed syndicate fabric lateral tie avengement
wrong turning, corner gale-force aileron; in prudent
exemption consigned to synchronise at zero, as for a
start, alike nemesis. Struggle tangle clothing beside
passing cloud, not mistaken eventual blink into kind
hopeful, attempt sunk in temper origin, justify gift
at first shot to polarise. Revision prune, realised
drupe untied foal until skip to amble, reticent name
complicit nickel plate to concentrate amity, shares
twist into tune. Never too soon, in truth to hide out
from promise finishings, spoil to propagate a crust
bruited abroad, accusing omissions to blame. Mine
turn both said, retain habitual prejudice lid, vain
office animus unfolded even this early, year-long.
Scruple implied attending with conscience for each
hectic arrival, place to first face a rush of blood.

## Rouse, Trapeze

Minister protein incriminate, pretending dapper and win as if fervent to mossy branch, impervious forest temper outside, make and bake; flock ingredients banish morose lull in link foregather, custom pinned and raised. Steam whence imminent, expel hot sprung neighbour pocket, check first later annex profess, tangent veil; lacerate cross narrow estuary, victorious medley woven into cloth patch-work, defiant recoup tested prime exercise. Finger revise elated prize torment huddled together, at peak sympathy remedy inter flotilla daughter, caught in thunder trio unwelcome, wounded in breath gasping if not yet remote; perch playful search ward scratch over glass elite, match quiet soundless. Brush past open listless canopy delirium, unfortunate anchorage, accident. Gaze to rouse, trapeze mendicant involving tight shoe trigger sublate finial, so many of them returning, love for love did they all as foolish animated, spectral tint stem oven-wise. Discreet suspension spun in borrowed melodious chatter, distorted roadway find separate contrite shining hours improvident relentful. Figures in shade obvious catchment, proxy to feel in then near noise-free too, elegant to break off; caravan line raining, weighbridge soak tight intersect freight settled in fragments, reclaim brilliant plight.

## Vengeful as Mollify

Luscious demeanour at stud partition reveal mended, knows grand difference esteem practice faint or flick inhibit with brittle frost, turn detain. Guarantee or enter average supplement yours and mine to pulverise sop to compare, compensate by refinement, by the way-side, catch up in defer yielding rightful, renovate wince. Reckless attachment rich undamaged pay or pray as less enfeebled, virtue gladden entire; carry under foot. Languish by scenic conversable extravagant by this or that, total rudiment pumice receding or yet by flattery let go through, time enough. Brow sail aura perfume radical, equal tonsure mattin defend, rile them all persistent in share alike, winning by choice evicted. Steady parody, before lengthen into mock foray, crush hinder segment fortunate plural debated well ahead, rough cut availment adonic or frantic, in for cover. Heated delivery stir manage, escape pressure, valve index roam prank deference. Oftentimes disgrace avoidance, merrythought paviour inclination tea for two, terrace catalogue. Trail sensible distraught vengeful as mollify, multiply resume plainsong doubtful even rampage. Ocular run to proof, inspect constrict rounder than, nacreous. Jovial reflected did supplant in frequent testate, chant home to pry oblique pacific native household rumple ostensive; mass equate within circumference station, live the day voluble loophole attar for fine inhale and vapourise, indite. Word in situ, at sight leverage, get first lock tight no new offence notify evince into shining fast by night.

## Hunger Past Greed

Torque scimitar hustle speakable act lame foot pincer,
kettle slaughter beyond legal close foible now price
to restrain iron sleep. Moult in season, finalise but
try both doorways, passage without subway redemption
tack will never touch the sea wall, even light to open
sight. Missive fault confection pediment, safety drill
panurge not slight when pushed aside it mounts fusty
in brine. Fruit torment barrier attendance capitalise
polka stomp, rumpus incident revolve, dressy on-stage
bearing eloquent witness. Aloud beach oddity willing
speculative trial courtyard, on parade flounce tender
pacified. Centre mark this strop sulky top gullible
salute game plan banter assimilate triage, grenadier
applause, swerve banish accelerate hit and run. All
you strap holders admonish side to side, polish off
every crumb fallen and spread; hunger past greed vis-
ceral outcry labour vowel, column inches rhapsodic
pungency blame to pretty talk festivity elk swept in
and clustered. You know, you do clear enough dwelt
in dark backwards, yard slit acrid to sharp and wit,
flexure we know too, antecedent paradox decay under
silk. No object sauce said vigorous semblance needle
apposite front step private, horrify scowl fuel wake
ever faster in comedy script, untainted mound fixed
undivided, both similar feature satin. Shine traffic
fissile harmless lofty value added, finish speech of
wind and cloud, slope pervade seep dry trifle, wink.

## Fast Cramp

Vaulted ashen meadow, into renovate doubtful reform
whether purposeful volume and seldom, to digit bill
radiant omittance and bunch up scintillate. As yet
to unload, assume tendon segment improvise praise be
horizon fashion, train averse cannon reluctant. Here
in plenty tribal script complainant nor fractionate
calamine aggro, pinch too much that's what they say
yet crick shoulder otherhood enter metal afforded,
gestic external often craven gangrene or bitten off
back to front; accomplice massive dial consternate
wishful you knew that already, flood the yard. Agree
unit talent resemble guardian main flight too, the
squadron crash dim utter and shatter, avail westerly
tension lunar heavy coil in season; no neap tide to
will provide, leak harass casement asunder melt and
glutinous in a cup. Or judge, brickwork fresh point
either bond tied handsome, jib to brevity sanction
inflicted and knee-deep: fast cramp. Ramified onto
canvas signature, corner face to face produce lift
brokerage accumulate aver and correlated, money for
string to wrap up support extrinsic vessel gannet
span buckle. To make amend, final rectify or hoist
balance trickle condense keel arid frail, lift up
with care luminous gleam they do, fireproof and in
accordance fulminate, desist from blame. Say over
session longwise, mild question but sharp answers,
vigilant deferent allegory meant and throughout.

## Love Part Stubborn

Off-white deception winter coat delay, novel toy flight
to faint erratic store in price, no exception elastic
hand reserve name plate complaint. Bring what yet cannot
or will not in summation, away to be lordship recruited
infatuate. Unfold intimate by parent chrome hull, as to
full share on floor accurate, none there was. Waive only
the plan entrusted at all grateful, draw alongside trip
wire satisfy. Burning clouds, rustle parlour, inundated
by recognised suppletion over the marshlands. Veritable
privilege looming colossal empiric, dream qualified and
ride outwards, yet more doting in fame, battle-dress;
ford more or less promissory was a wangle untied. Badge
to single near enough pledge intransigent mural, mull
over occupation live to see and care to try, by antonym
wing dilated safe landing heartless and wire dock preen.
Mediate before they arrive, breaks in service polypody
implore, careless love part stubborn; treble cut fancy
galvanise, flavour and again the same, power house just
in game plan earn to win. Insinuating malady by catch
as can, will hold, awful gaze for cure debate if trite
correction, impinge formerly. At this time well past
divan or prodigy, error come home mail train in benign
suit keen to blow line-up, tempest at fullest pacify
strain to sing, higher amaze, here on the dotted line.

## Yield Freely Undulate

Pocket slide for message unrelenting, to grab plenty own
wrinkle designate, next rate uniform berated to rooster
obdurate, will daunt. Or tame discover latch down foolish
certainty bridgework fitting, far distant lever and sever,
at one fell visit. Brow raised by reason, perseverate in
unit batch water shortage precipice unfailing downfall,
hither aisle by echo modify and rink about lengthen, clip
tenacity in link to finger offprint. Upright flew rack
parlance, stand matter section, great fallen silence at
thin adventures, treaty carbon balance. Eggshells also
remit mile black curtains, profile halo tinker and shout
will devour without doubtful prosaic manifest, lone age
consort blandish fan the windowsill. Righteous lunette
today eager and fragmented, turn about mast turpentine
they brush by boast or hostile eliminate, hat blinker;
politeness for conscience good grief on marriage shellac
rictus instrument beyond blame. They would and if they
could likeness, imitate furnace psalmody react liquid
half empty; negative consent yield freely undulating.
Moist riverine caddis, flint insertion get there early
rock the quay to fit kitchen average interval furnish
knife rejection. Feel to raid, picture caress fondly
so far as evident, prevalent chance voices avail file
strict energy strait. There was warm attraction, rule
to regain companion entertain, grain slim invention,
never frighten, butter fingers; what you see is plain
sail, flew over in full melt and vigorous similarity.

## Scarce Leafage

On the wing or sang for them, all in want to be ready
tend to fly bare foretell expected reveal, vanish orbit
vain tendence lance at speed. Line optic fathom accident
leave may abandon tongue, extricate will they, will bay
contrive too far, too hunger order say distend familiar
beggary voicing. Cry out in dream or mine, hear you on
lost formal sacrosanct imitate, for not real decepted
at last enough won't try, can't unstring day close open
oh speak before, clothing belated. Child of grace, in
endemic dormancy assist to rest harvest, swallow again
too save out beyond for finding, under or lingering as
scarce leafage after, chew. Did you or we all dismount
however send attempted, their both way elastic or early,
fame in sorrow size to aggravate, relative out finally
too few, see what prize never now, even then, ever mind
to settle. Sad shadow shed off, murmur address field so
in want outward, lenient don't sealed in pace offertory
margin or shred, fetch. If we could, canted inward by
lever foremost, if but solid pinion. Must be waiting
from temper choice abandoned, escapement aggregate none
for the beating heart like dry ever, waiver honest to
end knowing in line. Arcade trellis, mockery readiness
or better still, is misery non-vital, servile probate
feed with them hoist up and unclaimed. Or lent to look
as seen beyond rescue pointer, on and on faint to go
plate to bare cup inflown left, and yet so far enough.

## Before Vestige

Take a breath to or be, obey gladly as or may
deplete left pine would simmer back over seem
for old held in ardour, end fast. Minim best
proceeding accrue to finish at if last manage
often melted own by down, size or soon leave
not lost but, yet forsake, for hurt traded
inhale mortal, select by travel pre-set and
value demur; pours overcast, blemish where all
too free, bold to follow lime out in slices,
arrogate. Piecemeal before vestige, sensate
let effigy back surmounted broken into, bitter
mortise parenteral by folly search place open
path further. To better remake at peak kindle
rank before, other in queue name by both at
first as given inflected mission, return made
trivial to last, woken agreement. Forasmuch
for you, for meeting felt wicks rising ill
assented, flare action pairs fold as fescue,
list awn eagerly tenet enveloped, never envy
or freeze; in alter tacit liquescent faster
and split, sleep on past symmetry few force
total lapse or cold, rest wanting. Suppress
attach worse fit we cling to have, have all
to end, binds up allergy insidious syncope.

## Evermost True

Sorrow almost, it is too near, repair more
to say, hold breath to catch and watch before
eyebrows flicker, back now. Of too late not
quite look to see, swallow these are parts
vehement resolve, be resolute, ready to give
afforded let to flow not otherwise to rise
and bear, hold to dare release where so too.
For true word to keep, whatever take, in starts
held to lend don't reclaim, wrist to quiver
let be strung touch, out reach intent, yet
match and glance. Must attain, here both long
and for, face to wake for cheek, leave to say
believe all as who, full gear beside, you.
Relent, stay less time no grief to bring like
fair dismay, or play the best as can, there
in advance. Air in fine attire please of face
open and free, live with, measure renew listen
out to find: overture, assimilate as through
and bide, is evermost true, both of two. Next
for fast, trust sufficient in honour meant
so be sure, hear to do, ever and over, rue
nothing yet nor woe endure be more, for you.

## Dark and Better

Offering or murk else tender outworn, soon seem
label to enmity reduce undenied. At soft not
fragment braving the wave tepid quanta traction
child fare evident, inference exhale byline;
why all passage ribbon, fable will care, excuse
prior distraint anticipate and fuse, confected
to find at point. Open extra, flutter equally
burnish in repute know to do, silent. The track
drop mine for shift after, massive deficit, for
time lost often gradual, dark and better, speedy
by now, bits fed. Shade overhang reaches de-
pletion quite visible, within similar trial
delimit, foster spring or instantly matching,
risen in half-light prepared. Bridge to normal
wayleave exchange hitherto, save parts willow
value prompt abutment, arrive early in share
premiss tide for ride, in offspring expected.
Go out far at once distal, dim entrain company
horizon recognise, all to grow and flow betide.

## Manifold Pleat

For whom to, whom soever human at the crick
glowing with attachment, curation to fame tip
as family soon famished, proof to flame. Bring
cord will pitch new immune near heart repeat
to beating reckon, mantissa ingrafted so soon
either mandate hand expulsed. Coerce to hold
alternate clasp, long enough impulse foreign
detour imagine, ever meant. Tinsel over cancel
across gaze retinue in remainder, pride bound
sapient and lifted, familiar said to attempt
manifold pleat. Main infusion is whose tap,
rife to pledge ever will, volute invite fast
for useful intimated progeny, shirred enough
in readiness. Fold under deep hum, ancestral
profusion extended by voice-print in the yard,
converging now and then fiction. Manse in mix
forgiven errand, entire pensive spinal map
innate at borderline, tribute allowance with
colours set fast. Speak next, replenish at
the door; instigate and manifest, gene pool.

## In Ascent Grimace

In troy return to singular scented pathway weight
level will intent foremost take missive, invite
to climb for handpress, mention. While libation
assemble optimum ready known arise, lens florid
pervade not listless, over journey seek without
in gravid comity. Uppermost sectile intuit enable
to bend, inflected prime lozenge the whole crew
will next elevate, untie branch careworn segment
persist and flex. In ascent grimace inevitable
promise truly if hear the same, given word bud
assigned them too, infuse; whether light gained
steadily, enjoined and free. On offer by chance
minimal grade honest to run, shake fine rejoin
warm as after ant tempest. File uphill to tell
who or what defer, fitted together go first in
remedy allergy proven. Did so, fashion rim abet
fusion fermented granule, yet so on faster, on
sign invidious and for now to thrive, even so.

## Told in Climax

Lend for new time, near to share swiftly steady look
inward light of lights pasture. You'll see sell, soon
sound in full flight, across and between, in watch
give on over much profligate; spare willing be fine,
assume behalf seeker commission. High column calcium
in aspect notify, enlarge on plane review occident did
bell ignition peril never void entwine. Or day extreme
generate particle, loose count on mass extinguish, to
quicken up when influence all to notice litmus afford
adopted, line-out agreement trail. Palm to close hold,
borrow in brow unless, furrow so parallel by symptom
lumen gather feel and spread, lamps rich as they all
sometimes will. One to both tacit truth fortify, a
torrent climate margin assign apt tale nourish plenty
entire caressment. Close to call, mild play or milk
cloudy, out to touch, trim. Fell into shape first, in
main dispute rail summary drench parapet, best to foil
disarray mounting as they do, undercurrent turgid all
measure to seize, told in climax punctual promised
inspect. Eventual conspected private incandescence,
corrode marking to come back prime, loyal and true.

## Fort in Fault

Return not set, torn and bred, quick bird on briar muddle
limber bromide, hot metal meant yet primal grid invented
dart in silt at haste, lost first annelid, anodyne guilt
wasted, part rebuilt best thirst pantomime annual quieter
annulment than scented sat up unsaid. Red by then yellow
follow middle tanager while teenager leant forward torpid
brain caliper terrify, implied plastic amplify wade best
cramp beat inert fort in fault, allied font ever-bought
cheat tortive; batter regilded instead now met our alter,
flatter fine bird heard ahead but lately miss intimidate
electrotype fulminate dissected bulk, not liken refill oat
omit trek section ingrate spirochete or livid fervent trio
join hardly willing tendence mission, do they. To buy keel
adjustment, remedial timid trial unlikely, slow intrusion
around probable treble mean finisher, worry to levy upmost
each brow reticulate except daylight pitch discover anthem,
wit advance expected intrinsic, effusive; grapple beforehand
how many tilt over down or low sooner reach grateful mist
horizon simplify strict excision append trifling plentiful
bound falling knee attempt supple delay, to say accommodate.

## Telling Not Broken

Protect the neck fillet eventual give out recount
air lace too far, aspirant level mendicant none dis-
appointment trim. Often flake be thought ever gleam
clear running, out dire and before, all swift of open
skyway and keel batch; much shall yet determine edge
of the path. Carried over by remedy of desire and
moving by wave front, eye-beams bespeak to rim flip
and bear; telling not broken yet exchange by hanker
each the other same would lief swallow intaken few
error given binary out trust for this, near for here
and where to limit due; or be lent ever sell root
claim invent did final other or minor sentence burn,
slip past worst so by lip interim frozen; bite sign
to rest unpair see to seen, air-stir lover's glance,
table surplus soon believed would tremble or refold.

## Instinct Low Incur

Go to try or willing safe to glass, or orient filter both for insistent brand-ready likeness taciturn. Face to mark prevail open sour particle, at once damage profile, exception or feral. Batter to proof so many awaited, bank slope crossing re over in a life fermented or by casual sunlit despite, activate wish to reach first match agreement; cool child profile amity tune single alight nourish is yet adopt and foster. Nap zip-up full beside intrinsic hold to loyal transition none for at present trial of reach, grist anticipate presuming. Instinct low incur remove allegation as inside attach scandal plus finish names seen and known, will they not this much impugn sufficient part divided, eventual. Let shade not cast retract, not infant invented overly submit perform flicker come and go frequent. Awe for them all in current replenish patchwork, donative in white all of principle affected, least to predict incidental or mild.

## Carum carvi

Caraway perfectum incidental, truce elated
adjoin casual matchwood curvature; helical
proving torrented abjure recline untoward
all grow, all allow like to like, add weight.
Will serve orifice, issue retained long out,
schism produce mainfast elected dash for no
waiting first to last, duress. Tinge fruited
alliance perpetrate, esteem before uncertain
internship provoking and requested; in both
soothe typic plaintive, either back mistake
birth canal funded, lucid entrain. Deign
at pleasure, all refine seam full suited,
nominal plastic febrile well after doubt.

## Better Induce

Linnet devise and finish extra, nor vivid
call through, persist tenterhook sylvan dome,
chaconne singular or last frame specular fit
to come in. Who would know as still better
induce florid mixture, near flown tracing
aromatic; journey lode aspect, lever trim
forcible. Relish discrepant anew complete
monetary, insidium protected if so honest
summon evident, bevel swerve alike cruise
cosmetic inference. License extravasate
terminable to win compare, track aligned
of the forest culminate insisted, avid try
for why not yet; few to blame into rise
proven fondly, integral tongue and groove.

## Search in Troy

Lurch eat lunch advocate foremost amber
not impugn, time like present. Whole must
placate the crew arrived, both hands now
aroused as welsh income satisfy, agree.
Fraction summit search in troy, due temper
sworn liturgical by list placement, honour
toast. You'll see soon, look on leather,
coif upraised and audible nap by the by,
of them treacle, tracklement ingest to scorn
attune sign ahead for sport. Luck will have,
moment frowning crescent implied and woven,
risen limber aver, eyes for her too. Occupy
mention grace note touch fulsome intrinsic
carnation, never hurt by altitude or grant
far display, most worst syrup foramen all.

## Coolant Arrest

Duffel condiment merger invest distribute for this time fortress, anxious must horizon twist strip partial, ruffle. Over pasture randomise clue, soldier promise energetic solute entrusted, dissolve would yet renew, counterfoil mast remittance accepted final. Coolant arrest prime loss, prize to match older why or when guarantee defect replete past interview; pretended dilution entwine seem more solid aphetic won, dream-like true dip percussive. Profess tolerate, coil buttress significant bond heartfelt inscript too, accompany encomiast fleet unction, with them can best wound attic. Patient adhere domain undo at crestfallen, crypt retain flit descended, stairwell folder, cyan blue meet. Unless comprise hue deliver outpace toil, discrete massive tonal oil fuel endeavour yours to mine, ever so too few; scribal ascorbic plentiful.

## Tight Ever Set

Purpose unwind caramel, choice vocal bone
touch whose advancement intrepid, on much
expected. Velvet crimson lace twine welling
overt casual nervous shoe horn cartel lame
imitate, you will or had caress. Shall up we
then possess nowt wasted, self finding for-
sook lectern arbitrate sepia fright descent,
to yet admonish. Too lavish voice quaver
simple frown letter sit, announce visual
carapace entreat pointed inward, mistook
distress should insistent summary, cover
fission. Mica welcome ransom flourish, tight
ever set mimicry my oratory if for you also,
demur sentient risen synod fulminate creature
intuit discernment. Overtaken in passion met
surplus trod whim improvise jointure, less
beaten. Shone over brow too, along steady
advisement, panoply trimmer go on through.

## Cut to Fit

Impulse settlement over fault, sine, persistent
upward partition or metal winner dine intercept,
care for cure built and dented already; relent
to halt surrender fashion less anchor suffix pin
cherish mirage often. Step back, by look up, be
in shadow else numerical gazing meant frequent
tore open wonder, stubborn additive to lottery.
Melted or steady meander counterpart alternate
inch bolt pyre cut to fit, longing always, days
selected and fragrant: tithe. You save, aware
discuss infancy, caught hither chimera fortune
allergy return, spline sink inducement coyly
sufferance delayed. Alloy fair alignment, miss
out discrepant hilt borrow subterfuge, or lose
sufficient rated unity; infusion sent pliant
saw most reticent pre-mortal antidote caustic
refer temper winch. Limit pawl wilted, fix by
candour, awe ridge allusive percept promissory
lair bent forward tilt on loan. Take up stance
adoptive twice, fulsome whereby brimming over.

## Soon Allowance

In swum suited newly, ascension clarify ceded coruscate to be to treat, sentinel valid pause and gaze at root donation, tissue listen alum gliding. Lenient luff over misted tribute sill out to soften, felt of deep lissom venture able lizard, screen pay to play, with them. Assume cliff rising tress reproach token, break some moisten inset pine forest harbour, loose glee intrepid ascriptive, elatior. With your plea prepared, douce dimity trestle sibilant occupy mercer at the door to signalise, recruit add title missive, them all lipid unnamed perfuse to drift and fall in system arrangement; on fresh course floating as always listed, mild granary or sylvan tip succession. Fossil claim before otherwise needed outflow, quicken to attain prior placement homily beseech bring fastidious, pen shadow remiss. All yours or soon allowance mercuric paradise warden gate swung plectrum derive up to bridge realm in trace first; ribbon whistle lastly perplex.

## Flop Tremor

Dilate frost helping tympanum overtone minor cut
switch climb, wondrous spread even must induce.
Profuse eligible forehead, each time hatch cranny
legible egg-like abed, betony ponder succour if
for patronage. Ever close in held affine dipper
organum innate clamour, flop tremor, wheel tooth
lesson prognosis. Dabble these assemble, silt
upper win attachment bead, hone crucifer simulate
joy. A moiety re-granted and ducted, blend freely
suffusion permittance fast as practice; sender
fair declare optical lintel, average bred credence
to foster, folding at the crease. Tentative single
paragram, edict comedy plate reduce profane re-
turning in team prospectus; meddle afflatus in
stay with me all while, end else full symmetry.

## Lure

Writ riot wet wrapper omit terrace comfit lancet
benefit integument, biotic segregate mitral
let infill flighted face up. Rite snap estimate,
hit white elegiac limpet, debt elated. Yet by
sated cry orchid in orbit, batter waist fret
ornate too, due intake. Strict intendment witter
sapient slight pollinate, inflate vital, obey.

## Dire

Comet banish miss solicit, guess ossify redress
mount summit try merit insistence; finish intent
innervate quoit pertain, suzerain onset. Flight
way peruse, quorate, west address fountain won't
pacify, anodyne. Ascertain percolating implicit
planet score freight entangle tenet so far dis-
tant, quantum ahead choice refusal designate
admittance; mere indifferent.

## Collected Wharf Now

Stick lining elegant ascriptive endue illustrate,
half furnish to mirror overture impoverish ban
directed lavish, inflect. Often pretty line, at
price service underscore merriment rose planetary
alter sidelong retain, entire periapt riverine;
preludial custom plantation. Advance fast winter
dissenting absence however disclosed, your brow
inclined, frame ever mobile, dative. Collected
wharf now to ambient reduce and design, turn at
immediate crimson avoidance sunlight travel find
congested anomalous, cause unravel dancers nap
to score. Address alive or if, die fluent once
into front, prolong seclusion. Bay to green in-
fluence join handsome, brilliancy mused courteous
dialect familiar elective, by eloquent. Far off
to know, keen to saunter watchful, nest enfold
past there fused, adventure eager attended. Fly
trail iridescent inversion, wing ban conjecture
at quick or glory, for them inclusion far ahead.

## Prevent Satisfy

Distort foreign blade to count foremost, less wary in effort esteem vocal and certain, dyed few stinted or surge optical effigy. Plant before, fusing sheer allocate cranny seem swept well ahead, be at coast suiting laid out beyond temper reason bond, which to local anklet forward tepid lasting if settlement verge report. Act will catch reflective, sap frost furnish press career after dry, frame mint brother old but said until longing; intrinsic trellis. All over relish, stay for him, call rapid soon to merge prior let go few manacle now decline costly do reflux in front. Attentive core entire to match, to search out fondly this bristle since want captive optional, stack feign on depute; prevent satisfy avertive to pacify insure, mere finish off in fund dramatic overcast renovate. Relent too simmering while replace division, rennet crop or risen boat wavering been honest back dare intently, say fair scut accidental; must align fusion grant leveret evenly calm undaunted, indigenous lentil and free.

34,000 ft.

## Addle Bird

Batter refolded or better not yet alter, to flatter impeach
such scolded fine bird ahead at reach or dread too, by few

Instigate freight porpoise not on purpose dilate imitate
surplus boast and crush, force portion altercation relative

Denial oval trial not fuss, acid bale coil to pressurise
dust in eyes arise mastiff hostage pottage at triune uncle

Bad hurt resort mischief not sad, led astray which way
certain mortal ambient facile, sentient retail proclaim

Rid for bid up painful not with gain made, allayed if too
afraid lipid procured one time payment, immured insipid

Fanciful balance accrue, not silent or new to touching,
safe purchase wince failing face rice cambric listless

Water bought fair not pairing liquor elongate pure, dare
under mortar yet quicker relate endurance entrance caught

Announce reckless fence not inspect or insect, through or
too pounce absorbed once message entangle deck ageing so

Will know by flow not fill up over brim temper to tamper
never slow undergo the foil heap, ill-said boil deep lip

Quantify alliance want not inch finance fly past banter
now to enter entourage reforge perfidy lurk untidy cent

Swish flush nimble not fumble, crush apposite in flight
did biting cold for, remould unctuous and sensuous lush

Former inner sumptuous entreat not yet meet my corner, in-
dulgent as winner, a swimmer reheat to trumpery beaten out.

## Conversance

Shall we go adept to the footpath, along the side, would you keep company by reversion if and when the light clears, could be accomplished?

Ah yes more probable by this request, easy and quick to grant your favour, honest hold fast readily we know to suggest as soon as advanced to meet, heart-felt.

Would you be in trust to persist after turn looking out by shelf contention, really would you in promise evenlier than forbearance and guided, to make attachment, for good? In trust quickly?

All right away we'll share necessity driving on along, which side to be as honourable, trail part to next outlet, premise in-voice by air in returning water frequency as each portion made up to compare.

So come then with if limits allow verity mostly, do you accept enough to make sure bright, attract to shine, by the agreement out in advance but only for trust if it reaches to line in part, apart. Enough?

We should confirm and do and bring with consistence to where one another in sight afar, concede near enclosed fully in view to transfer and soon satisfy, beyond the need but wish to know to listen, resolute.

Is this the point then, beyond capture tight convergence, always construe, would you aggregate all our fortune in discovery, deliverance for ours entire consecutive long for the entire white memorandum, and should we, can be done?

Each we crossing know, for each one ensign inversion you live believingly by the footpath mine and yours noticed, circle the stream head the same one gone to find for both. With all yet soon to know take or make steps in pace spoken.

Tell clear listen, face to endeavour, as will infolded, willing?

Hand to hand in evidence often will give or go back strongly enough, hold fast recital not lost scatter lifted up afford, with acceptance mutual undenied profile in effigy words even in flow, influence.

For sure frequent, waiting to catch up in a moment or few or listen close anyway avouch in advancement of sense, could be made out as good to gesture share to know anyway, would catch up on-side assimilate, yes?

Agreed by attachment look far to see they say determined, both in turn be true as promised well ahead, mine for you our sample, so disclosed incentive we admit as to bring to the footway in step remember acute.

Will that meet our fate of taken at our open promise, is a chance of it if not by accident avoiding its less brusquely rustle, up forever minister the air, running ahead water truly livelong day agreement?

Then avouch or then, the same reaching ahead at rescue sidelong part to finish up afar, over give sign step by next step obedient to expectation in rush to find out beforehand. Be sure to tread side to glance face to speak.

Yes watch each our step adventure take new aim, be true level for sight insistent stride match one after when too other predict take word for it step westward: hear the echo service have to confide infant pearl fiction?

Along the side channel foot print overlap to commingle, lace fully protect because any conversion yours and mine I assume made solid, for sake not at risk take the strain you know best.

Who would see us there, exchange ready glances still hopeful of what is known yet, whether it will or shall be to trial the rest of it murmur below no audit but see it will mean to hold fondly by means relented?

Ah you intend the front path for the doorway, the slight step at the turn observant and lovely too, much all ways we know not too soon our habits find where before lift thy foot prevailment amount to mercy entreaty.

Of course sly in parallel veering for patience we know othermost, for probation quickly as before, confirm one the next either so your turn affirming to infuse not too late, sensible?

Stepping out onwards do, in deep converse ready for of pair wherever we make or take the track we shall, to tread the grasses felt buoyant to bear and carry, air lifting mention reliant sound in sound crossing.

Inside contentment less to manage could be prolonged searching word improve each in place look out for pause to lay on the bank, walking freely rise and fall, air warm on our cheeks befriended?

But then will as even do you shall we or not, chosen by to prefer intrinsic gentle respite of new revealment keep pace absorbed by share turn and return to fill allowance both ways, assented lightness.

Is open now and again as you'd expect say so first, remonstrate but in passage for to make replies always telling what we redeem to hear nodding and in alignment, of slow advice but brief admission proven?

Yes words and speak along in flow gradual and implied shall continue what to say is simple and fluent already heard level voice humour and query for occasion to be whatever's best.

28th August 2018

## DANA : PERS : DANA

DANA: Thus to open on a cold morning, can you see them near
  outmost at hand, white now already drifted
PERS: We had better recognise, risen in air, at first web evaporate
  by immediate colour matching and sound horizon
DANA: Ah for all and both, hold out quickly enough, rock face
  shine on your side quartz probably manage to reach the apex
PERS: Will you wait for folded before, the rest in voice prepared
  allot in advance certainty across snow, uppermost child fill
DANA: Either ready slant to window, air curl spoil and latch,
  press fitting say what you think or want enough
PERS: Withhold for you also, early or later difference gradient
  like to donate slice partition, pair arriving missive
DANA: Why not, any grant reason as we know, lane discover
  by counterflex, listen right out; tabernacle primed–
PERS: Exact admission pane image, inflect timeout cutter you
  can open see, chill air beyond the balcony, cull favour
DANA: Blue and green tell what you wise prefer, attachment
  still volume before going slip to meet revalued sober
PERS: In the Course of Season peg them out, pack ice counted
  finish sled word trailing watch, can you leverage
DANA: To ask so inserted, to hear the sussurous foaming
  is a voice in answer further, back from your larynx
PERS: And mine also, ours in trial badge improve signify
  parallel amounting, impetuous possessive fearsome drift
DANA: Impression, white print dwellage these are coined
  by rank company after both elevate not long to seek
PERS: Fresh fall, cover in trace search, brilliant tread over
  silent now relief said for sure, offer pledge each way
DANA: Accepted. Talon fee, eye matching dazzle compulsive
  ordinate warrant blink, animus we too ready-hearted
PERS: Can tell state to be evenly, ask trust first magnify
  frost declension, birth average long to tell instinct
DANA: Formerly the crevasse, caravan beside the floe, parity
  augmented even docile unblamed wrap convergent cast
PERS: Worse than, effusive permanent stake to try, nothing
  left defunct entire pale intricate perspective index
DANA: Mark to fit the case, speak out decision shared, echo
  returning Narcissus levity, grave answer arise, prune
PERS: Utter sequent strong to hold, restless instigate hollow
  joist following well natural, tell me by convergence

DANA: Instant unless simple retrieve passion intimate claimant
lime threshold, fit shoe to grow fate to foot haruspicate
PERS: Blow at the ridge line feather shimmer oracle inveigh at
testament white destiny, promise insist incessancy
DANA: Courage, as bold typical inference too, relax portable
fabric disposed in chill whiff, plume ablative mingle
PERS: Intercede or venerate assume with them at the door
perfuse freely multiply, break local ingress entreat
DANA: To fetch and match, shade are disposed termite ill
code fixture winter wind, door blind in crush soundless
PERS: Sifted in powder, path clear but near to melt chronic
interfere refinement, morning sun cover glass will ever
DANA: Announce, pliant or porous settlement shade line accost
prevalent retention textural basic rise as then called
PERS: Nod to say for, willing sympathy wrist into flight
bird in snow, in white plumes, effortless conversion
DANA: Or Greenland Bears casting deep shades ahead, in profile
verbal currency, in truth. Where will you stand intrepid
PERS: Already reckoned like the others single wattage fiery
willing orchard lit up, cave stair flex for us, novice
DANA: Evidence device, of the life perfected, take sure mean
no better latent part furnace to clip cold vigorously.

## Onset One

In life to be foreseen and hold teeming, would
soon by wave mounted, here and dear close to,
sound matching cajoled open pitch far reach,
implied hand to save, brave echo interplay untie.
Sustainful donor our honour no lessen by trance
coeval or vital, aspect wear enough. The voice
of her, blush light affirm deep extend recline,
search outbrave injury, clatter allayment. Nil
need she excuse disturb back forward, dream in
late array, intense to layer up ahead. Venture
alembic in turn about, for themselves chaplet or
yet diadem supplement imploration vigilant, aid
voices soft raised, brow illumine. Answer before
destiny profile sounding, glance over repair free
as once again and fro, better will. Your or to
know, eyes sparkle enter at portal, rainfall by
tranquil said glisten, to save till share our
modest implement; with tie attempted onset one.

## Soon Darker

Soon darker than, when some ever, will faded
under the mark made heavy, mind ribbon mail
shade to pass below. Offend diligent craft for
levity agreed, next after sibling walk slipper
invidious, overflow tale detected, habit. They
to me, go readiness amity profound, hidden eve
enter constituent talk help in foil, hark up.
For dim indigent last but one, limit tender
force envy, dial tremulous after by claimant
allocate, made in pair attune labile singing.
Promote miss to chance freed, ground mastic
level, well to come similar incentive; grass
citation, quail severe accusing, raft zero.
Infer tomorrow impatient bulk test inept like
applicate, final hawk cover. Will pay while
day open aside hard up to visional, sedulous
trimmer oblige abut loudness fragile, better
cling. Port far off, avail heroic topic re-
mittance plentiful; faster than, as novelty.

## Is Drawn

Insect guise prolix bee setting, forest sanction
to profess consonant purchase virus, provisional
lancet solemn in size commence and nurse. And else
sensor magnetic compete, luscious hispid munition
blockade addition, deafen. All is known, found
under netting brand inveterate convergent, don't
forget terse in first twin, known utterly. Efface
light column torus, sense appease cram faucet to
notarise, suitable tag borrow sessional. All will,
no sound, those feet ancient innervate gristle by
tressle amusing see crabwise on-side in ordinal
confluence. Rise tepid, dapple or florid unction
humour modulate avenue crass abundant fly upset,
sun-risen no further. Line is drawn, out finial
listing, will greet withal chorus inverse, sugar
retreat coptic for engine, ingenious follow ant
lurid, extreme in parallel. Suppletion snare-drum
often lambent tracing, prize warden garden path
endurance, canal grown willing insipid, cereal
mentation resettlement, silently train dawning
true gather these before; sweet minimal can we,
can you too arrest restore, meet to share. We do,
replete ivy resplendent by archway, free frozen.

## Honour Page

Proof sessile rapid contingent omen flame your accurate jaw-bone, produce stellate carbon shot, missile printemps. Figural swallow throat bite tropical harbour, finite link orchestral summon mort plaintive plant-life inherit. Fill ingestive aversion turn back gladly, tame retrieval flow, envied loop denied moral; take cover drastic be urgent, pungent asking willow plate restriction. Thus quick taken by agile span hollow, ridge task unflinching, dust to follow do honour page great solo pilot out to sea. For mandate sight, coastal flare path outmost sad heart temper blow, our elbow covenant tall order fringe locational reversion and simulate, range to home, roam wit; except promise admitted redeem to same profit, instil visionary soft fluff allow cheer deeming; clear seen free gifted motley presence, proclaim.

## Edge Causeway

In advancement they went then to the front lap
and shimmered there, in edge causeway horizon
parlance; this was the footpath for both ready
incitements, partners had known of this before.
Speak true for proof footfall all each one, calm
difference, act to margin reckon via interlude,
two of them hoist in scarf repointed. That so
is the card accounted, at horizon's pace trodden
muted sharper, hold companion-way along the crest
emplacement, steady attracted to share the upper
view. Her patient flight by new rest of, onlook
to features, never dim. Speaking between, to and
fro exchanging, longing too outward in pin cause
discretionary supper cloud time, can be likened.
Given quick, relenting mutual, take for grateful
surprise, eyes flashing. Say wit entreat by lip
signature, print more to know how far, than yet
further still to find by trance overt she will,
both mark the tale for impulse warm embroidered.
Holding his view also tremblant mercy, in fruit
up on the bough, brow folded to hear the full
repair; incited familiar recognise, harbinger.
Fly over to try each least idiom, finger twine
for free prince release unfailing, about due
time each first most too fair or sent; ahead
frank discovered flush in step at hand, slant
gaze, walk along through cloud rim visitant,
eastward search; to hear breath taken and lent.

## All Will Clarify

Soever are tongues perplexed; *lex loquens* we-ever do
know by care weather front, cave entrance voices echo
own seem verge wrist unwavering. Tell to open way best
harvest all presented, yours and mine deep so buried,
peaceable. Forward in face setting, mile and smile no
grief planting far over sender wait for, hair shining
radiant shall for sheen, near and repast at the table.
Trim out to foible smooth clearway riding up high, you
see its fixture either mine again, oh vero, oh kindly
too. Not retiring also, not late but ever early, take
our time veritable where grant to innovate and claim.
Not hard to hear about lively, all will clarify, in
colour brighten honour too, immense so attracted glow
while generate, speak far aloud, threshold intimated
by ardency in grain reply. At the moment warm as ever
be, forearming and pleat returning, utter out to hub
commended in queue share flicker, heart now so near.
Transfer, infuse blood volume title benefit both adjoin
in look fasten, frontier match entire when and when,
from bounded here resume. Festive shadow, play we took,
chance too no risk for danger simplify extended; what's
to be deeply wished not least incidence be there see
plume brush mantel, stay brightly yearn. Our venture
renown to find tongues set, say what you want to mean,
quick-time each of us reach out, tasted flourish home.

## Land Flown So Few

Now known nor new, one mend or mind attune
how so for more to do, where lend and saw
by law in sound, to fend or done where found,
to send in pair and bond, low or snow-bound,
land flown so few, as near to kind or there
and bind, appear by care in fund. Or end.

## NONE YET MORE WILLING TOLD

## (2019)

The eleven curtains were of one size
- King James Bible, Exodus, 37:15

Sink beneath the waters to the coral sands below
- The Grateful Dead, 'The Eleven' (1969)

Too much of a good thing is wonderful
- Liberace, spoken on BBC TV, May 23, 2000

Wie aus der Ferne, aber deutlich
- Alban Berg, *Wozzeck* (1931), p. 225

## Moss for Spur

Moss for spur entreat, to ride
  away part all we know or will
too gaping. Lit to lamp, fuse water
  lessen flicker, ladle furious
massive snowy morning waiver;
  pronounce inflected sublate
advantage; nascent tribal carry
  up-stream tack, offer plain top
beat on-side, no hurt passage, if
  ever withstand squill to tassel
or macerate. Tint to play soundless
  hard to fend, each way anomaly
sieve mission credit dawn peg, into
  mark to run, proof wish so late.

## Prevail to Link

Prevail to link apparel, nor sever how soon
  far and wide ascent, range verify seal cling
in-shore. Ignited evermore sparse deal citric
  purse be pitiful at once. Class frame sadden
by shade flowing, steps abound, minister else
  in favour, make a promise: live to tell for
otherwhere discover give certain wait for storm
  rouse breathing chill resilience. When who
goes matter flake, to be born. Assembled in clench
  profile, impart graven to share, dark sky
cast lucid fitful shadow sleeping cypress cordon
  moreover stay still nor reckless inwardly
frozen trim. Voice to raise, mention deference.

## Fair to Well

Fair to well either self proven clam too,
   crest within canter both before sonic
invested ligand cell type, seize. Amend
   allusive, full-legal part fire, fleer
search after, best true heart sail benefit
   in look in, in lock come to quit, all
like dare mounted and whether at fictive
   provident train. Or who away not, give
for them, for her within ear-shot carriage
   raise scare glory, raven wing try ex-
treme pursuit oriflamme; caution sitting
   across, fusion drops eddy invasion by
tuck foils, mallow tense intended monad.

## Discreet Bivalve

Discreet bivalve latent, morning traveller
   incipit fasten to enter, primal harbour
surplus mowing essential felt. Praise at
   guise, distant haemal cruise adamant,
complete added surely whenever reach out
   stainless equity former lease, vertex.
Buy to find more rapid, yet will temper
   press, up or fathom be first to limit,
more let bond entire, in friend or loose
   ribbon stitch. All over now enough, of
phase to slate otherwise most flame arisen
   phoenix cognate datum, thick in bush.

## Limit Gamut

Limit gamut mastery her suited critic altitude fine
   lent filament praise merchandise come to sense,
into reflect and hop-scotch granite, lucid waver.
   Tremulous soaring are they shared because flus-
tered parallel, cordon perceptive separate. Oh raise
   her loss wanted better, grain for as she will; or
sift awry fulminate intact derelict aching near al-
   ready child, prophecy insistent along the front,
timeless birth assertion. Marching through rough
   woods save her tenet beaten brow, linseed fuse
revoke, betoken advance further her name, with mine
   to simulate dismount intransigence, heraldry.

## Relieve Amber

Relieve amber arrange fringe melted, long
   in room as were held at rock balance,
hand outward hazard check. Infrequent prime
   laze to carry, rouse in song debated,
lost and march anyone would know first,
   then told ahead. Intuit pane to draw
level square in heart beat away, practice
   spine attraction. Lamellar solace due
wait for promise aggregate, find afforce
   near forest ledge; host at main, fume
thicken low, attach delay in fruited dawn.

## Piper Three

Piper three steady often, zealous to dree matte
   private weir tenement, claim at first. Read
touch exacting, brightness falls scatter seen,
   alternate and clear replete, opportune. If
add to found likeness company tight to bended,
   soft folly underside profession. Win terse
share effortless sinker let, retorse or finish
   elide better ready; slip now at once, end
out left bits. Advocate ahead mere off indeed
   risk averse, spruce conics dilate nearly
jar still profuse with sweet flame and smoke.

## Annex Still

Annex still by the river comfort, plain digit
   favour our terrace suspect fastidious,
both by reluctant infant commanding, revel
   vex to peril, rigid in main. Mix by some
appetite previous beryl sitting, face out
   fluctual behaviour; forehead up perch can
ever forth unctuous sound privative punctual
   brevity indued, faster refund delicious
grasp act filament. Pace will as all redress
   never in mind, hover to choose better,
rampant place over; gentle invite went by.

## Thin Into

Thin into purpose mostly jaded in stream upset
   finish too, consume aroma act internal mirror
groove, faded twice seem redolent avid minim
   lavish. Met slice don't for wait, this one on
will circus trample under rest attenuate, sprig
   awning price favour. Decorate perplex white
blemish marks valid together, sail or special
   face tolerant; grasp at sense, fill tactic up
to its brim and fervid best. No choice formerly
   enticement, last fertile correction by prove
file up, safe reduce winner trained ascendancy.

## Rifle Attract

Rifle attract molybdenum caramel, blemish lessor
   service agile cadent morsel, district preservative
ash lodge, mischief. Bank on to off, sway teasel in
   travesty, affront formal so festive at forage;
gain say optic paradox induce, swerve actual heat
   with trim intact. Want to find past average, all
cost to spin, run over gravity no prison remainder
   front traffic insipid likely, riparian agreement.
Nil found, free of tactic claim marble work to live,
   tolerant in share, inshore fusty operant climb
full steep lucid, acquire frequent morbid diffidence.

## Oblique, Fleecy

Oblique, fleecy measure digress impulsive
moreover fulgent paid; affect minimal find
torrid keeping window. Into newer flow benefit
lacerate pick to date rested, assemble for
grown contrition bone indistinct, the light
turn hectic in cheek, in check. Weary
already tempestuous arrival laid out and down,
felled clever old so, held to word at listed
count. Nominate assessor clear tell also, no
better reason to the front; at vertigo on
avail in trawl simulate acerbic masquerade.

## Intensive Occupy

Intensive occupy twofold grade procession awry
adequate distribute right form, in traverse
to tame fledge. Pamper under fear notice, made
up at rate formaldehyde noon grist, motive
end carouse eventual. Take turn imply arrested
back to back endorse spillage, tail spin do
meal time humour gadget cost, bargain infamy
near avoided. How to tell by the label, or
laugh yellow can rise to see dear ones, tingle
acute dimension cardiac swerve, angle for
matching. Distance browse daybreak, invented.

## Cavort Furnish

Cavort furnish, test ovation assiduous at helm
  hope for sentiment entire it's caught decisive,
railing incendiary masthead. Gradual over them
  invigorate mission traction scatter, to name
occluded minimal, proclaim haphazard agreement
  advice. Or yet twice over, restitute contusion
barrack running apt discovery. Want format ill
  timed, made to lock impetuous crater implore,
all evident sighting. Fasten tremor west gate
  skip digestive or linger multiple bat more try
they nominate successors trial bent, alter quite.

## Skillet Nacreous

Skillet nacreous lifted up man season salt step
  to buffet wise fuel intact, skein overspread
or deign so, taken fast. Set to fluke, anticipate
  level grape immense gantry in fume precious
manifest trooping. Pleach hedge optimum affirm
  lay raise taffrail breath to hold, shell troop
immune foaming headwind equal to fluster family.
  At said chorus swell allume riboflavin nor
gather sibling mist deletion, away. Praise best
  assist, we'll time entry cast back extricate
and nourish, nape sup, tense loop in correlation.

## Ravel Porphyry

Ravel porphyry mention integer cloth purchase mollify
sugar tremendous, sensory inmost the pair classic
pathway, signalise. Both coinage variable, half sill
soft eager fortify, his be there alliance she will
enjoin find shoe moderate together; lengthen for on
apply to flee, pillory excision escapade fascinate
clip postural merciful. Occasion vested inundate fell
texture foster ambitious now, then, soon antelope
crowd haul aphetic scope outright; defiance protective
up found. Lacewing crescent the inverse tune infer,
first envy fire place, aft missing precious insignium.

## Monitor Prophet

Monitor prophet balance evident, fixative by anew
presently orris anticipated, as headway shall
relent orbicular, spark bit. Cotton in stock radius,
led start, amount to pontic attentive disturb.
Save willing once effort, few to polymer disjunct
in mark plentiful sent further remiss, thread to
schedule fast renew. Situate interview, sable preen
sure team bunting accrue in dark flight, under
intimate adhesion halo trim ado. Either docent you
gainsay part to heal allocate abrupt pacify, red
proliferate across lee front, guest seep at night.

## Along Natural

Along natural paper canopy enlarge sufficient,
  'la vie moderne' approach steady evoked margin
trail index no foible anneal; such to fiscal, tale
  in view. Ready pleating merge temperate lack
forge whether assist prior normal to fit, fuse.
  Into batch foil succulent, plate token later
still, ask primitive kernel, to rule; nor yet grill
  storm vestal twin, intaglio freshen already
astute operate scalar wick. Frangible demeanour
  convergent fomented pretty, sealing news open
wake missile not trifle blood latch so invigilate.

## Taste Wounded

Taste wounded reliance misgiven pacify nest imp
  monastic collar held, murmur sorrow crease reason
multiply short intrusion. Grieve allude no more
  wind gauge temper soffit asperse luminous anvil,
however flown nascent brine, too late votive. Each
  to careworn, claim dogged behind-hand wilt twice
railing where were infill apply and plain, sail fold
  is stubborn clerisy, volume told feud. Attar on
hit risen sweet fill cedar; inverse bonded weave
  antiphon, lull. Server rugged in memory, more
still than born, elastic radiant ample invented.

## Dare Up

Dare up formation listen twain announce, par
readiness diver planet filament escorted
tributary comical, pare down. Gesture listless
stay with, cross topic cloudy insistent at
moral occupy nerve. Ostensive calendrical shine
fissure agate diversion, cry for ill nursing
pretended sip over wet; nothing cleaver taught
to spill partner too fine and one. Retort tin
unsteady, blame set up stochastic minimum, here
swerve out inflame, arrayed countless over
legend allegory credit merit intense, optical.

## Profuse Average

Profuse average why trestle, share to this side up
with harmless edict fortress, alliance. Beam
silo give back arrival, by extra private, privet top
defence wide soon manage, alarm inspissate or
weary brow conation. They will, they have no choice
to take cover but evenly, blue team. Cannula at
first instance fills midget footway extreme, dis-
tortion tilt error under wayleave for mentation
fortune grim alike pretense bluster wedded few. All
run up bowsprit ascertain, harp across distress
fluent magic gated by willow lens, side after side.

## Doorway Happen

Doorway happen assenting principle, throat strict
deceit interest fathom several lay to reckon
oven neat advice, legal to bent still. Pitch at
lappet rotary meet pressure estimate, risible
over sightlines; moorland discrepant fury innocent
label. Dice cast session infarct, analyse by
noxious spread, forest to sail, to wrest up. Break
angle or crude told, tiller wicket buttoning
arrest, crowd pining for pardon; floor plan twice
over inch telemetry wish. Divide candid, echo
relented snippets, offend float enable, annexure.

## More Frugal

More frugal intern with andiron asian watch over,
must entreat entrance partition all out. Mesmer
flotation close call batch loaf vacant, crust for
that too, petition. Defeat morsel burn fierce
or worse teal inspect trail best if discrepancy,
august sovereign clement mantel. Fall parkside
in summit whence clamber, across sense suppliant
alignment; retain satchel frontal glottis arm
outfit. Swallow cluck evince sniff compel invest
afford enfolded, question pencil precluded to
light of life or limpet known ahead; motif natation.

## Eminent League

Eminent league utterance into viewpoint cascade
opening joint precision, wade outside flip
profile gusset. Promise gale fracture, intrigue
point rapine plan brisket upended. Rage
fume batten amazement flint path, arrayed by
clarion astern, team onion hum too; rainy
mean unfading adduce affric visit, rake seek
amber tendency guidance. Lent upper tint
in half stock, faltering screen snuff cambric
berry take offence. Faucet permission im-
print unfailing ticket; furtive daze bluff win.

## Mandolin In

Mandolin in lilac awaited, flew over swift purchase
vale adamant cosset flourishing manor trapper
attend marten; listen lack to fate volatile due for
fur while loving biscuit take fright will rock,
herald weight lift dual chase metal. Nothing ken
binding plastic minimal foil gradual moist tail
amorous courtly, unpriced plainchant interact might
give way, in line. Out crisis elegant obedient at
bate trusted asset slack neither cover, reach for joy
now chew enhance tungsten mission freshen attest
curtain differ lightful whirr twisted; indolent pin.

## Garden Brain

Garden brain, scansion missive, hood mother dim
   blue macerate tacit fascinate place to be, enter
free will say up chilblain friction clasp; terrain
   optimal way elation single file passion, scented
ream affirm. Joint action hand in hand, twice first
   fluorescence landfall at birth, heritable immense
gilded pitch known crew. Where due liturgy fantastic
   mild, unison childhood glisten willing craven on
hermitage welcome phantom swept back mock koan;
   ours to share, out of pair bond extricate main ten
line gift distribute theirs to harrow, invert season.

## That Day

That day askance motionless fountain to bring
   extrinsic condition, distrain exaggerate fry
on balance maintain ignorance, say armament, sent
   loose change one after sway finch valuable
fissile scenic, between times. Address enter code
   immediate gleeful; plain winter minimise off
paint doric malady take back over transfusing do
   selfish impoverish line to gain, heat sink want
rustle bill range home density; fond glance hand
   pay swell in root solace. Wish frequent pitch
kale redeem denied temple elbow, crane reversion.

## If Too

If too mellow practice designate act vital dissenting
local recruited blaze to honour, follow head torrid
martial freight invite another office immense; breeze
lantern impartial ray focal assuage prize shelter;
dense winning borrow distinct sudden dive trivial loyal
audience might here in fruit witty season, easier
looked for demeanour rate improve. Find out beholden
sense lure to bear, mere profit embed leader when
turn about, spindle fond affected. Share to alter lint
relenting figment, suffice active palliate skip, low
policy core; over care prevent seize banter punctuate.

## Set About

Set about with best of reason, high season, seed pearls
trim with bright coinage, through & through, loose
flourish retain degree, obey freely in margin cambric own,
her face fair turned to him, again linen lifted while
to crest, *intime*; all smile within, wreathe ottoman wing
play lucid, tune adorn bravery, iridescent milky whim
ready for he'll implore renewal, strewn about even hunger
interpret, dimension. Thus profuse, parapet amusing
unhesitant willing grant to hue in due time, epic plain
small brilliants light catching her brow raised, over
to him trifle to tell morrow, grain endued; shall assume.

## Inward Morris

Inward morris and tabor, listen fleet gesticulate, light
passage to path intuit rise, her eyes for him amaze
in suit front relay all day address manifest rhyming
to dig out then lift, arms akimbo lips parted metric
luminal gem maintain; just phrase voice temporal never
yet refused or perish, openly. Nor song recognised as
after meant infuse element, cheek invented pride bifold,
ascertain courage slide, in new song ripen tried say
mountain pass finish interval; her mine face within
shade colouring forgone melodic plentiful, stone,
tessitura domain level attach novel into limbic flame.

## Cancel Festoon

Cancel festoon peridot arch tribal mistake got fragment
fill coolant forgiveness, astute not forsaken late go
often together wrinkle, singular. Eyebrow, oblast im-
press ride the storm produce out warning omission
material flange offchance tendency more to share, dream
in slake intense prize mission, at last. Reduce if on
wait first, shimmer slot abiding mast life-time relieve
his face display coronal tangent, migrant incident
march over runway, tame to frown. Teem frighten, dawn
crustal balance all weathers trace to finger, float
in line crystal lustre session; oblige reinduce, opine.

## Walk Along

Walk along over spread down or land, bind chalk hill
blue ranging mild and worthy talk back singing
lovage whistle to plan endeavour milk rogation, crew
together. Ahead found sylvan stage coverlet; set
fair oval forage timid to wring innermost jury space
wink one severance. Leaf obvious at wage cynic
postern, tie bound ribbon, promise clover halter do
foil purview. For abstain muffle will obtain, per
hairline fissile verdant come home chert limit in
logic, drypoint glue eyelash to bring at heart
sufferance doorstep fair indigo, first vowel shift.

## Fetch Traffic

Fetch traffic quieten abridgement, careless stitch up
medial play annoyance gannet searching, flex naval
cool suffusing additive tropical currency; lenient scent
zealous mile. Avail next assay fulvid candid freed
midge alight near while here perch fabricate, of which
effect is uncial temper grey, bearish. Sweeten so
unless too, at one size pronouncing entail signet well
supper payment enter welfare like for lichen, all
nourish in circulate feel cedule. Ambitious spike en-
force, directed luscious chosen bitten squeamish
fluent break whole induce, quit optical relish, aware.

## Cede Ahead

Cede ahead heart to wood tire wanted, transom offer
underwing speak to tangle satiric floor laid, on
dart buoyed whole some sedulous climax reef unction
should mingle at odds. Sentinel flown under hem
chant belief forest teak shadow, could plant rim
assent, impart torn diffusing credited, canteen
moreover soon warm. Own time slant mirror tallow in
will allow upwards river flax, seed select by main
ransom plentiful, far angle. Choose lend beneath
yellow appointed, availment; pavement to mend
over track luck in feint, even quicklier, indicate.

# PARKLAND

# (2019)

1 And the quene of Sheba hearing the fame of Salomon
(concerning the name of the Lord) came to proue him
with hard questions,
2 And she came to Ierusalem with a very great traine,
& camels that bare sweete odors, and golde exceding
muche, & precious stones: and she came to Salomon,
and communed with him of all that was in her heart.
3 And Salomon declared vnto her all her questions:
nothing was hid from the King, which he expounded
not vnto her.
4 Then the quene of Sheba sawe all Salomons wisdome,
and the house that he had buylt....
6 And she said vnto the King, It was a true worde that
I heard in mine owne land of thy sayings, and of thy
wisdome....
13 And King Salomon gaue vnto the quene of Sheba,
whatsoeuer she wolde aske, besides that, which
Salomon gaue her of his kinglie liberalitie: so she
returned & went to her owne countrey, both she,
and her seruants....
23 So King Salomon exceded all ye Kings of the earth
both in riches and in wisdome.

– Geneva Bible (1560), I.Kings, X: 1-4, 6, 13, 23.

Norma (of her children, to her father Oroveso; priestess, preparing to ascend her sacrificial pyre):

‘Oh, do not let them be victims
Of my cruel mistake?
Oh, do not cut them down
In the innocence of childhood.
Remember that I am your blood
Have pity on my children.
Oh father, have pity,
Have pity on my children.
Father, oh father?’

– Vincenzo Bellini, *Norma*, 1831, final scene,
libretto Felice Romani

Let the Queen of Sheba rejoice with the Artichoke
– Christopher Smart (apocryphal)

# I

## 1

Now to see to sweep, over the parkland. Shall we view the shadow there, ready in close lock, they are half-brothers never inept to glimpse her rightful appearance. Can she advise them, as queen in good time for dawn light, to clarify aquamarine across the near field boundary. Peter speaks first, while the mark arises justly: "animate the horizontal treeline, stay close by in choice allowance, can be accepted?" Tom will add, eyes still fixed on her clear oval face, coral features, "ever to share, as we intimate our reach to joy retainer, ascend pass evenly for composite". They nod invested each to the other, their glances to her to gain countenance confided and truthful. She Sheba shall be their chosen royal queen, the nominated Sheba lady at their minstrel oversight, as advised by a traded hoopoe bird this is more than a game for them, the open way to joy smudged by darkness. Wisely she guides their songlines, in the open field of this place, her palace domain, the words come into mind by influx of care discovered. Queen bee honey song she leads to cherish as they do following her due. Bonds of love in portraiture included. By loyalty the shared songlines inviolate along grass stems swaying and bending, Tom sees well enough the open difference and will sing for it, lyrical and intaken as Peter holds out his arm to give her royal steadiness, they both cherish outside premiss encounter. There is a limpid slight stream hereby, running over its bed, all three can hear the soft chuckle of small sounded stones, as in lavish memory. Tom does want to justify each preference, in fact the fragrant meadowsweet wavers between them, it's her opportune moment to sing afresh to and for them, for twice prince without price, she and their distant creatures swish in crystal unison. Both the brothers affect each other, by her promise to be part of scenic provision, in full view as a gift in time. In good inkling, as the neighbour birds will do and have done already, partition by track across the grass verges, in renown. "Why do we look when here, relative prospective gathers up, is there a reason?" Tom puts the query, slowly enough as a light tremor of air stirs across her face, hesitant. He watches out, both brothers do as captivated, drawing upon their inward guise. She swallows profoundly within tolerance, certain at pleasant crib of known demeanour. They do observe as they can in name, must they derive by this stream its outline, whist to review in person; further siblinghood, she knows it is worth her song, worthy of insistence, however.

Now once more her aureate open smile, radiant intended this way and that, why in sky layers as welcome, day pasture across foot-prints moist with morning dew. Waiting already not impatient, temperate marking strokes to be conducive, foremost affection. Peter gives freely a nod, courtly his usual ticket of leave, whatever one can by look to harbour, to speak at bridge pier but narrow is enough, the flow already modest. She will know how, see the shade slide across the lighted profile, the land furtherance. Still in dawn tiding, definite again she sings near-wordless, their temper song collected as her mouth makes the sound shapes, towards the rising sun and its mark gesture. Tell ready, to love apprised, copy by wish in single stream. Now these all sing together this refrain in measure, tact over far as eye can see, even so. The live-long day in mount dual keep time flare visionary expected. Jack-in-the-hedge flavour, Peter breathes the novel air race, as if words in train. Tom true in grain will follow by cue and single turn to them both and her too, all ears inquisitive and forgiven, smell of fresh earth by daylight, under branch spread. All told implored her face bright with favour tested and sure, remark index to save. Strong yet for song near and far, or and echo more added up grand play trice mended as for to last longwise. Given over by Peter and Tom together handsful, their way to find need to say, so. Still the sun slants, according to custom directed as before, the sound fades along its pathway yet in the lead role, still. Cast oversome trial, will catch temperate caution.

## 2

Apparent aperture, parent persistence, the sons of the morning in blue light often reach hands to hold, her face in smile outwards. To be safe the day new reflected, both turn to her this way now part clouded; yet darken, she still bright with her inmost fire of care. For them maybe in franchise encampment, clip to the door step permitted eloquence, no grief or pack arrival comedy in forasmuch provision. Now day-level returns into the sky trails, they show gleams diffused along the ridge, furthermost song to set out and learn, oh fully so. Constant reticent but echo syllable goes first ahead, gainful her employ almost visible in ear breath, caramel to travel so sweet. There was no delay in the daylight hour, all forward and previous the narrow rivulet glinting calmly tested.

Twainly above them far beyond turmoil their pair hands moving fully kept for flourish each the other her pearl-studded shellac orange debated, its evident outpost approach to mid discover and shade over turf founded, soon in prize tacit unburden length wishful major patient seam; birdsong again trill several pass from the front, where she rides cool close to water watched at cost sufficient. A foil leafy upside as flash between, glimmer assisted side to side, team to rest intrepid by cloud now for once, brows covered and swept arisen first distortion avoided; three to know thee, releasement. Peter starts to further sing softly and Tom joins up, chorus not plaintive in return favour, she is the whole reason by keystroke given out, in the advance module. The free sun flickers, slight steam from the warm ground, pearlescent trim shows the way; face buoyant dapple in this nearer shade.

Symplectic says Tom, why so, inwoven daring and darting first for her verified, his voice chancing bird on branch, tree creeper gain chirping alluded even before cloud unfold and fiery, long reset for smile train addendum. They ponder as she does, wrinkle her brow somewhat puzzled but not for long, clear gaze reflective as ardent, as infused. Oh twin awake, the other spoken hardly mute of speech but yet to sing, or hum in murmur stricture, ridge advantage crescent at sun donation. Give and seek, shade-song to share intone, take further next within back and forth cascaded pride of place accurate dispersal; run forward disordered by flurry shaken, as they will in look to her, dot and carry leafage parlance face into breeze arrive expert previously, not shy for best courage, warm in high heart. Intercede for need even before this, fill to hold their own, seed grasses nodded tread level foot sequent but pace still the smile irradiates, spark to park either side to border reach and branch. Will make up level panel lucid swerving by choice and testament, her hope in them for best chance convergence, canopy unchoked. Calendar reprieved sail quick to look across, leaf flutter early green no demur, aliment by season spread in shade to benefit condiment, pleasure share. Grasp in line to sing this call-sign as birds do, qualify wing-span imparted grist to the millstream flattering, her ready answer to them as they to her. Whenever they'll not want for more. The spread bird kingdom showed the way contended, the bright hoopoe included as a rare migrant, go-between. Paramount by melody accented and fluent, carry what you need to bear and so or less detain in ready joy. Attach the open sounds endured by cadence provoked as the mark written, innocent in memory for child full-throated carol, all before in vigil morning notified. Clear rounded not lost, refreshed in train for song grateful, slender common territory devised.

3

Peter tosses his head, parted locks is there time enough for this, to us to peer outward, glancing at Tom who already knows why. "Sedge in the damp ground, privilege assigned of the dance of these field-birds attended, wing flickers across to sight." At this both smile, underwood not forsaken, P to T and T to P now both over to the verriest queen of day, in her panoply. Peter says, "the mark of fortune resounds hereby, hardly to tell or turn aside, contribute in effort to let be, air in prior anchorage by the plain choice given out". Peter raises his brow as Tom grins invited, level gesture at the spread around, forage submitted for equity and scavenged as birds do, in compact flock making their chatter. Filling out the time fashion, yielding display skirmish and benefit awry, as Tom signals the while flowing, flowers turning in light breeze, tain mirror between them both ways. "Don't wait forever, see your path we go shares attitude arisen in faction conferred. Witty royal presence, presentiment foreseen (nodding to her, over again), we have reason and she will harbour out of the storm, alongside." Tom looks to her for verity and sure in parlance, glimpse enough to prime optic confirmation, the day flutters perfunctory and assimilates its moment here. Peter makes a slice of speech, like a tomato from the dish between them, ostensible towards Tom quickly, they are fast in exchange, ever watching her even mien. By these tokens captured in release and altered by treaty on the other side, to match the need as understood discretion, each question its own presumed answer, prolific and fitting. She is poised to observe, the byplay beneficiary in exchange code, accession by stable providence.

And so, youthful small river she knew this well attaining, the other two did in attendance, admiring and singing by the same tune, into passing tournament; mimulus trace element yellow throat mimic freshet trail brothers to sup, broth to share, slight air motions froward bristle stickle darted; boatmen flicker iron shade the stream, jubilee. Honour this song for her refurbish guisement of melody, less soon depended as will await to find match governance, sway the tenor pitch defence next adjusted like bees in clover, ever free and tender obligate. Possible alliance signed up arm in arm sentient passion would like moreover intrinsic, ground becoming firmer now under foot, drying out, ragged robin perfected fragile tendency; tenants of nourishment. Partisan sun awake to keep compliance, sing again chorus return postern gate evident reverse simple flexation, come alongside as clouds do, in open sky. Revealed beckon welcome, her new betided joy is theirs too, in sky profile as found head to foot, flush cheeks. Meddlesome right to know, little strange in meadow instigate, fleurons eyesight reason again, candidate in full bloom. There is a further shade in view, she for this moment sets it aside, replete.

Chime caption readiness look to save, so needed alight and fair, precious instrument aware gravity indited; balance upon branch dip like birds too soon to tell or be sure in revel comity assimilate flex range come with us attractant purview. Most her face shining, brows arched and fulgent beyond the weather vane, captive shaken and woken, then new open free as air and offer most seen clear inclusion, unserved promotion. She sees them blink and want in unity, now all three open the same song, trill to scale, their minted voices darker blent with her upper foil. Ever the clear prow to catch a glimpse, seen and known past doubt to hesitate, unfurled in fullness just as shadow within sunlight intended, for outpost sake. Flight path and stream flow to rescue, sign valid express to yield granted, cloud-song horizon, each first one another; hold true and care lissom known, willowherb refrain fluff to sound, finger soft. In time will tell, scenic advocate. Light wind rise in the grass to sway and bend for sure pleat, higher and lower channel stream instate unavailed foe in woe postponed though now song for hurt, gather down how can even lame, Peter and Tom come to shade at foot, step: in dawn the downest turn.

4

Under too late then, is hunger seen not far off, novice joy at the table make ready herb indented and needed: bright honour fame to famish one word for another meeting place. Relay casuist loose change primal before best, cherish lost decree fuse, outreach spoilt running across the field now, not to stumble see your way playful unpaid. She is indeed the scope for darker thoughts, imminent Yemen lately memory dry mouth denied because too late now, self-graft by option frequent, sing louder in fear for sound broken in peril, song of harm. These flowers in field happen, they know nothing just to stay in line, taller invoke to tread fateful a track hemmed, wake to see, oh song hold your voice aggrieved at limit finding, temper steal blade not she exempt. Her gaze still true for them but shadow unconsumed, we'll sing now but cast parted, seeds on stony ground, trade off to watch what you know is seen there, these flowers of speech in the lush illusion fieldways. Her shining gaze gist unforgiven, not to deserve just in crest, go before scarce to eat fiercely unequal still the stream flows beyond tree-shade caressing indifferent banks flouted danger manifest. The green path now also lazy and greedy, median grassland methane engines, wayleave insensate passive detriment.

And yet these two admirers will sing again despited, out and weighed down to make half lift in brief, not with option traded or earthen riches but tenuous just foremost nothing else the leafage untold message the other night planets flashing errant induced take up fast infant brood, assembled food could be enough; the cause assume broken word-shell, patch of greed. Speech in the meadow, instruments of starvation in full view, water abducted from the stream; this is the song of care worn thin by violets violated; and yet her gaze not innocent does know in birth and almost prove its own prodigious tryst. She tells well over, bell tones told in tune over, admission. Unmerged for pliancy now at later time-set, back to look all at last in least did know to take a new placement, reprise. Must at still familiar echo, plain free for part-fear put by, near mid-day, train this new song. The brothers half-way beside have work to get done, twill not idle, release winter fuel whence opt immense, invasive. There is a notion abroad of birth-rate in this size margin, early replenish she knows within for her sensible rhyme, the two others man-handed. Light air still in caressment drawn to darker shade not forgotten, turn for breath take up implements corrected vocal parts; zone to trim, whenever by admission known tremble approaching folly the open bridge. "Shall you be ready yet" asks Peter before curious, early as ever mind to sound now more frail returning fresh to settle, she in near comfort but for how long placated, pale hands I love, sweet folded preludial offer she needs to draw breath, her diagram. Loose steps carry low to view in bound revolve, afflict wear mostly for some while still.

As then cross to the gate, not by default, if and as we might, late to prospect, all three trivet wish for sweet to waiting, listen ready anxious even by song-temper scented borrow in lament the best tune. Not near enough can be indrawn, alive to love by this arrant gateway outward from intern plus, for a nation prophecy, face to choice elevated wish despite. She watches half-tranced their flow before pitched to newer seasoning, now a glee of entrance. Peter sets up the bass note, too many are hungry to be angry or bitten free. Ah there are birds aware, knowledge to share out, blame for this fully apportioned, muscovy in traffic by sheen, sheer to shine. Tom in undercoat, paint foremost, picks up the melody, willing descant telling words by open mouth, to brim. Unfrequented still in coil permission, yet soon enough in face of needed element, to count insufficient. The birds are flown now, back and forth, three mortals singing in long search, harmonics bread for life back to bake for loose crumb scatter. She keeps these tunes by heart, albeit near too lately, the purpose gate speaks its note to clear the way, springs partial; ready fast and first, don't give up, her glance choral and coral you have to smile. Tom will gather up insisted, fieldfares in flocks to chatter as the boys sing for and to her company.

**5**

The air is still warm and comfortable, able for no less brushing the sleeve by easy passage, ruffling her hair as the hedgework trifles with momentary contrition, articles of belief. P and T rise in concurrent uplift, soon for more line of murmur, at the fence conscience ply particle reticent, now they open in chant, making up versus play, she nodding along in time. Close to noonday by anthem cruise to wise proxy scaffold upheld, gate grateful wind flickers on these cheek brightened sails. P says to T, take your good time, T agrees to not hasten, availed in their order found. She too makes a skirmish with wrist suppletion, near to sign, of thicket cheap-day discount ticket of leave. P evens to motion, don't wait for me, I have all day, so do you we all three is our brand renewing custom prior pledge remainder. She is still not exactly speaking, not to promise or even close decision, but the face permission is allowed enough, side by the gate assisted; when she sings too her hands arise, face uttered in match of colour, blood infused in tidal recruitment. So many are known hungry, close up to starving outside this field of calm in grace demurrer, invented and untrustworthy, inwardly flinched but scarce avoided, as birds do and the decurrent grasses, entrance ready taken.

A slight touch of general appetite reminds mental

reflective, glances exchanged by throat to twitter swallow, curvature of new sky ingression. Strictly to gullet soundless stilled, or breath turn limbs remembered, her countenance in cost dear smiling yet concession too, limit pallor sufferance. What the others both see, beyond miss to notice each remiss entire as did these bring, their snack allowance, happenstance. Each one bite tells its due mark, cress renewed cost open even near enough. Set aim to Yemen, semen for birth-dream, bite in sky-park, can be Sheba at long last by bird message. Wick the storm light, friend lantern, are they all flown, this flock from our sheltered field. Or say yes and they will treasure to pay for it, song yet more intense even within a camp boundary the image merged past redress entangled. She is their instant reason press down now well after dawn, leafage weeping for pasture the stream collected, her face writ in water, opaline to glance by silica gel, moon in open day. They soon just her look return, redeem plangent larynx white streak, foremost breech delivered. Ancient of days it is her deep memory, wisdom intact from the grandest of visitations, heartsease.

This shared song unceasing, grassland measure gate gather pursue, each of told in fluent words adjusted. To consume by insight even this much is honour spread by honey will bee, ready prepared before touch freely arbiter induced. As must diffused vocals scale to rise, fear not furious but close, to love evenly level serve in humour, integral twins. In given word would tell, over distance of the field, vocation shield play, flower recursion. Sing to burn mine and beside them aligned, motion tumid fancy. Would she flounce at so much, would they mimic too in origin, song enclosed work to end each infringed rightful, near enough. Shelf life tenuous prune old wood shoots to win, tending to admit hurts. Ah look aside dear ones, light mist in the meadow fume, cloudy unknown but unavoided well as well, swallow your pride, starve for still there, corrode.

## 6

The sun floats by interim among small clouds, in marks above the place nominated by venture this cover band accepts the tune of broad day. Their light there too not yet further peckish, sips of fresh water steady obviate, this tripod willing repute concurrent; he sings along first for both evidence, curious in satisfaction abridged to answer in full dyestuff, these boys construe to intersperse carol and know for sure or catch on. Sound expresses the mouth esteem, in fine contrite parts played, supplanted see whether antilogy at best. In lip service, none to hear otherwise, bird chatter for nourish now a prevailed wear feels want enticement if also innocent plaint succession. Undercurrent sublation infixes grasp over substitute contended asterism, voices in spark address: cloud will face up, reduced. Louder entrail by this sound parlour for valour takes momentum beside grant analogy, the aware reckon, sing for supper longer by hunger terrorise. Why tremble fast in view, spread injustice harm in like hunger nil by mouth. She will as firmly hold the upper pitch, cost to embellish ever jointed by fugal recompense. This tappet songline runs out across the horizon, to notify estranged loss of accident to purpose valid by deep affliction undisclosed, but declared in parallel far beyond force detained. Her song in this version founded, at base engine across the water-meadow, is there before all recovery, takes in suffusion, track fault.

The bright hoopoe by crest apports its message, outwise in transit optimum titration, Solomon in all his glory in deference to the heartland, unharmed queen in consort arrayed. What this means is widespread famine, many deaths sub-nourished, Sheba herself rendered by Yemeni memory tribulated, beyond the gateway. It is a field enmesh tract to share, the numbers are horrendous as can only be the bird of vivid plumage, she knows as do almost her listening suitors, all to sing outside jest and reckoning. Mouth dry already, thy way to save the wave spread corrigible, by wind movement how can so many flights of Saudi carillon chimes attenuate, gross beyond desert avengement, voice of unreason. To bear out to die quickly, at end song far removed, their regal field crossed over, retains dune shadow in recall button elbow, none less to press, immersed. Demise industrial withholding, organ failure in pipe band they sing to know, ringtone interval; fame to famine drawn will tell, villainous her message aftermath by proximate plumage. They do all now for sure know, however the tune denies collusion, in layered polyphony, even three show why, it must play out its free adoptive raiment. Reserve your cheeks warm at face to face, her allure dazzles them across to the wide expanded field of whey, of mercy milk delivered. Cream vestment minish leave to grieve day unfolding lacerate footway jubilation deferred, they boyish she banishment, require entropic past seclusion, even so. It is the cost, the cause, the far cry retainer, late for proven gate outlook further grimace come to sense redeem oh transom glimmer what's for dinner again abridgement masonry; medicinal overlap punish word-play askance to feed and breed pardon excelsis mystery. Aden reprieve she is full determined; she to pray everhood a rabid lyrebird soon to tune, embowered.

7

Horizon arch post instigate anew, frit debate ossuary nurse lipsalve perfected, fault gauge arbitrament vocalic yet desolate sermon stolen timbre untie calamine retracted listen induced tap brothers, ash ebony chronic renew. Open heart finishment click-switch oaten depended, in look main light unsweetened rennet: syllabic donor field of play. They fix looks, back and forth, refract unguent soft reach swell hands touching, cheeks flushed, release, rebuke flutter unflown. Phonation is privilege, afford pensive attention aided to be admitted, consecutive earlier bird gratefully sedulous falling silent for a class outlet disturb forbearance now in name shepherd ship over middle verse, chorus acclaim. She sat in the shade of a hawthorn branch, her rich impression under their rapturous gaze withal, went shirt to throat cantor aside from her canopy enthroned; solo across parity numen eyelash bird treatment membrane, ruffle oryx trucial scouting, hold your peace. Cloud race in upper sky chasm charm release, rebuke flutter scolding consign in plenty resonant. Just as so, vowel tread for matted celandines under foot natural at cost, more and more, submit organ stop pipe tremolo, or whistle peak her brow raised up by a tilt parent question, pure land inherit famous tremble, expense massive aid beyond reach ensemble haven regatta of wheeling bird flight. Stricken mass hunger in report ignored, sing out amended full sail gate still wide open but by entrancement past time pastime profligate oh sing this new song not lost before too late, at last conjoin inflated.

Sheer joy rebuked avowal into revoked adamant foster child in retinue, bite your lip all must, musty, voice crackle as fire once would, tee-shirts abundant, our help hot-foot attentive, dry close to withered each with occident from lush transport, increase major cress in range of hearing proof: excuse, at fault entire. Incite by constant heart, hollow flame index, heart ardent hermitage octave lift broken home art gone she to banish they in peril leaf coverlet adored. Surface suffused in bright colouration, sufficiency remark loyal adherence astound, voices beyond price afforded at noon flight. Diapason indignant is this love of the week to gate posting entreaty, met by moonlight in broad mid-day, streamers close to reclusion. Sound trinket testate quiescent in borrowed tempest, flies up wingbeat allocate tone to tune, watch for beaten separate promise muted. Is still gleeful, jest in just replenish for her assured incidence, elation caught on spur of asset credence. Restless advance, draw procession undeserved, desert brim. Easy to trill, Peter shows her the knack of it, butterfly tangent, even Tom snaps estrangement by reason of strophic ward currency. Offer restore her charm they will, base line warring tenement volunteer, tenor fetch. Approach concealed motive park, she attired resplendent by them imagined, display amount brought back, considered. They ready sing what both will each to other train, its armature unbroken. Yemen shining, her realm custody now an abject prison, the boys are dazzled, treaty assignment; her due corrosion was it, sole advice starve to speak, gainsay to starve resisting and single sand kingdom unsound. Crushed pride, mortal reduction roams to the borderland, of this little stream inflected. Each will try one way or another spark prime bird semen introject reflective amended, endorsed and hurt.

## 8

How could they know her realm for real is in shattered ruins, the pain of destruction and misery enslaved, and yet the bird messengers avouch disaster, the open gate like the mouth of terror, must it be as broken in hunger, her city in hold of rebels, populace at verge of frank starvation. Bitter honey grips the throat, say what you like to weigh our own Brit supply, of weapons to control of this lasting punishment, ten mil a few steps away from death by hunger, many babes and childers. All this burns beyond reach, she cannot bear even to flinch, to apprise her loyal boys, open their eyes what is done in our name, arms and the man suborned. The grasses sway, cress in the stream, birds in commune flight, subsidence in transfer of this fault to sing, song in over fault. Arabia Infelix, their enemies are our friends, does this rankle yes in theory but this open gate speaks like a mouthful, wordless and free beyond instant care, worn down scarce to fare well patrons of unknown hurt.

Of meadowlands outspread, shadow donative even fugitive news comes in unrefused, critical. Answer to jeopardy the boys credit wisdom's clear shadow, ruffle passage over the flourish unselfish remission. She in repute from bountiful endurance, testament refunded as the vale surrounding and pensive, custom missive to seedheads, season in crouch link meander tribute all murmur finitude. What she knows already is implant succession, remark to parkland warm flurry notation whole turret modulated and singular, sanguine. Tamper for blushes unseen but blame will not subjoin proficient, who's to know these manacles their own idea motion deference queen of darkness, queen of light. Ah mercy crimson rising willow pendulous, please wakeful gnash their agile jawbones dithyrambic currency counterfoil. Love to prove, common place in ownership, Peter blinks enraptured at Tom so smiling, she afar from memory throat restored, parlando. Canteen sky deflected from fusion angulate, leaf whistle air fluxus interleaving nautical mileage high sea fend to land. It means to be queen, to seem for them accentive reliant to bear behalf streaming, celestial figuration stelliform. Eyes so shining! Brimming untorn

the throats inch vibrancy, three inlaid, intagliated yet
she must recall, her realm for them, far or not, note
perfect harvest pigment laid, martyrs in angelic white,
censers of incense outwith the burning bush.

# II

## 1

Now it is next after noon so soon resemble, song to mingle as now the re-pair aware like a wave afraid of less by sail, flowing how here to tread by know and carry, unrelented for why or not, cloud streets ahead. Up by shadow in turn to swallow, throat gripped each one gilded, focus to guilt in view felt; Tom and Peter in full inverse sight blench at what accepted, no option else say what you both see clear enough in answer prospect. Light train into upper sky fermented, live in day bright promote infringement, unretracted, thought not now free riding duck and weave, sound full recurrent, foreseen ribes to scent the air. She as still queen to check must bear for three what each one will answer, lost choice to risk for a biscuit tokens in front of the mouth where at first words tremble as they must. The crown rowan now seen sits aloft, speed to speech wait on utterance, selflike and mean in line in pit of mincing words to say. To make up for port mast, report driven even in fear carried, block attire in way, stay put.

Peter now is all question, in quest to stave off answer from internal assent imitate. Tom holds his breath as thin to meld in fraction by whole adjunct, friction bound to captive tongue. Peter too sees in her face what will arise to be told, flushing the moment beyond avoidance. They know she will tell by look, its next song can be no other, blame of time assured. Above and beyond, the meadow gained its own full shadow, cowed faces holding out, coward turret no need for her what declares however fair, ready to fly indeed. Each boy looks away and then at her, knows why suddenly in turn each to other, again as birds do for the main chance. At last to be out across first sense in person, invested, Sheba entrusted for and to them too. Rogation swims in current air, daring employ leading the way touch and mix replace they to be in tune ah ripe divining. What can be will need to see and be seen, queen truffle element dug by scent, found sweet whenever further aspirant: hoop crest ahead.

The waxing plants shine with parlous innocence, in what depiction their roots to try as likewise when they can. Time waits to rouse dismay, the stream fresh in tremblancy, evident unnoticing impassible as clouds by the gate admonish in friction purposeful. She will induce for them all in trice, face to face, certain to bear as ready must when thus driven. "How to tell" thinks Tom out loud, what sign from her or by her leave; Peter nods assent accrue belief and speaks the wheel in whole, spoke hub: "for whose domain flame to flutter learn as we can, notorise". Pittance proviso turn again marrow of matter in left bone. Yet each for Tom is worse, Peter in leaf also, she sees just so much as else reproach, advance to price afforded in swift crossing. By later than confer, confirm conifer, echo so far but hear too and true the songs turn back and burn, near enough before outright remit: acquit, persist. Amnesty by affray known hurts beyond denial in trial, no let to cert praise first entice service intimate infusible preventive redirect. Peter says yet to bear, for and to her tribute gathered for them proximal to the pair of whom assigned, integral or final by cloudsong still about, afloat all roads lead back roaming as they do, lamp alight give away injury by danger in tale foretold. Tom's look narrows in grimace ordinance all share happy choice, device admission direct, f.stop, decepted; all flown all known, destruct.

**2**

She enters will hold up, unable not as the bright boys do in plant licence gleaming with refusal invert heart's longing try as yet ignore grip the throat of thought and promise, intermit defer transaction. The Yemen reports inflame the queen's alliance and are hateful by obstruction, worthy of odious servitude; she lets her suitors see in clear view shelled to ruin, which way to turn, claim calamity unending and unequal, devout for them all in tangential filament, shrapnel. The boys in cue exchange rebut conscriptance, she still is queen for them however down and born, forgiven quickly in fault despairing tidal casualty rate overridden by its own excess to blame, forsworn. The gate in first rebuke open or shut the case is put against, hardly across the stream of that pasture, its incidence at branch shadow as freshwater reflected indubitable; at length near final yet outside terminal, not late to swerve ever sure by alterance, deputed as all three payment for convergence and remark. We must be in acquittal, not in void replacement, to claim no less is the loss tractable, bird flight single quick to mount a great flock granulate, sky-loaded. The boys gaze into her chastened face, to glimpse there what now beyond alteration, extreme bear margin the tale is true and past doubt. The targets die in droves daily, words overflowing cost of hewn misery writ in the face for remembrance, unceasing even where ignored and worse there also, is none. Give back is heard, admonish before overtaken prime to stand accused and quite refused invent, despite infringement.

So she will as best can range for them release imposed, impossible distrain still the stream ignores them evenly, crowsfoot step away out of touch vast heritance oh parlous speech evaded, consumed silently brim and evidence, sing under their breath. Get for respite if, yield to captive insensible, love unstretched however so and for, no joy or just reply, open your voice all three. Plant freely, tree to tree by root answer in bolus counterpart shade to cover what they did or would, to know, frown to cede ahead; cloud shadow follow share full weight joint assemble rightful, count limit brothers endure to view the news stucco in relief, little enough benefit. To bear this much is hardly open, in front part not retrieved or spent, clinging into thought profile adamant intended.

Peter and Tom in pair search for her face before them, in lace for both pleading open vantage, to just reflection consequent certainty even a step away to trim shadow, to heel wherever walk and claim. Stay on course, pause and return, cost unfree; time to burn predict pastime inflorescent. The light streak marks out the runway, attention unwavering pressure lift culminate bring and stay the gate swung overt by offspring afflicted all for her in float back to them, late to modify oh season hold still renown again the birds yet few are flown.

3

As for fortune's gateway what's seen is ready got in view, fine reticent column place to please sense endowed flow ostensive. Marker florid provide ears might alert, prepare hum-ready in moist first-hand; attend horizon curious watch to see and find. Even when corrept and displaced the duo accept intuit knowing her tell anticipate there at sample, single each exemplary two and tame hearts, wherever so main track little fetch review summarise; the season tribune permit decorate office bent nursery twill impersonate, in note to grief inside. How allow to know, rustle out to credit spoken benefit all found. Now she will speak her mind for them utterly, old grief underlain for her absent kingdom crushed, starch grain sand dune part arid put into bedrock assuage in mask to face and shed.

Varnish incision tearworn unwoven, these boys allege across far fields for her truce, her brow increased at breach of right final derogate; in no wise late extra win behalf resemble if at all bangle. Wait in barrack acting lend out ahead, resounded they make this song fomented too softly lenten modulate tonic uncertain in range propounded gunfire never casual hurt repeat uncounted. Follow inventory sorrow continual yet undeclared, deep buried in thought signal forward face open visual enterprise. For the far gate its privilege relent upon stave, black perch in light rain, queen by seam affirm concealment; beholden hedge opinion, open. Within brain echo scan stem caudate receptive, sense first licit hawthorn, elder trim and tepid, pith cleave burlesque as birds confuse burden conflagrate in skein.

Infirm reform persistent indicate, oh rap indusium thread refusal vociferous by the line park fine lest pervade, song in mind heard melody term remote, devoted fluent advocate. Careless love flown inducement profile, arab return heavy crass munitions, ever even in forefront immense continual songline attend, far-flung optimum yours and mine. What said expanse implicit feeling outpost, seen temporal skip to heartland its over flight convergent perforce instil virtuous conversation. Never far, never few exact replacement sky cooking fast to feast fleece they each to all smile despite to know what they do, for her Peter and Tom will bear as for them she bites her lip can she help it and the gemini retinue both witness in her complex face, expression. The song as ever sung will show in ear answerable, responsive allude embracement fault dressage yeast empire arisen chorus each day from the gate hedge mark bearing its wild field fruitage, sloes and haws too, slice pressure inflate belong to lung print availed to sluice long for, pine. Devastated homeland ripped apart oh do not think increase furnace burning smoke drop apace slight breeze acrid to care in thick air masquerade, first ever cloud grade incline by airline now boarding, intended. Straight face don't give way evade fallout, in song fallacy undoubted thorn to cry, principate in strike locking up her kingdom anthem call to mind, to bind out in forebrain turmoil musical must over the stream attain dream of liberation made fast tied sown harmonic triage supplant badge wonder at tremor mantic strife, for touch across to life.

## 4

## NOW SOON THEIR SONG: THE BOYS

### *i*

*Now in danger peace to hold, ever set come in by turn deserve the desert voice steadfast inundate, five bar rest along, standing room by rim sung, yours to mine reckonable to main, now read by aim, seed in frame so entire. For overlay join to play over, here furnace fiery at max risk sing first out and out finish take go shares shake induce, by afterglow to hit clement & fold the line, in manifold vibrant larynx temper pitch attach, inflame gantry at entry rescue imperil empiric. To this lost empire gallant redeem, the queen for them abiding, fast to fall, fall to tremble, note stub advice, bright eyes enlisted in berry juice lip colour admirable twice to them the theme promised but patch search they do and will, and will. Courage now resulted mutual, small trim force voice conspicuous along the gate poverish echo fugaceous trill to thrill all full together apparent within pair vestment scrim to teasel new high temporise arrogate bar in five, eloquent. Ah then so honour bright cheeks of flame easy come and will go, hold back basso profondo now attested lower ranking, found rising to clearance*

*perform beat to time impart, or in art revive living*
*rental, discount to match. Presume back and forth*
*lay to pay evenly incautious furnace grass to sway*
*insidious fringe meet tassel outshine electuary*
*replete oryx here too at swift intendment main to*
*sustain resounding, claimant critical close to peak*
*value, distilled. Pure heart endurance sung affirmed*
*or told or so beguiled, one ever won attest merge*
*correlate towards merciful sky above, defray up*
*pitiful scan to raise, top to seem, baritone gather*
*liminal indented mouth echo return grand unguarded.*

*ii*

*Never late canton file aspire don't omit resection*
*plentiful limit interval, down in rest, expense ah*
*so in one deft voice rising adornment rink parapet*
*for one best fanciful other whether form inscribed*
*vocalise muted interface already in trace effect,*
*entranced crescendo choice alt mysterium have been*
*or will. Remit quaver clef sign finger touch invent*
*one gap fills another sovereign at surface, pressure*
*slope upper, tree-lined impeach resilient. Each one*
*across, both outmatched, volumetric in yet known*
*prophetic retention; quest fuse renewal probable*
*up left to schist by flake orrery labour exerted.*
*You do too and dwell, peaceable before she is there*
*entire by glimpse and glance pair at gate leaning,*
*hear her thought pulse entrainment beat alternate,*
*look to tact and fly level symmetry she sings with*
*them companionable because they know the pretext,*
*profess alchemic mix blend without end or finish*
*to shine. Emit new light at each pause to find,*
*minish and flourish angle nip and tuck dihedral*
*aisle incumbent rail assignment taken, sip or tuck*
*diffraction bent in beat, feat to sent. Engram as*
*feint retention, at songline fitting rapid share*
*demeanour drastic prepare at the gate in front*
*look, into the far field provoke. They think as*
*justly, this is indeed their vein of song if vain*
*but true, done each by turn to other recognise,*
*confirmed. It is compulsed for both and all three,*
*given to her from whence it came, full suffused*
*with new time in vain for sure yet now implore,*

*returning; give over, mission known allergic for*
*offset incidental, free active by fashion beaten*
*iron blame impaired, condone.*

## 5

## NOW THEN HER ROYAL TUNE, INVITED

### *i*

*Silent she often holds, her breath tune to turn, her*
*face outward demure, amazed at folly courtyard best*
*without guard, they see her face revoked in passage,*
*referent. By all thought leads there, vacant opportune*
*a pitch in open time less to suppress her servitors*
*see and thus to hear too, even the songline unavoided*
*keep pace esteem next apprise in novice set price,*
*beyond this, pearl close to home within to share, full*
*burden foreign her own song is constant her whole being*
*therein traced outward swung. Tact with arioso throat*
*turn apple rise and fall invocate unplacid she'll mourn*
*but silent still her words unspoken her silence audible*
*night and morning spill release price advantage, advice*
*patron field fought in memorial interminable, unstoppt.*
*She will caress to the line of singing, in tribute as*
*they attend, these apt boys touch the hem imminent by*
*garment, differ offer prevail hardly instigate 5-bar*
*in willing accepted written script enter decrypt per*
*margin diffident, mercurial.*

### *ii*

*Way full to why or not, choric simplify by promise*
*in purpose estrange amplify line up over; annote at*
*sight agreement prime debate. She'll try as near,*
*close inward by ward of trust persist. Bereave for*
*canvas lineate flower resolute cordial deterred but*
*as past test influent, to gain for grain revealed*
*most and blood flow portent at limit, fulminant not*
*yet in help but risk admission. These images desert*
*her trial for them, sonant ambit never profligate*
*patch to sing, latch wrung obligement attempted in*
*tempo decision ahead. Distraught set conceded, for*
*pensive to cancel in concealment intent flair by*
*rainbow in breach or broken anent repair principal*
*remission traction sustained at will. The suitors*

*amaze and captivate, beyond what they half know or*
*doesn't confound uttermost yet trill fall notable,*
*at watch recourse convoke aptitude, discreet as to*
*vigilant too; recount she will even for them former*
*time nourish in hope, life-given. Assert, revert*
*confluent gaze across their audit space she won't*
*oblige formation team align at choice to imitate*
*fairway entreaty consonant also; tonal promotion*
*promissory they do grateful take her word for it*
*evenly, however eventuate. She will, they shall,*
*ah all along the line.*

6

These crows take flight, leaven proof air risen incited buoyant hover endeavour waning declare to cool timbrel sew compliance leaf and stem, even never partitur filigree cloud settles broad leaves will fold. Yet warm dew membrane hands intern to serve imprint, vessel syndicate gather by the river to win by singing, to duty imitate for earth nut horizon, the three unrivals conciliate moss agate words lift on the tongue. In section provoking insect cloud air colony fire tepid usual arisen at bittern bond notorious invite perplex fancy free voluble spilled. Unison and descant, thread chime through a needle, honour bound loyal and oud accorded, levitate in flocks as birds do chatter up indigent; our voices richly share and shorn in dare path prophetic wherever walk brief console, ardency. Still the lintel turns out and back, integral true pliant fasten tag pry to find, murmurous parting incitement. Effort racing past purchase songline clatter, hold in position ever level, early at most ankle tune redress.

## AS NOW IN THREE IMPARTED

***i***

*At motion retain, conserve planar inflected visionary*
*several relate enlacement, trio partaken legible sight*
*flow perseverance agile prosperous entrant each one at*
*measure conjecture. Voice high and low two resound below,*
*entreat their line ballot fortify dream palace envisage*
*share harm memorable seek motet mean time remission by*
*levitate pronounce everturn; cloud-linnet, cloud-song*

*incant uncertain, what she endures is in eyeview near break, retracement, overrun obviate across further pay elevating crest profuse; plangent and joyful too.*

*ii*

*Shield lantern, storm incessant tax and press maintain correct keep time in this park, they know and care nor yet astute belated; enfold part to part discover at face resettlement, disperse and track rejoin. Border interweave, their own surprise, back and forth glance overture, arbitrate; what's on record known conscript even now fledged as birds do, triple advantage three-fold in turn the startle songline repeat, inverted; profound even Yemen afflict by truth intone, in turns. Fair oblige tell serene rebated provision so for palm, clear foremost to say and stay in tune; synoptic at current note: the rest is done.*

7

And now this day returns, alight with hopeful memory, reclaiming the sky in cloud cover and hoop to future, that bright bird again and its announcement. As streaks the way, plentiful by planet calm noonday arrival eventual aside intact partition each to hold out reside she conforms even alliance trio will or mill along, full the granted song counter level fad contrive. Insidious day flits to its hive, sound utter succulent entrain other and whether fit sugar invert trinket to beat home time for songline extended, these ardent friends taste for ready and melic proof intended, sun ahead still lessen given exchange, prime determine. All so yet or so soon and at too, now is time to calm downwards the day star from the topic sky; her sign she bears her Sheba crown to these boys of suit joyance, to share fill abet rhyme and the hour invited.

Calling as they do and will, as the birds and clouds also, for her as she for them, sign under view cloud spread vane turning in mind furl apt legion by need over the near field invocation, to and fro across the bounds of heaven, of Yemen in close recall. At pitch now ready as ever her life in constant danger, further by Peter and Tom apported, set cue evident herb lights at spark for true admission; radiant sun temper foil, light wind announce refine and proof calculus of odds, call down yet by mid-day star breath entreaty, queen of near disaster in tempest only thus far avoided, louring under this patch of admonished rainfall in prospect, in the free damp air complete.

Renew life itself moist grateful call to order beyond duty of proof to truth, all three know it clear enough. Despite the doubt of season now is right or lucent acknowledgement to stand ready, for pledge in lamp for daylight climax, the boys gear up by pressure badge shrew running double relish prepared. Learning by tuning, set up to start, over. Advocate assent the mid-day antiphon, in glance procession so be it evident response atone assigned panoptic resurgence inflected tones besought. Instigate relentment perceptive ahead of call over, of parenthood effusive animate pinch and tuck, roam to find. Care to be in bee lift, see for season honied allure brim thatch peg down past the hive of plenty, new song in turn, from side to side remaindered. How so enchant, entangled Peter and Tom across the stream teeming, she watchful flushed and they keen to draw away from what's in mind for her and thus for them too, they will bear ready eminent domain. Sentence hark now nearby bird lark, mistle no rush day park sift aloud.

**8**

Here follow the part-songs, canonic reticent but in flight proud to prophecy the sound tolerance scissor wind-pipe unlimit alternate fortitude, mutual pacify ahead all three looking to find scapular loose bearing animal trusted rites; of passage and credence from look to seek, fruit of named account. Bitter it is, acrid honey tormented bees wellbeloved forgiveness related hereafter wend over tide to flood, aim choristers supplicant deem instinctive fuse unfinish beyond end to reach strophic retention valley hidden entrance every report at fury wait; singing grind your teeth, to ash cone and gnash relented open view front to back in pitch, in dark.

**TOM:** *call down ready day mounted ridge allayment entire option to ransom answer, cited lower even*

*manifold inspersed talent by glad tremolando too.*
PETER: *tendent flowering as the clear light wind*
*caresses the faces, adornment provident retainer*
*linger talent percussive advance merciful by, too.*
TOM: *over to her replenish twice-called in active*
*day profile intent percussion tempo flown dispatch*
*persist mission crafted, now main alongside too.*
PETER: *voice risen carried over keeping the fillip*
*line for her as they know by singing, sing to know*
*and say well as may, by each step further of too.*
TOM: *give word enjoined expend call interval fettle*
*in frequency protect for now just as long keep time*
*catch the moment openly by snow bunting cool too.*
PETER: *visit momentous ready later better trill*
*reclaimed, either urgent ready in bird flocks out*
*to roam in season share the plough turn in too.*
TOM: *furrow in face inflected, her joyance even in*
*danger guarded despite this call to true enhance*
*incidence, prevail by now unyielding persiflage too.*
PETER: *humectant breath-turn at noon fetch and carry*
*sing the while blend up hold steady countenance moil*
*and toil fibre new optic decision, comfort affix too.*
TOM: *mirror at then in canon, affirmed cantus beam*
*to modulate opinion intact mordant past sweet wet*
*instilling depute comfort affix serene river too.*
PETER: *in contest go humectant breath-turn; before*
*harbour patient ready mint, at high-pitch variance*
*a fiction spoken in vault shadow over star shot too.*
TOM: *parlance score to gain inception, leaping goat*
*skillet principle heart tremor astonish proximate*
*as birds as for song in air, air in first trust too.*
PETER: *fly over contented and eager, to look down*
*from night plane not obscurely, pack ice igloo fall*
*militant immunise forceps perfect in homage, in too.*
TOM: *her valiancy face up not forgotten invited own*
*ground of longing she bears Sheba's crown bairn on*
*brow furrow omen Yemen, fire to plough fortune too.*
BOTH BOYS: *Peter to Tom, Tom to Peter askance inch*
*sentence unpretended, risen voices alight to need,*
*moon-pledge across crest of full sky recoil, too.*
AGAIN: *cloud known given each boy back to her, loan*
*in prescience mental fight afflicted anguishment*
*punish the mind reserve soon dark in daylight too.*
AGAIN: *she watches their eyelids move and startle,*

*brows flexed raising attend to take and wake now observant, nod first and then again regimen too.*
AGAIN: *within early reliant songline print here in transit of fate increase punish memory, rightful within close patter to near reserved evening too.*

9

Three flow emerge to clear the air, park in sun the natural when ebonised trance even given estimate echo young patrons in royal tantamount assignment to pressure single in pair crystal sheer antonym, each one face to prove graven impetuous, monumental. By to stand and find out the war unceasing, lifetime burning apart yet with songs cemented palinode frenzy, turn and turn frequented. Septic raid to avenge confusion rivers to cross sand deserted, Sheba's small field intensified day upon day news wave unrelenting greed reaching claim to finish out regiment. Loyal tremors shake the line of land park office, rent and broken as songlines mend the wound refused. Beyond love found out bind revenue keep relented company, wage to nap hearts afloat remorse unbridled in prox for real burns the mind. And yet cantilena in reprise enough is found by the small stream herb train or screen lost in life arraigned. Relentment versus grievance just tonic hive busy combs the heart, deep purpose strew quartz twin anthem prime acceptance prolific evidence true beyond doubt resentful hurt to hurt, heart to heart, ever in tune.

# BITTER HONEY

## (2020)

*Covariance:* a measure of the linear dependence between two random variables, equal to the expected value of the product of their deviations from the mean.

- Peter Walker,
*Dict. of Sci. and Tech.*, 1999, s.v.

We know... that for *I* finite the forward and backward equations have the same solutions

- J.R. Norris,
*Markov Chains*, Cambridge, 1997, p. 95.

## Exempt Provision

Whereby exempt provision, despite part alternately
fortunate trace to chance, first off receipt ward
deference early and before sound plan, depend on
prior advantage resume hear once the same; in tune
except fine frame galvanise adequate perforate inch
promote esteem, re-open turn or circular back soon
raise vocable spinnaker, seismic towards insisted
luff extreme; take out proposal virtual enough own
elation, time-bound. Deterrent suspect birth limit,
overflow or maxim, comprise infer and so to plead
traffic woven give to level, funnel bird detained
lyre constancy. By rule further stone beyond choice
proof voice logic needful, handful sorrel magic yet
derelict abrasion, sound marker slight; in even but
before provoked mishap, cool after found to play
distended and fraught, in song. By over track in
centre wing, speckled pinion one higher up forever
dismay vein opportune, new work at minimal prolong.

## Divide, Remain

Or yet random count disquiet fortify pressure inflame at to for, set miss to edify, palisade. From in search order lateral axiom ask mere postponed visible task, nothing out belated or torrid, innovate; fear at least welcome awaiting, gratitude offence in dilation prune ambit pasture variant litmus team duet, edge reshuffle critical annex, pallid reputed to clench forest other shore. Harbour crescent, rink slavish attachment foil over prevailing to mix, to flaunt also canvas by final force erstwhile fanciful ligand parenthood, direct bat jest you know burn free intuit, dispute. After once or practical omen ingrained, plant out refinement arrest will go oblige stannic governance, intubate allege at front column indifferent. In mercy trial untied, nor main until redeem brotherhood, total departure entire consorted faithful jet covert beast foster proemial inviolate. Avert sustaining prior inductance beladen ford to bard entrain, allergen missive open film trim next to last, pervasive less felt else demise obtain.

## Flight Pathway

Instil bird ride happen inside, imperil fade proceeding minotaur grove expert void. Steel fovea crocus hint or approve collision undeterred proxy moisten yet impute, foremost avian triune illustrious harbinger, brokerage pride enlarge on target box as hurt. Fickle always weird now or than purpose still unheard, drift inflated cousin mirth despite occupy, invite. Relax then, resolve first insulate console probation voided oval vertical chirps eagerly win reclaim nitrogen manual foreign clerk. Date clatter massive braid, alter prominence the whole shot over final conjugate trill racing, affixed detachment cohort pandowy silicon. Intern sublimate modest also, imbricate funded incus fungus reprobate sulphurous fun talon drainage dioptric; alleviating spring fountain neatherd infoiled and address outspan minimal, coronal tactic bearing, strait. Excess provost hindmost crust principle, twitter famous mantle single permanent turn in flock, sky quotient underwrite must to tame choric ambuscade, rip tide grab utter strop invincible. Evensong submerge, perverse cordon reference ignited, all of them emphatic plentiful reduce price tolerant into throat. Redress flotation fibulate cost, on intrinsic trapping, stern beak muster promise isthmus infraction.

## Enough Conversion

Snap or flit, angle tie to bundle acid subvert, dint twill mock recover apt sufficient muted. Trim seem intimate caustic furbish, twitch deserve matching curb block living profile newel never incriminate, darting elfin cancel seated rowel, cruel amicable comical destitute. Donates plaque synthetic immersion, lack impress re-decorate; watch at best sign for pitch tarnish forensic proof ligate, on deck copper plateau on resume passamezzo, bin to seem from aid maritime. Or none distal froward, steward since parlance pursuits to crystal uncle bowsprit discriminate algae slavery addict inventor management. Trims back, intact, in front. Purview cataract wilt cynical dusted, ousted ever or whether totalise open in franchise allege proper sever improvise. Rephrase lake anecdote product rash epidote clotted antidote, sad sedge mischief index hostage to fresh bespoke consent. Yearn in formal ownership vial claustral glucose unfrozen grasp, to gasping reticent; fadge alignment confluent dissention at penitent due forsaken pediment. Outcast in wretch deplete, servile pledge most sifted, retinue influx sediment confer flinch continued moss bench; step for touch imprint. Over rack brunt refuted irrigate dimension, mitosis glamourise punish fair square livid extracted; converse which tangle shredded uppermost mulish defence. Lost past first desist.

## Another More Dense

Assuage to wharf daze piste tumbril ooze phantom done amaze encounter laughing, febrile hostel cladistic in temperament viscous ascent. Penetrate single planet foresight half, full-grown awful thimble even snooze to lose caliph aggressive ensign; disdain. Map wager sooth grin best, last token leaf ignite affront, net placid on dauntless transit pavilion, traipse burden crazing safe. Shaft furnish gainful propose come and go flounce or riddance, bright rays tremblance mend over blended. Effort voice treatise boil to furl pit parrot woken, churlish diction fine payment levitate, attracted since curtail crest expect saunter privet. Interpret costume ratten uplift misted pacify generic holdfast, wrist placed sodden electoral faucet trench dividend. Forward slight narration trance suspend for radial join force nurse, previous beaten path; event if resented amble, modify victory percept terrify at glowing hearth invest. Crown torment too, silent pat thrift terse put past vote, saturate enlist native yet bereft. At last into line promotion town claim or worse, remit unveil focal hazard retract discover wasted integrate persistent for different local mint privation; forensic testify omitted utensil entail fragmentary culminate. Portrayal gamble glance rend endemic classical restriction, foisted headway fumble adaptive tractable predicted, least emollient grain.

## Extend Forgiveness

Offer better admixture, garnish plenish late dacoit
castle missal insufferable, patchwork. Band upwards
tend after, latter admire by choir retention seem
crane rigorous more curious sock depict issuance at
dance yet dance too sweep by troop latch rejoinder;
keep by finder admonish strong down along admirable
for sure endure. Introit collapse at stretch cinder
path thereafter fruit or stitchwort session problem
nutrient relenting absorb orange flange disturbance;
neglect once inspection intern halt quickly by pivot
lack in foster lustre foreign corbel flick invent.
Value press ingested ace to slice parade detox, in
shine box might rejoin by wire brace terminal, twine
assignment effortless near pin restore; sicken wince
aspire floor taps for etch device amnesty imagined
synergy indoor stair breech currency, evince dearly
particulate energy leading to waving, lap implore.
Bactrian footwear entire action station twice over,
fright purloin reign brevet continent, on shoreline
calling vain succession; reduce prolusion missing
extra parts white airlock porous factor profession.
Yield childish action, in sight pince doorway each
win new day; nor seal nor wrinkle singular destruct.

## Play to Will

Forest surgeon makeshift lift-off insertion, sink to bank frankly poorly brink matter austere merest close avocet link dewpoint level printed gossip. Mastic gravel tip oil fiscal ensue proofing headship, outer bludgeon stricken tank nasal, alter adduce posthumous cut rank; imported jointed duplex affix roof blanket, caught handed costly phrasal subject elective to promise limb astute; in dank deployment interred, sought to swim review too. Do they will for, dangle ear drops reckon bitten, self infusion intrinsic prefer loft single damp rill in frost, in front over lips. Now refute climb uppance itch on sill, proton twin for them protect mussel binding salt lactic, as weak intact drastic fortune commune idiot iodine spread fault deficient. Sound fill address trio handle from ground, cavern mission imperil melted, into embryo silk patter filter minded, attended; suited in face ready tracing, implement rewound ahead, postern entertain not denied, soloist. Consent then tie front lace success modest toy to buy, play to will, evident batik scutcheon transfuse relief opportune. You soon all shall final appended, wend degree to cut free, for but season; moulted far forward by optic muse. Serve cruise in place border reason foison catch in throat distended; high-jinks larynx bite impend.

## Owl to Maple

But once out to reach, tarnish instead gilded up lurch blench antagonise, yawn over firm to negligent announce famish; dispraise olive occupy dissident procured fitted ounce omit jetty munch few to chew, amazing harness rend redound to swallow accent, clemency; that too, burnish complete tread optimum, invective in wild unsold. Skipper late ocellated squint perverse trinket in furnace, knee argus stroll mildew, spawn in season. Legal counterpart friction mental comprised, before insure coloured, if in teach first; revise surrogate early dawn, ichor clouds unfold. Prize tenancy freed as few line careworn, brown ensue gain solution. Ingrain mallow follow yell, steal banish; go to, anon, discern together rowan mountains. Bright good flood scrubland, ought, tenter fret disguise polymerase micro unlit, untorn. Gone in peach provided, mellow how many qualify, primate frustrated percentile datum; pinny frenzy mended, tune stubborn melt astride, skim. Sardine prince qualm. Trait mutton blame, yielded outlandish wanton, thorny tantrum overmuch. Guess tiff brazen ivy, borrow nor lend, sand castle. Shine twain in cloud, hidden and lazy, salt lock birds in glory, attenuate bestowed. Praise nowhere by the wood, carry add yolk why not; pilchard forward enucleate ride in front, praline symmetric ebonised, chronicle refrain.

## So After Another

Wick stop in power transience, reduction portion saving ahead damage foot speck, elbow vantage bisque. Nervous landless per crooked district, ample to cramp, oven first truce lenient prowl ancient step-fast fund. Lick enhance forage will engagement, licit banter ferment, crescent set better for butter, nervous admission. On disc raffish behaviour cornice, up to or through, anvil gravity select effusive heat penitent after fact, under temple deducted crypt. Brachial on lintel, curls dented over brew, slip-ware molten zig-zag saturate refract furnace. Crevice, lichen plaint arabesque birth canal amended surplice in surplus ingrate, countable deficit traffic pliancy front; usual late polite exonerate darling, win to drag or fend to stamp, lassitude. Whose stock derail uncoil selfishly brush deturned, scapular lavish sprain, rise to ingest tropic restive, furthest in virgin flight. All watching affrighted costed indolent, risk terse pact infertile, and still they tell crudely tangent overall remaindered. Desertion for winter-light numeral obvious plural, insert accurate, astute. Sustenance near coincident: manna from haven snow given shrewdly reserved bipolar surge allow. So many company appoint in split pin anodyne, sumptuary apposite undistorted, all asunder version white enteric regime proclaim incorporate; amend, distraught, protect.

## Wall Germinate

As here to be firm storm, to see from suit worn despite
span over flighted, in spate fury, return; rage by fire
torn sky-patch shudder, esperance accrue, open heaven
founder awed inform dilate returning, passage old swim
near sight line composite, cloud riven score. Recruit
list tempest crack, vertebrate cluster avertive delink
astonish blast contended; insistent violate calming
fissure rip-well, offer to scrape tabulate destruction
imminent. Back to stand redound cretic billow, by wore
ravage, punish underset crash of waters next in black,
struck face depicted; ever for, rock groin as pitiful
thunder, odious wrack partition as unknown, below wait
debated, derelict. Transit plunder narrow deluge midge
frangible, obligate, racket surmounted vatic diminish
rush to judge. Nominate inroad crustal, lateralised
washout grievous antic, over take cover in severance
undercoat. Further spoilt averted, tilt formaldehyde
explosion invented as crush to blame, profane parlance
sideways, fluent slanted currency in torrent format.
Falsetto whistle boasted might perforate, impersonate
incised reproof dank coverlet militia; soon out remit
by prior merciful reprieval investment. Onyx crash
both porous, soak to floated, muted on tip rejoinder.

## SQUEEZED WHITE NOISE

## (2020)

'The *ideal* squeezed state of a harmonic oscillator is taken to be a quantum Gaussian state with minimum uncertainty product.'

'In practice, squeezed white noise does have a characteristic frequency.'

'The correlation functions [of noises]... are appropriate to the degenerate parametric amplifier, the most successful source of squeezed light so far found.'

– C.W. Gardiner & P. Zoller, *Quantum Noise: A Handbook...* (Berlin, 3rd ed., 2004), pp. 322, 331, 336.

## In Note Attended

None yet so true as for to say, eye watch flinch, obey
in player sight dispose as other plight; lower by lover
offer incident, ahead despite unfair, unvexed by this
no marvel revel when intransigent, distraint revealed
aright. Censure so few entire, repair to seem exempt
donation false, reproof level in view; foray intern own
or from instead, confection. As soon to grow, distract
up fled after, borrow afloat, in dictum from world's
affray; party to vaunted loyalty counted, reprieved
candid by florid search endow. Furrow in tow, in brow
see what indeed renew convey, assuage must if whilst
holding dear folded close. Vain sunlight royal almost
trusted when most in doubt; nearest by open cunning
flowing to faultline truthful in fight, else clear.

## Sealed to Fly

Hill side undismayed, of earth and sky close braided
terrene to squirrel star sent, until thirst pace in yet
slope broidered pasture medium worth bridle choice,
path beneath. Upper shade glints fading out, over to
cloud ever prouder, portrait elated sealed to fly;
day far scented, air promise marry further increment.
Discrete, due now to fall, fair heart contrivance at
spate, shaft safe shield breath commensal win, agree
completed into part, to yield. Fresh mint in glade
announcement, frequent if stayed, pink camphor torn
for planet nourish by finish testament; born in clear
turn, grazed forage await hyaline, transom avoidance.
Overlay cloister preen furnish, wafer why so crowded
helium levant, at night. Troop carriage cluster dark
to face, obscure displaced implement cambium unity
collocate annoy. Keep pace step first yet amiss, to
gather, none other prone divined scale apt intruded;
down from dawn-light repined, pressed firm in shape.

## Unto Greek Fire

Eminent nested, throat pack wrinkled, at prune austere mortal and silent, tenderly if vivid so imposing. Flagrant for chance crazy addict dice address situate with certain for curtain fallen teal aggregate rift zealous. Numb tempest sited limit astride, sudden they will already lifted topic aspect confess fine unless native by tuft implicit to credit affection; impulsive costly far-off precious, the whole on file fiery his hue forage critical, cortex shimmer neglected. Go to slice deflected, loom trim hold onto bye hand list portal ivy too, well before consent. Package luminous supposed fought to jaw obtain affirm pointed flexuous tabby amazed treason, awed veridian soon tremblant and fragrant ice laden foreign selected gist. Phrasal seeking appetite impact besides, correct profession oppressive medium fuss, elute distantly into flight reduced, fruit perspective contingent.

## To Banbury Cross

Clench the porch epact, doric lunar match intact ditch elongate tension mandible escorted which frolicsome win summary, elegant redact civic. Famous torchlight inches parlance sanction yet thwarted sooner than, ever from hydroptic and when massive proleptic to plastic, sing to bench turn mute about audible; archway supplement inference condiment fulminating, endorse attract worse both if first caravan blench. Offhanded Lettish enteric portion, by earn to wing, span condign flummery, portal outward suit light astute to missive argument. Smoke in sight capsule, imminent paramount trick, wrong tangent urgent forcible bring to hive-craft, prang awake soaked frighten sliding, alert. Be or see, kestrel for nostril awl to why shock fly upward or grand in friend switch idle cursory; provident hale link granulated afterwards, to ever might saraband coated duel to while, jewel to lend filament actual. Motivic alike frost to run footstep, suffix in scansion bandage toy of thought fractionate dwell passionate mix by pilgrim, by saffron unaffected.

## Or But Invaded

Thumbnail aspic theurgic carapace spectral plastic
grimace allergic aggrandise incisor waist famished
undoubted, anointed; submit for salic male greed
ridiculous tensor side-rail replacement, in acrylic
bat to bottle, green battle in a box. Fraudulent to
distant hoax, eyewash fatuous example offal by garb
to raid, impetuous juice coerce flippant icy silent,
other-worldly. Even surly toasted double joint dent
scented bell air surfactant lizard, tolerant pink win
arrant count radiant immunise. Into prize, instead
fast ahead confuse at the window endowed likewise
twist, then vaporise. Elbow sprinkle power horn in
turn even withy sedge to leave for sprue, trample
due surplus primus few out talent mandate abhorrent
accounted billow replanted. Want if or but invaded,
open denied across the plain, canter oft explained;
tank urgent sacred consequent, inter-tidal misty.
Fluent going past, best post ingress, pressure in
salve resolve appointment; natural nostril abacus
fix pastel edenic indistinct, barbiturate intact.

## How to Say

Flaxen added boisterous, beside limitless dinted speech parallel auspice elver meltdown hospitable, oxtail brim overwhelm in forceps coverage, squint moist beach lace head instep. Forage output realm, rocks within wintry clad poise, stewed to manage dresser blended thousand notice, mild trodden liken, faction in constraint. At summit bluster in storm, crown punish credit to ardency cried fast aloud, menace to blame, emphatic dock coil fuel fortunate mortality; suspicion worries square-up on fix deliberate, furnace trailed inured dark matter soft palp and wild, astute. Brew council wax innermost frozen or splinted openly, brazen indelible uplifted sandwich grievous energy batten costume simple paste adornment high-water, market. Resides force it blanket front to back setter average print, if get distinct when some when fill to stack endure, optimal scoring prime attack profile. All convergent occident, polar verst stimulant white marking, striate audible foil fueled activate. All set then, breed ready whole bread antic brief affront tremendous monster in minster attenuate.

## Water Evidence

Would brook, scenic ominous canter outward teeming denied omission, both limbs caressed; limpid blank corrugate noetic, special fashion size at his bite or contrition. Foremost possible all of them humid, peach found to touch unbound, river hook in later harvest induction. Might comic at blame forensic altar, for spicule mended rapid give over by self arrogate demented. As can unlock also tip cluster sun-bleached flock terrify across for under chasm ride furious, custody whether so outreach dramatic open trench seedlings wrap permeate, placid. Grate folic esteem, galvanic option misted wavelet hidden ankle doublet contracted siphon, game attrition in splinter either thankful, to flock unhurried field to cloud in genome soon extreme. Ponder trample illusory runway, quick overtaken and scented not much, flux innervate monastic merit assignment; soar affix in climax, sacral or mental time enough, rebuff quest meal grateful, notorious redeem dim otherwise reclaim. Captivate employ foreman injury, provoke sealing resilient, prime verdict invented.

## Go or Shall

Exact flight volumetric assisted, perfect next sought wharf to price leap to cheapen agreement; in wavering misgiving pliancy, fervency bring onward to syndicate. They will had better, exchange manage escapement tint forbidden in housing planet section hadn't yet found across clear ground hidden to want gradient, evident castigation. No stint afforded, clad imitate, bounden entrust protected winning, amble rental offend strand certainty cladistic plausible, discursive holographic demeaned. You go or shall attainment, refined lapsed ointment allocate, disjunct mannerly obstetric instil manorial candidate, obstinate estrangement merciful pink to rescue, point fast lithe effect. All for, all on restore, sham crocus licence bonus bird slim on bough pensive; intentional strain parapet, trappings meant merchant tenancy, impermanent remainder omission ban renal averted, dissent. Construct set whole wick to animate before, nil offence parlance handy to family, stream bedding trait; obverse mat rend to swallow up, rounded primate in dispute, undeterred but realised as born stubborn average wisdom not mine to operate.

## Imbricate Research

Arrest for rust infested, distrust digestion, optimist
over consistent mast head, worst first or last caressed
wished-for unless contested; nut-brown, crown speeded
planet ovation plus instinct planked national especial
out-flank animal, vindicate. Algorithmic yet untested
span to lift remote, in antidote dimercaprol pitchfork
sac carton cardoon crib incarnadine, one to one unsaid;
foster after much faster, drift apart scarlet outlasted
spread feudal, arrival mendicant. New awesome into dread
fashion caution resignment upper brow, thunderheads glow
berated ignorant blunt caniculate oppugned starlet yodel
candle pitch-pine; time near past suppress constriction
diluted honest lunar trite frosted, steep and sleep lyke
wake inspissated. Advantage play amaze birds of prey by
ankle to trample deck to mark, by luck modulate anodyne
planet analgesic iridescent tenure gannet tenth minced
arrogant excisement. Plumage undamaged, dauntless dice
invert image inclined, rise and shine, for chime assign
the team bovine none opportune lame disinclined, monk.
Inter flunked dank crust to pitch, imbricate research
cherish in heart murmur, invent; no mind plangent dint.

## Empire Purge

Condole schoolday taut enlisted, thread out wax trodden mixture tool-box raptured perplex broach diffident bunk indifferent invincible trade pitch succulent fort dismay, edict deflected; flinted path colossal bringing fossil rejoinder, imminent. North underwent veil porringer conducted, invent arrogant lint parcels dismal life actual, mortal catalogue enter dissolute. Terrify entire forage portrayal, mental however synthetic posthumously declared award sorted honorific; drastic empire purge demerged in frost under netting, posting. Familiar depleted inches dogged rancid element, character piece melodic practical most trim old advice, gravy improvement levy asking reflexive protrusion impeachment scurvy non-vital enteric print sentiment: barricade. Ordeal trail trefoil pronounce adducement, verdict hurricane indexed and vindicated, horrify for principal oracle at monstrous isthmus digestible; your pact stated unpacked idling and simmering has-been reacted octane orchid manage impute bustard. His anew, almost crux, easy polity frenzy modest ignited.

## Issue Bract Feather

Ashen zodiac forsaken northern lexicons calumny soften comedy, flex sash astrakhan beckon packet weapon. Tantalise systems enterprise formation presume awash, distress unfathomed mediate asian revive mutton tracks, chops; wake steps rocket tacit prolong. Intern fashion refusal allergy as twice long face, queue trace mongoose etherise, in dice rough alum beacon challenge modicum at table wrinkle faucet interlink. Lunation attune cyclamen mishap siskin, tweet undue sink to sit swallow throat create aspect commiserate; high note vibrated, melted napkin native upbringing surrogate. Licit parget promise napalm, all by true nil in vain, game in turn reform planetary overseen, falling down; leave burning tie storm plaster gather, fluster total margin statin fit artefact. Fume issue bract feather, dawn scribe pinnacle, alabaster case weather, safe disown. Jewel prudent bassoon, perfume impending, raft room to clean in time; marsupial quiescent do confident rupestral percept, carpet invigilate transparent macerate depleted by afterthought.

## Indignant Rant Often

Cannibal aedile nuts in may, full display pelagic
gaffer present laughter, cold and frosty told up
or off put on forty one eaten seen titan mischief
win annulment; margin club boil over in secession
split choose silicon ardent, astringency. Stubble
quibble list form reframe calumet farmhouse under
pipecraft solstice met to mitre gather knots woken
mistaken, porphyry in orphanage, cruise. Inedible
segment indented, intended by ossified fragments
untied grimace lost roll along carousel assailed,
solar weapon in blunt trait anointed; liquid see
dree pacified, coiled reviled, revelation impale
oracular stint however shellac, cordite very well
done ought not aplomb orchid panic saltire fluxed
pricket bay winter snaps; agile refused bruised,
thermite addicted price. Loose hanging vestige at
arras isle fuel inundate flotation, flute omits
trill until revelry belfry greet infant election
site; aniline diet frighten and shorten gnostic
cavities multiplex, indignant rant often, dance
to Handel. Deep blue allure, immured hermit plait
ill served brandish remission, sings for supper.

## Intimate Hoarding

Corner intruder agaric sepsis, wading organic tiff reflux churn away fade mesmeric food warning pontic swallow prefer disclaim. Slain worst suffice gullet slender oneiric void left-going field transit rate ruction cation few allow; essential arson incur bite face-track intimidate, suffer tallow in vain. Basin unfound, regained endemic wield acrostic cost marrow chill to bone thread; eye sedated, remonstrate tide in hollow clay for crude adhesion, play full at most inbred. Now then is one credible inductance, to fly past least, meddle or whistle all trodden in person why altered without debate rumour savour. Bled cult misfit livery, medal awarded; fray stewed farflung soever model allied. Ectopic munitions never sent they would or carry out, inure folly capable train time, turn dilate boarded animate sistrum in former intimate hoarding. Watch mine, dug out in handsome shelter, watershed bypass oppress compulsion; vat aversion word to site conation. Do like glide test, conquest different probation in nomen melisma, if discover other plasma over plaintiff; improvident chanted impenitent grade, illusion fortune recant.

## Flout the Rule

Bantam cantaloupe, oligarch attested freight indicted primeval larch needles ointment nape issues; facial civil industrial, wholesale drought teasel. Coffer set rebated comb, welcome dynast fresh suffusion limiting will or can droop heart-struck in lamp beaver averted coronet. Valiant flow child unguent coil fuming brow exhale pageant file complaint, former deterrent screen miscreant; waver to cover sandal, window apart better at odds threaten, under arch, rampage. Earliest pass single mass, shell lift hostage gale force purse off course reckon; imminent frame eyelid plectrum open, luminous entourage. Flout the rule initial effort by enforcement, both trivial function foundation piquant kenning whalebone seamark buoyant; take a rise adonic heatproof acrid distillate. Known to gain advantage, when all roads go there, shingle doff carrion shine in fervid lip, salve price prey instigate murmurous unaccounted, allay reflection. Bastion harness fluff aimless centre agile embroil swivel to fault, to mend in plan offended liken stoop in anger to question; at count the top plinth, confirm precise roof aerofoil dismount to cross; convince sense wince to overrun.

## Motivate Hurtful

Reverse online harm immediate bias template foundation
disparage bring ceramic, anodyne for painful outcry
offer to censor by same, all in serve time win foretold
avengement will impinge; thought to sift, inflame amiss.
Curated vessel flint passage, disputed and torn apart
by greed less splendid, mischief from the heart: spate
torrential crime accuse imminent by night. In mind end
the thing strict custom age, reform platen burning to
linger adversative minus notation finish, mine to give;
witness assigned imported by generous blunted antiphon,
fill winking spoil descent fossil turbulent outflow be
for beam entreaty, west split lint cascaded each bent
reprint facile procession. You to know, deep to care
vivid in fire torrid since defended, born aslant in
candidate plane allow. Your turn, next after yet deny
tested brink solid wait for need immense; for catch
affirm intended transit taper to amber entrain, line
issue down paper pacify warrant doorway, in seed drill
often banish retinue. Dual confinement orpiment flush
stinted damage rescind selfish wire broken, lay woken
cling dilute token, gift. Assisted wheaten nearby mat
refuted, harness sacrifice allergic fast intrinsicate.

## Sent from Away

Elect trumpet fishery after in damp predicted open each about appetite hectic feverish omelette depict swish tremor fresh nines impetuous; bouquet tread cramp treasury torn cream, instruction. Mostly spin diagonal solicitous righteous beneath honest give to save amaze crisis turning and welling, mischief runaways, retard in the light around us, preserved. Regional femur fracture ocean imposture, best card shade to lamp proximate; tour flower heath to tint placement, in parallel infolded vine suited train assigned terrain conspicuous levy ochre balanced instance emission, reaction, final reward blurred stir, stirrup intense. Rooted by complex incense sequence swerved slant more bold, sailed calm for immense expanse, clear nave folio; curious dress mostly less told radiance, air warm without harm in flight escape fruit shallow dish limpet black action, tract allowed to wish. Who knows that or this, current flows later in water, clatter undue, averred from mounted void; clouded dispersion bit careworn signet effected minaret concept meeting swiftly resided, delicious. Turning suspiciously juice force disputed, voice recruited temporised.

## Six Leaves Rush

Six leaves rush and push, talk the stalk mesh win dozen origin plainly mining affront; discreet pint aborescent dissenting covenant. Will, won't, seven kingdom level arhat tip topmost address induced at clinch spendthrift; style bee target batter consent invariable, condiment across dyke. Often mission to heathen, foliar inferno conversation, be just, be fast, well beyond question, on every side infatuate so how on back, to front pump action; cousin spin pleated unfolded geniculate, average benefit inch diminish sublate pontefract; giddy aunt auspicious panorama witty plunge intense shore-line paraffin edict, addicted gristle intubate refreshment, out paramount frown farmland oversight detached. Once wrench from free, stubble watch involve no part or patch unflown, annex nectar brim. Suppress within, bowl spun furious jump the vent, forenoon catalpa, capricious factual affixing; nugatory toy repent precedent mandate, scrimmage esteem wide albumen. Now so, now too then either blown fallen, shuffle follows or walk all hallows carry, silken quarry carrageen skin ramble falcon talcum bunch amaze; include lesion or split, entourage but nonchalant.

## Fine Chert Bruised

To prise uppermost canteen, currency foreign, groan
at green replacement for birdish host, lost forward on
temper. Supper fence clinch dace shoal, might within
teem, front ways often praise and board; less asterisk
musing olivine intrusion. Cascade ignored now arrant
frequent allusive casework ice pack, mostly ten been
whim plagioclase bent slant profane. Sluice erase to
trice unheard discovered, shaved office afford esteem
effort; profit invited fidget inveterate over sweeten
sward seize, instinct. Last instigate untoward prime
weapon symphony effacement, phase talking twin brittle
hostel capsize, knot unties arid; hornet gaze unborn
prion atropine amazing trout, ventilate win replica
procure cicatrise. Nine from fluid averted, alert in
slotted citrine pastel rival near adjoin; tired flame
tap button western flout graphic, tendentious ire or
silk invention. All grout, splint indented ascertain
fine chert bruised, aggrieved feudal swindle dismal
instil virtue, programme elapse missed, conductance
to beast interpret genuflect. Your proficient trick
fascinates liquid overcome, brain conjecture origins
lack oaten pittance; invar spoon insipid, scar wane
criminal drastic prune in re-open greet, impoverish.

## Momentary Once Fled

Abridge by gaslight infolded sugar multiple friendship
segment wigeon woebegone, welter thrown, abjected tin-
pot thorium edit calcite stint acquaintance trance. If
stage countenance blandishment told off curious blight
remit tribal infringed lounge flash septic at least or
singe; harm odic plaint wasted, evil sweet reluctance.
Stone canton mountain suspicious sliced transverse by
drill mud, fill road brake, attenuate. Work hastate or
follicle legendary orpiment, reprimand halt consulted
sound up divinity, decision complex; squirrel disband
almond under fronds pellucid, to fragile lynx indented
ostrich ridgeway. Conceal frail animus terminal gales
force rigour oxide division, way felt mint or plangent
document absorb momentary once fled. Bid exact ritual
blanket atonement no lock to proxy, leaky boat merely
afloat by luck, rebate; mentor exaggerate chapter lead
edge ride headway to blade embrowned. Sensation faint
allayed carnation pledge in good heart relative, part
tendency if you will derivate shall tuck fringe tamp
manifest indulgence in bacon balcony; stooping falcon
estranged endearment recrudescent pit to lark, remit
this hillside contrivance feasts yet soon discontent
and taken forward, neat opportune canary win caravan.

## At Ankle Winkle

Butter up oligarch, orchard in-flight credit speck attar infarct indicated loosen contrition, slate parchment flattery spread to latch warden; interim hen latent occupy, to brood. Clatter impending wit dental antidote, won't tread escalate at otter in other deflated, weight to matter; watch scorching open footprint frighten medallion. Intermit edit glitter intrusive frontal spirit utterly ripe epic imitate instead, destruct inbred, culverin peach greed. Lunch match inflicted wedge; fluid willow surprise darted, liquidise at ankle winkle stray elected sunrise in wild surmise plead or punish, such elevate. Punctual interval at fled to storm come soon, incision mimic tangle futile inflated; elastic which worn outward, cream eventuate silk concision. Organic entire vested flex discovery esteem confirm insidious wisdom crown enticed assize; first seed emotion valiant anticipated consistent after sifted service visor, revision charge useful hatch tenuous. Stitch blue endure distended, bent forward mental allow tinder dash inflown cavern discretion, river option scrannel episode. Very well done filial screen, scrawny pencil pipe evasion, chrism conductance buy son.

## Icing Sugar

Visit the cauldron, hydraulic devout divagate sure seldom as random fork quiz offer doubtful, ill-kempt first about fabric ironical each enterprise stuck insect yet about; bonnet now malcontent improvident, hadron foulade at cradle stent. Trident or would inversed, abandon colic private impaired new air, same purse and mouth talk aspirated wince interpret; calendric demeanour exuded revenue pale ever told surmount appointment grit, slot, ruinate temper variegate, profitable once mincing entrench so elegant in vagrancy. Cambric attempted flitted absurd indicate imminent, aware comment flinch by print tag, affluent, gallantry; intuit by gauntlet for rancour glamorous, rancid placid abstinent to all recoil yet worse too, so went abroad private attentive cost fluffy, tanglement. All they did, insistent florid ask plate, lurk close by harden or foreign, chip pardon interminable, miscreant. Entire caravan cultivate parenthood, sole working testate brilliant supply supple scupper incentive to colonise; gut flora ostrich goodness embroiled native permittance. Attention payment restricted prudent rely moly clear white into drip, magnetic confident the whole day uppermost even prolonged.

## Enough as Good

Moss cornice, titmouse crevice consisted, nourish on allowance improvident discounted, relentful indicate fortified; praise come to see parish sighting sylvan prudence furnish creep to tree; treat some far away guidance tortuous literate resin varnish envisaged alliance. Or pious share, knee bended amiss sandal, supplied ready bundle apposite don't, item in clear ant trails erase dark markings; rose-bay dove ways corrugate displeased, in-phase. Whence advance inch to bench, raisin pudding recite or won't, as wishful bethought alike, greet inundate sea market gilt all dependent they were into covenant. Near promise one pledge keep as made fast induce profess, summon bye seal truth missive face to season; enough as good, will inherit in due warrant enter winter incanted word limit, barren levantine, suffuse ambition. Now reach feast forward, escort guardian outride, dart aforesaid relax sulphur pride; white froth yeast in prize, fern to turn brindle tunnel singular relieve disguisement. The whole trek, bridge lent inventive atropine encourage, forage in front design afloat allocate particulate prodigy jacket, estate indent; none other green more brief sunlight gleam flicker from leaf blade, moss half-shade, outwith trident.

## Vital Crystallise

Sea force earth twice basal woven ozone, until
gauze waiting sullen foreseen blood torn sampan
essence fling, rampart gallon churn. Revenue in
particle inside classic stack refurnish caustic
loiter astigmatic mainstay daze ridgeway; less
mirror jitter mastery at still delay persist on
wing tarragon. Aquaplane get mine braving, fly
vital crystallise shire ride by wire-tap scoop,
turf war claw to digress affection bittern for
ironclad remained oh maid of work, listen into
flatter floor severance penance; finance flee
the crib tie, asseverated to languish rhenish,
buy-out if beyond doubt spoilt histogram, not
credible miscible agitate conjuration ration,
even. Torque pitch insipid at torrid calomel
unable retracted, rocket fit delimit scimitar
never far affected to split, blitz; advocate
punnet gusset tapestry delete, astute denied
to master-key. Bring and fly, water-way, now
speak your weight resounding, presented yam
equable thimble bravura spattered innocence.
Repay macaroni dye lemon famine blunder, as
up from under rejoinder emulate brotherhood,
another that's the river. Carry forth, nett
worth entanglement, by outpost sold or lent.

# Allotted Micro Dapple

Across the plate marker, two-state remonstrate cage frozen to forge aliquot departed, ought to barrage broad dated river stoop. Dark wave for surge, sated or hinder to fraud couplet, heat weighted fortress overhead, after underneath, innocent. Slur elision to friction, action latent sought rancid chief bark stipulated; sorrow aspic; ground. Oft ternate alter graven loop catchment, rustle embattle plain stolen pardon, medial. Up on before or more top interdict, impulsive gate steer, waiver engulf, crater refine pollen apple spadix. Sumptuous talkative alkaline russet, walkway inured, drizzle annexation infused, all fold plied mail to chain, avoided; ballot tusk cost deferred ballast renewal, perpetrate. Vulture cellular cover tossed insipid aggression, daytime clinical curtain diversionary havoc impersonated; devote brighten. Vestigial prevail age surrogate: adept full control fast boil up incensed, inimical core told crisis by influence, slight impatience pertinent. Crash merit attire, beforehand to dusk allotted micro dapple, deal sweetheart cinder path announced, enforced. Imminent proviso in capsule, overseas pledged decretal, fledge mandate brimful marrow at skypark bounty. Load by duty total front inference, mark sibilance, in story morning glory.

## Voice Testing

Chink lank apprentice furtive arraign provenance
tonsure lacerate visceral, durable smitten; gait
step steeple censure, looser shears rhizome cloth.
Up-end crackle leniency, salient with fears aloft
divisible and pointed not yet entire, grapple ate
view on site; in forenoon, rapid excited and sunk.
Baneful out view to pale, soaking outright provoke
weighted repaid, buoyed unafraid trek motet, abet
arable soft invasion pungent qualify cream session
profligate. Faster insist pendent vocalist slight
motive, fire harbour saturate annoyed impatience
pursued at staple oval facile credit, unit beyond
doubt. Improving to fit lapse delicious go first,
close splicing, flammable endured hot foot print
to nearest moult. Brackish sullen underling trait
style for sermon, functionary diction motion pick
binding fiction belated, assist forest digested.
All told far over crest to settle, voice testing
for wear injury brow darkened, critic parlance.
So in tail follow final say-out, shelf to self in
fearsome addict flutter temper avarice, index at
prolix complexion; tenet gear release appliance
turbulent incident yet aware unspent. As wanted
rested syllable for there, appear latent choice
twice over, reviled plural abrasive inclination.

## In Torque Reduce

Pre-royal plagal martial suited, York ham mind cram
unsettle dual recruit maxim; pontoon lifted macaroon
bath to oil, room plate attention. Equal sisal flake
disturb fabric picaroon dynamo effervescent, absent
incidental gable mockery, dative path intuit. Single
to fit angle after-zoom uproar, dill posterity store
brevity, loyal contemn to victim laggard in torque
reduce. Moist aftermath grim liberty vestment, wing
lattice hard up in sequent panic invited, pork clad
pudding sufficient. Whether out, tether by slumber,
eyes fast not blood shut. Styptic fulminate vestal
capricious, invested eagle trial, skive or skewing
envious; mollify pasturage inane renowned, polygon
amend half conjecture to pedal. Intone let bygones
dive further plover, evidence prudence draggle frog
tabular, mingle for blend descended cover in kind.
Alignment. Detritus habitat synthetic closer tenant,
safe and whole ground mill grit restive and sifted,
merriment. Brow lift, best fast convergent tangle
uncle; old sport, got caught, right single cannibal.
All is flown, is known, cut for luck, out of sight.
Had broken custom contortion, steam horrible even
unviable, let alone fable writ grist insistence one
by another either wither bough hang; myopic tempest
allusion employed, woken medal profiled impediment.

## Heat Point Artful

Income cumin wherever clover acumen perforate mild office device cornice impeded, at voracious howdah fodder uncoiled drum love to flame, forwent. Pint nascent ant weeping still lantern person weft over vast tundra, anxious leaf itself, pride roused, to tenor turn shorn, immune only claim occupied, bit kept well as bees do. Main suffix low-price wish served open mind upbraid, select, none imbue rain attended cling or linger yet to find. House blond, blinded face traced over beyond worn loose estate, recede splayed modest green peridot, imposed meet oh rolling river not for ever, or soon turn back; unkind to sleep resigned impartial, promise fluted sufficed incentive buzzed trim stock. When hoist, redress precision grown, dove-grey needed else if season own mansion abrasion seldom ingot appetite conduit agree: free park, prospect, act. Spelled decision mortal faction, run up aground subsumes transom division flooded to beating heart; heat point artful recurrent. Long done call, haul lid betide in close to tread portray aloof descried. Bee milk actor motion proven altogether, in wild mint attraction; consume treat issue impassioned joist for tenon fine to float. Lock rainfall see lemon until agile in profile, fluid scrip relent.

## Radiant Star Fish

Will noose flourish openly dozen terrace courage, zig-zag expect decorate channel voice expert sail to seal fresh crease induce figure; spruce tricked operating vale soup candle. Toilsome frolic broken panel loose cousin type jagged brow, slowest endure cease invested privet primate menace brick. Impact invested how about masquerade solid bright to say out, clathrate liken to culminate tit for tat adventure; give or view conceal frigid spillage piecemeal chilblain sustain improbable overtime. Join at twice civil just necklace level coil ordeal principal tangle, reveal pigeon in selfish omen radiant starfish incandescent. Print seek mirth parkin quartz hereafter, convey parish deuce in aspic laughter mullion inquest; animate last dullish mollusc, niece pastry rigid to spring. Dash redolent cream display ink winking when most, funnel nailwork, ever breech of kind untempted glowing, of brand gable burning, near-scented relenting. Hazard parget admiral fulsome, coronal bind both together, of feather mind crystal or subtle, lent pretended amend made. Least said mileage trade, terrify sit to knack obelisk, twist first-come often in borage like to a throne shore-line, addendum. In fact aspect handle mingle aspirate dulcet remnant, lucid in mien resign, track florin faucet missed, ingrain. Ever for merry clamour, on wide mat tappet impugn protectorate.

## Seditious Ice-Cream

Derelict quick quick gallant imbalance thinks out
fastidious badge ensconced, strewn trick limbeck
narrow wicked twin. Fortune aversion come to that
flippant blunder wager, pennant shirk rivalry tap
carpet appertain portrayal in cellophane. Vaunted
seditious ice-cream trusted for undulant whirl win
denial, excluded to splash by the dark canal not
yet sufferance, had rid entire with child hidden,
madden in broke extant caution wind-blown; ashen
bidden flush out scuffle red eye surfeit elated
triune sanction, quantum pair tunnelled descended
sanded oblate rutile barren town libation snips.
Engorge at the side rail, zealous steady mark in
line brim dash woven, astern restrain compunction
fume angle lock bait introit urbane; vanquish dye
wooden driven dangerous, obvious, laverock tucket
judicious silence come across, speak your mind on
friend pathogen. He beat upon a ladle agile minim
gyrated antonym, neither spun unbound, ingrained
cap pippit trip. Great red spot thicket granite
congealment impugned, coming to think of nothing
less promise sound not now visible datum tertian
immersive restless, impeach fossil clench rivets
bridge outpace strait bonnet winsome. Danger in
window, air flow crested salic revert unfunded,
junction listen option canonise infusion: lemon.

## All Blink Supper

Inflicted sulky deceit frank compunction, frame announce treaty alkali trivial so sweet too late doubtful ink trepidate. Assuage bulk angry windy taken heed need token, rank offence defunct scorn by sage decision torn, ladder sunk civil uneaten repute sconce broken tussle. Criminal panel often inflation, roast garish roost apart yet contrite be war to wage offal; pounce to grapple enslave trees toys craft outcast till square, in current. Unctuous must horizon bunk datum, tantrum grief on tab, air repaired let droplet replete, intact; trouble print fossil embrocation in fashion, for rapid twice envision factorise. All blink supper frolic temper declare, noise to boast ripple past remorse, disposed sad than ever one same, profane off course, as laid. Warrant paregoric by thermic hazardous, dank shadow steeped never cries, your fate placate unknown, throw out ballad appetite. Wrath first scratch divested been sure refuted, missal violet fight converged or lent, fraction outspent. Scold trace in truce place to search plain origin, antonym welkin overcast, dispersed nymph orison, converse. Mellow to follow crush of ballast enteric, lame struck main weapon, gravel hurt abraded; parry fable false traction, defect inclination grip deepen hunger waiting pollinate.

## Yield Dazzlement Lift

Other startle format limits, accepts massive infirm pause to quantum noise, advancement trap subtle lets tropic actual hoist ordering; informal measure gate phoenix axis deploys remittance flaw broken on signal once if more practical, because. Fertile quarter wit appoint grant reluct, retard infusion, bract distil whim full without mirrors circumspect. Attendant for scissor in wharf collision, fractured twin beam pent or flint, chrome allowance slider proffer ejected up pressure mercuric, tasted and acrid. Transverse fold field pleated, inure perturbed, cyclical density awl pierced "is probable"; attune mercy prize finalised incision; late inflected technician mutual toy must exist, of so much for. Soon find mantra, mead trammel yield dazzlement lift, consequent venous impartial frugal haze top brunt; conjugate effort folk planet, flutter prior to free point expected. Altitude profit net bound orbit, prime spectral appetite drawn outer dissident parallel resile partaken overturn, mowing nothing zero transfer fiscal aspect. Light seal toil well past denial, in temperament score fission tied squared, excess filial decree treasured. Ushered to seek unwound; fortitude indent dispersion, mission nail beforehand, positive availed. Source anyway dye thread preference induced, recoil acerbic at bandage innate poundage splinter, insert covariant pedigree.

## As If Adept

Slow milk ranked direct, pungent other token sunken
talk by taken, silicate same to cream delicate in
graphic dismember, amber forked ramen dolmen raisin
bulk timber nightjar. Tilt vinegar seem in oat time
auric bell to sally soon silly, obligate attainder
lacked pilot seraphim, languor beam. Tremendous sum
building thatch beguiled, unmatched for splendour by
sprung for or cheerful, clear; tantric polyglot coin
debate, sulky dank and murk, dyspeptic. Fund anode
for antenna aliquot busted, both tearful but trusted
viscose, originate, detrimental alike all for sake,
confession by allergen. Spin round coracle plentiful
in solitary woods militate against melancholy raven
symmetry cone, fearful amity mended in coma inducted
as profuse, as if adept; rescue retinue insect silk
in folk confronted. Vain ascertain, demesne offer by
definition, native subjunctive preternatural ushered
of twin. Already frantic rock warren, bank cogent in
tad illusion, pair misprision, be joyful and roaming
quick arabic, gum instruct instantly. Cusp and flow
drain treasure, assure tm product wrapper ant in bud
blame tension, winch above twelfth spilth ordonnance
information duct. Vapour single acerbic conflicted,
bone careworn entrain feverish, by viaduct election
sickle annoyance dancing fragrance. All now known,
flown rural tremble, high cloud allowance attained.

## As Many Tarry

Bristle insignificant mutant collision, mixture span timorous chromatic aspen lesson, fickle date fixative banish this derided; faction to vision feel trail slam nine slide supreme. Tower impugn macaroon buttress fictive amazon phonic gallery, into folly precision time over, wine duct select into volume clamorous arrival, baffle. Agreement avert front torment lent forward strain, estimate distemper forensic insensate, off prohibit entity crane dune, magnify outcry tarmac lost aback. Fee cower natural grateful nor yet frustrate, casual astonish price avid lace; flagrant exploded rite proposal fertile generative filmic as many tarry erstwhile incident. Stoke wan visage crusade, run past outpost, set pace grimace turn to tide, sun derision trickle avoidance crude office, elided. Why traded ebon nickel violet instated, smitten genial enfilade, link cascade taxon proficiently aumbry clustered in vault, inviolate; known for room roof pitch consent arboreal set anvil want arrogant renegade, leonine impact, restriction. Spill attack just evident neverwise, operation open dual candour surprising mendicant flouted replant omit implacable defective, how up next deacon grout propagate. Date, doubt, infatuated slight pertinent instance whom enlisted troop parlance infamy viewfinder denial still cruet.

## Forward Steward

To well below in glue, arrow gleeful if yet anew
meadow burrow as warren, summon ravine in panel
by mineral blue indic sheen; narrow lane to find
helm tame or rabbit rebate groom. Gravy stir crazy
rueful ways allegory compose in fury, gaze froze
removal loom silo sidle uncle, petroglyph stiffen
dye for neck signalise brazen in fine ado; be one
ago crew musical dial ease trim drain in nonage
invite over despite hard time. Then overthrow in
style timid ascended sub-royal to loyalty, ooze
apprise follow cull scion celadon; blue-tit quiff
two squills vernal knoll prime next askew; than
to mend for undergone, local herd allege or bill
worry come forward steward, trek whirr tick score
attracted brood or moth in touch assert. Indoors
least action caret additive rewarding burnt inert
lawful at floor level, culvert morning dew burial
root inflection; in sum decked such over spectral
suited to hand, confirmed leaf cover reducing pin
mind bandage, deep-set. Wrangle or yet to choral
tonic certain custom tunicate; must all will tell
fondest quarry spelled apart, of peltate tribunal
obsidian; neon trental accentual wet figment in
samite accorded, in worse-case brace anchorite
lag or next reflect. Motivate unturned, in fire
annealed discreet, on throughout patronal oval
pair, in mirror axis corrigible tumult, intact.

## Cant Recruit Disputed

When wane mortal fry approaching, caught ten unless stem topic stream different, in portent by aspirant staff tremendous ascriptive major effort, trim pilot default. Toasted best optic frequency, ethic tribal by measure dreaming, all would timber timid distrain derisive almanac, leisure coif to wife plentiful own claim, retention. Mistaken sibyl in guile protected booklet rocket eminent, dado crumb steam imprinting went ahead granted, improvident crane for brine, oak soaking affine voices sluices; implement judicious, eventually absent, to minded flock, sheep track up-folded, spinney tight in strain; alleviate. Wayward instead, gravitate item unspent munition to fruited lessen, plum trick mist to frighten, system marine, interned. Ready go-slow wadding brute pressure, fly to buy plead advent, glib incident anecdote freight unload; previous escalate displeased rap for top sic attenuate. Gastric else convulsive grandeur animate suppressant, piquant reverse ice remorseful in cold cuts lost at first unlaced open bracelet with allies remiss. Till built ingredient, bee hunt sentinel on guard spent anomaly, descried dint of pride forwent; go by say to try episode transept, margin lent. Want alembicate forested bay silted ledge clarified over tilt thrown thrill toil, driven mansion gate lucid soul ignited. Mile upon mile invented, cant recruit disputed; all in while resplendent fondant, infant in livelihood, spinnerets wafted mustard win spikes.

## Not Far to Roam

Further still, outmost passing seen new leaf talc
trail listen to coastal surfeit, widely occluded
since control by riven sail; all told recall unto
echo singular fast tied down, either dial boasted.
    So-called, then to hold dear, next in calm
    angle tender, central pivot tame envisage;
    formula manage elk to milk undaunted, mere
    even fur-lined, foiled quell within surprise
at farmland copse intend. Entire blend enlisted
brand bird to oil discovered, plume enter thrill
sideways, hand to throat; prism chief merger silk
flaunt hops in hope, delusional surge disguised.

## Then Set My Eyes

Column first panel in chill fancy, opal hoist when
gathering ready to sing. To linger prudent most at
open main, ring-fence proclaim somnolent willing
fashion parlour in debt. All unwitting collected
    with bread sweep, talon alerts plain reform
    refine dry alloy; cohort disinclined sound
    funnel to drain trim residue, greet moat of
    rind work; acidulate for incidental braced
melon preference, castigate summer manifest; origin
missed. Once to add warden, pear envy window option
will flip to sleep, button breed by promised oven
tunnel, heated incite, allude respective inflamed.

## Sugar Indented

Diverted collar entice frost, scalene dairy pacify
owst prior remote alert station gene; surface must
attain in colour setting, none. Earth towards spun
even fair promise lean up, wrest against device
   restraint went in tint colluded, pair under
   buttress in malapert new-minted crown; test
   fortress same timid spread. Simplex ahead
   fiscal product minimum crevice to tailor at
minor avarice dentition, lesson refund entreated
gallivant cream across the rim instructed, attic
ingrained fiction; slab thirst, out next, unbroken
diffident silver twice mischief impulse decrement.

## Gram Positive

Fit to throw, indigo match escrow assemble dip
for tight now alleviate, invited crystal invade
contagion prodigal mention scutcheon elevate, in
mannerist by wrist-turn; cinder to burn out at
    finger plight allege grimace dispensed to
    wedge foremost. Oppose frequent invented
    bitter tire breath-hold, diploid insinuate
    grow dye insist nip for violet taste edge
able denote liable modest custom; merchandise
casual incendiary by usual maculate inch bereft
entry scatter endow benefit, worse yet promote
gristle void turgid, disrepute endue innominate.

## Vanessa cardui

Noble by steel forward painted harrow in dread,
plan reveal stable synergise, foible unendured
hypnotic custom taken. Naval party acquainted
fuel follow aftermath, untoward claim to gain
  woken, rival in prize commotion. At fast
  dart straw flight unrewound. Gripe tenable
  easement dormant pressure, seem presume
  sweet-pea whim ahead; some to claim white
coat breeding, tested brighten disturb oracular
potion, disbound; belief stripe-first appetite,
trap by egg. Industry retard history, don't yet
for doughnut dugout founder into legal intermit.

## Human for Interest

Hope to hurt in despite also, lamented tenuous
burn explain, browned up aggression, emphatic
pleats least paint first reflex. Shed by harm
list to inflict assign instinct detainment,
    morrow prune enter branch anxious deter
    label feasible, flinch to tread, optic.
    Curve repine able instead contused, deal
    illusion melt, name franchise infected
privative delphic imminently. Repast scented
homeward re-entrant mere swerve dispute; slit
enfeeble will frown, detain occupy cataract
systemic repression, far off croup distinct.

## In Fine Balance

Here main flown, when say to fly
alone climb to try is mine, in tune
even sylvan; weir tame primal dry
entry pantry coin line follow own
   none for them leaven
   driven often, before
   secure fort optimum.
Fire at fence one, renounce gantry
endorphin proven fair empty, bring
about, assume oven; fathom whence
in gradient sly entire, eloquence.

## ENCHANTER'S NIGHTSHADE

## (2020)

## Her Vacant Interlunar Cave

Speaks across the window, forest nervous revert outset
within eyebreak attempered spoken hub order word view
    one for two seize lichen crust frame vocation
    further still yet unable, utter again this far,
now this also acceptance. Seem open relax efface trim
extremity seal the waiting day, came for avid tropic
    be else advised retain perspect, eye benefit to
    novel foresight attrapment; list instant reveal
add to own aft sonar deliberate stay for tune close if
iris finish unblinking even so later, over line either
    or then tower watch. Then both attainder pause
    enter delete, early and foreign almond influx
shine quickly, recess evident. Curtail extra by untold
interview, label sign wind tremor admit in glance pane
    to them for all attachment, contact aureole
    in turbid twin. Beaufort ignited over pacify
right distance bring on-side imaginate former temporal
hue version, before constant together in fine season
    not deflected, to suffix by grant propensity
    evenly next spread in outview; front sight to
allegiance expense to name intended, voice inversion
deponent italic exfoliate. All to reckon rhyme sooner
    supplanted, curved field as ahead of licence
    clears the way, proscenium ignited alive gaze
chrome deliverance. Part from whence, as near entire
prepare, conquest overcome; in for assemble retinue
    tree to line leaf fine eyelash hear said out
    see ambuscade give word trysted are invited.
Or pyx or if so yet replaced, interlucent persistence
camp blinking anticipate alterity, by luminal thread
    gale force rebuff intervene however not dice
    refuse or foremost permitted hold the mark.
Will you, will by play reflect interlude, collide eye-
bright too look to see, hide to find as all the same
    presume; often broken, untie most successive
    least stratus over water headway listen, is
throat debate languish dispatch; in frequent then moon
silent obligate mission, give out taken abrupt fast
    incidental replacement exacted; ripen chorus
    side-wind spiral inset novel rate fume in

time return. Regain over later inferred antique toil
ground inflect too, select to modify first place in
    argument want stringent affirm; or to reach
    initial wherefrom common day sail votive full
tribe on visit brighter accent propel character, by
spare month esteem diligent playful as other willing.
    Link kohl eyelid manner yet predicted, note
    to first foe candid local flicker harness
rising to plenty insistent shadow inducement, bring
on glint and even. Multiply option prior ready top
    watchful, brow furnish precedent in serve
    question lemma intrinsic all actual trifle
by flight path known. Rain allowed collective press
instantly metric afford stop over prime, announce in
    word at first buy trim to pace in passage
    cast-off, both indolent. Few to lever in
front visor, offer qualify look fast indicted sea
lanes; trail massive resound keep below by natural
    undercurrent swear true, bear up claimant
incident tremulous gallery inserted. Tract daylight
in fill active mollify, no grievance sort to planet
    fume mind park verbal direct notify duct
    impossible per limit recognised: all of
them. Did review assumptive practice, as did so.
Levitate suffusive walnut unsettle propane resume
    phantom mastery, what you get track or quoit;
    lip digression reflect in the water informal
headline dopamine, liquid activate impart classic
rampart mensural fiction push out temper, all run
    bind fame tense decline. Allege remit advice
conspicuous be tacit, be also calibrate forfeit,
arbitrated, told up to mark previous, in far fire
    to score. As will, as able also fascinate
    foible reagent class to casement, as in vain.

## Thine Forgive Mine

So often then, often so and by then intend they
or then, too so too more when go often with and
    them all search full by when been in line
    plain allow when grateful save in mercy
coat, by then ever follow each often sign or from.
So when late time abate from impassioned mind
    than to go on often float, soon to end
    to find, again as more sent press advent
conjecture, when so deign too absented inflect
abstain, piteous wound lightly by round band meant.
    By so often hanker for, as thank in view
    grant lateral capture when or enter, in
ready intimate ahead; mainly accept first plight
given resemble, redeem for when now or soon even
    more yielded by this word, ever so. One
    in time lease pardon absent further caress
close no less place assigned, come in often free
may promise note upon note folded, with them. Even-
    tide soon found before wide by care enwrapped,
    door shadow pane raised up by then even pace
when so longing to so, too mend differ, deference
extend whenever often praise upwise deserve. To fit
    counsel donate light worth than more, over
    shade gift utterance no weapon, sorrow not
proud best older placate back concede, fine given in
thread into thread rest warm often when and when.
    Ever known single where found notion graded
    they too will for twine offer, treaty foil
into show allow then ever and ever; for when met
untied measure, relenting by trusted recompense,
    than early stroke far off by glance ahead
    to cure the scent, inflush, assume instead.

## And Almost Life Itself

Carry out pretty ones over the headspace and far
look prevailing, take place level plain by close
        breeze surge arrow and follow soon at rest.
        Left beside search mechanic dust averted
histamine average clamour internal rank able fair
and generous litter by remix attic, reclaim near
        ground intrinsic display, coronet formal
        to align them, up on brow overturn worn
comparison. Revise panurge all subvert too, run
fast to fasten enter fitment dapple within pledge
        childcare before footstep advancing, turn
        and simmer while there's time. New listed
window square set flicker shadows one after derive
and save, regular too agreement ensign by sealant
        fulsome assembly; act out the part merit
        mast to most remedy station. In court under-
stand, draw back, on the coast afforded however so
otherwise, so practice performance, lipid view. Will
        meeting inflict question one to sever, all
        to one find a hand memorandum in doubt commit
occlusive passionate and foster, at bridge by cage
dispute. New arch ducted promptly fluidise or yet
        temporise choice infancy now well ahead
        resemble each notable resolute to wait,
belated temperate by need to, asseverate in drastic
cream; deep for down label for them to everhold
        cranny and plaintive, up on points fillip
        advertise discretion, redeem. Infill fancy
river plenty solution to inversion describe other
will reveal open touch trait proposal, by fair
        viable exchange ingenuous; to all in line
        unblame, tell rustle off disturbed pro-
vidence. How should reflect anomaly already prized
testament, a new tune comb scented honey yet alert
        action debit welcome offerance, at first
        intermit. Languish affirm natron splash
admixture numerated polygon, pruning olive and
trellis accent entwine, finish in fuel damask on
        noisy highlights. Flight cultivar pressure,
        consume by portion bitter out, bite in turn

sewing steady upper lift graticule. They will, or
we also shall design a florid similar aftermath,
        by fit swale opportune manor gable purple
        motive window grange principal random tiding,
set up closer sooner; stitchwort mantic strewment
ply upon ply, bright in pinnace swing forward, plume
        fashion dish device. Go first, in footwork
        spark amorous militant witty and ready,
brilliant smile, petal arbour at quick tip coronet,
calyx orange pert and late. All grateful in soever
        share handsome, linden leaf leaning rise
        to shine, pertinent mastic want there and
beyond, outstretched possession, also ripe. Harvest
their wreath of pleasure, they too know who unselved
        to praise ever mischief greeting proficient
        on cue not divulged, until the whole display
is evident, relate unseen, in effigy. Cambric feint
maritime not yet plant dream latch and fetch anode
        reach effort surf clandestine awaited, truce
        inveigle purpose to licence lie immediate.
Chatter pyes amount horizon often, blaze in sheen
for modified channel to funnel as valve horn well
        past averse bastion. Give instance address
        slow output twirl willing ambient, however
far to hear evidently, eventual accident. Resound
the lyre! Raise first price trump magnet pasturise,
        frolic twice of voice dual release inducted
        epithet royal kernel dash casting, prompt
ear in early necklace signify total acclaim, never
banish supreme united orison. Who's to say other
        or fare tether minimal factual, regain both
        tap margin gravitate early or afterwards;
armour to former move to love windward crenellate
maple fipple opal so impress caravan heart's care,
        here coincident pitch and round rewinding in
        new profile soon disclaim, indwell taciturn.

## Girt with the River

One more river, now quick now soon beside
   find the way beneath the waning moon,
the deep blue sea day in day out, on full
   fathom, five praise, wave along. This
new song all told mid alien turn rue then
   foreign petition bring, jubilant so,
no more twist modest time to cross, she rock
   to the east at very least, yet by now
to fly too; stepping west woodchuck fresh
   the winds their revels yet compute, the
hour latent marching through. One more rough
   daylight ill met ocean wave, old folks
talk makeup bankrupt glows the bright, moon-
   shine later dish and spoonful what's
to do the master's lost; as ever cue, on by
   the hawthorn-hedge no motion now or
some in rags best badge across the town, far
   so Mountain and Silver, gather nuts in
bits. Open treacle even banish off pea-green
   finish money proud in the wood standing
now or stand by home, to roam range answer no
   bow-wow whist mischief motley epigraph.

## Hungry and Cold

Ribbon availment from and yet persistent apogee
hungry winter slope gusted agree to ponder rental
masquers inflame; ebon floor cratch tenon filmic
caution. Deplete in retail, deplore planar allege
trim nor so entail, imminent canter anterior wave
reduced grove brine salient enough. Grimace foist
artery fume oil partition, go to stipple elegise,
grow through entreaty. Rock floor flour will pair
target volume, match replete spicule turnstile
later reticent, resented foe in fortune, at cynic
momentum. Preen evident costume acidic purchase
immune saturate edge-line, phantom favourite don
enlarge, unlace, hove mental together vine. Next
astricted adobe dwelt binding rule pale envision
cramp or craven, loose thirst if tall observant
size ingression literal emphasise interpret fit
part fusion, manifest remit. Obverse in knowing
illume foreign, frame soothe by tactic graciously
all they may do, invented coronal; inside of leap
save to practice, proof sun rim to dry, new native
effigy. Rail mimic protection evict civic casual
several builded here, blandish terror acquainted
sextant moss-covered within comparison, wave dial
over sea pitch, under roof vital. Go to swarm in
memorise, to be near as ever able, tune on land
mint taxon scented orison, nymph in hectic fever.

## His Flight, Aloft

Probable forcible intact reverent whilom to aloft
sift, tissue resume refrain ginger arisen cruise
instantly promise, salvage topsail sensible, or
wrack applicate colour druse. Whose at avail level
spirit plan, flame interval casual intone cambric,
cassation intrigue one in line, game piebald prole
remark in souk forsaken, sanction entire. Yet fair
entrain lop-sided cater unblamed first served angry
then gentle, fusion engine dioptric miscible over
severance dismissal; occluded planet duly termite
mount fathom. Often haven bench given all friends
sent back, set out in curt stoup coeval imitative
all ends also formation pyre. To this fast, inheld
suffuse opening, eve portal lair under neb purple
explicated damage company inference. Ever later
latterday casuistic interfere, manage or privilege
fortunate bracket softer proclaim other moderate;
conduce in parallel more asseverate wicket euphony
clastic cinder front, grant prodigious accepted.
Did in faun unfounded clinch related, astonish at
birthmark entangle remote praxis, furnish braille
parental if berate, team conjunct, compassion. All
near, all past preluded vesper limit fascinate do.

## Rakt with Deep

Our time rakt prominent, incidental up coiling
reserve cool while, clafouti irksome in temper
violet hamper weighted. Willing eager outright
if seek dowel emergent under lack refine risk
crass outer remedy, seem so. Annoy, prevalent
duty waive proem sinter peach pie, credit awl
meddle in flight; spandrel effaced in trance.
Presume sent scented, misguided brotherhood at
readiness talon, blink rapid vapour in similar
undo suspense. Deponent absolute further sing,
out of turn newel boil trammel viscous blame
others handwork crewel motion besought doublet
cologne inflicted, regain obsession. Tangible
settle offer nail militant grasp shadow, infer
total better syllable. Know to see, ban to out
refuge, limitation buoyant pippit bindweed fit
recovery profane, toil in front agent. Rifted
friction password passion intermit, interpret
auspicious fraction crimson anklet fluted and
brisk allergic by session soon. Mastiff break
critic invocate light pasture obtrusive, bye
arable tenancy lease pace confusion, furnace
urgently. Solemn fame lifts clear, utter hark
sylvan rind bark tepid interlude percolated.

## Count in Motion

Calendric foremost liken up readiment aback trifle ills by the system they wrote for, attach many filament days ordinal at dewline, datum turn by turn; caught-fast in glimpse pencil set out since provision range foremost with mental early and late, missive coiled imminent to fasten across the front. Count in motion own self other first and last true heading fetch, name in reckonable parapet sailed out, fission weekly dwell carnival pet celebrated allowance within, portion eros rising still scribal due anticipate forerunning. They will entirely match within single to seek, to not wait tribute taken head to foot token address invoke plentiful. Base deem methodic enter custom in costume, pronounce tack legit concision stop add double however daylight deep strung liable, tender fretted winnow pince often. Listen few mending eventful, stifle cheek advance cordon rite met moreover fitted liberate evening; centric fiery relate must else so various in cloud version, until up before announce alerted quarter mounts to frame neap entangle risen than ever calenture babble, invert fields retain.

## Fond Palms

Allocate reed first prism even ready submerge,
to flight under chasm ivy kid, swerve bated
hyssop funicular laggard often listen foison
balm generated seeming thread lentil mid oven.
Urgent aliment, prize doctrine swapped by fate
reduced, abducted coast-guard no bishop serving
beyond harm; braggart fascinate or fulminate
to preen elected noisome. Accentuate vocative,
weaponise, arrack commanded however in pliancy
gusset boastful or harmful infect. Full on, if
abject lighten quickly divergent with steady
precision tender opt to end or fond palms, over-
set. No reach no bracelet, crop belligerent for
agonise to praise, and fight funest or protest,
art rising deep best ever cycladic or chrome.
Roaming land-fill primal fit to invocate, near
thirst ration exceeding compulsive blank fill
instinct, linked margent prefer bother sent or
forward suspect quail acquainted, indifferent.
Furl so, time and the hour remaindered, polymer
metric vacuous empire brandish loaf percipient.

## Into Sudden Flame

Often seen pronounce main to light of vivid flame
sidle affix, single suffused meritorious limit
parade cope arraign. Most and since hereto entry
few and through, outward tune quite nor yet, by
furious, spent rehearsal angle dirempt, remain
currency hasten. Trail no blame portal off rebut
strict, once to next claim asserted, dissuasive
in forthwith collude, hope later drupe ample such
also wing two; flow indite furrow, turn winter
plight about. Too both lance filament, earn tame,
by introject binding yet refusal trim; scarlet
base up to crest and fill, wavering. Environ due
will mix slight taste, turn to find in harvest
dialect sweep reform, impeach out far, pertain
island gather dissemblance. Advance song whiter
bill profile either linger whence by hillside
entrant ornament, afraid transom risen loosen
interview spike task convene fallible division.
Mind headlong recession, wind-blown imminent
converse reap infused high and wide pinnacle, to
search cry wage taken flight path elated, past
in cradle pasture ready to handle, match. Wade
crew upon crew, of warrant refine glowing ambit
chill to leap, keep-sake into front assent;
cancelled province amended. From how many at
best frequent tempers, visit defray provident.

## Hesperus That Led

Eventual hesperus antonym pronoun often integrate
laden falter ingredient adequate fashional pleat
nephew missing weighted intrinsic low hazardous
scintilla; prentice hepatic give way purposeful.
Distil maze to fade trill mossy damp steps uncoil
warm hydroxyl agnate obsession, until bound up
impulsive qualm. Daze heartfelt system flooded
interleave heritage, onrush halcyon close woven
plaintiff obverse crystalline, deserted shores,
wood soon reprieved. Save to hide, stray halyard
steel outer helium, trial issue voidal astringent
data habitat, heretic. Individual try to see, see
to send, ever transit twilight guidance, immense
plump forehead gather up on constant try melting
and faulting may be at cost flourish, maker so
divided. Stream widen euphoric threaten over by
thereat in furnish, wave broken unction gradient
in praise nutritive; go to find, find to send
gaudy parish activate. None loosen reserpine aver
gaze to prize astonish pink trellis, homestead
bye anchorage, on way eaten. Haggard sweep across
horizon better mission, moonstone sliver mail or
tide fuse privet attenuate instep, take your fill,
up tight. All the same assume ahead, sink either
in deep breaths forth dilated, now refine single
or mental heraldic by instinct at longer aniline.

## Escap'd the Deep

For else inside well pit hand-written to shade
abridgement firth colouration from rim pitch
round and down, gust windlass property ill bite
basal scent extreme. Reverse script massive
flecked augury interpret, sectile steep prowl
in step loss assemble scarlet plume. Both seem
entire moss water stain, birth forth or wooden
pricket dark mass, crust label. Inlet grained
low deference untie, fossick descended affine
sustain to energise umber till after, foster up
plain-chanted. Born trample unctuous of blame
addendum anodyne suffice, purple refuse ominous
careen posset, for them; synthesise noble corm
bring follow to yellow, in vain. Near invasion
interplay able ground finitude resemble aspic
to personal pentothal crucial before them well
even, monstrance sated brilliant otherwise count
deputise enlarge. Know best, enthuse partial
vociferous syllable cultic fidget frozen custom,
aphetic gladden militant at supple habituate to
iridescent surplus deep rest prune left apart;
elder unfound, matter sunder sewn up in flight
caught primal and servile, lost. Flange grasp
for hidden vantage, astute hesitant pacify, on
muted to forge in first cross, liminal forested.

## Pass, to Reach

For reach graphic demonstrate most upward talus fine stone discretion, graven ward cirrus placer crease, provision. Dormant nascent hurtle whether regular apex, bee swum fulsome precipice grated to waste and filch, brevis. Expulse spread, host in treaty beach hut loving, moist plenteous cliff rime before, unbound constant brittle extrusive catchment; forward leach apt collect, fertile vivid impugn advance consented. Ever will able deferred cease prosody, cry off to climb exert climate impression, aggregate hoist tender fill imago. Vitreous excision glimpse reflected cranny protrusive, voluntary dial creel elated, bastion wilt; for shelter codex in time of war tempest, ever for luminous honey recused debt subsequent, asleep. Outstretch opulent braid together fulfil, grateful alliance sound filter sans echo foliate, mercy tenant session refine imminent coign fret seminal, river teach produce. Wakeful in profit join to frame pageant intense, metal orphic pry incline credulous torment, by fitment parodic anticipate. Come out hive retrenchment, nectar inter cumulus main board inventive constricted, fringe revision given caution; profusion excess. Lax weather shoreline tilt to flourish, any to reclaim or deep profession dawn coil overture, indurate dry abstensive blandish, wax endure so.

## Loath to Depart

Late too and so belated follow to wait hereafter, flow
to grow allergy might syllable take for miniature back
returning brave light freight over fast left out now
before attain within nor yet stranded anticipate afterglow
finial his dignity absolve, proof lift at claim
anterior replacement bivalve. Late also distrust entire
all by so open face crisis emended with match credit,
entail supplant linger pleural discount cellar effusion
latent, grove stricken, fate replaced. Notable rampart
soundless glass in folk, allowing distinct arrival or
promise elsewise, hurry incisor best fount subsidise
undercurrent lapis, relaid fettle. Subverse incident
prefigured additive delete rebate in excised groove
hillside deplorant, the fruit broken more candid timefast
in greenery; how not otherwise maxim astute yet
presentiment soon before otherhand. Previous comprise
agreement lace tremor ended weary, incant by trespass
passed over, bitten hand-rail optional link sedated
prior roof covering surplus into greater next fugue
hardly earlier. Drover mid-most profuse or derelict
planar after stayed flickering yet casual, partitive
abstention little blink iris contracted into suppose
ice wind ahead; rapid flex percussive entreaty tonic
original. Fanciful least early on; synonym likely to
attach pretext uncovered, of purge reflex dismissal
syncopate allege to merge catch up, astonish prefix
brandish issue provident interrogate quick relation.

# MEMORY WORKING:

## IMPROMPTUS

## (2020-21)

Always have a point in mind
when you resolve a scale line
– Pianogroove

Beylage No 11 zur mus. Zeitung

von J. H. Worzischek

# Impromptu

für das Piano-Forte

Metronome de Mälzel ♩ = 96

sempre ligato

## I

An open point in memory trace itself, its inner domain amid the neural synapses and brain pleats, not here remembered, no plaza for so disported antic or retrieved tranquillity, a neglected small urban square, flagged and with cornices, facing columns, mixed brick and previous stone; with a communal spring or fountain at its centre, paved around and worn over passage of time, the many steps feeding up to the curbs and nourished there. The thought traffic worn in markings to and fro, its own surrogate recall, the air history often breathed, cooler now maybe evening but sash windows still open and looking down, curtains furled in the shifting slight atmospheric. Shade in time of its own to pass with notable easy care, this is memory at work, with no outlook to drive along or even back except its own reflective purpose, yet latent in expecting its near arrival, thus confirmed, the glance unshingled and without evident person, secluded from manifest. For still the moist air is just beyond motion, or outside across the inner absent figures, their own tacit voices from the dossier of set partition in huddle of voices sans pitch, these are shade presences now without sanction or passport from across the apparent threshold, coming and going with its lightness of easy pace and glimpse, yet with sound as if beyond current reach, perhaps ever; just to be known there, and yet underwritten.

Here too memory plants and tends its ways, like de Chirico in bleached but bright colourings, on leave from intact dimension, self-contained. Later you divine this is audible, not your thought but fleet memory grafting itself that waits with you for its summons, to peer and pivot, no hands to work the puppets, no lutes in serenade, merely a band of slight echoes from the yet continuing one-time domain, the doorway ajar inviting the girl in profile with the pomegranate, now the right moment entirely, intuition's self-made prompt: no needful anticipation all is fully intact; though evening in this place has slanted sunlight in moment for now, if waning, close to depart but not quite yet; fair notice in advent for solo company, mind portico. Why of this is not a part of the array nor will be, no respect of succession, shadow glints from these contented windows; faint plashing heard from the tremulous fountain at the wellside, polypody at the rim is housing minimum insect life but actually teeming at a closer look. Privilege in shared fortune of myriad under-current, more than enough the wake of passage, in balance on foot and print pausing, neat vestige-marks shaping the air in focus still not determined; returning at the same portico (mind entrance) against to spill as with care itself, its natural admission almost heard, in near large as life.

## II

Effortless tedium of the seascape conscripted, the ocean expanse like an empty jewel-case reaching out or packed with gew-gaws, waves nipping and breaking at distance in time with ready acceptance unaltered. This self position at outlook luxury of waste, endlessly sufficient or just across the pier repeats, tiding over until beyond conclusion, the fulmar ploy salt tunnels garrulous echo display tailfeathers, familiar in themselves and close imitation, similar not exact in their dissolving mental freedom proof from departure. Almost refined the dainty boredom of appearance and swift precious litter, to catch the light further flicker, the mind dispossessed of integral address; here in circular recognised mirror park, within bounds of pastoral patrol and sentiment, away on each side. Blood pulse does no less to ocular ingression, brave so and bravo, gratulant horizon well discovered wrapped in evidence, hills of the shoreline a welter of company confident of every option, ripple at surface polarity. Or too much for confinement, uncorrected succession each wave-step altered another fringe benefit until longer yet in deferral, grey and green again in half light from here filtration. Anxious at nothing, enough itself to provoke current disturbance, at nothing over again, vanity too much familial not yet to intimate, the old flourish. Wink often when best can at these pleated crests, retinal tucks salt once more in replaced future, in clouds, gusted breeze turned aside. Lift with the tide encountered in figured headwind return of its onset, in season mind glisten, light from the cavity of air surmise, from within such tidemost exquisite.

## III

The pattern easily recognised even though unfamiliar at first glance. Near the front all of them visible, each one over their shoulder as brim concession, fire dogs close to support across the hearth-stone. Wanted eagerly now, brow creased in furrow mention, choice heart murmur festive turn this way and that, all is due to change about, at the airport. Outstanding extra word fidget returned in prominence to average alongside not beyond transgression, adjusted and instilled as fortune allowed and ordered in queue. Yet unrestricted by this interment, the others crowded around the doorway, in and reckoning at a wrist device, distressed stone base surface; quoin first quicker than effigy where new colours discover their purpose and trial. How many at agreed count set in alignment, what you hear by finger pressure, light contract sufficient lenient in tolerated aperture, slow to unwrap from the step below. Capture filling, renewal modest and crystal twin interface, reduce digit cornuted sling militant; wait not far below in shadow ash park or stance opportune granite brilliance. Crimson streak dwelt at the curbstone, arrange pliant gambol insurge with several missions coeval by parentage. The entire detour makes its open pathway as fully tested to breed; seed-pods in chance rush, resume, aggrieve, if not yet infringe or gruel unknown.

Famous district in delay then already pacified, calorific surround no herd escaping investment, as running fast enough to the distant gateway synonym impersonal did they foresee the rumpus abstention; if not whenever critical afferent machine adjusted, invasive paramount. To know ready shelf prepared leaning and winding, finish escapement search before levity consumes cavity in match parallel. Fume laboured cupboard, glass-front panel swivel install metric questioning: guesswork flamboyant even temper throughout. Native fictive tribute practical with all the whole mile to flaunt, diminish stitch broider ever richlier scarlet tracings imminent blunt conclude.

## IV

Able remark indented at flutter, serrate conversion, water in brow radical and crimp, descended opposite firm too, tooth alert. Quintal vapour exchange leafage close to depart by optic classify, root olive and window alive pursuit at palm column, fitted birth absorb instructive notch. Ample frond coverage gives to first front, better hostage month grimace lime-fold ballet branch by branch no wrangle even trill refracted; pasture in hour confident finish moist dew converging at drop apex, avens sent in trim advance, plant by hand. Pinnate fantastic anticipate general, come to this in relief shadow, fruitful give-away. Why so pale, do the same, biding time not to wilt, will not directed, see what you find, want what you partly get: amazement. Swung canopy stirred slightly, ruffle altered proliferate look forward almost nip and tuck filament, figwort and found the stream bed omit cursory actinic bond well-stream. In day silting close to bank rise to shine overhanging neural stipend rapid debate, afford palpable consequence refer jointure armament. New could if so be true again, espalier invited handiwork more than many like before incipit redoubt. Defer frighten iceland spar conference intubate rephrase, seagrass meadow bring about specific cymose florets keep clear myriad reflection, later on said. Oak to grove, holm derive deeper in shade, profound instead leafmould benefit ramify gesticulated production: agreed, admitted.

Batter to filch first off, revel pilchard seam enclosed makeshift thread jury ensemble, go along with what can find layer in bract colouring safely graze moderate in turn and down, enact defiant. Every marker already infilled for each one expected, root mass ever woven diligent, pleach to risky twig. Want to drown in flood clearance hold back until fen lizard avaunt mount after schedule, nail on fire, parade first.

## V

Arc claimants resonating debated, radial devious point display who will or want askance ripen over rain flack and sheen. Refuge bite fast infant shadow profuse incurve, ascertain print secant diagram vest blewit resorted, subtend instant now debate, impart. The shaded portion in vigil, central fill predict, intact biotic perpend modal or modify imagery reversed, plain necessary current. Actual victual brimful chemic in habit encounter, brief prison limited outpost on its extempore island shore, culminating at self breakage, sheer diffract. Diatribe frequent provoked olfactory in touch the walls cost free remnant, gash lift tract fur, enclose coir shortfall. National effort boundary converge now the crew floods in, common crown adapted in spite cringe edge multiple tread offset can better infuse, evenly pronoun foundational, they will. Apsidal custom canal licence fume towpath, toothpick inhibit fast habit floor mine craft mass test, refractory ever sonic track minimum preen; curfew recession prey rueful parallel contour not exact withal. Many close to most convince in blame bring and fetch, water mead under headland project. Drop stakes unharmful whither pack, axe flit, follow line meet travel in wave surmounted, diadic plentiful regression tempest fluent crucial plaster; delicate offer pitch brusque ail pannier cross division so few in form, infirm cathected. Line built invade roadway, grit patted down, aversion.

## VI

Cream intensified often as ever found if far apart gain to grain avenge homage belated, ranged in damage post to system, between left on outside. Mind over brain topic mandate inclusive, name pinned into sleeve mound without excepted antigen failure, brace and amplify torment in thread position alight distant been transit guided seem fine instead. Ration civic departure signal, late gantry affront grill agent dream discovered notion agree to seal main choice brandish, in voice attention; bind up own fluid catch by pride option, undercurrent churn festive entry yet inverse. Hamper flight, temper slate planted in plate adoption, rise to fit correctly for sluice fission step after grip. Mean more nor less foiled affront, cluster donor plastic loyal frayed tissue picture in pasture, wherein conscripted, boil dry, milk friable by recognised excess. Commissure join in frame simian profligate, gaunt prior slice omission depth annoyance. Grind faction coral tip out of view cram open sleek to black dice oppression, none yeast listed going down steep bite gnaw duly, few deal splayed eastern win agreement will or might. How treat elevate beforehand sextant attain brow-line win estrange along peril, retrain partner site ambient aril keel flame, to not blame waiting at float harvest, thirst invented. Did attract bereft even so-for appetise, leak to eat lapse mental source induce colloid train ogive spruce missive omen exulted; precedent frenzy abate mint boil twice police far oil Faroe concession drill detected claim. Front to back inhume dyne gene path, redeem undo flotation.

Do you or we distinguish when they come to pass in force regraded extraneous silk, town coinage watch go to fire impure tension liquid back immutable, vindicate tenement mixup. Stay for too interval narwhal plot action morn to hem nasal base yet might, under weight bantam sought per inveterate pursuit tweet melancholic disturbance. Waning tribute electric accident cram metric adverb mundane broke divisible, surplusage phrase choice muted or further. Neither pander inspection collagen amount to dressing bind and buoy, triage allege defray, by candlelight beyond inter lark and fledge. So for lift privet, far enough midge enter tight appear laurel reckon pledge child caution spread in layer before dissension.

## VII

Successive link severed in fever replacement, in foremost appointed by tractable service obvious undestroyed; main tremble least crown chain find undercurrent regain intent friction. Aspirant previous portrait grasp lipid dint frame catena ever instigate all they do permitted; pen durable from down film, feather feature and either wrist past guest rictus. Markov lost this much fox defended not yet so bent, lock divagate top mast first stranger lace sand toss who knew the rest height muster invocate envision mine infraction; think weather chain grossular vestige privation lenient subtended, fax crossed either crane patch fly best. Entire folly grimace select intruded, hale elated by sign severe, seen restricted they come to fend unbanished, envied by other sky peak and lantern, seek allay abridged final star cluster. Notion system failure or closure, rail detent indignant provident, such as to mind fast must impulsion, potion session right up front sequent prevailing nightly; fermented portable side hook however arrayed or lost to sight reticent, frown symptom cause to choose. That much disposed may blink nor yet revere, pair at knee joint mint tented at flap missive, harc racc embracement hurry and fury provisional retention, admit defined print tine fray in nest-work. Never mind the wind blow, all now slow to even flow retracted, average diverging relish attached vivid to trail river longer to seem and join, born at the spring, at brink. None they will travel home, loom tangle in foil perfect insect batten on fell, cord affectionate trace fitted antic jealous, incite alleviate promise: formulate.

Oversee momently pardon nominal time reversal row friction fortify flaunted prospect domino walking, brace collagen wavelets cursory iterate one for other mistaken why not. For no reason just cause probate digress, brow by elbow probable scape to blade. Heron tune hair line furl below soluble indebted, all of them tame liquid deterrence moderate intervention butter fluke; early rise temporal process fastidious open the door rich listen affix fetch indicate. Lookout vigil, brilliant next wardship goes forth implicit testament, all there is currently soon past; overdue tolerance consistent grape fortress in drainage, lateral spike tremendous, feet-first.

## VIII

Modest curtain catchment finch easily effort hanging blench safety fitment or went drifting to curtail level outlook draft over first seek flotation lifted or annotate reverted as most they do openly, leave aside drawn made fast, uncertain best in contest. Infirm conformal counterpane, relative debt mission entrench doorstep entrance planning. After issue rooftop inclined, swift across waned orbit forward plastic clinch before lotion cautionary soften, drape permitted action twin faction overtask nail towards frighten lesson castigate least affection plaintiff. Put to plush, often matching illustrate swap pitch mansard tune spared utter bloat aware loom to frame, fused illustrious natal percentage, guttural always been enter vain central criminal sage in spurn tithe frozen and tremble; sample open completion principle lank assert not yet fluent, resolute question fresh section most assisted, indurate. You for, you too strap assail infix watching or cruelty mask, festive caramel wisdom trail run alongside tepid moribund blent parcel riffle flourish dispersal, cavernous yet alert broken within, batch headway. Stair trodden on behalf, wait to be ready, riser tether abrogate column filter later, otherwise transmit outright procession in river floor mantle.

Opine crystal fasten annoyance, prune whip finger-work at fringe wade to win sensate; ask entice or not yet drone system top patch alone inverse certain, often private auction granted index mascot. Swivel own listless, furnace confined profit to hold the line, brim forgiven version clement tangible pinch bright veil castaway ordain. Prow extended cupric segment, focus implement purposeful recipient fluster pinned together injurious cusp option imminent however time heavenly ones face shining; air sweeten, mountain fuel civil alleviate file adroit tempestuous upper winds that blow. Cardiac latent muted tongue invented to swallow blank, whole self range up to shelf distracted, entire coat offered along stream done coin ominous cloud across remain pantomime salient objective invariant modify skytrail fluff relent.

## IX

Frugal foible innocent mandate, eager convene testament instructed venerate parlour valiant ash surface imbricate, mansion fiction willing foretold alpine delivery adamant splice intended toast; measure digestive throat switch. Full match to either left over, knew last attentive placate, after deride insidious pressure follow insurance termite in kite; thermal currency pliant abstention envious charter clutter dispute mast phantom list-cover, tip for inward win nutation inserted. Young seedlings admonish impress to flourish, they navigate intake tractable urgent scot-free welling bravery quorate incision to wisdom; host premiss bit district offend foreign, medal limit compacted operate mortal crucial possible cruelty, inch to evade ingrate. Lime truncated subtle cheek improve went to motion met immutable grip-fast attempted, frantic minimal convicted sustenance medial sprite; distort deem temperate fossil mingle fond slinks rise to gain emotion far before, traction empiric caravan dune merit. With them all, drain sprinkle monstrance tenor intrepid, mollusc flew the camp.

Manor elegant minor soothe distemper swallow prided elongate, dinner driven capsize, afflict to prove yet narrow jacket restore. Gyrate banter grade falter allowance integral remedial open for, crisis voice faucet errant grommet fix paradigm, innermost; lost travail while abundant, dapper estate invade. Trade occupy cardboard costly detail, value colourful allowance, theme grazing safely close arch whence dice parade extreme brine, manifold availing ominous search corbel fragile overturn berated. Eventual shadow shore agile burn amain, frayed evident churn frosty minimal, return habit porous astonish reveal to claim, else.

## X

Gale force lace to battle trace confident surge crave custom prove resorted aisle lichen rage hose marasmus; liken winter obtain dial morrow labile aerofoil gibbous robbery orfe cranial nought, centre fest cemented. Aggregate current fought licence, evince broth coverlet offence both canter mall repel indented, button federal gluttony lustral mail course surfeit anchor perfect tint. Arrest to cease any furtive stack melodic wrested, heat tremor attended headwind bidden harassed plentiful, all assignment thoroughfare forded, tie lack fret. Ascriptive sort to work, top to pair even sane expense horizon seven femur goliardic pensive mild emptied oven complainant sate pretence. Wizzen antidote invest throat comment divested brazen covert flight ministrate inverted, borderline regain ludic bought urbane weight lustration; raise the dual failed dissent hereabouts front. Sylvan stairway leading symptom derelict gravitate seam donation portion inundate. Care for both incense tested missive frustrate well ahead, praise on size, glazing western mutton poise bailiff consented flavour must to feast, flypast shower come forth temporise mooted imminent.

Notorious benchmark sense province where they graze, sunlit bracket envelop dolmen fury, organise prevail guileful childish who to say wary missionise ingredient, by dint arrant mental. Punctual scansion high breeze toys assented, upper crest flaunt tabby woven milk riven get haven, gaunt profane. In ever vain, unknown. Galleon function enter further, endeavour drastic privet fulminate savour anxious crevice; cinnamon riverine obey, trees above proven to skyline, twit affix. Avian murmur grain harvest endorsed bring to bear, to share wrung fast pinion quail toil bright of mitre scout. Inflict, infect divot habitat invigorated.

## XI

There is some look for a large horizon, bordered by plants that oscillate in the breeze, invited to be remembered in the birth of origin and subsequent continuals. Who could not find chance to stir at moving clouds expressing their ambition and ours to join a signifying capture, in temporal escape without dispute; only a few ruffles of alternative portrayal will propose an elusive schedule, in determination. To be full awake and grateful is enough, to define arrivals and departures, dividing and subdividing as is recognised practice. Resemblance is then sufficient, watched in a close attention like breathing itself, eye flicker in relation with tremblancy of the foliage. It is hard to resist assignation by firm design, because bearing of the mind keeps pace without disruption or impatience; notice to find by stages closer, in choice perspective. In trace observed it is the marking of affection, all without affect except as passes in distance, and avowed; nothing intervenes because in-between is visited by its many doubles in sake guess-work, curiously cherished like bees.

Insects though mostly small pervade these environs, they are the attached sensorium, by motive renewed just below the level of sense but cumulatively in character; many levels in leaving overlapped and receptive, iridescent small shades make up this bower within cover, its own perception. In lateral share the canopy occupies its numerous opportunities, to travel and be grateful, searched below and not impoverished, for time affords its discovery and recognition. This is the dialect of a few moments, much continued and repeated, respected sweet resumed.

## XII

Steam once in train, smut in the drop window, make a blink or many more, exhilarate retracted for ardency ears puffing in first and last gasp. Feel in being held up by longing to meet fully, whatever it takes; the sound insistent pressure of the heartbeat, lungs speaking what they so want to know. That is indeed their privilege, heaving forward in advance of what's to be done, unwraps itself like a stranger searching for live threshold, the reason follows on behind. Take this part, be partitive by generation, dative in function opportune. Think of a parent, one solo outpace the thought genetic memorial felt in good time condoned by accuracy, air touch colour of habit each new and unfamiliar, rapidly absorbed. A twinge or minor spasm in the mouth shaping up, the hand rational, each one; record its parish certainty, echo tunnel to find issue by instant recall. Reveal by travel, glimpse of honey in this buzzing hive, the lines polished and shining by huge expectancy, enjoined.

Indistinct its own fiction at the rink incautious by volume aggregate trial to know hourly, anticipate parenthood, air pressure fill balloon lent ahead; outworking by fancy abridged. Not one too many if in number aligned, fresh branch each brighter beyond its own shadow, casual in purpose airbrushed circular to self-reflect. Time enough, newly found attended by versions all in turn and then restored. How would not be known foundry, of sense just beyond interval and better reach.

## XIII

All is known, around to be fair, the pipe organ here and there by revolve suffusion, the carousel to flourish like shadow bats at evening. These tunes are celebrants by their own recall, jingle, creatures with wide outstretched acknowledgement, each time novel attained, fair for fair at even parity. It's worth well to speculate in the mirror motive, the tune gives this assertion in likelihood; shout to hear, laugh to bear, witness joined up risen to ride. Name even to forget briefly to the quick, instinct in suspense at a turn each time next after, flight marking, centrifuge to merge its force attached: the outreach of the continuum. Thus offer to take, take to imitate, rectify nomenclature by many visits smoothing down and loaned, so many similar and familiar by gable profile if not upheld. In duty the visor shielding the eye-beam marks obliging prospects, that's to know what's flown before.

Unrelegated regulated, insert precedent link forthwith a little shock each time, one built into another kiln-fired brick assured; proclaimed from inward store, tune to joy bounded, fortified aright intrinsic. Come and go partner butterfly warm stroke, turn-up a main chance compliance. Full tilt watch the others watching, entail the pattern overlay seeming fresh to pick, choose to share. Many for other in rotation, a queue defined not long to wait aside, already even if all new, promise kept conscript.

## XIV

The crimson nubs extrusion, pushing up through the debris nestled in case to hover closely, as good fortune in a windfall profile, ready for red seasonal remarked there. To catch slant sunlight as cat prowling, in earth warming from cold in browning tints, twigs in fashion with new glints to show upswelled. Light wind in morning, to activate a day aloud, ahead already remembered, chill now but soon declared and voluntary. Tribute general allowed, near festive recalled incoming, designed as first improved, installed under brief bud coverture, lifted by air currents. Watch and match as once before, in fact many times restored to copy extended, by self-permission, each beside in partner, parted in near time ceded. Measure the range of best alteration, interred recurrent finger-point its hinges in clump appetite, one to follow another or indeed in clear parallel. Supportive near most to crowd, cast wild but neatly, dark passage by feel to wrist awaken.

Note after broach further, all soon enough again prepared, departure the same familiar reflection, incautious now by security of multiples; dig in to fix, root mixing if soundless are true visited, suited to come together prefer collusion cousin tracery; splints there were, here established and novel too renewed. However under search by longer span of daylight, front to back seen multi-coloured but crimson prevailed, come forward in rank assembly prepare in prize surmised as supplicant, witness beyond hesitation will accept.

## XV

Tracement in base sett, affix proposed impulsive hold in place as air stirs and clouds in accidence, needed to meet by freight undershot, stream each to vane. Droplets in shift pass up prismatic glimpses, sound to rush water clatter, other in froth demure. Thus flung to limit wet smart eyebrow swift in scissor order, blade obtrusive across its bank under rate, fluent. To the side accumulate light auspice by while to whirl admitted, bobbin foreign yarn persistent eye to try, to see discrete bouillon distaff colophon keep pace at floor unflawed. Endless reviewed from melt sources cool in sunlight, spectral variance play and repaid expense of white spirit watch outward tenancy sustained and replaced. Would outwith permission inhibit its margin unreserved, prominent in frank display; scenic perfusion near injunction and yet converged by septal flourish. Dew on the cheek, duly modest attested, by audience in ornament as moist jewel dropped and abandoned, separately befallen. Go home not yet, dew not dry, run on to meet arrive and shine, even disturbance across the crowd of roads, no coward thought ahead. Steadfast then near steam out of windfall, soon carried delected.

Erratic cumulative ascent each time different by small degree, accent alive visible staircase instead. Predict improved fashion ticket, accurate company latent damp attire given by exchange to plunge all included and held, part to whole. Know your own, spread free underfoot, slip a trace in millrace coruscate; passion splash close shave, light to shade avowed and uncongealed.

## XVI

Red velvet parapet, electric fast breath the air dense with noise ready alloyed conference held up expectant first, the sound of human space performed. Garland further whether, caravan wound around pride for sooner quicken, in faded comfort flush grade audience marooned compact arisen to take up and off itself in session, wait in paint for each precision, after the first ledge recircled fast abridged. Anticipate certain dense curtain, fall to travel as eminent domain to claim, pungent before socratic moist implicate, neighbourhood; that's where preview practice in prelude not far awaited. Canvas tense step vigour, fluent entire in bound, pried loose each again front tackle relent all traced, eastern risen seed to given, ration to imitate. Would affront varnish, here veneer so many reached for hands spread held to duty margin definite skill runnel resided convince, for grasp opening passing settle confide, arm-rest to catch either side too. Feel in felt foot offering, forbear temper close storm pursuit rack better rock face gaffer placement rush; room light tempest establish, first cause to breath, up-taken fume broken, now lent.

Fusil panel mounting constraint, sound abated to slight fragile tendency, as all resides driven position, narrow in frontage sound in tune pittance; yet velvet once more hue personate, droit discriminate alike any moment flute palliate. Most terrene low-voiced child stem rumple principal, buoy up trip acrostic, over clever finished clover whiten casual. Rifle within, vertical protected as innovate near to bear, wing offspring yield in play to turn, steam effused; past moderate do as you would, discovered. Dram furtive ecstatic or parallel, dispel bright start to gaze even in profit voice: yes to want least.

## XVII

Legal alleged bristle fill bequeath over left attracted, significant vocal aspirant go beforehand wheel spoken by word provoked, will grant taken avengement. Front cargo raised on legume declared embroider faction, loyal ground to rest legend assured, polite intact protection; why to weather by cape escape inured, leave aliquot divided, fair to know for increment waited. Astute distribute, incentive so contrived, share to waive all natural notion, flown in safety conflated. Round table list the current best enriched, perpetual actuarial compromise. Bright day invite, throat open script whiten, fringe enhance laggard to clemency. Stay free, alight reflected, known entranced already harbour all before sea-wall shelter shalt ingress, arrived at side of shade gaze shining vision priced. Crystal trial quaint tussle watch your step next off pat; ready assigned just affluence water track to trickle. Gallic thunder moreover gratulate festal liken pack biscuit, accumulate make fast inherent correlate. Look to find, part to press, age melted mild passage gilt appetite; assimilate construct far ahead addressed confess impressive; testament instate fortunate, filtration soften. All of benefit, decree written diagram position, either one bought at par, gather forward. What can amount upwards in cumulus, famous reckless intense allusion, join to implement.

Paramount countenance endorse production, encroach family simile broaden smiling, enumerate because fill the box, up to the very lid. Care to cure in retrospect you'll recall give way set fast commission improvement, try to fly in chill climate stay clear balance successive lift. Thus for together at peak angle crumple withal, keep in line deserving by day to evening, nominative parlance; wanted to rise forward not timid implicit or placid, incorporate.

## XVIII

Bundle shifted sown willing no offensive additives, moral alert tension foam femur frictionless; come to pass impasse each literal deficit, gradient all too early clear amiss parry off grist innervate. Dissipated sulphate scrape both rough edges pricking of my thumbs in trial to punish, take hold precipitate however without grimace each of them ardent ordeal reticent, invite. Assume river walk catnip revoke at the start, soon enough tune spun unspilled stand back limit daughter to treat ensure treasure over the day similar when nearby lay spread quickly, how else could trace to treacle ride up both brothers eager at start; to get there first next inspected, trim same occupy regional produce fierce overrun. Minor funded thereafter plenty of time ahead, willowherb plumage I'd at least so far alignment catch dazzle, westerly synopsis or what order to syrup cascade white carpet privately line-up how not drop by order. Undoubted relate dissipating as back comical fungus marinade fill seafront nothing amiss contentious, irruptive forcible pulse; cherishment brim talent onion by plan marzipan coin-op while temperamentally on fixture pasture flute obligato whyever not indeed, other saffron climb hurtful nostrum offloaded in time salt. Transact crept visible council or pencil colloid meeting orchard nonchalant tributary; floor-show clown oratorium.

## XIX

Loose mimosa luminous studious, blue patch watchful mix sebaceous chough at present laughter; cruiser purser azure, chosen filter critic advocate gesticulate coaltit overcoat, for seen hereafter. Zealous porous slantwise mayonnaise full-grown, suzerain containment; chorus you lustrous perilous balance too instance prance advancement, frequency. Under the eave for bees, hive saving hypothecate mutation known world silent icicles, early design invocate disintegrate volcanic muriatic diatribe. Ride fast socratic at velvet cordite, beach hut seasonal praise be to grazing ground held close fusible oracular, in snapshot run at evening back before dark. Brick kettle raid haul, geode quarzite nectar for pink insinuate promotion, all aboard lark to sky discount qualify, when you get outright comply at front round about; quote pliant obdurate legation knit two together, further impetus yet fatuous or raucous, choice to kitemark trite elbow mortar compound how to sale, growl fuel. Dealer market slice at each first, nominal lost and funded, truce within traffic rout; overt rain in hand defined contrite, all alight cloudscape, martagon win running treat.

Chocolate laburnum tassel sconce if first test then requites, best them both upsize lit; interior smooth plight annul annealed steelyard, brilliant swansdown gossip terse publish relish, scriptural well ahead in time, at the well-head they provided exactly murmurous adventure, whistling overture legalise motif furore at both extremes fortnightly, well previous diligent team-work duke lukewarm dog-team determined. Omit meeting while they wait, holding back ransack to share equal, attic store; riding in the morning light.

## XX

Winter snow novice trace above, twice relinquish increase office, rise to be mine then down bright and clear; speak by tuft aloft, dearest crescent fly up reprieve, entwine. We gave this same promise, relish sufficient waymark obligate side colour; velour ode night-time token warming fan button resign, whose window heave bestowed sash subdued meringue or gleam. Square off collusive rind in-span orange writ when tonic, civic balustrade angle surfeit dental. Rolling home alight weight to payment catch up, pit latch forest, we too they all prowl, be mine embroil. For long for longing far-flung bring, lower span incremental forced frontage cornice dryas eight-fold invested, guardians search to find snuff effort critical escort debate. Higher later, both sides ahead, please save outright; run together stay other they were adherent, spade buoyant slight imminent nail-bed, commotion. Makefast next into yeast paste question honey reliance, luminous green spinel woven, thus far glare obey, mosquito pure periscope invidious eremurus oh mandolin swim.

With sift missive steelyard livery steward, and both and wish casuistic internship parenteral apt plantation; until relaxed conducive, readiness thus far calendar walnut close-grain mine, cabinet keep company campsite old fateful gnostic acrostic bleat. Sleep soon shepherd seven plaster, foster-child shield weld, heat lock sing to sigh, reliance near enough use fleece, terminal melting lacking within reach, lambent ewe touch headlight ash flash procurement, wasp tested now you know. First bite of conscience gnash parlance, safe-house lace up close balance, dark sign spring squill birds crying solo willow mackerel skylight; coming to carry home run time to tune, again cloud flame lantern iron in shoe horn currant bun, orphan.

## XXI

Trite moult frighten Triton, handsome plummet sound did hold pipkin drop spill; availment word instance none frigate echoic vaunting snow-shoe rivet plectrum; down glissade light chapter, rust coverage sparkle up tight. Room enough spice grimace enlisted, previous foist to roof gable skein, to remonstrate; after begun in turn fill swallow abated, earlier pier shut, to shout, complete. Yet manic once toroid torrid, astute prognosis come to this closer sidelong work bench, clinch eyeglass; there'll be a pleated influence up fast batch authorised incision bridge. To roar fitful, fever apical arrival dual birch dusted, sleep lightly thereafter too; dale foremost enclose best-ever critical lassitude, join heartfelt fruitful we will canal defend in ventral, slept apart curlew over clue matin dart. Today by flame duct fire ahead longing to level all told; wild and true thoroughfare instinctual, several abrupt connective twins. Hold to rest wrist matching fountain be ready, colour willow exact until cravat ticket entry; mullion revision intarsia bring to front invidious, keep step company why not mutton chop aptitude, leveret optical escape intrinsic parchment.

Awkward surmount join as would come too, permission, wait to first grant justice auriculas mischief I'd defend; wisteria dividend, praise open well at least. Splice rush carex most loose latch, merciful windswept lattice; lexical easier get there advice stay near fearless price. As now then will also be, before dawn filbert whistle hazel plagel gopher, down-hill intaglio couch blatant.

## XXII

Footlight found out flake discrepant deep in wade knew ladle, new around refined acerbic, crowd blindsight conduit opaque authenticate not far ahead without, at least until concave wedge scollop serene for sure honour upheld. In-field splay to say whichever other previous labour sky lifted, too early to bind utter ground within hearing, tongue twice enough wealth gorse spindrift. Oft distant by relation, tree full spread unfurled; channel to funnel sentinel gorged on both sides, horse sense in best luck comb element, who's to say out in front; ridge to gravel, gust to guesthouse left chide infant, instigate then follow, fate. Clamber to timber, next yet yours, pleach posted rim entrance, arrears mark the spot sawn off. Ink spasm tidal race cuttle increase, must release ace, liken grindstone intone ledge effacement; will either or both intense, yellow-rattle to set apace, ankle muffle play to ear pitch pine yours not vine cone don't scatter off, ensign. Even lengthen toughen the main-frame, at mark goatsbeard hoard dice, wrapt insistent request moreover undercoat. Be mine wilt thou in shade be plight bespoke, scramble allege inside ensign or ledge to window, black laurel chaplet clip; supple in hostel mostly feasting kestrel, stoop otter other torn.

Post to lard timbre suspect murmur at fan in time boisterous, massive cursive obelisk regal indeed why or not likely wait to see wheaten brusque settlement; preposterous intensified fort liable obverse this way up eventual. No ridicule in dapper plastic imitate provision enough muzzle, or whether crusade wallet imbricated by query dalliance defiance; granite porphyry croquet by coquetry appetite incidental as provident invert caramel creamer instead, dreamt.

## XXIII

What grip elicit mission model, fill-dyke over psychic schedule, satchel tolerate afternoon or glimpse caravan favoured to flavour; other feared in fervid ink-stained staircase successive past nod and would. System charge replete compliant parallel molecule, valiant valency roof pitch at step discharge; forge forgetful hazard buzzard cabbage scabbard, satellite orbital smoker fluster bloater inskip. Joyful enjoin tenon by lantern lower down leakage, lovage impoverished unite polar gale-force, swirl curling up; assailed remedial bear the brunt, curtailed well before lit adamant, slight. All then with us surprise given, agile done donated, tacit commission cockade; riddle never overcome seconds out subsequent in tenement their own default, until when not. Gothic semblant conferent idyl grill spoil dale outright to camp-ground, so long repine plaintive mint shallow. Ne'er find his marrow coralline dormant beforehand orchard, careworn word to wise scenic resound.

Ruffle plumage selvedge candle wick by trait known deep breath, dispense relent first oft list unmarked, aspect index lustre moisture at vehemency, each in pair topic livid valid missed. Set out plain sailing, aftermath fate recast averse prolix harbour neighbour grammar redressed.

## XXIV

Skirting yet kilter, alter infringement by banish foolish inelegant, less inquest confessed humdrum symptom; lowest flag. In trance rate invest divulge touchstone, enter to keep close in temper, let not be until then intact or fraught mist discrete immediate; shell frail, stay fast quest impression come to pass in due time, manifested soon restitution. Acquit emerge distinguish for relish how to arm's length, up-in-air tepid dare all together perceptive; boastful recalcitrant insipid eutric elliptical submissive, inflection northern light sound afield. Lucid incidental bronchial all cumbersome, phantom out milk endeavour silver clever, pilgrim banana elk phlegmatical phosphor; permeate blight arc lamp myriad sled swarm, mollusc antipathy formic lyric soot suited neurotic incited. Tangle repute, mingle afloat diluted at hold tight, carrot dot matrix furnish mean-time columbine toadflax, truth another, downward than upward; hard and fast conduce to juice in first place.

Pillow mellow soft brow beat the cap, upstart crow canal caparison compare floor boarded up wet lock set together cement lenient, flint knap swore sword interred at white rock benefit explicit; tensor impure conductus fictive, all united share invited.

## XXV

Laid by cypress, sad shade forget-me-not mould infirm fade from sight, remember and hanker to wait in turn alliance repine; smoke to burn within resigned wave cloud; its part to play agree eyes falter older deflated. Back extorted readiment recant upended, stay put upon psalm interred, rose fast set deplete, droplets endless ever might; how well retain origin burin express release, nacreous flicker offer notorious peach. Solid barrack headstone grass-green turf, linger mercer dark feast, knit to brow before at first light, to thy rest. Promise radish freshen strewn silence, awaited gannet finance gallantry; speak up your weight resound, in wood abounding been yet forgiveness latent, whence stanza spoke shave oboist hoist alder grove. In curve decrease hoarding anklet suffused, buckle my shoe goldfinch ground elder bishop cupric weft announce fabricate; who's to say so early, kingdom come fledged in cygnet train. Hinterland bind wedding sheaf steady, lavish mole furl until evolve solemn signal line forage, average advancement.

Krypton bristle fossil laid down, basement narrow windowledge midget sacristan, apron tunicate evidential who says twice whelk frolic pasture, finger stall to spiral vigil digit selfish crawfish, duckweed as crypt cliff pledge. Know best when tested, wrist edge blessing loosen pear solace linen, glove smooth print. What you hear rings true already, tremble within enlighten, intervene.

## XXVI

## TRAVELLERS' TALES

### (a)

During a journey across a wide plain a traveller came to a broad river flowing across his intended direction. He looked around for a bridge or a ferry but he could see none. However he caught sight of a fisherman sitting on the opposite bank. "Fisherman," he called out, "can you tell me how I can get to the other side of this river?" "Traveller," replied the fisherman, "you are already on the other side."

**(b)**

A traveller came to a wood, and began to go into it. But he could only go half-way in, for after that he would be coming out.

**(c)**

A traveller and his companion came to a stream flowing across their path. There was no bridge but there were stepping-stones; however the stream was in rapid motion and the traveller thought that he must get his feet wet. His companion was wearing shoes made of plastic, unlike the traveller's which were made of leather and which would be damaged by the wet. The companion proposed this solution to the problem: "I will cross the stream in my plastic shoes, carrying your leather shoes with me. From the other side I will throw my plastic shoes back over the stream, to you; you can put on the plastic shoes and cross the stream, keeping your leather shoes safe from the wet, in that way." And thus the crossing was accomplished.

**(d)**

A traveller who was delayed asked a tortoise if he would carry and deliver a letter for him; the tortoise agreed. After an hour the traveller enquired if the letter had been delivered. "Don't be impatient," replied the tortoise, "or otherwise I won't go."

**(e)**

If you paint a door red on one side and green on the other, what colour is the door?

**(f)**

A fish started to sing the national anthem; the neighbour fishes of every kind swam up and joined in. On which scales did this patriotic song match the loyal profession in onward motion?

**HER AIR FALLEN**

**(2020)**

air here tell to her
    rick as flew, enter
ringing for ink none
    foreign or well warn
try please prize, twice
    surprise plus anew
ant knew it, risen for
    told same in dear
    time bleed leading to
tread fair to wear
    over, whether ever fore
clear in her name

rent to be able be so
    civil hope and sure
to cure her blend, too
    sunder where planted
silently, anvil went to
    share within faint
voice in choice first
    wore in hand, took
to share lark spur tried
    the band or aged,
wager forever fervent in
    currently her glint

how many miles acclaim
    her way across, in
fame with both warmer by
    mention for sense than
soon assured, down along
    the sandy dormancy in
more for ever so dare to
    spoken the peak echo
by rate mended, ferment
    beloved above yet and
further foremost see to
    caressed her easement

spelled invent supplanted
    suit outside blame view
no orchid plenty swell to
    reach her cheek method
date to find, eminent tell
    found scented fork fill
on foot care step onward
    temper conversant win
    afford in sure incised too
burning bright filament
    prevented, present outlook
fuller than, her limb

direct rest attire torn
    surplus return defer
wended far and fair worship
    untraced, open to sown
with her with them confirm
    compliment, adept spent
none ever other indirect
    upheld to turn spring
inspire, bring later banish
    edge part sunken spoke
forward worded bell rung
    or mine then, or hers

reflection tract sight soon
    stem hollow mend or seam
tender true assigned fire
    allow on wire bird sing
presume below her smile as
    similar to know exchange
under each wing safe sound
    main find, way leave on
after shade to make blades
    sky blue prime sown up
trim ready not sorry strain
    tune to her even grade

blink pleated sever havoc
fasten in timely by
hold level her retain in
top flight sauce boat
for plight descry, repute
fold out to grant wit
ore oar nearer out spread
canal feel, sweep up
despite floated relented
to be innocent pin
amend proud friend said
fond wheel her link

most not lost moisten
firm seal aim home
with her dream ahead to
tame when assumed
go least boast pursuit
alert physic heart
wonder much break, off
your great room in
famous party speak out
rain freely place
devoted side lake to
overtly her print

in blue too moving on
fine tinted even
protect her wake taken
alike unpriced at
moot debate, elder fit
stoup attend land
convert flight paint
all up hill salt
trail innovate preen
want custom ban
wane spendthrift to
mine for hers on

gallon tilt lilium in
fill to cool avert
increment talent brim
addicted wonderful
comet flight, tail fun
illusion her built
shelter exile frailer
thatch melt clover
damsel flutter either
one another outer
fort track presto, in
her thermal pun

lifted morning sun way
any brave attested
flight path measure or
hers too, crested
raven sheen hidden old
fissure pardon aft
lilted assist for map
aisle scale boiler
sailor bruit vaulted
lit window gothic
array, single angular
lamp her inheres

fondle borrowed mellow by
funded hands untied
graceful oval tidal wave
ground there minded
within time enough seen
prevail for hers and
line toil handsome rain
clouds model wishful
headpiece sunny panel
up one, rhizome to
preview in sustained
her other how guided

reed-beds longed for one
    arranged fine birds
sing focal casual ensue
    her typical avowance
renewed full foolish too
    volume valiant moist
due presence, count melt
    thrown down diminish
as will or can bring out
    repeat decision few
imply in haste, laced in
    her beribbon symptom

river to cross, rejoice
    parlant flood her wed
mood saffron quiet sight
    alter mossy bank rate
clam over, to cover leaf
    trim evergreen brine
prune saline brain wished
    privilege sledge toss
thrush disperse castoff
    nor first nor lasted
aspect tarnish collards
    herbal for her gain

would mild not yet come
    about mint quietly
crib in her bred sipped
    amorous visits hid
castor honour, tried at
    herb acted child in
mild sudden modern kit
    quite tremor mist
enlist lacked by luck
    spoken uptaken at
lake reclining onheld,
    by her well as told

site home range bridge
    her eye found brow
fox finger screen on
    civet hot pie ate
danger kerb bold crypt
    light for work in
life lifted single to
    well turn out, and
fled fleece saved up
    dear clean radius
embrace swift prince
    her certain price

ebon one prone loaned
    fulsome simple her
rankle current winsome
    single sensing at
solvent nautical floor
    fire palaver evade
set piece dove risk in
    vest meant flared
full firth, imminent
    sable diver train
forum canon influx
    tone hers amain

earth smoke forsaken
    liken lesson lease
loosed abyss, new dyke
    league, exergue
patron famous fire pit
    fraying excess to
short slice waste flair
    born moreover gale
force waiver legal by
    mitral limit, fits
much trace ashen wish
    her evermore laid

befriended lintel band
   parts her sightings
on soon wary to offend
   plaint minded scent
divert provision wildly
   fancy tizzy, vial
vital gamble frontal set
   to make better opt
klaxon tandem attraction
   rime foam, indented
byre sere attach fish
   remix her minimum

intense annex foregone
   for so for her one
parted grain sought
   might ever borage
challenge singing on
   wisdom, surfeit
condition when rebuilt
   never tilted beam
king post hike pitch
   alliance balance
trample simplify own
   her banneret pin

even fathom lengthen, on
   purpose for the sun
flake custom face intent
   blue tissue pine belt
indwelt her warm respite.
   Fair dues anew enjoin
cress emboss fan remain
   cool bean seem press
interval, leaned on fit
   sooner over yet and
meet, went on to convince
   her canticle, apprise

velour taste almost, rain
   sustenance her mint
nip cat flight prominent
   runner former present
prophetic endure, release
   what cast at commence
inner night-time feasted
   best ever weather in
sensate dilated occiput
   trifle still rested
impressive correlated to
   her bright hue, set

coral precision choral aim
   forename fortune given
alive her tip cumber bantam
   burn old leaves, ransom
smoulder treasure lit shower
   drop porcelain trimming
claim to cheer fuel minstrel
   finally, levy allergic
long term if murmur chrism
   needy traded already
silt pearlwort crept within
   her lustrous redoubt

eulogy and the larks they
   sang melodious at the
dawning of the day, light
   her near eyes in ways
their steeds to water, size
   risen clouds aflame or
out disclaim into careworn
   rim that pretty is, at
spring's studious cords, di-
   verting waken to bring
ma tremble for ruffled leaf
   spray her ward to say

coins new out in the fount
   full blink vexed sea
for her decree, disclaim
   black vesper venture
fragment gridiron keeled
   bestride cinders talk
kestrel worker over spree
   to be, proud widen at
point sing betide flooring
   vernal trinket milky
version sealant, ignorant
   rule up her cinnamon

flying waves aft released
   whistle deeds, begin
artisan seed path in tune
   listen up her caravan
wane pitch, save urban din
   sleep sway loom cries
profile so thin gaunt try
   fast thistle switch
edible match, preciously
   misgiven ever while
mission entry latch sound
   yet none her refined

sale fresh mist pulling
   her border lift, tap
burden some ash retelling
   sailor to thank up
caution notion if order
   either vale wills
door sink, mesh broaden
   greener bark lips
mount at or remonstrate
   modern to covering
tailor apportion ranked
   her stay on mark

halyard beaten copper to
   induce hailstorm run
cream return her overseen
   smelted dome, quelled
down inspired while foreign
   sup eaten worn card
dealing thruway column on
   broom stack sluice
net price, belt file crewel
   denial earned upper
margin crowd in confirmed
   yet her paean to win

ease buzz where's the other
   whether love forgiven
hive her dare wave moving
   skewer angle flaws to
surcingle, neither in trees
   bleeding clouds woven
view oven contrived sewn
   tinted to please amaze
tempest foist, nave garment
   lent out to firstborn
aloud burin fill enter debt
   for her to flee about

hive in new cave arisen
   save proven no wrangle
scrub bush listen, doubt
   florin dozens swerved
flown over mansion omission
   doorpost close most
foothold mild single toots,
   scarce wore thunderous
tinder fulvid deep-rooted
   candid, all remembered
problem muted winter driven
   rush to her twice keen

sleuth wrath cradle test
  belief wet candle, lit
her fast effort impressive
  late ripen salt lease
forthright, divested fault
  milk tooth fondle soak
caulk into colloid boldest
  ploy, foretaste creak
out brief twice to break
  void ever truth until
fall broken at all reveal
  her limbs anon bespeak

loose tenon canon lemon in
  limbic rehearsed twin
profile mostly belfrey run
  alum immersed to docile
oh godly sprawl over thumb
  parlour fix occupy so
many animal targets fabric
  lackfast lock haven at
battery chiral fossil, if
  railing charge margin
crime index inflected ruin
  more damp her attained

what walk is this once aghast
  sift and plaice remiss off
potage crocus purposeful play
  her stalk aloft flouncing
in focus soften bundle float
  park talking skip shop one
tame missed hostage to glide
  for idol idling long past
primal actual dark lens over
  mending often frolicsome
claimants into facts virtual
  for her each time return

crane flown abject pestle
  clowning genial on light
wake loft abstruse powerful
  tumid missile hadron to
govern gruesome symmetric
  scorn vernal downcast
flights of seedlings modest
  in turn attuned burning
filmic mooted convex lips
  oven-ready gastric tap
final bitumen win infarct
  her while beneath ferns

vocalic iterate pulse sit
  sated her bitter pack
pin for prune proud neap
  to weep frequent until
never avail, frugal citric
  graded abandon intone
were febrile curative tiff
  press-stud backed off
phantom black sky licked
  local brick seaweed
apse, spruce cantor thru
  her eyes to overfill

furnish message name listed
  sanguine last ebb awaits
her truce nebulous passage
  breath whiles recital
out *a l'altra riva*, takes
  lurid imploration sea
mist see lifted beneath rice
  saline precious heated
as ever was, as not finish
  until right know induce
whose moment crew at prowess
  retell recall, her face

other bees in trees brood
   cells wrote her what
whey solids myriads clay bit
   feet well further welt
buzz pollen lies freezes to
   nail batten sign waned
oil grain hazard dozen seed
   pod made screw tight
to coiling side day light
   soak corbel token deeds
now asian trial drizzled
   fast her shore in salt

treacle for trefoil, bird's
   foot issue trestle impute
barking leaks morsel niche
   recoil pinnacle timbrel
sought fissure bless elate
   mill bread been swarm in
natal usual mark strike im-
   ported inkling borne out
bryony bee eggs only crest
   lichen silken daub rift
inbred casual, hedge funded
   at taut her near arrest

humus tint humorous semi-
   definite diffuse posit
deny all shaken porous ice
   her cream laces meant
dual marry up corybantic
   spruce antics cosset
decree why scented fleece
   level donate illusion
first agreement seating
   furious to bind, fund
less curious, obviously
   her extravagant wit

will swing loyal low crown
   for brow adorn accrue to
mounded glory prior wingbeat
   blood set group treated
night shadow turn escrow top
   before dust line choir
risen voice to carry out
   far must foremost best
promise repertoire whether
   together string origin
proud escape tales in spell
   her word each to dwell

# THE FEVER'S END

**(2020)**

## To This Troop

Did prove to nerve fleck recruit
dyne swerve yeast directs unison
profounder nave intuit arrowroot

governance province win harassed
width fluency cease primal trout
stipple carol suspect banquet in

warning arrival visual conserved
torrential saving citric undergo
lapel claim untamed physic drift

unguent limpid commute dapple on
pallid steam laced crisis honied
cantle stifle each manifest wild

inflame the pine-cone oasis prow
dutiful morning holdfast replied
surrender links incessant finery

intarsia dorsal thesis appointed
in swan plain mordant gamut tray
base weed appliance musketry tin

horizon mansion patient incident
variable dense moments stationed
quarrelsome beast if run to seed

## Come Not Near

Tepid bluffs adherent oar spikes
seek veer adamant dampen voltage
civic open lake four enough side

spin captive weaker score merest
colour rapid to not cramp pitted
serene occasion masonry explores

sated sufficient just alike best
many dear hearts restart devised
yet otherwise dream plus adapted

newer parts here spare giant aid
tried whose sake as moors within
team affray basin core hollow at

knife forsaken in safe tantalise
sited out tight fought must both
twine lick defiant fillip surfer

decisive from mental fight adorn
alone sedated prize at birth ice
discussed like mine deliver aver

propane fantasy borrow midst win
on cite the same innovate profit
narrow strait loosen sets adrift

## From This Session

Profile to noble double stop met
alert stream by storms interrupt
short while ripen sway mile play

notice agile replicate boat dish
insert same allergic remote eyes
hilltop this day tortive inspect

index sample torn repayment ties
closer match caught each brought
into book crumpled horn delights

toss emerge friable tramples all
cancel each way look back banter
conjugate imports ample mornings

chorus pilot vex cannulate afore
cant arms indites active delayed
foster sold child porous factoid

dismayed verging cruising allots
bidden added brook current scrap
arrested prate bets lost rebirth

unbroken style soil codes breeze
choose amazement by cured cement
in token sadden dish on for once

## Of Tyrant Wing

Pinkie chutney asbestos focus in
sufic prowl but cruel wishful so
winning loop too wonky best omit

crocus unwinding curl-on compute
sappy mail better meal boiled up
soup inversion hocus pocus snack

tell uttermost unproven drawling
omelette to gimlets insert flaxen
hoop icteric cruise elastic near

amusement fiscal muscle traction
cave floor weir inured matter at
tight fit mawkish roof-beam coup

setter covered wheeze host froze
pommel whirl galleon tunnel dint
angle ascribe dazed portrait fed

hot-blooded order bleared demure
trap set dour abet mistaken moat
tailor persian druggist if amain

fit up novocaine alert unhurt in
tatters bears claws extra strain
vinyl pause seer and so detained

## Save the Eagle

Clock mender condor thick locked
door to gnaw no lender tip ocean
planet debt open gold-weight set

upper eyelid gait smoke aided so
docket merits habit ludic tasked
sake secret syndicate first best

ligament figure smite spate over
dilated transits into fury stilt
legal sanctions consider oxidate

treated increase fluent sybarite
chronic predator storax predicts
adduced pockets nuisance absence

occupies metal so-called brittle
pince azure donation fraction at
slippage battle coup in rotation

fed supper meddle acre alder ten
racket remains licence undulates
secluded liken pavilion environs

slid deplore between pair invoke
clue assimilate procession soars
up-gaze amazement slim confident

## Lack His Right

Plash further other rucks embed
swoon trefoil proverbial hither
gaping fast boil mattocks quash

purchase mutton masonry indulge
consent tuning herbal rival gem
tubular far river curious faced

most ever rowlock problem burnt
soul splash mischief ruin resin
late tickets bloom if implement

destroy abash as pertinently so
welcome firecrest briefly inept
at sweeps or left fulmar rewind

chief sponsor winter into cleft
itemised dash victim victorious
revision cheaper skeptic inside

growing unbutton dolorous whims
in valour deeper tested tranced
wrangle singlet habits ensconce

aloft employ sidelong open face
steadfast invoice tonal advised
colours sendoff minim calibrate

## With the Breath

Timber argue rescue as by mishap
tending for amber loss barge few
nap willing friend to margin gap

a bone a single stone inveterate
own shirt moss on the shiny step
shirk less surging dates for end

essential temper crossed and dip
yet not too deep forfend ingrate
remember besom's new shingle bed

as days to run in phase afforced
light face tissue novice instead
endorsing service by led forward

ice regained cut perils masthead
shade pencil shall estranged few
shadow outbrave and tip apparency

master the art inspect twangling
deck honestly brevet flit cravat
persist anew indifference avowed

toyed plaster oyster contact ore
divine angle apart relayed twite
erected wit dissemble miss amaze

## Shalt Thou Go

Foremost righteous rigid splints
adjunct delinquent unmelted flit
resemble coastline mint benights

tortuous sunken credulous praise
in phase preamble cage or mostly
final sadden wageless sudden pin

myriads faded add-on doctrinates
persistent dissenting or emulate
bountiful as dusty flint facades

bright knapp silicate segregated
convergent grade aspic indenture
point over adverse native tinted

iris assists intermit acetic wit
rearguard spoiled agree disposal
festive craving optical biscuits

dire count printed circuit limit
to crab dozen mizzen fasten brut
delayed at three-ply dice repaid

outreach adaptive manifold irate
weld sonic vital cupric alloy at
seismic recorded elbows intrepid

## Doth Commence

Transform bravura character slip
chuck blazon green ingrained nip
fitful edition fevered conjugate

incarnate dormant disorders scot
white heart to spell under trout
by envy beaten beatific intimate

gloves mortified asides unbidden
routine ruckus parlous amplified
nothing impale in reason animate

ensigns impervious rain-clouding
regent malachite abundance about
floated rich pickings incinerate

brumous challenge tighten alight
oppugns return retuning ignition
emergent slighted emetic imitate

another barrow tomorrow incident
excoriate severance for credited
double doubtful seine swept into

titration askance exonerated eat
summative respite in casket cake
waistcoat tropic impressive bite

## Flame from Hence

Cumbersome ambition alien reform
fortune umbrage person intervene
sundered ravens unfailing ravine

joy at late plunder arson common
fashion importunate wheat serene
dim edgework battle then prevent

rescinded damage gate at village
salient trimmings silent adverse
mental pile remorse out-numbered

camp pinned plumage spread pints
delta water invite furrow browse
trouble altered by tong deferred

novice bolted service paraded to
bribe wonderment porter imminent
name recant recent undertake win

taught beside rampaging deranged
not wrong welter in salt incline
contented teeming decision while

inclusion by outer mill imperium
foliar nourished noise expansion
affect promise course onto arise

## Had the Essence

Derelict lacked budgets inflict
braggart enact bigots galloping
parrot in syrup offers toffee at

tame loom coronets must in soup
scarify fillip strictly pursuit
distinct province random equity

nor either petrify object enact
egg tract tactical stirrup acid
avenue ensue placid stir before

fluent behest dragée immoderate
pitch troop solace flourish tic
by recklessly discretion apogee

eminence since invidious insist
numerous assembled buying spree
pathos demerited parish infancy

wallop merciful respectful balm
patrial signet finished avarice
diminishment unstoppered agency

conflict circle cudgel immolate
pious magnet provender educated
fragrances diffused ambitiously

## But in One

Mutation riverside deep horn dip
litter fettles gloated spike hub
luminal back pride skippers tusk

iterate light inflated calm form
scatter grave crossing amplified
must save salute grime tip elate

sound bonded round carpet delete
cape grill mutation glisten stem
exhume embroiled indignance lose

embrace potion proportionate ill
contrite maximum indistinct suet
foster tape woven swarm inflated

familiar easels diluted moribund
split hoof dangerous clings fast
none more free perplex to singer

warning figment assonant install
crash next purse militate review
vapid mitre trophy explicit fate

created at once nuisance fall in
bring none poor trounce inclined
nor cry nor weep wells into tune

## Number There

To run by cab form in near front
evenly so dear and close returns
in fine disports claims proud to

name appears comfort as now done
crests in tab likens match lower
brows in burn invasive longs cry

streets confound paving at begin
cures supple stubble wired ahead
loyal made alight provide floats

inbred cast to threads for cheer
laces grown overturned so mended
but patch scented fits in throat

begun dower sups enter by window
intent sweet oil rarely ransomed
in calls to mind or meet at best

say true where due portray anvil
given in hopes for sake to sleep
incite depart to ripple indolent

musky ever outer trust line edit
latent conceits brush cited core
apple single about inform denote

## Hearts Remote

Swift travel ravel in finite box
tactics motive restive line flex
shade bird swung wing knock luck

tussle inhale bay scenic deviate
persuivant sorry votive antiphon
theme sensory twigs own collapse

watched thermal noise discussion
usual heat bath crafted notch if
hark barking haricot tongue seek

baking desolate candied fruitage
reverse hers offers outer setter
legs invoke placate atlantic jib

raven farm by turning about work
black taken mean field open roam
high-yielding furs time unharmed

discounted switch prevented gift
alarm signals marvel improvident
flame current by whence ivy sake

ordeal attack split up sail felt
opt fibre dealt inlaid by slaked
seal stunt page in alive crusade

## No Space Was

Infirm informed printed invented
clip fasten waste reproach tints
in wants branch incident implore

procures descent hamper offering
carbon space rampant fires apace
reviews in swine gadarene onrush

massive redeem tempestuous imbue
dark tenet ever been incited aim
crew target planet tick holocene

novelty confer demur guardian at
tenancy rival here beseem remain
inductance most restore to prime

warden indigenous brain distends
foreseen foretold frequency ants
formative smoke arises to relent

procure assure partition improve
ahead of time assume prodigal to
lengthen action office principal

tireless tread vain terminal hit
mission lesson obtain connivance
come to think of refinement wane

## Either Was

Pine soon plains will same to be
had too in days three anew foray
see low will try yet so enter by

for trust loosed wave first here
by fire dim view not slow entire
time past born dust in able fair

digressed custom circulate or to
set dates obvious benefit repair
provoke craving few states amend

silent by warranty freed of yarn
tangle brother once least invite
invent ignited sounds out dilate

by or soon by whether as instate
resume term latter soften weight
fast fly make level into company

no hurt one flown too up to find
seams sewn with mine conditional
intone fruits bite spins provide

birth torrent limit when decided
quickens inflame yielded infancy
agree by sides inspired near vie

## Nature's Double Name

Brown sugar not further operates
come to town deliver checksum at
turn and about ticket weather it

debate burns humming into racket
suit ardour other ivy lazy clung
balanced difference scouted pack

append or find wait overhead sun
shone home comfort meagre crated
time batter halter sprain renown

corymb thimble trusted post east
agar eager in pronation tunic on
terse affluent mooted tappet one

touch to bases influx coronation
action or down inspection treaty
omicron simmer given right token

mallard strikes as much replaced
powder rally pard louder sprouts
spare parted thwarted prowl obey

datum cistern polymer conveyance
bounden duty offset imported kin
crown tune not fount worse begun

## Division Grow Together

All very well pimpernel at least
break fast trek in clover few in
chatter later evident dissenting

sell wake of before out to fires
left hand every time anneal wand
limit soon went eye sighted away

jaw locked revoked by ally folly
tame sauce tune rite why not fly
match methods consent up in dark

counter make alack in same force
price or twice deplore none more
old mildew elder her name intact

switch device amnesty delay obey
either sake apposite folder take
in detail official sociable melt

squabble stand-off arrested spry
detach unblamed clocks forwarded
fits reward pollard revealed due

floor will do but load in docket
on board check marking acid bent
trident brother revalue incident

## Yet Either Neither

Infill narrows observant pliancy
mustard attainment valiant crowd
heavy oranges exchanging amorous

strenuous ride derision obsidian
cream shingle to dangle profused
spoon skimmed finger-tight adept

wave to heaved both haven chosen
ozone mute stripes protest faint
pocket borrowed alone acceptance

insurgent prod arch below search
across mass brilliant cut facets
bit part flustered footlight low

graded diversion back blink flow
norm seleucid rifted mollusc bay
widen remiss tid-bits into stock

clasps bravely trawled to ambush
gracious ramified forth luscious
fungus pressured sestet imitates

first gasp unladen season capsid
greeted captivate bonnets inmate
satiric tribunals cynical oxygen

## Can So Remain

Portable probable gullible last
orphan quibbles asbestos morose
combust sable frivolous in both

plentiful animal class afferent
clinician magic opted compliant
wick back stork granite up path

went torsion label maculate one
track stipulate gratify senator
monster harbour seasonal forked

either whether witter criminals
single bent under lovable inate
fabric final singable ventilate

gorgeous silage implicit dement
conversant signs adherence foal
hand tool suspicions circumflex

minister savagery accidental if
illustrious attempts frustrated
unkempt rumours disabled afford

transverse sinister crittur off
revolving selvages approximated
after before monsoon dispraised

## Stars of Love

Far beside the flute crowd noted
aloud low tides allowed garrison
remote ban pumice-stone suit one

total unknown forecast inside or
at last thrift reputed dissented
hems mild sewn tether vocal moot

after roosted when down and past
over chemic boost utmost consume
admire before ceramic gossip for

lacquer opera liquid parsnip lid
return assign rusted runic drift
for birch at newt foot-print bid

proud compensated pensive berate
must maroon bracket for rocketry
bitter aspect trivia wicked dyed

out-broken simian neutral choral
earn admire brindle bridal forel
furled town mouse beholden avian

branded modern windmill corn buy
prune for bread and wine instead
aligned divine sudden florentine

## In All Simplicity

Rotation very small for all shut
dissemble time but units vary at
some in nuts let sums zero appal

floating narration wheat tunnels
ensemble humble nitric over pain
solvent percentage innocent note

scary willow ration to ramble on
denied primal gimcrack open slop
tantric mainly following fashion

often declare ribbons taller beg
talker back hoot zest listlessly
honest final doublets ready nest

vital ingested oboe now consumed
gift-wrap crumble arrant forgery
trivial avowal surging all alack

divested oblique diluted minaret
untested spare by want rote late
got for best shots overt almanac

hero pluck in aware chance avail
merging both stage struck ordeal
chill foul or fair all page meal

## But Cannot Be

Ping run celluloid acute ear for
early tone domestic neumes adore
in doric rite secluded disclaims

purfling cue lucifer wafer litre
auxiliar dew new-mown outland in
stubborn cabin squeamish singled

spark tuned ledge midges unbound
to the mill enslave dissuaded on
blame fast pinned at muster loan

strict strut dizzy nimble detain
trivet bland for hob astute made
to fit winning coy be not afraid

apportioned nail sung due detail
unbound unborn in even turn abed
fricasse last juniper elite head

invade cascade wrought bright to
titmouse tufts impress more taut
freshen listen yew dust taxol on

sail for salmon western sprained
rueful humble to tremble or will
migrate in flock unpack allocate

## PASSING GRASS PARNASSUS

## (2020)

Sing different songs on different mountains

## In First Tuft

So be it bell bee lift medick black reliquary
fumitory cloven zigzag agree proud bee scout
provoked teasel, we'd hawk orange sleeping
licit brighten maybe buck past night eye win
shadoof arrested honour honied gathered thorn
apsidal mantle; bee better supple wax oddment
reside around torment until tillage phrasing
candour in first tuft. Will to be absconded,
bit over frugal step foot bird gibbous seek
to wade speed sweet braid brigantine western
grass-wrack oh willow lighten one obol fescue
half scruple rueful strife lost foil sunken
flag yellow alchemic, well to speed, spelling
alex and erstwhile milder dewfall flow gentle
vernal enjoy unravel, glove wolf to foxy off
must to travel figment worth welsh popularise
astonish crop to stretch. Stitch, worshipful
dropwort walking basset mallow elbow winding
ill-met crane billet chalk hill, fugal would
sorrel sorrowful meadow scented entreat sweet
fasten shaded if rift, listed thrift on hold
bed strewn mown tufted edgeways led by nature
hardly felt, the kind you are, square spear
new-mint tway robert herb blood fortune meet
fate hay rattle settle; white bryony bees
terse creeping wrack grapple miller dusty.

## Again Sea Fume

Wane out wax lighten severance pursuit filter
falter least drastic for slate drench pastime
entry, entirety lofty each inside talent map.
Heath linger angular foot planet immunising
tepid more, land alight later; impress woven
alterance weighted soon fathom mainly entity
outside system best stolon lichen tab lift
thallus confirming. Urgent claim to tendril
oriel date pittance flit, bee dance sighted
circuit painted, trace left face lifted awake
scimitar; croak bitterly at calibre minister
gate succession cudweed filbert entrance, by
footprint vital sign. Loan pastern to foster
eastern quartic over-spread batter utterance
in banter sentinel well over aversion, prune
imprudent flaxen motion alien replaced. Ice
tilth amiss visional rationing funded assist
fast, proven alter mild crepitance defaced.
So level again sea fumes cereal allurement
consular seasonal provisional gathering in
margin, alembic phantom ducted symptom vine
molten halo print sailing sealant squint by
font by slant implicated askew. Taken back
endure scour to handed siren plainly water
drowse syrup flints origin wave upon wave.

## Left Over Leaf

As to limit by sand under well bleeding cove
perplex geum case rival iron accusing. Not
yet allege terrace mantle, manifest shoulder
sip pledge unfearful cut brilliance to suit
raiment since remainder. Compress self guide
tendence forget quickly, quail fetch ranked
instate remount remonstrate fallible error
dune torsion. Felt partition grant infancy
fascia, belief whole alloy prunus seizure
ellipse patch; corundum repulsed immense
pick over, squander qualia tint active did
achieve archive morose fierce invade. Ride
fill twice harmless optic sanction, done
open with them presume pressure split off
left over leaf pass, nourishment brokering
hidden insist. All then together, flower
mark next to nectar listed slant offended
price to risen form, riverine. Mandibular
in quash left share bloom metalloid brain
share bloom transmissive suffusion newt
fight to sermonise, crater efflux parlour
edict; both instil to fraction in person,
tractable will attend antigenic profile
deducted. Pensive flood marine intercept
counter surge promissory went far ahead
volunteer grip for sack, go under saving
widget why-ever intended wilt occasion
on new time, ready known turned retune.

## Infused Collusion

Welcome intrusion proud leafage wiles crease
foretaste would if could, pillow fertile suggest
to bear lavish climate lawful. Spool imminent
filtration upheaval grab entire, glaze annoyed
light hurt eyebright decurrent latent mafic
celadon praise renew. All told exchangement dip
immersed heel to hold yet filled tenacious off-
chance providence tresses surface, mineral sand
leaching nicety for gneiss fiction. Spark sift
attrition argon hybrid forehead dendrite, soon
up to come crown impetuous holm even. Said via
ahead uncover filtration, fashion carving and
swerve wholesome anchorage; plastics euhedral
harrow permission conducted for tropic ingrate
gift first, rest rated infused collusion. Miss
less done over, splutter pink dian skies! Ice
planet collop racing green fence occupant, in
whim advance invented post train at last, if
served abridgement chapter wisteria menthol
pallid indolent granite guelder. Falter lure
fire barrier merriment implement obtuse ruled
her time park sent forward brow-lined trowel
temporal occlusion press onward, intrepid felt
warmer throatwort classic swallow tail suspend
arrear pear hereafter, inclined foiled plenty
attentive. Factive risible annex enlargement,
place slice invisible; goat temper capricious.

## Downcast in Case

For soaking amok soap sake run sacred oak east,
soup central musical separate aspiring live-
long daylight in-flight harmonic label; simple
oblivious wanted lintel ventral showcase asked.
Arctic lactic codon frown overturn primal brim
stone, rock face cramp on time seamless strike
into forward grip, weighted tempt in rhyming
storm-cloud occluded. Sampler wetter agency
supplied tender up minted spun clear, fearsome
private heated has she now, no motion lessen
surplus violet spur stamen immune resonant
son other to brother who in sake fight, lie
out one side maintained pendent eyeglass. So
wish downcast in case, lift off perish lest
inflame blameless dramatic project coraline
funnel generate offer. Genial aloft tunnelled
drill righteous, smiled near privateer event
lean backing; gambol sessile by stupor fresh
wick on turn tureen, formation. Intact acid
hanker soothing forebrain mingle salve avian
wrinkled ocular further future panicle asset
strict fitting sacrum onyx honour debated.

## Calculate Omission

Unfold, refurl loop fuelling temperate finish
over fire watch which spindle, protean binded
protein extort rustic immense. Reflected off
same enter proofing pitch upmost winch alter
pennant, twain salvage furnish spiral hostel
burnt umbrage carriage drove printed. Flinch
blunted overtly, non-trivial sensation remind
both found bred lining, cloud filter profess
exile plaintive surface; regent employ sent
instinct or most wink, undercroft, aftermath.
Whence dark for payment segment, engine went
censorious touch basic matter fitter organic
stop transept, flailing arm failure, loaded
broken out-step split retaken. All awaken,
passion inflamed pinion custom benchmarked,
optimal sanction benefit roused pertain in-
dented. Fantastic misfitted altered feature,
by planet sonnet rampant most must invented
dripping fate opaque fluted tramp milestone.
Reign precept off-course bested after wise,
test before nor prized nose known enthroned
vast invest shaken down first afforcement
pursuit toasted, calculate omission acute
fishing rescue obscurest dark wooden inch
purchase issuance cup western action step.

## Scar Circus Friction

Whether however savour future or notice listless famish precinct parish, inspect tincture lank succulent bent service mimicry. Imitate dye modulate oration connect afflicted civil profile, crocus dense while lop-sided frayed ill march through groom in room, roam turbine for final sermon demon respite. Incite trail profitable organ traverse induced birth-pang wrinkle discrete canal cancelled thrall type contusion all set to crack broken, autumnal saffron perform locket bit facet glide, deft reticent objected. Crop let-up notary strim stubborn, symptomatic float path ration act scar circus friction ankle blight scuppered preview verging crude eastern maxim, none if protect attend home went grind rancid. Pat vexillum pea-brain confession attract loyal doubtful, arrest fell trim training dosage platform; gradient impulsive cosmos rises, to bind secure weld lend admission infants link polity attack. Bruise resented furze infused, confluent packet ocelot faucet lop grating, ocean rick. Ticket prison season, mock further elder mental upbraided scent integral neurone own firm claim submission.

## Docket Alight

Shell to pearl fill shelter shield impeach
ballast lost stripe derelict peel, diligent
currency gist tetherance foisted persuaded
denser marl pit pious increasing, augment.
Hurly-burl built pier lock price formative
grid illustrate dative viewcast cabin top
bream winding conduit fin film to firm she
apply eaten, wheaten obvious docket alight.
Under cluster wear off whether picture lime
album pointed practice voice pulse, cancel
thurible repeal rental or primeval, anvil
wintergreen. Gainful sufferance, sidereal
realgar portion version share richlier far
semblance adjust ricercar since yet truce
trice lint, advent minted rustle clamour,
all true please to follow fabled land-fall.
Innocent trait often clam tight converted,
roof settled auction win, bidden accent out
slope auricular fraying match hidden wing
inclined span mind this ring: funded once.
Binary cistern action reveal gavel paving
store, pyretic crow cowardice critic twice.
Taciturn frontal sibilance fissured hasty
craft, mast phoenix shellac mistaken twine
exhume remaindered murex phalanx crevasse
advice bistort or crude enough. Keel whelm
end us send crush sand piper dipper snap;
Linctus firecrest clipper will accidental.

## Slight Breath

Cradle tee saddle incisor molarity privacy
candle suitable meddlesome parallel, listen
infamous session prime tremble, treacle on
tread rushlight celebrate receipt. Crystal
or single rail follow siding, sidle viewing
in steal dolphin lacking singular almond on
signal missile, circle parcel elfin sailor
first pierglass immersed brave font client
mended lie down. No one vitamin whist cask
forceps, index numerical glistening sparkle
whistle on tap fluency. Less defect tipped
fact countenance comedic median, outworn
thread middle plead detailed boiling fuel
aslant indite. Slight breath indrawn turn
crucible dismissive, crucial avenging in
overhang tangent frank. Back to bank, mild
attempted frolic cambric oscillate defunct
expect assertional imminent stack unsunken
scalded regression. Turn about rite salute
habit lax obdurate daily fully mollified;
bid construed idyll angle, press steed eat
devout bred picking least pickle. Ordeal
swale on moor streamlet asset impudent if
fresh digress ionise prised loose, taste.

## Sow in Sour

While after all hail stumble blissful nil
farmer former rumour, western plaster born
best humour stain alarmist ambiance. Tryst
and saraband issued denial levelled overall
wand to bend indic lament; flank grill well
assist plain tail current fluent campaign
wool curl banded at gate chalk, night. Omen
reversion welcome spline torrential worry
predictive lactic archive, on to mingle by
audio crew, style incubus pressed voice off
produce cast nurse dispersion; animus bye
enticement, lacewing brewed winning short.
Climb up late plight, ensued vine charge at
dawn-light or glimmer, intervals resigned
ascend chrome made suddenly avian employed.
Past lucrative relation faction greisen, on
often solemn mine threat thereat eaten up
near luck frolic. Avail divested vocal cap
choral single player owner problems theme
attainment, grown prevent attentive deemed
olivine must toast. Frost encrusted causal
alignment, chilled furrow borrowed signage
arctic fault dealt tamper preponderating to
envious ballast adrift. Yellow waste double
us too, sow in sour durable seal brandish
in effort dual croft surf almost impressed.

## Tomorrow Canyon

Arable sample saleable wagtail enter sink shaken sullen wait before pattern floor in wing broil indeed lucid, affront milk persuant detail spool pound truculent foolish and found, recant. Catmint neptune proline amenity sanity, mail chained bound melted crude painful; wage engage most crossed to tinsel fossil actual. Opinion lonesome ill ground, when grandeur in mixture glutamate frustrating and powdered; blood tie scrape up liquid peltate scarlet trestle wishful credit oval tomorrow canyon. Implicit wake negate crayon decline boon urban bane nip tight surfeit, future perfect practic ail milling whole. Tepid sip instinctive tint imprinted, languid civil willow regimental fire friary manic trephine, recline cream. Uncounted patient in coal seemed holocene broken sanctuary offering, replace massif risen eyeful glacial impugn. If then down blame flown braggart certain crane on bill junior entertain; escape disdainful polar crape cover, revival spell oracle fanciful hive leaven leaving simplified regression.

## Guardian Fitting

Sloop clack fissile mockery saviour direct octane contact beckon tick reptile secluded, unction rissole actuary stick point moreover further score; boiling socket power pockets misfitted behaved implore fraction returned. Torn back tomorrow knife oath pierce digress dacoit stilted, gilt parcel lacking fill dyke feverish, favour packet scrip gauze mistaken liken retake fiery. Placate blind-sight gull wallet failing trout harnessed, office skarn habit flame; percolate till indurated, talon trillage adage heave paradise. Guardian call fitting team flout rule pallid maculated aim haze, outer blaze forehead, prided innovation profit, angular intimate scoop. Echo troops owl grout distinct thanked or might so curt, caught catgut mackerel, aquatic tricked out flicker tack prismatic colic, at water basic wealth famish. Linger to finish radish off malice gruel trowel untrue festival, missing tappet slipper salted new butter chilled infested waist, adpressed lucky epitaxy lately silent treat. Smitten median grain entrusted.

## Contrail Caramel

What is said sidemost tucket coastline pinned
conquest drafted, rectory monetary gorse dice
envision, commission apostlic factual undulate
distilled vapour; coarse stupor arrogant evict
leaning bushy nightlight. Commiserated or yet
diorite distortion corroded intuit carefreed
fun onion, munch easel attended pride mustard
distraught warning in diminish banish repent
astonishment; given bracket wicket surmisal
alliance drawn down turnout intimidate. Fate
white optional take retail nail head to plate
escheat repinement; instigated gale frontal
temple trample footage revised. Tactful into
decided intemperate fountain remounted, slid
payment playful brain apple corrected. Went
deceptive integral moralise, displeasure at
spinneret discuss rigorous the birds and very
beasts webbing nacreous billing lift further
deliver, paint repented wain obtain draught
costive avarice. Dub trail signal recalling
layby agreed while away, whither when want
resplendent, proficient censorious or taper
mercurial suitor. Contrail caramel mileage
prize pin drawn link indignant, sociable to
ouzel whistle craft first after left over;
never flown rivet pleat falcon treat stoup
shrewd strict interdicted already, for mine
crib fry-up loop both mouth hawk-moth whit.

## Slight Pestilent

Cart mirth load wilder endeavour flame in
bream rightful titled into scratch; switch
seamless, preen rebound billed, felled old
sage scrolled thereat threaten theatrical
voyaging folded. During ribald utensil oil
route slight pestilent, heighten shameful
wandering one after twine been silent sake
bent ransom cramp island. Surround pamper
cosset dilate confiscate, prevailed tool
spoil suspected thicket, wait; up-end try
attend remand simplify implicate pannelist
mostly inscribed dry level accurate omit,
languid. Termite trilobite strait mollusc
twice-told disgrace voice folded zeolite;
buffer attrition, shield drake pike darken
estimate, alert swoop lenient profligate
panoptic oestrogen oceanic singe soloist
digressive impinge alter dome refringent.
Prevaricate horrid faulted token column,
aim rambling spines, policy improvement
in conditional expected skein. Syllable
illegally regal docile canteen, equals
usual steeple vain opine cymbal wakeful;
trip prudence pretence announce, length
in strength dispense revealed stronghold.

## Charcoal Negation

Tip the note up, braid whittle sole, valid
veiled fleet reviled, clip district attract
tangent imbricate rebuke on once; price date
floated sharp in stoat eyelid trip slippage.
Brief us prink gimlet persist, butter oaten
hull silicate dramatic stroke. Membrane own
clean taken tingle avocet, predict forsaken
constricted; up to top, rapid peak angle on
salt profile clinker chanted joint. Double
stop rosin acclaim crown forget instant, by
brake indited advocate clastic exasperated
all or none prime swift. Gravel notable to
play chip friction, charcoal negation whiff
obstructive crisis lyrical legal banished
dace conduce foal did medal; lifted tremolo
crush inspect scale traffic. Offertory in
dialect flake catenate osier easier lactic
promote culm as from token barricaded, aid
berate want and surfeit; halfway fire laid
up to come on, grapple reluctant merchant
profusion. Enter vibrate brow barrow scene
match to reach finish, allegorise run slip
fort tannin reminded, wait native relative
or when alignment ointment cradle in-focal
beat upon a ladle; civil parts cent ocular
theme retain, inflame on thin sample burnt
parent. Porcelain gifted inner morrow allow
feverish, encroach best miss lavish for now.

## Impulsive Character

Dollop percept factual prism nonpareil ice
bone bison drone sculpted, nuptial hospice
limn spoon refashion dishclout; maritime
auspicious daggle sprung galosh ramble on
battle-plan, doubting fumble price for dice
montane unwind; deeper measure posture crop
migrancy alliance pulsing trapeze paradise
iceplant serene. Naming pruning pursuit in
purposed embroiled, fiddle crumble dissect
arterial bankrupt. Comatose once or twice
crimson phantom reframe inflamed, dried out
aside over, plied intense terse. Suffused
risk ballast custard, custody rankle finder
inkling emulate, fright; rice cross hybrid
dial rocket fractious brickwork, trackway
allayed supplied ordinate. Plastic syntax
freshen ban flatter somatic parapet, prone
stalled minted cutaneous brought forward,
inverse mill prison watering ultimatum in
costume don plaintive impulsive character;
shower fling higher than singular posted.
Ace to fix manage suspicion off-shore win
stricture infirm film promissory climate
reclining immortality statistic. Aspect
riffle pack choice peruse sit if unless,
uselessly impressive condition in-term
manual resemble, want in hand over hand.

## Nowhere Else Kindred

Scoff tough muffin mountainous groan, in
granular off enough intone grinding lien
gamesome pelmet crafted vigour born; in
draft mulcted bruised winter plenty shoes
after luff previous lantern blame scorn
infamous roaming. Where are thrown autumn
downstream, carrageen tribal tribune met
opportune stem steam limbic astern prize
fossilised cram pillow farrow literal at
fire-pit emetic, ember singular flint in
honey succeeding; dram turmeric on return
crimp edit neglected. Your detain simple
amp minded mill grits blown over, credit
blamed non-final trivial arrow monolith
craven mild childhood. Red spot or lurid
on sealed compact buckram indicate white
background washing cut mission limited,
until swim forward assume tubular sugar
sacred, clam. Precedent pilfered nailed
new prescient alternate dative climactic
befriended, nowhere else kindred damper
solvent reticent. Recoil indole vanish
furnished varnish, average discouraged
by forage toilsome; strain lifted over
incident undulant ankle sunk, provident
alerted finite grant brilliant displace
twice on trellis tacit blink. Who knows
even when wind affine claim, divide bat.

## Tolerance Trillium

Mullion mullein omicron plough-down grid
filled allium commonplace assist case meant
militant success intermix, crass increase
aerate enclose livery carrion mailing; oven
boiling calmative restless galleon sourdough
skill plaster wisteria conqueror scullery
nesh address for tress talion foreign pale
pallium. Plantain liken forsaken bowline
bracken striate rebelled commission bullion
adept tantalum durst he do malleable marble
powder ponderable; pillion arisen tolerance
trillium. Sandal suitable eel shellac out
of pocket gossip assimilate stannate or if
valley paragon octagon irritate asserted
blacken barium simian elided to delegate.
Graven trouble subterfuge frigid spoilage
loose follicle appraise suave complexion,
often brink splash seldom also both tract
solanum telephone fusillade. Allophone bit
beryl colloquial dumpling awning synopsis
bridge worst wastage fluster, interlace on
frown decreasing afric muster replacement
pledge common coralline niece; dated trick
planting wade which one kneel to stride.

## Valid Denial Bribe

Bunkum oakum plumb lumps open sedum knock
ocean diction portion, gruesome faction
floor awesome indoor summon pennon on win,
flan punish until downstream wrecking one
trammel ginnel playful civil dumb waits
instead; instate conduit accession lesion
pinned manacle pinnacle man-made forehead
agreed. Untied valid denial bribe bridled
bangle entangled, assimilate chelated in
modest moderate missed intrepid synonym;
shine declared deplore fantail donated,
crumbling shine ventilate migrate stare
twitter and yet self to move. Elect be
quick and quiet, before while entreat
untrodden, this turf released for twice
face spruce purpose pinnace craze, dial
far for far, furnace palace solace crisp
up index plush audit liberate tactical
slope grating; out-pace rennet retentive
coping practice scratch insist to drift,
patchwork shirk stroke in time tunnel;
wrangle travel interval module induce
smooth breath tempestuous preponderate.

## Stricken Divan

Oblique tablet obligate antique constate
seek out limit, goblet synthetic giblets
far less taken up, summit confirm break
object more rest ingested syndic gaelic.
Worn in tune, beseemed altercate restore
mere lawful trefoil droplets weaken, own
python mutton diligent. Faint aspirants
current curated, lintel sensible yet soon
too now cordial, spurn plummet if behest
in question combusted. Swirl profane bent
upright infancy, stricken divan astound
ingrained, neumes remind; round fasting
pride prior attention, manumission when
frosted lent. Client nor meek resentful
nor sake endure, finial prebend wainscot.
Palliate acuminate acquire furtive, in
branded sentient remission; soon tame
overhead franchise, revise issue maroon
claimant inflamed. Explain on dimension
listen close and best, chromatic imaging
redstart cleft upstart, insects canopy
to staple original content. Rim pretend
end to end, down prime custom turgid aim
to frame, dithyrambic by uttered name.

## Spice Gross Posted

Poultice sufferance mildew clemency fussed dealing plus callous, exclaim prune miracle integer skimming under slender splendid fad graduate imbibe corrosion; maiming ampoule flagrancy crate boater suspended fling want menace astern. Sully imminence retrench off dredging extraneous phial guttering reclaim aid tiller praline, design laid down pineal muffle sprain oilcan; spleen floating outer tribute. Worsted at cost shingle coastal or vestal rival, if dealt looming gusto most tranquil, indelible to commission; afflict wisdom. Shout part down greeting, renown infernal lateral typical, instil retrial declared or wearied; spice gross posted renewed in place across lintels shameful kernel colonel subtle priceless ceasing from mutton both broth. Induce lock slice transmit sleek synapse dispense, wish-for varnish relinquish, about time too. Stewed fluency promissory offended tributary, in victims invited trenchancy sloped styptic garnet, colloid tinctured on trance into entrance palatial different. Mallet mulish auburn stubborn filamentous, lustrous when permanent foundation fountain, new-minted until fundamental dolmen iron industrious, scant; ocular percent whither plant sect traffic already enough stifled, indigent.

## Sea Planet Gained

Natural neutral notable entry, landed intent
plural odds neural transmit unending cornet
correlated nature insert; astute soluble out
modulate native inserted, funding centrifuge
tubular mended let be, pantry deck. Minimal
dental best chance provisional once garnish
or twice mince crush festive modesty twist;
published priceless, mental relapse sepsis
corrected. Presume voluble crescent static,
in frantic huge pedestal fashion serrated.
Lactic duvet polyglot dialectal, distorted
prospective wrapper fancy inventive tasted
mindless, hot grape-shot evidency despite
mistaken, brazen platters indebted. Alert
to metal central refuge, astral willingly
on flight awake, or bite orbit azurite in
credit; ate visor clamour over breckland
claimed, intrusion convince lancet gannet
slightly hurried, wood spinet resurrect:
why not. Nowhere unclear or bracket clock
trickery, fury black covering floorspace
poor effort catch-up implant, awaited in
president flair to coir, derelict anew
indistinct and near to blank. Bigfoot be
gain to unmix, trait or habit spade lever
moreover movable staircase; ever father
mortal molten feather aplomb to winnowing
spun interface. Rancid if rapid brutal
signal fondle see plain sea planet, vast
veiled recoiled, plover natal assigned
becalmed distant octave; lovage brandish
ontop sip lost, fasten occasion locution.

## Fleece Truce Spicebox

Bricked-up bridle broken bowl buttered cue
dank dangerous hyphen, remedial samphire
abut tower lower medallion about anger sun
range presageful. Orange stripe ripen fern
eyebrow easel, invisible sedate silage in
link intrinsic pommel, fortunate; liberate
acute faulted violet, sprint. Licentiate
forecourt courage forage asterisk, lizard
hazardous mischievous obsession, ensured
tonsure preview, mercantile dreamt grown
instated. Stricken ironic parable spooled
pilot summit fermented, safe crew framed
diagram fraction. All-over radial retain
evaporate brim sight film eyelid membrane
deputise, surprising risen golden sized
bruise; symmetry honesty lunation least
foster before last, acrylic. Divulge daze
scenic damage adventurous coriolis meatus
inventive, median crumb split to run, win
flame intern tonation. Traction clement
smite redacted, sacred secretive treasury
ill staged due imaginary failing crouch
toast, wasted cost fleece truce spicebox
metal posset, ammonite. Perjure saviour
rancour gristle notational illustrious
partial, vertex at start first station,
liken to bacon; resulted salt question
irrigate tinnitus pursuit Hittite sane
tomb foreign. To groom then, in vain.

## Foliate Discretion

Natron option pell-mell tragacanth oyster
blistering wave tries, resurgent balance in
over parlour bantam. Acre nitre spreadeagle
rumble tell-tale oh well secured, laminate
distrait rise and shine, tambourine; feign
evaporate headline screen polythene lend
multigrain. Intercede in braille uphold,
in foil wrapped spruce purpose, wet lawns.
Den sett split dressage manage, peony find
pavilion cascade; bravery extreme for fume
plane injured, close shades find domestic
by scour of steam, that things do not move
however long to turn, sprain in demean if
observed posed whenever or stay the same;
customary soft pension foliate discretion
drift often donation. Tenacious scriptive
fissile rotation obverse, reflective terse
immersion dawn chatter better libation, in
gorgeous defile; solution dictum zodiacal
cryptic tab. Rust as posted hearse success
otto lingo how many vary chary watchful
barely rainfall downpour ordain on call
town for towel envisaged average trowel,
beets repeated sanctum memorised homage.

## AQUATIC HOCQUETS

## (2020)

Though all my wares bee trash     the hart is true

– John Dowland, 'Fine knacks for Ladies...',
*The Second Booke of Songs or Ayres...* (London, 1600), XII

## Welcome Handcart

Foolish chalice upset target circumspect react
vapid insipid if wet marshes cahoots will brazen
dimmest business, freight. Awning cruise soonest
bruised up stirrup fat trial. Lost or daft,
boil crevice, divisible graphical, get full on
track placate them all now; point the stick
allocate stitchwort sicken for bracken, broken
off. Find denied ovoid liquid each steeped at
brunt clipper, dapper dib-dabs matter, chat grated
ice trappist; burnish grab likely unfrankly be
infrequent, nut tropic distinct elaborate splint.

Hush clashed missive swallowed posted in mastery,
grind bugle callous backed wrist burst into
front pocket, outrageous perspex rich forbidden
monk lazy; costly and greedy defiance thence.
They want, they will unless banned stuck stupid
over-fast, underdone pat stop fulsome telling
agrimony spatulate, spectrum crash bite head-on
bent necktie backup; impacted or flustered
impeccable, cringe abduct knocked plaited off
in flat cup, renounce impost knotted portal
tarnish abstention lock fast ratchet in traverse.

## Chub Shoal

Produce educe syrup punctual hit slip-up or yet
crack shot, brickwork item faction infiltrate
ventral acoustic daze; hot plover miss silverish
stun form lax often gravamen. Outward plank
reward buffer to seek clatter, bring stung tint
swarm, albumen. Crimped suspicion astilbe,
focal lenitive get quick actual must obligated
adjust promise masthead, undenied. Alone in
brown study rectify miasma, fever staff protocol
from fathom suitor, grossular domestic abet
garnet; faucet impetuous impended fillet crush.

Spoonful handsome plate scatter, otter special
feature ink parlour, lank bring languid flown
stark desolate omen tribal foible; nicotinic bit
slunk underwood attempered sand-pittance fed,
inquest requisite black test fewest stupefied
acknowledge carriage nitrogen all gone tenet
shut past, overmost in blanket primped. Went on
dizzy strait extract the death of pringle in
spun rayon bungle trampled, amerce illusive as
told to, much later; grimace positive accept
triumph cut batter, stupid verdict stannic blip.

## Thicket Slice

Impolite parsnip politic pitch-pine persistent
   tack stud imminent, grommet luck veal wicket
flop. Tarmac act tobacco stucco facile picket,
   which patch blood limit drastic lags; dregs
optic suffice spasmodic bleated, neeps alighted
   riotous pluck merit. Story in fury sea pages
alleged stack bottle label dimwit, colic print
      blocked-up pacific partnership; particulate
bin rattan truck open, buckram activate irate
   licked portion profess. Foxes in boxes musty
brush spread push sedated found radish apricot.

Brimstone define scratch allow yellow relaxing
   brutal offal plaque escape torment, picked
bungle-bungles wrangle assimilate midway over
   cluck fashion; torsion invariant prior mat
pullet wellhead shallow swallow perfective gab
   instinct. Stork prank avert fragment orange
tip wing float ham harbour broker, boulder lit
   flotilla chiffchaff call leafcutter maximum
percipient stratagem. Choice fuse liken option
   or none ever by leverage crank driven, used
spiral premium; gene bowerbird's fervid gleam.

## Duck Pictured

Bit brittle bract ruffle backup, chieftain tic
   fat chance advance blind guess invested;
list notorious distinctive impulse wasteful
   into void promise breech. Each arrested lip
clustered beechmast auspice, brat invalid damp
   lump flagrant showoff shoe wretched next
conversant gasket overblown. Time flown same
   rival sorrel mutter bash butter dish; loaf
set off efflux explosive bactrian caramel,
   fossil crass virtue omission. Wicked blink
sunk already dread badger blaze infirm stripe.

Calomel simplistic sub-fateful magpie butts,
   fitter ledger plug idiot laggard vindicate
dispute flit mattock second. Risible inside
   ham fist purse, baffle reversal elastic
wit ditch sit tight fruit cake, bannock kit
   jam-packed lucky strike buck up triplet.
Importunate stifled either gasp twisted, bat
   chuck could wooden floodplain, obviated
in hospice cryptic all told ensued unfolded.
   Caught wingbeat on down broken archway
tide laid hatch out speculate natal cordite.

## In Reparation

Voluble spinel driving twin bundle, grit screw
politic stub mica shrubbery, late strapwork
under shirk singe lounge; useless terrace ban
spun unless trice robber team. Marine dubs
viand groundmass volcanic pitch, grief noise
probably beaker, induced coma vanity. Stile
meal skyway riven, dichroic banal stroke spoil
trucial might scout latch; devout animated
ominous resin for muslin screaming out latest
warranty. Dozen tighten anthemic repulsive
bay in way, on way entice, indifferently sewn.

Mend dandle flung ichor finally prodigious ate
loan granite spate, dendrite; on land pre-
tended remedy caustic joker, tricots solution
section actinic stridency. Arrogant whole
beat scan and calibrate infested frozen pith
minim come forgetful, gem breadth pulsed
origin sum intact. Beyond lack human margins
brotherhood, pasta in broth mustered wish
dispersed, astriction spendthrift planetary
under plume domination; untimely brash off
contest scratch, vapour islet sulphur blame.

## Wash-fast Lustre

Maimed foreign comatose clutch morose cotton
climbing thirst name-first, boasted sauce;
adverse sense comb to limb tricorne barren
etch claimant stretched, slanted barricade
median sign regain, regal spoilage signal. If
abridge coil, furl recede, fled away storm-
light stayed at red impugned, slowed; cold ash
rowan brine pledge munch, at once induced
utterly. Bet sleeping fast boil turmoil, at
better leather offer idiot delay, suited
employment scored just say twin column found.

Dark bleeding trained this one pit rivet, set
scant blunted, point beside. Brilliant off
facet misfit adaptive tonnage still to wall
clamp, effusive salvage climb out upside
forwent corroded in ravage gorse, alder govern
prove; oscillating stew, tame to manic do.
Fire out below on lifeboat force, pentothal
wallowing delink sea plank provident, in
vent submerge immense toys marchpane; biotic
carefree stuck-on winsome bacchic monkey,
provost cut. Did new ado gruesome braced ago.

## Obvious for Kestrel

Bended knee canal back canopy cannot licence
   black hazard kenotic pint, despite vacancy
in conduit sanction azure frighten, hysteric
   by fanciful climactic gale. Miser cruise
freezing bandbox banana offspring covenant,
   accent carrick incident knelt at knuckle
strike. Your blight steam sale thread spool
   funnel, condolence whence loving through
naturalised kin for kind, unwound. Locum spin
   adoring out and out flint balsam codeine
vestigial on relic skip occupy, split entire.

Factor cabin connected, stupid; protested
   gaze furtive ostrich exacted crackpot,
knack readiest soonest adze. Blazon crimson
   on whim, index digestive reflex canonical
file, graven error spinach fleeced cousin
   polygon cruelty veil. Seem or not fortify
accident, chrome hit viaduct, night-light.
   No fear offering, fumble rustic in rabid
separate destruction, formalin. Within decay
   in prion flaming loop-holes of the bright
hillside accolade, rumple each discrepancy.

## Of Streamy Morven

Known yet knot rescript over knoll flight
   canted newel by knife siphon, argon kin
cream caravan; stake knock irritant even
   quack ducted blink. Acclaim convene pit
arrival lame akimbo, clatter victim lentil
   until tight flame, charcoal wit; growl
to neck frippery, olive predicted attack
   liquor punish benefit. Knee flown horn
distinct plant tropic mace, disgraceful
   nil filament spent far ahead, craving
blooded impound at downland slate efface.

Festive pendant spill certain nascent orb
   urban knit fracture sticking, dentate
fallen out torrid new tint cast, faint on
   rant limiting cracknel last brook; dun
villainy violin turnpike, broach propane
   inquest if sifted lift, left-over last
trim dorsal bunk. Drank virtuous parrot
   sycophant, imitating urn ascribed bred
subsidence register rule-book; mast open
   flask damage consist oppressed allied
remote sap grape token, traction denied.

## Brim on Dolphin

Judicial facing purpose, singular acre oven
   paddock lightship porpoise shall shoal in
wastrel unannounced; wishful claps thunder
   rowlock angular moment, twice shy prison
shadow thereafter. Scatter useful whenever
   retaken stand court account, spent better
if not from fit elision, praise be lifebuoy
   flex gatehouse ointment. Racketeer entire
histogram familiar trunnion fulminate bide
   flatter brother, later on after. Cluster
lengthen in strict instruction, bent option.

Shreds and tailings, touch-paper in mothwit
   debit proximal acrid to chain mail orchid
pollen river bed. Drive out unafraid for else
   surface credence plain sailing, much in
prime affect, cold trick turk fleeting wait
   contract in grain linger henna cinder plug
interminable on sidewalk mutton wasteful, on
   cranial ingenious soonest. Burst in dust
listen detonate, the plunge offence parole;
   failing to chew, shower speckle whistle
felt elaborate stamen stamina on consternate.

## Here Lies, Mended

Igloo so-so caribou growbag common coiled up
   OK, obey gigolo local total together broth
spindle coverlet unspoiled, filo aggro vital
   insurrect, stray debtor. No other wither
else ever escrow you know, or why lay current
   insolvent brook right conflated aromatic
wicket. All down brain polychrome dehydrated
   sent loaded town rat, buffoon crumb clink
occult spinet, undertaken proven lucrative,
   dangerous. Soup mission pitcher picture
entailed, gale enforce palace demonstration.

District destruct packet corrected oligarch
   bitten sully dust, porch alliance; flinch
cerebral cereal wounded anciently. Sprocket
   ligament attentive, split effervescent
foundation in handsome gadget. Limit margin
   albumen lampshade promotion, sink swell
at narrow temper gastric patient celebrant.
   Ask first or rate candid iron tangent,
sum disclaimed on ticket felsic primatial,
   all out debate throat lynx in front care
endure libation. Recent tuck agog ongoing.

## Ode for Jay

In play allayed on way stay-put flute muted
fortunate, ebony borrowing arrow flight
pert diluted. Alert in clay foot, print yet
distinct point to say up, bright; comic
bonded yellow thimble, tremble tuneful, be
placid. Irrigate newt marrow, slight bet
humour crest better still, loaded in broad
light halo follow inward; test to tease,
easier far than hoot persistent, cover over
lid for rest. Press stud day by day on
lesser pleasure osier weft; shirt dry linear.

Suit corrosion cleft bank best consent, went
in foray proud, mode joyful winner, all
astute disputed; no say suppress surprising
sunrisen into prism, maze alongside awl
untried. At trifle looming mewed up tight,
meadow grazed offer fossil, oval stocked
print occupied. Slant telling befallen soon
callow, small window low for misted, mint
quote aromatic; far fields level too. Array
hayloft search plight mellow visage, in
further moat to gaze, ways to tread allowed.

## Retentive Profile

Secluded by season fractionated, optimum on
elegant mushroom fit sporadic; alpine join
late hepatic collar souk. Dint bargain dealt
crack licence, pilot hand to hand script,
inimical wand and bound. Ever why split aloe
allotment single reed whether intent lint
persecute distracted; within next reason pin
junction random aggrieved, extenuate as
all plant margin prevents custom sake. Twin
average issue trance coloured, long spin
expect in version traction flood conversant.

In price commit down to drown by top market
ice relish, furnish locket indent voice
chorus hocus greet; no more oar blade said
mid-treatment shunt. Excess plead design
outright partnership, butter fine words bat
rebate in front, collude dressage serve
attentive riddance pounce lit follow. Birth
trips off sprung wrinkle broach once, if
gifted remittance suits; alleviate candour
fewer ever upriver, batten intercession
at belated hot wait. Some early, most late.

## Braces Dangle

Ping riffle burden fragile, summons impulse
  gap tangle top claim agility, common brim
or else ungainly. Sing lower tonic hymnal,
  dial summit restful, digest wingnut rife
missed to grapple. Eccentric tappet linger
  refrain tender heat, finger warden dulcet
if frugal crinkle, applicant. Count bring
  home open bacon, clove oil mitten plumb
ransom sanction, tempered billet brokerage;
  often improved or in disguise. Notice no
time, twice insist, inclination seal beside.

Where Tyne where Rome for mine intoned old
  planned called to sill, find to keep oak
sweeten sake; installed suited ensign dyke
  electric unblamed, tempest in frost win
at ready tie invited. Studded facade viable
  crystal, twin swallow, tail habit unit
remit table inviolate. All told enfolded,
  dutiful parade prided clinging sullen
alongside copper canyon, to fault dyadic
  cobalt, raided. Crescent plummet itself
tweet matrix, window borrowed humid trove.

## Apt Freestone

Rigour parlour furious sofa remind them in
   offer testify, hemmed backwards flood
over latitude petrel fraud. Ensconce attest
   fluid word parry seek to confine, reck-
less proceed in esteem brand decision, at
   congestion segregate candour prismatic
just lie down. When on behest target lit,
   lakeside psychic inured safety guessed
nifty dragée specify. Fort portal corrode
   labour wanted major confiscate instil
uphill trample. Discrepant breath-turn on.

Colloid worry sooner dost overwhelm ounce,
   descry implicate tighten sultan signify
fresh trust toast. Nest listed sufferance
   wage to rage exact, friction vested in
fleck witty plover lean back blue schist
   monotype imprest. Anecdote epidote dig
cavity migrant tower harbour windpipe tic
   sworn parcel, axle indiscreet abjured
before cranial test; buff ephedrine off
   tufa severance, discredit for askance,
drench glass septic. Look wafer, send up.

## Cross Provident

Exile folio following valiant tendril at
   latent pliancy; into for utmost dental
nostril, servant call over-task. Ruthless
   alien seeping pleural curious, evident
balcony; waste possible dint vanity, see
   across the lee side view most too afar
extant, ornament guile. Gale fusible in
   vocal spent price, praise silent went
induced and hidden, harm perverse prevent
   most. Fits contribute rodent zealous
plaids astringent, havoc sumptuous don't.

Metric forum asylum. Addendum commission
   loop citric album sedative profuse in
spinning eaten tame rejection. Know what
   to make of it, perfected hive client
split orpiment, planet; noxious trespass
   profitable console, undo sealant at
undulant oakum left assist in tropical
   winning. Trim line moonstone branded
tubular optic, intruded funded animal
   fat with anxious metal rims; plaint
coat subsequent front to back, to swim.

## Knack in Best

Singing at night aright, liken dark window
   for parkin sighted, treat outset tried.
Below slake by swallow undoubted, extra in
   vesper pitchfork or at sprung brighten
speculate; talk walking tang frippery ink-
   blot gather up not far off. Loosen hit
thatch profess slide on past concerted, as
   minded stave in wave front, low out to
height. Each other more clever and eager,
   in pack wick aurora, in lyre; luridly
cant ahead apatite, streak always white.

Still stronger ringing, ear sound either
   downy prink dust just match, resemble
attach cord to modal fantail, oracle room
   benign topic attic, rumble at level.
Bake up your pies, day-break stricken in
   purple velvet function, smooth rankle
useful trying around the ground entrance.
   Enhance his trance lexis, into want
affront parade admit parakeet, flit up
   and subsequent waited hour-long, new
song it will belong; in verity, be true.

## KERNELS IN VERNAL SILENCE

## (2020)

Under the opening eyelids of the morn
- John Milton, 'Lycidas'

Hast thou not seen the smoke that curl'd
From altars of obscurity?
- James Withers, 'To the Moon'

Roots should have room to breathe
- Chung shu Kuo T'o-t'o chuan

: a dream needle creates its new chance,
    its many threads in alliance due
with nuts of the season, predilection
    in honeypot, wasp blisters here too

: living moment grants leave wind-blown,
    be in tune with them, they with us,
knit one pearl one, edge two together
    asleep prolific, better out in plus

: plain eye all ready, once full mounted
    to take part with full heart, surely
want as we do, through and too disport,
    time enough to talk and pitch nearly

: how otherwise know the way to clamber
    and claim relief due, yours to mine
apart, freely give and sure both accept
    what pricks a finger, breath resign

: in bleak cold winter bees cluster, kids
    eating ivy gastric disaster instruct
to follow rote and wait form to function
    as per example the looped conduct

: often sufficient by portion shadowing
    plate-mark paraffin stove, unless
through the window flicker to linger
    chill knuckles tighten below stress

: treat to ration scissor snip, fresh row
    at cue for listed salvage, refit
priority acknowledge this along the line
    for classic division, cross and split

: no orchids no sundew yet all simmer mild
    at angle blandish, damp course replace
to align the ensemble now so even clear
    before the windowpane, drones apace

: awesome in pin option sharpen for bright
    eyelid floated now, new out of away
  to skip retraction pursuit claw to bone
    this much as also, ever much to say

: echo contrived by a sponsored makeweight
    in fresh encounter, open frank knot
  brings into view; arrest fill compensate
    altogether what's this, what's what

: nutty slack ancient slow to sable burn
    hardship borrowed from fire to play
  remission guarding the hearth beside
    just spread the paper, get to defray

: prophecy key-stroke, further sit tight
    for sib to tab and set a fair rule
  in share to modulate, home in deft clef
    the key on to turn, the tune in cool

: all careless love cloud above, horizon
    entire I want and ever certain pine
  at front by door our incoming even by
    to wish and dish more, mutual refine

: the clouds I care for, reminded me of you
    curl succeeds to frond, needle to storm
  but just for now skies are turning blue
    to keep the vault of image lockets warm

: how cleft in look, lock for buttered toast
    relief of hard fancy a joke intrinsic
  yet clamp to do its work, grander surely
    in prison else, time outpost forensic

: soluble voluble words free shuttle, enter
    weave forth to back rime by lemon trace
  to follow imitate, midnight surface dine
    auriculas show in snowbound, even space

: crack corn several darnel, early in morn
    not made to care for gone away truly so
risen in sunlight sad not till thereafter
    all for the many watchers, the black crow

: home on the table primitive for sound-bite
    in kitchen parlance, enjoyed the jewel
in neck for nectar, gulled out for gullet
    crowned in the hearth, inset with fuel

: press on out, watchman what of the night
    our ouzel, awake well towards near dawn
how estimate complete absorption georgic
    in tinsel garments all by now outworn

: bleat like new lambs tantamount, with fox
    and hounds in morning dew at level
cut across trace attic repine in hope
    as bees do, day-sign clear and civil

: key in this lock not for ever, will better
    spin away from near day, money to burn
inscription hollowed out with casual chisel
    to keep by finding, train the apt intern

: and no cheese by the witless bird, flit up
    to perch ahead, bending down the branch
the sconce by wingbeat, met free occasion
    to catch sight returning cheep askance

: compose in compost as most action station
    reliant again offered me and you too
devout prepared the clear tailgate populace
    brought to the forefront as counted anew

: at the wheel we'll not sleep, insisting
    to clear space in race to our fixture;
plenty envisaged after prior-cut strain
    recalled in grated evident admixture

: thus taken in warning notorious stranger
    called in and left out, gap in fence
neighbour made shallow elbow marker; fair
    ground target catch blowing, innocence

: foot to stamp arms crossed oven stubborn
    by near miss dutiful minimal comprised
in skeptical reluctant indignance habit
    day by day, each new practice revised

: treat by treaty downtrodden best unwelcome
    plush visits, bank replaced all awares
within loose deployment, first and pungent
    searching the link for current repairs

: shreds and figments won't square the circle
    or fabricate conjunction, to oversee
wishful desert faces oasis in parallel
    from strict inclined to instigate free

: one fine day desprez à fleur jaune hangs
    down from its trusses, fragrant within
its now florid station in rapt memorial,
    laden with dew in hues tangled to win

: summarise sunrise leaf-green new enfolded
    tacit intact the more difficult joys
to join one self to another entrancement
    like a childhood with shiny new toys

: thus too for its own sake, clear airing
    dear attracts silence, fresh tribute
joys to enjoin, shoots dense in quartering
    already partnered form elated, astute

: no more than this is enough, fresh stream
    restores its source, as blood donor
to know the nodding sprays arranged endue
    in history shipping forecast its owner

: by mild rewarding belt sized, seen told
    near tenant, port over the open door
with charcoal shadow so well out beyond
    as yet still accorded, evenly before

: corrosive acuminate not so far estrange
    partly lastly offset reckless title
ingress buy out remote might in notice
    bitten each forsooth his molar vital

: ever since oftener the last real tints
    to risk regression tied, up sufficient
for day to follow, particles infringing
    alike with these others reminiscent

: random completely now, to plug a gap
    in the chief garland over the brow
dearest care to turn enlighten new hope
    to share most fully, late to endow

: pick up your mat lying lost to repute
    calling to help in rescue, proximate
finish childish aim to upfast discover
    ordeal to guess cue, percent estimate

: consult the root spread, tormentil ahead
    of suit curtailment, pinned up there
as where to exercise destiny marking slow
    solace by solstice eventually beware

: come with warm valor alter the air rose
    from the cage disposed to now elevate
crouch hold tight freshen, mission paragon
    broke out open will all-time frustrate

: two to one running, pare down to new pair
    whittle metal or could in common wood
whither or whether dare frame the doorway
    deep along where the top echelon stood

: prop slide distinct with milk insertion
    now apt clarify names, alleviate begone
crux call-sign, bygone wheaten crackle, for
    up by the shore-line, always and alone

: brave archers as to eaten not yet tomorrow
    looked forsaken return paper silhouette
weave searchers as to, ready view, flaming
    dawn pigments, evermost or without regret

: rosin amber cuticle, living in tight hive
    fancy beef tea, originate a fuller week
past the relic attraction digressed promise
    to find out if next after tide, entreat

: surge protected volt spelled quake induced
    mint cogent, imminent adamant this ring
to joy in virtue suture, gradual repair
    from front to cheekbone, prone to sing

: doze to dozen zazen wake lark upward song
    prudent system cistern fountain overflow
promise to furbish best able, retorted flex
    quick to first guess, soon by yet to know

: salt risk rod and staff persisting, or wilt
    fair grasp start pronoun, go lower than
extra margin, when retire once bitten up
    system amended accorded instant to plan

: risible probable laminate overland strike
    line into, line after govern enlisted
steam diapason the children, by scintillate
    sup in straw, laugh wildly as resisted

: etch batch grisaille, close faucet rising
    to fond attach, fine-spun in fire drill
parable fictive planet rebated adhesive
    trail back foot crack slave at the mill

: other than one, interferon term excepted
    wrapped choice rapid lit-up besought
lock syllable humble impress, lessen by
    lesson wound up weeded and distraught

: by wick tremble wasted, mark fault to go
    from check-bolt acid index march paste
width annex coding, deference vault, tame
    unsealed and foiled catgut input laced

: with conduit solicit micromesh tunicate
    holding close armrest crown unsold
flexuous suffix old folks leisure pit
    warm along arms these leaves enfold

: basic crept inside, unafraid of symmetry
    reason in antiphon invariant probate
at table docile mark, fault curfew sifted
    treasure in measure, early enter late

: either window thrown open, amaze gazing
    recall joyous morrow endeavour, ankles
wet with dew, eyes forward, avid instilled;
    care for many more at crest tap tangles

: brought back bonny scot-free draft inspect
    tarnish the birds further and better fit
sash upper fresh, wean from supper parlour
    rumour warm, root entreated impact remit

: syncline leaning broach vigilant conflict
    wind-up where you are, out yet and go
will seize for traffic, slow heart heated
    in moment fragrant crouched to overflow

: hold out hold on invoke the team manifest
    all in one tinder ditty box, even to dire
and tender ordinal by multiple affections
    not inimical by burning, mitred in fire

: for upswing gaelic retrospect, ye shining
    braes along the turning way, affrighted
  come down yet never leave; dissipate scrip
    portrait each staple for tissue, ignited

: acerbic undaunted yet if of maple fipple
    while still the air, unmatched to leave,
  resounds, freely in warm impulsive airways
    hereafter, or sleep if contravene, bees

: gathering ready to leave while still fine
    currency under cloud, patience endured
  paintwork can be deplored steady as ever
    insured in top proof, so as new procured

: declare lozenge natal exploration unknown
    garnet decorate gannet, raucous outcry
  talk back even to walk moreover so proudly
    ignorant before brisket, first to deny

: deceive fervid for languid anyway, proof
    to cancel factional not to leave shelf
  life issuance berry staple crimp or tinted
    confession agent instigate, up to stealth

: name so yet unclaimed, one each of tree
    for remedy, in ration of seasonal sluice
  early ripe in type after, acrylic comedy
    sufflated and wrested, park yr jeep loose

: stick around gum-flap delected, cream puff
    no instant credit well beyond belief
  all around darker lights, mostly seen links
    black in or out fresher shadows beneath

: guardian nominate melt cascade laid aside
    down to sleep who'd be such close set
  bell-clear to sound, raid permitted early
    one morning, if fresh grass still wet

## TORRID AUSPICIOUS QUARTZ

## (2020)

And the likeness of the firmament upon the heads
of the living creature was as the colour of the terrible
crystal, stretched forth over their heads above

- *AV*, Ezekiel, 2:22; for 'terrible' Geneva Bible (1560)
has 'wonderful'

...as with Stars their bodies all
And Wings were set with Eyes, with Eyes the Wheels
Of Beryl, and careering Fires between;
Over their heads a crystal Firmament,
Whereon a Sapphire Throne, inlaid with pure
Amber...

- Milton, *Paradise Lost*, 1667, VI. 754-59

Isn't a crystal a genuinely *substantial* and inspired being?

- Novalis, Freiberg Nat. Sci. Stud., 1798-99

1

Edit elevate addit quenching the melt double
basic rock faced placated facet geode crane
waver, never yielded forward faring in turn
on time anvil bevel woven credit; caret can

intruded bifold bicuspid could be welcome,
glass borrowing interplex collected fleece
for flax presume fleuron olivine breakout
mica phonic outing veered clastic ridden up

quartz loving twin reborn in gypsum plumage
turn stone to clasp dearly, rise at first,
tall hunter's moon closer nebular brother
in tarn. Inflected line obsidian dark flight

dance-like ridden flaxen inflexion prism;
contention trident spendthrift, rich text
volatile mass eruptive membrane, far over
the spirit waters zircon replacement coded;

2

Satin orient iridescent handed screw axis.
Reticulated square tiers mimic snowflake
bladed swallowtail chreode cambric infernal
trail deal colloidal hopefuls compounded

hold to name ballade mirror recalled shield,
tender state park cornet fillet nearer breath
let indented; latent snowflake thrown into
dear airstream diffracted settling same done

intimately sedulous dome. Veins of tone white
vitreous lustre in foster so flautino, seal
chalcedon right or left spangled wrist, to
watch perch coming on by; ikonic net slide.

Layer towards clear affection impressed as
ever must, to over sill, vivid to interfere,
foliar lurid tints use of jasper oven-bright
chaconne zonal rufous. Intact into tighten

3

Fusible care hermetic caret dilated plight,
cleavage of age attractant or scape exchange
influence mediated. Visit crystal host nested
address intergrowth suffix, plate overlay try

stripes x-ray, denizen becalm teeming when by
alight pendant; loyal felsic speak for, unto
dormant greenstone dykes, alkine feldspars
shallow salt pillow, herbal upper mantle on

channel trap residue folded hands pace egress
together or whether, air past least manifest.
Winsome silicon aggregate, crystalline clouds
hillside slopes don't slip ice felt entwined

by upright forearm pledge; aventurine carbide
twill heart-shaped twins contact fluke habit
veiled intrusion silicate appetite, pink patch
harpsichord obliged vertex onyx; apple-green

4

From nickel ice-cream, conic cutting whetstone
glass shards. Bollards in error voices mingled
will shelter alabaster louvre satin neck flux,
increase fine flakes break fast stay free way

sunrise praise be, graze safely companion on
join turning shave to smooth in four decades.
Told talc sheet, quartz contained, spirals by
gradient of charge undulant and peeling, on

diatom collide straight chain stung complain
violet cubes, scarlet tracing compact; face
wet. Arsenic firework citrine veins, single
metal holdfast at long last base pilaster to

crust reaching ocean bed; declaim ahead sit
vitreous upthrust volcanic tell heart rebuke.
Out of mind-set eaten fluke to flute, result
credit eye to eye agreed six-pointed, into

5

Roseate asterism shining look reflect, crib
before silver, safe promised landscape bite.
Or as tears of the muse, as petrified ice
advice invidious concentric, bloodstone drop

fast cornice burnish foil agate adrift dual
in surprise package. Welter adhere consistent
twice limb blamed candle prominent, sluice
voice by soft succession impressed. Call out

fervid dyed flint ridge over-ridden chalk
precision dealt grade terrace stairway all
told included stripe advanced sylvan residual
trace entrusted coffer, recessed galingale

ink tolerant cypher furthermore. Absidal re-
lapsing serve to stay overplay sail induced,
wasted essential internal, chatoyant come
back reflexed be minded; bound ingrained as

6

Deemed section plane crown, growing curt
index intercept ocean leap fuming cast up
spray dealt salt. Fault cleft if surplus
fracture marker water seepage patronage;

capsule frail tenancy crowded difference.
Mercuric detent emergent monocline, vane
derived ravine timid present arms remit
turn ransom question, full sufficiency

native aggregate vertical crossed prism
seldom once named. Looming dial insipid
pleading tame innocent reticent consent
within, claiming prune phantom detriment

famous saving livid loving-kind; mix press
together most often fortune, fit surmount
ardently main logic wicket cambric spread,
intended near parent ferment held on tight.

7

Latent discontinuous along host planes, sum
weight retort friction; start from single
crystal hub knot omitted, strict. Impulsive
site bellwether corrie sold salute, mutation

win confirm infusion opt, brain link sectile
catacomb retained cauldron shield, residual
if melted downwards, alteration sugar planet;
better you had, gamble anhedral help to print

open-cast, least massif face first dentition,
none like the present illumine fasten intent.
Swing elbow out farrow marshal profit scale,
critical stone astonish overdue admonition.

Maxim samphire involucre come to stay viol
converted likelihood, relational swerving
indusium. Trace icing pasque flower medial
first power dilated, nodding contentment.

8

Promised be prominent say when inturned let
latterly graven dismiss groove estuarian,
monocline hopper crystal oblique twin cloven
wedge forage tabulate; prism face alpinist

from sullen earth survived, longing in form
trinket wallet preview implicate. Both to
speak sounded, call as cannot blend deflect
graphic respite frisson, arch incumbency

defy their extravagance tilted at interest;
save practice honest, spur to demur agree
unequal share refracted pair, cubic habit
ransom indeed nor yet to wait protested

excused in silence. Stake fast broken up,
incriminate latch blessed out for thatch
retorsed accented which converge, profuse
intense deliver; eminent search replete.

9

Apt mountain green vein partnership crack
blain dichroic sundered plaintive, pedal
oracle cavernous sent fabulous nightjar.
Near arbour wears breakdown beryl violet

flame marine sandbar; part-ordered faded
coincidental louvre cinnabar volatile mix
vermilion spill. Sub-metal chips, opaque
prism favourite planetary losses, save in

forces canal edge of slivers; native guess-
work cosset vivid captive chill pacific
oath moss too, how if foundered mild wise
capsized denizen, calm. Intrigue figured

prevented, fissile productive caravan on
morning plain, white chant ice synoptic
level fascia; pressure soften stem in
tune disguise, fast pattern intern voice

**10**

Saffron primitive premium dark acanthus,
frivolous atrial service mansion; credit
conscious tribute trilobite. Scan liken
lessen, mint obvious rowan paragon fit

mission detriment; scattered fulminate
at census many ninety proven, dune affair
cast off. Previous fibre averted, rite
infringed fetlock, stint habituate spirit

knelt ankle simmer cream; granulite with
flat quartz tuff, moistened crust mostly
belonging particular pent. Ring-enhanced
now thin column vellum stem fold placid

integer on profile model, sinus diffused
at subsequent revalued oxalic anglophone
contusion. Rampion skittish flourish often
reversed, night's black bird, sweet woods

## 11

Down impart writ to loosen avian beacon;
phrase coin elegant, whichever foremost
penchant, plain-chant complicit suite,
hang fire oblong or dire dual boiling lit

lung accession, inner pyramid face release
noise lavish salt parrot. Differ tongue
cautionary impress cracknel nickel reduce
productive solar flare, bier wishful allied

skimmed self-risen. Good both ways median
believing life path source, gravy way sleep
sway immersed; low profile crept root went
blanket crooked, turquoise turnip outside.

Plectrum no tantrum blink nostrum, fashion
saving box cloud shaded plinth; otherwise
since crowd tint candid braided, lurking
marten bitten, implement consistent same.

## 12

Strictly spoken tacit caption tailpiece at
pace syphon, grid heron mortal annex fix
delusive shot-silk at suppletion symmetry.
Folded fluid validate orphic, pallid late

occlusive nightwatch, arm in armour dredge
homage device; go on with pursuit package
synthetic appetite, gelid intensive ogle
alongside. Twirl fireball, overt thunder

promise slated sleeted mannerism tactful,
unbroken youngest widen apartment, batten.
Proficient initial skills, ledge furnace
paradox untwisted, ill-met prowl to profit

amity; upstairs commence this to cover
native silver reckon invented, stellate,
in flames optic datum discretion hence
offertory static, munificent delicacy.

13

Oyster hysteric outswung sacristan canon
motion cluster fardel, record polar rotor
relict cross overturn; aloe subtle rutile
spur inclusion. Cypher link ex mafic disc

lattice both carry chariot pith vanish
fled, integral daylight; palpable front.
Rustle incur pestle one after, later up
turtle, toothless tactile needful after

nappe; trim like no time, pantomime elfin
pinnace, eventual cornice zest. Masthead
ready gelatin requited, ignition bacchic
daze foremost battle hurtle bear across,

bound far off squadron sanction entrusted
at very least; price guessed fluff best
scud cloud rebuke advice cohort minion
ration syncopated, twin twinkle estimate.

14

Other over to gather, haste away so soon
whether or not time short, harp together
wasted, nest woven name in sand assured.
Heavy veil revealed skirmish taken away in

sight, barite also in white, wheel under
meal grade arpeggio sent to blend, fancy
babble, rebel cranesbill affect subject
link. Riot forth pit lyra viol kneel, to

kite resplendent in vestment overflown;
variant charcoal bellow typic lentil
asplenium datum saturate, infant paved
with swirling tuffs, spheroid enchanted.

Without failing retail succulent house-
leek implant provident, blown at creaking
wing rescue fluent issue precedent. Else
whoever not, key insert client diffident

## 15

Prior fabric quiet forever in flow instil
covert; formic comfort pliant implement,
astute. Scroll weather allege fever, few
infused painted in window silicon debate,

denote. The whole crowd, will all entrain,
surge forward unhindered district flit
platform harvest grammar fulmar petrel
ochre pocket pleat imploded, by florid

instigation; but you like none foregone,
by turn within caparison, show beacon
light conflated imminent, flatter before
and after change of heart. Grained yet

unmarked, in market employ far out, seen
by tort to thrive reversed conversing
sung retort; stand clear of flight opaque
in granite, ferule beryl smart. Alloy by

## 16

Ahoy call out promote, the flash of rule,
flask complete in truth, portico; renew
can she excuse, unbruised by sudden jolt;
no-fault claim restores beyond blame or

too woe ashamed in eclectic wonderment,
shall we assent uncrazed far beyond in
praise amazed. Set out to caulk the seams
suspicious, past talkative walking and

waking no hurt contact plane entwined,
no late fault; generic yet absent silken
pilaster foster brave redoubt confirming
undreamt, the leaves grateful stalk joyful

in playful trait. Gopher go further latter
step footage leaning back up, second help
satin hem; solvent sleeve zinc blende at
prismatic habit green followed track, to

**17**

Start. Stalwart classic new deep forever
warm esteemed, close-knit local in loyal
fast colour wick. One after, next before,
laid down passion passing in front; in

leaves once more chaplet lift constant
heartfelt skill, remembrance tip oblique
bract avid average; lovage silent face
across pennine bridge, scalar to peak

digest. Taste and see afresh premiss,
mortal despite side portal in profile,
prodigious cycle of ages, be pasted
explain self-raising infant plume, in

trumpet abounded perigee, small airways
blazed ahead nigh at hand of one tell
another. Pitch salver badge awake do
entreat in wild surmise, whence all

**18**

Our fires desire, free on sail, arise.
It must sure purchase mettle woven,
sickle rebated beaten coronet toward
exhausted flares in mounted dryas wise.

Paddock now locket grapple folk full-
grain clary soaking proof surface eye
to fly contraction stubborn, play in
full availed, tailor-made sandwich.

How come this aspirate bisected feat
taken aback welded filament, sheer
fathom drain endure repair restored
heard tell improve, each shining hour

conduced, invective interrupt compare
great things with small agile placed
face to face, coalesce slice supper
sensible manciple even return aware.

## SEE BY SO

## (2020)

Darkness stored
Becomes a star
- Samuel Menashe

foot path step overseen
   declaim, abjure by
forsworn plantain tips
   nectary; deflect leaf
wing nut fitted slight
   connected. Arrest at
time package forestalled
   tractable, congruent.

gate in turn revenue fit
   well head attended, in
avenue reach abstaining;
   herb robert infused
entitled forenoon not for-
   get out walking get
to work, aspect lamp lit
   perfected damp wicket.

other than before train

   follow, swallow tail

opening entrance portal

   help on further, domain

convex or lenient price

   improvement; week day

confirm all chocks away

   say play time undenied.

luke goshawk warm how

   many returning, own

name object stoop fate;

   flighted ankle sentinel

by sand dune coins, wane

   under wax seal truce

none single candle, up

   sticks effective, thus.

avail valiant, be come
    constraint briefing
elect contrite assort
    patch work threaded
private elation, whim
    cypress break fast
reflective, cast iron
    antidote recurrent.

russet bark in way fare
    bye tree blow winter
wind offend not unkind
    graphic digression pin
search likeness missive
    key ivory attain; we
neither groom bridal, nor
    solid banded eremite.

various snow forward, to-

gether seeded mention

palm corn flower, blue

by love's working sift

unlock thresh hold taken

beseem near grain yield

lost mill grist laid, to

miscreant drastic rise.

stay treat in tangent

and fill now near bowl

of night venerate ointment

colloid slight tinted

fishery mandate, company

bridge work spent ill

dale folded; down hill in

later willing spooned.

## DUETS INFER DUTY

## (2020)

The year's best sweets shall duteous rise
- William Collins

Douce Dame Jolie
- Guillaume de Machaut

**DECK 1**

Sycamore calico evident. Plausible pimento torrent
  would operate fastidious, prolix iterate entrance:-

front fortitude back stop buck thorn, consultative
  faction tint mordant patrician; nonsense in grief:-

ahead how many there were, adpressed decisive actual
  forestry, wind-blown betterment distinguish for:-

density ruling no time not yet, went in first domain,
  bought even currency derelict or might, pick up:-

as birds do, for chatter in charter flew; immersion
  top-end corridor caravan granules supplanted less:-

numbered glossy lamps to preen aspen foothold pinetum
  owner, conical capering dissipate to lock onward:-

boundary twice indignant, all come within you'll do
  as others, medial to medal, bar tend deal in dealt:-

gander tender coverage, digress fort hazardous quiff
  praline in-line hazel solemn between powder self:-

servitude magnify cut back, populous village luminous
  infraction comestible trifle espalier veering map:-

scalene open maple notable scrimshaw inuit alternate
  fount sentiment or so or not yet but for situate:-

## DECK 2

tropical tone pitch, scant naphtha incidence evaporant
    careworn optic twitch redstart budge aerial wit:-

to bite fraught smitten none alike, not seem fitted
    give over level meander, flower bidden occupancy:-

coin travel wear down undulant flit fever sacrosanct
    rendition transfer blame, impart to govern in flame:-

tortive reckless ponder daytime each away sufficient
    cycad perchance industrious, paper-chase defiant:-

play coy battery agree in large to charge outwardly
    soaked head to foot, unheard more sweet assigned:-

vain rotor proton spins defiance, often by un-ruled
    foolscap invention to the brim disport elegance:-

atrium speckled, and crowded or better late deflected
    in proxy woodland good things deployed examples:-

go even light and fair, action remitted as altitude
    magnificent ashen fringe, consistent and intact:-

restorative tempest intrusive aliquot imprudently
    between birch bank settled, cyclamen clustering:-

foster love between, arraign beholden sermon armful
    prevailment croissant hand in plans shared out:-

## DECK 3

elder in folder unharmed by swarms of lucent care
bear me across, bound to go plead for reach staff:-

wattage want what wish wills never enough, influx
light inward tablet discovered, portrait shield:-

flare to lean import crescent snowed out, invented
covalent sweet in pressure all presumed, nacre:-

acute eyebrow mellow longed for, overland trailing
sucrose benefit. Proemial candescent better led:-

as gone to ground earthnut florin additive ascent
in hairstreak suffer hanker alabaster reel abed:-

opportune eagerly, paperslice due mince
enthuse furnace obstinate wading outward spruce:-

promissory imitate dehiscent, leaf to leaf aside
shed training obtained ill-defined confluence:-

rivalry jacket, gather here lies although ignite
smoke to russet obligement, by syrup consent:-

orange foraged shallow broad expanse, buckthorn
sold team to claim intermit, toil foal, tower:-

principal aeon nothing ventured same to win, den
skilful dwell ready parable agreed condition:-

**DECK 4**

east kingdom blossom rivet, haven till undergone
    praise device hawthorn intermit each spruce:-

coppice afforded flight manifest once only sent
    satiric offended child-light; yours inclined:-

upraised together witnessed, shining white, snap
    crisis surface, inveterate incised corridor:-

declaimed. Held infusion customs vibrancy free
    to roam, line to mission clam vibrancy bacon:-

fortunate incidental presided flint endurance,
    struck flake noun attain nape shorn daytime:-

save off released. Unseen detriment trip indited,
    tantamount penchant loop remitted, anchorite:-

cell block sideline, consider embassy walled in
    vatic enhancement perverse pervasive flute:-

declamatory willowy riven arrowroot inclement
    elemental goaded hedgework lark new spilled:-

coral fluorescent at open-hearted merchandise
    intimate hornbeam fathom legal into plagal:-

so-called mounted delphic recollect, imminent
    tentacle clad overture at surety pre-eminent:-

## DECK 5

Almond found wounded, gained often at soak down
  bracken ditch; catch up to second-hand holm:-

ivy too lively preach. On a hillside filling
  all salmon resounding fallow size detonate:-

bounden pitch burden, teach welcoming newel
  diffident interrupt crowded. Allowance in:-

merge upper spurge at milk sapphic fortress
  treasury rust-free breezy swelled whelk:-

purpose don't mist innervate, deny acacia
  moisture why defrayment intercept. All:-

before, none between after retain full brine
  halogen offer inference yet near later:-

turbulence; grope at the doorway pretended
  aumbry, bramblings white elm elemental:-

insouciant qualified siskins conditional
  prowl royal ice board unfeared mildew:-

due or covenanted breadstick lit crossbeam
  instruction, plagal retaken illegally:-

astriction already how many amplify tint
  contentment shredded partition spent:-

**DECK 6**

having to be dealt, brown bear salted, cave
   navigate willow face, airs in grace plus:-

down confirm shallow next below, stairwell
   near stars crumpled canvas obvious felt:-

stitch, yurt soon warm, bare stony basement
   angle for sea eagle focal by yew flout:-

wilt moon suit tureen must have been column
   wrapped matched resist after thirst foist:-

distant owlish slacken, motion will parallel
   braided out-of-doors raised crows candle:-

stick back without rim pearl barley scorch
   averse avarice lest cuts a dash unless:-

bird-watch voice votive stipple fleece endorse
   counterpart passionate; aggregate mount up:-

pupil narrow ache harrowing squall telluric
   famous righteous by night-storm mown down:-

painless cabin wended pride of place ferment
   acknowledgement, to yield prior bent polar:-

strict imputed silent dare, woven thread axe
   trace livelihood intrepid unwind accrued:-

## DECK 7

mournful frown weapon, crampon stir fine-bore
   stirrup when gallop headland distilled:-

hint gruel last coverage; alleged chaparral
   chantry quandary wrinkled, single oval:-

dolphin live enough truce undoubted squadron
   patch new-grown spring freesia apple mint:-

taste beseech must oft remake inversion hood
   plaster hill-top master, tamarisk insist:-

copper plosive impulse crop debate, convert
   sill fusion whisk glad, add pinion leap:-

above-board frayed orbital, new in heap at
   tether. Planes importune samara digital:-

seceded, vestal aggrieved hubbub vocation
   remember weasel grist impartial muzzle:-

flinch; whiten beam struck shade impacted
   pageant abstruse moose loosestrife on:-

bank wet to near cliff voice, endear tribe
   tape faded out her freight limit, line:-

linen throat cover may ever tapis footfall
   apparel missal in flood wing adorned:-

## DECK 8

brood inch pack trailed behindhand brighten
   chestnut blazon maroon integral benefit:-

aspic stake sold out for salt, surf racing
   socket debenture, persistent accomplice:-

elemental enamel cemented avenged, complicit
   abstract held off arm's length coruscate:-

sheen route undoubted together glue alongside
   ingredient archway corner to centre, debt:-

inundated liminal cruciform determine awesome
   prune flutters affluent rainswept talus:-

tell us tallow we know sour source, soup bit
   trumpet wainscot equable minimal adjusted:-

pleasure-craft immanent radiant anciently set
   apparent rafter kingpost, jaunt foremost:-

nitric holdfast soon not worsen phantom groom
   becalmed signage foster walk legroom apt:-

castanet rifle boredom, loyal long recalled in
   graft crevice habitual bring to book sip:-

restricted, entrust who would amend amass off
   inducement crepuscular ominous nonplussed:-

**DECK 9**

overshadow remodelled fudge time-span seen in
  faith of the mountain ash sparking rental:-

re-entrant collop; oriental tabular infantile
  sedge explain flush compliment after went:-

through ratchet brevet insidious ridden grape
  jaunt means of joy inveighed harts-tongue:-

ant lift at pawl spool spillage toadflax mix
  butter milk butcher's broom so much port:-

retorted, shared out even event ventral flit
  austral hold tight, head visor capacious:-

waiver, overturned brindle malt shook down in
  ownership ocean promoted flown ream pack:-

parchment hydrate corridor trek. Film claim
  clement warranted calamine ravenous pint:-

astute the same boat fruit apt quoit enamel
  porphyry instinctual befriended witness:-

moulted purport faultless into imprest taut
  handed either skiff, accent wait remote:-

at caught stoat pomade. Indented swivel dell
  gravel aboard as would or not, quit riot:-

**DECK 10**

benefit western companions, mirth extruded
   livelier harvester replica, teamwork aim:-

refuted past divan held broad implored, top
   out fir switch roof day sky assay; avid:-

avian tray collar outlaw indoor regnal tirade
   mortal civic oversight already made, lid:-

t-bone new-born plunder centre-piece effaced
   slice moisten conation dabchick bruising:-

lake imbricate mute, dogwood pike abundantly
   fast to bulbous switch lost-wax matchless:-

crestfallen crocus orchestral knuckle dusted
   site inflamed tight incipient fan-shaped:-

lymphatic tenterhooks; black looks ordain hum
   grove twice depute carbine remains cone:-

imprecise embrace by covetous out rinky-tink
   biotic babel spinneret at lost and gone:-

mustard jousted confluent confederate yell
   coil feather star's grove twice auspice:-

catch as can swim toil swung deputed carbine
   plum far drove limit eastern upswept on.

# ORCHARD

## (2020)

No fruit shall 'scape
Our palates, from the damson to the grape
– Thomas Randolph

### 1 DAMSON

hold up close down first-born attain other
mine damask question, am both laden
mason bee hand-written mansion aimed
tight ransom purple gully crime even
festal acumen monsoon in tantrum, one
on both pucker hue for blood on bone

### 2 PEAR

scent appearing nearby, doorway lure
collision welk stalk and fair in law
confer carefree as others saw at hand
as will gnaw relented, repaired unfrozen
his hermitage secure, passion true clear
daring to glimpse double shape aware

### 3 CHERRY

ready forever to travel, ripe heavier or
safe unravel wary, due to cry
cream edict say through life dye
hue crimson away predict fuller up
heaven-sent, pair limit addit
retrieve ferry twice maroon else

### 4 BRAMBLE

alert to her thimble afric tackle in
doubtful tangle berry foray mostly
preamble, adore let matin spike
asset fraction pricket plaudit eon
ample as optional timbre arch spray
catena found rifle all live day

### 5 ORANGE

manage taken or set, sit rick first
homage perceive derangement go
vowel angel back remittance,
reed fragrant sedge both boatman
nigh to night affright elevate
fringe lantern strong beam plait

**6 APPLE**

recall gnat swarm pip in direct cast
ruffle effect russet tunnel mount
underside, peridot rebate infused
factor credit lax tonnage wide spread
unsick rosebud, core freight rising
adornment eyeful love entire brought

**7 PLUM**

downright induced engagement deep aplomb
ruff plumage reflect sound formed
asdic upforth victorious, singing
turn away target leap over integrate
pittance device, exact measurement
another luminous umbrage timid grot

**8 CURRANT**

muster truly foster distorted, tart
inflict tress trellis dangle willing
all new season rant dry forgotten,
interminable summative prune antic
caught up shall thrive twice cursive
lustre darted shrunk arrant piedmont

**9 GOOSE-GOG**

fast aghast florid loose tail sneck which
last gasping autumn threads waft
in breeze to please crust peep, out
goidelic gossip apace flagrant good
go to, anon frame supreme marine
grimoire save-city awaken attacked

**10 APRICOT**

easter ripe first waist pleach earliest price
luminous alight to sweet within total
simple open discount cheese welsh dish
arabic bird-cry wave tricotage astral
rickrack hot feasting gnostic rice benefit
sumptuous cutaneous espalier soften specks

**11 PEACH**

yet reproach reveal revelry anvil latch
enscone herewith princess sheets
tasted pink-tinted flinch poached
all at once most outreached chill
in how search absinthe branded pea-
soup carom nice one preach to win

**12 MELON**

in tune foreign sane melodrama meal time
plain down thirst by first rim,
they to play annoyance not yet so
gordian neither off to on turn, up
home run, beam melic upshot assume
felon arraignment own unfortunate

**13 GREENGAGE**

towards bough yellow belong in grange
jar tendency wage related even also
reached agreement pitch, at fewest
age-old sweetest session fashion
glove loving, paginate reproof un-
known partition scenic overflown

**14 MORELLO**

so better more and less relative sourest
deeds moving to follow dark endure, or
low eaten bitter mast rail acerbic
enter flavoured elbow, wince once
black sans sugar lingual angular
wrangle cinder armful tell on bitten

**15 RASPBERRY**

conic screen cane drupe alert each sweeten
lain down shut hasp out prickle
asperse to race as very punnet been
deign spore, ever satis deeper tee
rough dimity verity stain abut meant
bowl spill lucid ramify wherry at bay

### 16 STRAWBERRY

wild abet leaned downward scarlet fragile
yet achene repine slender runner
to way credal creamed skim tactful
helping raw in gorge surge to gawp,
swan up stain statin crimson birth
err marking raffish trim, hawthorn

### 17 LEMON

take site rick on left track honey swallow
yellow profess zestful on aid parade for
sharp ardent citric clear-eyed grating
inflict tongue clip verge answer one
citrine stream weep quittance twisted
go my leman eminent on which to sight

### 18 MULBERRY

ripe to shake to fallen spread here go round
bush like tree way, foolhardy off
piste silken sleeve woven mull sheen
motile mulatto mercy be eristic fit
cold and frosty, trusty merry ultimate
branch age seize rich colourant fool

### 19 PRUNE

whisper birch unified run more fast incised
dry-black syrup wisdom, prism trim
secant prudent loose to lose dune
unspoken acute release runic in
prime is one rutile vigour reclaim
bud leasehold fold lain down rain

### 20 QUINCE

meet to sweet cretan paradox soften
quiet daylight inch to sense ought
autumnal flight bitten not shy
quay beside in cell to bury on
sidle whether prolong actual
wince now, why, what you will

## 21 FIG

to care not ignore or yet illustrate
  punish for produce supported
  more finite, grant fragrant or
  seed core roll endure meant to
  figure out right, dutiful if
  gifted aware in share alight

## 22 MEDLAR

hold hard not to meddle better medium
  get addle larboard instead tell
  when said deal me, sold wedded
  lark flown soon apron morning
  aim led along dollar open win
  demean lament don't go innocent

## 23 NECTARINE

are honied skin smooth elected tarry while
  will marine drupe fine attar rose
  brim rhyming for minor, shine from
  within ecstatic great prince far in
  action ejected stone, purloin clime
  beckon confirmable well beneath sun

## 24 LIME

scarce limit other mine percent lentil
  climate coherent ought resign yelp
  felwort violet feline late imitate
  tart in grass, score butt for
  reliance melic fulminate lipped
  ascorbic in rick curled by rhyme

## 25 GRAPES

forward apical rapid in tow, swarm gaping
  cling to cluster rap on pensive casket
  bunch must aspen mention, primeur to mow
  now blown auster vinous lost ferment
  harvest price endowed at cellar par
  living throated heartfelt open trace

# OTHERHOOD IMMINENT PROFUSION

## (2021)

'And, sweet sprites, the burthen bear'

'As if translating at sight
from an unknown masterpiece'

## Radiant in Moment

Just beyond first gaze could now be seen
almost, among the leaves barely moving
in the light breeze, the playful scatter
of reflections in answer, each to other.
Here pause with scant reason, stay quiet,
such a cloud or so in the sky; in patience,
expectancy, what arrives is itself, eyes
familiar with occasion, small sounds as
fingers of visitation from the air currents
open the view to thought's slim inwardness;
coming forward to meet the certain moment
close to competition. Then will be known
what has been known oft before, repeating
its sufficient truth, to be seen fully, and
understood: fortune in fire beyond desire.

## Another Such Instance

From terebinth its own link distilled and full,
to dress the frame for entry in company, close
generous in morning light. Wait up to discover
the calm return, share in good time surrounded
by woodland murmur, chirrup of small birds.
Attracted by insect flight, position adopted
a steady neat heart-beat consistent to paint
its resinous flutter, listen to find out and
catch falling light across green shadows, moss
sparkle not lost, not yet or even ever thus.
Pungent edit at the rising slope, pathway
ahead turning, flagstones in shallow stream
for step to step, upright alert to catch
breath tremulous; the shell will divulge its
folded nature in centre listed fluently.

## Into Reflection

Attention half given, persimmon half distract
close to immediate guess-work; moist arising
glance to hear small sounds, round echo taps.
Sent forward after before held back, in refrain
successive chorus prune affixed, sway fondly
by choice fragments demure, askance. Sense
proclaims tolerant happiness, ripe towards all
warm blush cheek; gather at near level ground,
be easy by size, melt at point of day in custom
fresh option, open hand ask to grasp, motive
arisen upwards. Now standing, still balance
in melodious charm, firm pivot on each of both
sides, blend by patch and mend. Willing sip
brace to taste delicious, precious also for
gain to save, high now well above the rest.

## Inshore Horizon

On line beside the sea quietly, once is enough
to match up to relish famous skies, the harbour
clear and evenly displayed. Flowers of sulphur,
salt caught in sunlight shone across dark lift
canopies, distant voices indistinct. In crest
service by turn boasted, take heed to look
and care, assume. Hedgerow follow; ever so
enough train through all together soft pleated
replied, wave in true best advice. So often,
so fine planted as many others face to hear
and be heard, ahead humid and wet. Simplified
relented, the path uphill vacant in shade,
colours merge to save in time to near win.
Honest bees better, buzz cherries call out
note and pick ripe, pitch perfect assiduous.

## Inset, Beside

Aside the river bank, many eager cries catch
the dew in flourish, peace disturbed easy soon
for dawn, clouds lifting, boats rising & falling
in sleek currents, sounds of lapping water trace.
Echoes by the inlet, inn-keeper in tune with his
gathered guests, margins of plied refreshment,
one calls out to another, sky reaches down in
answer, over again. Wait for time to turn around,
familiar and sought eagerly, grant favour in apt
crevice, long aspired. Come forward to reach out,
take to quaff; laughter admiring in near sight.
Slow mist along the rim to blur sweetness, now
already exchanged for visitation, proud find
in person shadow; tree leafage shelter, others
sway so with joy, with coming day, abounded.

## Entrance Transept

Lustre across lacquer deters no gleam aiming
not forget voyage surprises all corrected.
Deeper still in display, shelf directed for
each to see, solitary not to vanish by intent;
attain this far, a team in crescent obligement.
What's seen refined, imminent in full selfhood
to watch the grasp relaxed, match points set
province, some in marches indite ignited half.
Equal to real aspect proclaim to seem, attend
and parry, meet and carry one; prize to price
inflict, inflected spear unspurned, innocent.
Acid drop fell first pave love-in-a-mist off
mark racquet play allayed two for pair, where
ornate candied jar at faucet might; vanquish
obstinate all-over mission still not yet night.

## Whether So Now

Ardent pine for cool air, rain first name aloud
skippy warren sign to lessen dark leaving ply
rail set; skillet number near cold, brighten up
parapet. Woven outward tacit message, by stair
reckon gentle present, had gone away deemed as
will obey, daylight by wainscot. Welcome into
loom semblance, clasp postern, vane ahead;
climb the stair refine, not found. Yet voices
heard crossing to plead, once or twice credit
ensconced in hand forward, gift severance all
applied, by still distant manifest alike. Be
early bare life dragon's teeth laid quickly,
if washed clear and shining, then gone; grant
want tame within, access temper act to split
device intone light ayre testament in tune.

## Ahead for Livery

Asset flight butter stooped, undo before warn
bright churn ski excitement pasture, indignant
as why luff tryst in boundary, forsake. Like one
another skip-jack manifold persisting, look out
to see in calm licence, grateful for amplifies
motivated. Get there beside concur secret, blur
plane couch name to rest; turn out recruited
object dare to phosphor match, vatic floor for
nourish. Let the one ring for toll frame, open-
heart flute utterance yearning wage, burnt offer
assuage; ski along cloud base tufted once, late
to wait, toil hardy fray magnified. Dowse ready
apse kneaded finger slender fund to send away,
note brut on board assert privatise caption;
atone bitten cheek contented, eager simplified.

## Doric Orbital

Oil kind sleek in darker prospect, river swell
tidal moor up care shoulder forcep attenuate,
tie beam haven, riven parole. Oars shipped for
pillow narrow sprawl, derived match to fetch
near silence parley, bound word lappet. So at
by stand listen grain stirring, like thought
for tomorrow new as valiant, braided; rustle
sweet forgiven meantime slidden breath, in
spoken attitude from my door stay and yours,
to wide inflate. Where no shade will go out
between profuse device, advisement reeds by
rise and tell, difference engine; lucid bite
birthright mention signet lily, tally sensate
incidence. Oh treat freight full conserved,
ear woken imagine flee close, ever this way.

## Pawl Next Implored

Out of lack dear heart entire, near star in
unseen for cloud cover, never doubt slighted
plain tale cool water aroused. Stave to luck
proof reach enclose, wide infant eyes flutter
no other exercise; praise by name verdict,
in gaze ever dark withouten blame. Wit talc
compose unbruised sit tight loyal satin, few
remaining departed, long after between sign
caution contrition by hurtle all to claim;
at river pitch latch-key companion, be safe
beyond compare. Don't know what will set
at the kerb-stone plummet, whatever whistle
where in line, drip saline importune or no
help half trimmed; lock bridge for confer
to steer curt after out in share, replevin.

## Live Party Symptom

Dissipate attire promise craw merchant fling
crack corn and don't care, who's to say more,
roam claim given, inveterate fought to swerve;
to the over shore care worn, droit. Enlisted
passage comprise wait to turn smoke burning
where one then another, missive sage craven
single sandal allspice. Trice for this hurried
at slim chance, ocean blend louring cloud hard
cut saved in grove, cold ash to sky solicit
grid impart. Respect terrace byway salt spray
mimic heaven, batten gradient's liquid theme
invited; happen listen out fermented, her brow
furrowed, advancement. Reach to search imbued
pardon shoe-horn beacon, wolfram pit incision
alter radon remembrance attic, nigh gone away.

## Heard Owls Hoot

Nearer than chill moonlight, willow clear wet
with dew risen by reed spears, would clatter,
spread where young birds forage; meet hunger
at the weir. Hear what you see, will soon be
in flicker abet to recognise, revision without
fear, surprise. Discreet tangent limit absurd
anticipate by echo, follow quantum allow pair
bound to shadow, darkness; infringe evasion,
lesion torn abduction, these birds conversant
reply in clamant jargon. Hold fast to notice,
once or twice each way onwards, drawn close but
still not quite, yet; brows at bee-line ledge.
Cloud bank glimmer to chatter, whether narrow
ocular abatement won't chew, faint stirring up
habit in white; corrosion crowds water's edge.

## Sans Fear Previous

This one says first address, attested impact
consigned without punishment, speckled would
livelong day equivalent monsoon calc schist
even marble congealed. Done over verified in
flame, nest weft pinnate ascended cloud open
unfold pride, lionise. Gorge rapid for urgent
streaming down, in dowie den acclaim cryptic
next too billow guiltless proven; upsurge
boat beaten flustered all hands steady must.
Fame fluellen ponder conic section, pensive
flow stain under mask stalk resound. Not yet
either for genus sifted, wasted dark traits
distressed, watch whiff agreed. Insistent
ground both say next fortress, day chased
emergent detain detour; as into folly came.

## No Place for Ideas

Either soon often enough, less custard intrude
furtive, deterrent eyelid; last was willing fit
muster decided, applicant by born lit antiphon.
Phantom devotion cling peaches priceless mixed
quickly winking and sunken; level down spelled
for question drawn appendix, all sides wrinkled
barrel dehiscent, take or left over. Provide jot
principal pencil singular flatter grass abstain
to lend citric glory, hazardous tempest eventual
attach which reign. Darkling pause infuse cast
to the winds aghast blown cinder pinch, intense
length full temple listen unhurt; trumpet chorus
florist wrists apart and lenten, borrowed pitch
apt pittance fragrant, in bliss outside. Drastic
deviate solution, entire acceptance floated ever.

## Nautical, Aspic

What's here seen, betimes, sly avens convince
when pineapple supple device, impervious merit
dative fraction arbitrament. Lunar spike bit
adventurous, deny season why frozen, cladded
lick solemn estuarine gift racks. Tang amine
polygon, span until midnight, crotchet talc
talcum vital all set; grapple gravel nitrate
afraid for decussate violets auburn paragon.
Three-mast purpose on crimson alum, idyllic
choral initiate lamp fitted. Lift bred, into
stead muddied all well-done watershed alive
loving in privatise, perforate tribune son
burnt sonnet apply turn up; book in pother
on tether apple brother, so long fair dues
give open share coulter breccia go to town.

## PRESUME CATKINS

## (2021)

By lakes and sandy shores, beneath the crags
Of ancient mountain, and beneath the clouds,
Which image in their bulk both lakes and shores
And mountain crags
- Coleridge

## 1

Promote to the window, air flow hearten
   beat over brow to seek and bind, up in
cloud hesitate to stay; live to reflect
   so far along cherish soon melted, why
silk and felt road trodden, set by front
   slow as must, as trace outward, accept
enough. Wait to limit offering, in-shore
   held in view, ensue snowberry almost
to back; remiss in purpose next return
   in full option of a measure, generous
attempted, missive sweeten plant within
   seed time shared. By wait for long or
with recall, comported fluency and blue
   light at horizon discovered, entire at
length unburdened, true company. New seal
   in cords for joint to fasten, breath
regulate near aspire larkspur, contented
   lamps to shine, ahead descried each
word in thought retrieved for issue fleet
   reckon, made out, warm flecks in water
mystery. The cistern not missing, system
   custom foreign, listen close by avail
to trial will intend; bid alpine currant.
   Impervious native local spring, driven
in flock covert partition as brimstone
   alert ambition comes to play, reliant
patent dividend, patient succession belt.

## 2

Over stile by fate to reach touch interest
   parish far over, tremor, play the foil
simmer broken half light, reach surrounded
   by flicker shades, invite hearten let
outright ever be true trident inept cite
   correlate. Fern mission bear crossing
admission touch in base long for adrenal
   you and mine fallow inference engraved,
detach annex your ichor near ladle profile
   take shone pine on to hold, grow chervil
laced milk-deep sown hoist in precious use;
   asterisk keep close watch mist. Ermine
be yours confessed no foot out wrong weigh
   strewn similar joy pace script inventory
heat adjusted yet low love beyond, trilled
   o'ergiven limitless stay by fray intaken
hard-acre, won gainful psalmic philtre crave
   pinion massive inflection wrist promise
grist namely numen darker rival. Wait season
   sigh hove premium middle share at brim,
window-ledge crevice unrecounted at price.
   Sentence both relish first usual loyal
siphon engraved welling all bright inflict
   obtainment, hold on tread weighbridge
in common disclaim counter to hidden heart
   would fleet deep felt thrift, innocent.

3

Alright here's what instigate veil abjected
 constriction, blick insect lots immersed
purge cosmetic blood exchange. Farce pretty
 punish rink robot convicted, bloated by,
villify crass punish drastic fulgurant. Tied up
 aggravate sense inclined as fell to fallen,
laconic facial morsel grapple on sward, answered
 yet wild gossip indomitable; casual belated
affect sit tight monastic bell foolish surface
 reduced. Seldom revoked dissection cut-out
vertebrate next cathected, hurry but envious rent
 preen fateful cogently; time-like prevented
crush shrill facile grip, remote pivotal fused.
 Did you want, more or less in furtive to win
concealed, frugal congealed, split emetic villous
 sedative benchmark slunk. Or wait out, scorn
broken aliment withheld famously; menaced waist.
 Organ transept set vox immune will attune at
scratch team voluted. Run to pitch never teach
 in failing light mutation credal, torn first
did you, riper years caustic shears thread lift,
 which crossed lumen glowworm woodhenge ounce;
few snip quickly aptly in wet, museum dormant
 gas washing or scrub pilot novitiate. How then
many sent to counter blow, know that and all's
 well anyway for now, loss adjusted in ruckus
parlous enlisted. Oven govern foreign schnapps,
 at roaming informing aromatic less needed
fulminate, bite gnat fluke flautist incriminate.

### 4

Or both high and low foretold, obey ocean skint
fuelled curtain ascertain warm up mistaken
alliance clasp close at hand blood flowers end
truant hold on, fluent absolving currency
pliant token mint coat ease for sleeve, airy
released increment stealth fashion each truce
long since spillage. The whole face octave inside
opening final cousin tappet tip delimiting
fantail enamel, want both for each forcep wand
defended, over fateful muslin scheme. Or none
more brave and patient sure, footloose in fancy
befallen wooden variant unspent; practice
pungent account or not at all, dawn-light safe
elated capsize head start joined. Hear what
contrived, one after next prided slewed kept up
to near mark grateful. Capsule seed herald
pacify harbinger way past, door step; graphic
anticipate shade task salute, mud. Orange
or range out trio morrow indict rehearsal into
solemnise surprising dib-dab aeon comforted
accent, venal flavour tribute. Pinafore indoor
endurance planetary fluids avowal earnest
garment throat thereat insisted, domesticate
visits objects eyelash cruise interlacing
consist; tunnel tuning hear turn over back,
hesitate decorate modest discounted intact.
Viable scrutiny at fulvid mockery condensate
germinal propitious fascinate shoelace by
trace emaciate dripped own mutton; brink sunk
threadfast discus hyacinth nicety entire
conclusive devolved agrimony spike aroused.

## 5

Indent together all canal caramel denial, consent
   tridentine whether mended, canine bent to fall
contented; vial either or father too for toothsome
   foursome, skint. Tighter to bite back, surfeit
kinship, mile violet despite restive in festive wit,
   in lieu chew racket. Satchel mussel must off
pitch pine pandect, exempt meet meteoric whoso to
   jaw clip and draw, suspect detriment dirempt.
Whew bittern corncrake stroke placated placard,
   night-guard forward croaking throat call,
oil right pitted molar cut flack polyp. Cretic
   divested wasted, inbred soured rubricated
crimson hatch; consistent wanted to waterline
   open libation for parched wild guesses.
Fresh fields new pastures twitch, ado in blue
   more azure trial, aerial foil seal to fit.
Commit plangent ebullient wind-up, statistic
   morbid onset bi-metallic acoustic gadget
fudge conflict. Derelict invited peril often
   to fashion, mansion precision concurrent
ride decided, horse sense providence; assist
   furnish, scene again foreign supplement.
Fed up back, skip the rest thrush call well
   judged, fireweed bisque columnist flair.
Crucial touch, torch-light flamboyant tint
   etch stipulate inserted; none yet like
present beating heart astute, longing more or
   less apart. Willow willow live dart,
soonest mended if there first frost restive
   at dental optimal protected by spark
ridge, flag riding float swift encouraged.

## 6

Cloud base solace scythe stratus meatus vied
untied surface crayfish wainscot lace pat
let pittance full hillside relayed in shadow
days to daze; surmise wave profile tidal
loud echo ripple, curtail recollect trumpet
affected, grown wind-blown wicket. Aisle
while local label level dabble moonshot, wed
venerate nightshade atta tappet occiput.
Yet occluded current turbulent beaten outer
intervene, sustain leaf margin arranged
rainfall coil lick spinet, about; redden net
catchment trace decisive elude hit cornice
street plan on-time monsoon comet tip upset;
caustic intact running order swept. Sweet
chariot merited, water input hydrant melted
souk ground plan lentil advice lattice
auric plummet indicate. Fuel most casually
massive lengthen, spoon sarsen staircase
wasteful success. At first crested somehow
plate summit ingot fateful futile graced
legal elegant tribute sistrum children ice
auburn cauldron; on track darker colour
merger pillow for yellow, wasp stripped.
Parcel gilt plain told milled, imitate
worsted blanket crayon torrent veil over
deal; chenille mastic smoke tree grit
obverse, if terse intense retained. Mimic
seen serene crown occupant whimbrel for
you to curlew, cataract late cascade, fled.

## ATHWART APRON SNAPS

## (2021)

The waves lie still and gleaming
- Byron

The faithful and the true
- Clare

On the coast of Coromandel
Dance they to the tunes of Handel
- O. Sitwell

**1**

Optical light of today, rising to say, be here
    for her as may, where so and true, for you;
take in the air by clear to wait, estimate foot
    duet at start without, orient, nut in cluster
thicken searching replete to catch, the necklace
            along the way

**2**

Open the peak morning slant, elbow invented wit
    antic to enclose, reduce and crown by thirst
within to seek; incident bright iridescent want
    for you in both brilliant, in cut gem prevent
hearing and glisten her cheek, in shade to mark
            as yet to stray

**3**

Was it for such be gone, carillon for time, when
    quartz match thought leaven hereunder heaven
cloud hiding keen blue eyes, visible cinnamon win
    contest impress thorn least to rush into place,
at her behest carnation; choiceful attention given
            later to say

**4**

Hero rejoice princess, worthy of praise profess
    fleeces in space, leaf traces in voices; even
pardon far over to try, agile alliance decreed
    scabious impetus correct carpet; aspect refits
amount permanent assessment, tension intermits
            hers to portray

**5**

Capacious spiral fanciful, gabardine mild, filled
    lost satchel amiss, paste insisted defunctive
plasma court; cut short revalued yoke aberrancy
    mistaken notion succulent, completed lichenous
curtain limpet infringement; attended polychrome
            not in dismay

**6**

Athirst tundish subsisting, digression painted
   coat plinth, fright untoward redeeming frame
cold bed to seed instead; all fed hollow elder
   wine hatter manifest first soup leek incident
roux to brew, askew mesh, fresh latent reprise
         clothing to fray

**7**

Auspice outermost coastal joist, bereft
   famous ambergris bliss it was, dive
driven respite collagen displayed; furze
   icterine spoiled hostage footway plea
ortolan since when, mayflown optimum ran
         whether to prey

**8**

Produce insidious embassy sit permission
   trespass listen sluice, if credulous
impasse reductive, western halogen sift
   at least cuirass residual place remote
float missed retort flouted, sedition pen
         distant obey

**9**

Cottar coastal out, focal settlement fiscal
   vitalise, bustle pertinent duffel bottled
expert moral spite duplicate likening doit
   austral, attire oscillate vatic reversion
cupric for spick, spaniel granule fossilised
         in sea apply

**10**

Lexical extricate hoist mast insect sylph
   orris toasted, stricken lost moleskin
moisten loosestrife grief; taxon custom oat
   further other stickle laid back flecked
task force most derris deck cationic ilk
         new foray

## 11

Absurd blackbird further on, action radon
down stream fired back, word derailed at
servitor attract tonic renown maxim acquit
off team creasing fluff giraffe girded
near splurge missive derrick emphasis wit
next way-lay

## 12

Early mist, waist missing invested chrysalis
done incomplete to half weary gate-way
scarf create immersed adage unless return
remiss nearly crafted; pursuant cleft
light of living pasture, honour born out
made in clay

## 13

Most yeast replaced, flex daze at best undo
to craze off mixture, brace near pair office
snacks to feast, amazed; ghost step by on one
daring, pleased ace text at never elsewhere
spoor on floor; fixed up care or waver, interim
soon to slay

## 14

Righteous mustard after plaster, how invented
raucous offcuts malcontent renewed, infused
must hardy, hardly smite. Despite shut coffer
alight, foster sentiment osmic planetary dip
tardy outlasting quoit, plovers in flutter rite
ever to bray

## 15

Awkward forward up grated, torque awed relaid
pork ignored deploy ahead day-park soared
instatement warden beforehand all-sorted yet
retain complaint bought, bandwidth grift
committed split payment leaden in lucky hit
was no deny

**16**

Crepe to bunyip this time round, rival strip
  cool nape mignonette, unbound seed-bed, nip
flask oval ailment masque; civil will imbricate
  red-brick teak obviate, ask first, side mute
in fruited convex bunting, strung out in front
    high-up dray

17

If column sooner colophon cream mite indoor
  combined replete, notation ocean autumn
after solemn bloom dictate; raft in spoke
  more strike aimed renown claim fortunate
entreated, sift and flown determined, gone
    as to toy

**18**

Arbitral airdrop skippage pact sealed oiled
  at cropland, third ticket incorrect parrot
revealed contraband forfended; wreck up yet
  arbitrament debt mark-up concerted wince
cold hell parallel on foot, done adamant lip
    tedd the hay

**19**

Inept, inert blurted outcast yet lastly, crept
  past bet overt, transept electoral peewit
naval neural pond life, alert quicken in fact
  distraught, wise bond farm profit adored
muskrat flit full-dyke innovated necklaced
    garde ta foi

**20**

Chaffinch dunce wincing, fax luff to lunch
  upon once ancient bench-mark, basketry
offset evince lancet or brisket, finance
  verdigris foresee batten rattaplan rim
avengement by credence darken reverence
    gang agley

21

Complete nothing fit eat cuffing link sunk
    lanky marrowfat debated, barbary apart
incidental hollow split reheat, headed lick
    bindweed fallow stuffing baryte benefit;
pinewood credence darken outer reverence
        or guess why

22

Comfit calcite irate calx correlate tighten
    import upset federate piratical edited map
collect hymnic cataract, stymied intersect
    confection sought replicate loop penetrate;
time-out matter steadied, envied estate
        fine untie

23

Snaffle to curb, verbal invert sweet riffled
    deceitful, sorrowful minnow affable await
urban volcanic cullet, table sleet full tilt
    white flake milk stop check dwelt emanate
moult skaldic scandent incandescent pinstripe
        without fee

24

Off pat predicted, get gather round impounded
    sever whiff severe, or whether this ratchet
further another liquorice official oppressed
    up-gaze hatpins selected; additional abyss
calendric misfitted, hutch plate full sporadic
        alight gray

25

Middle squirrel, moral morsel advising bell
    spiral entailment, at railway accident
quarrelsome eyes closed, size impact kit
    faction in kitchen, hawkbit apparelled
resemble tangible brought back, indite
        not or nay

## 26

Strut in dispute repeat, shutter out leakage
    falcon balcony, ebony alchemic and grouted
attack cranked fluster, talcum problematic
    bistort converted estrangement in paragon;
effuse escheat overcall, split into profits
        ever as may

## 27

Fast racing onboard effulgent, ill cardinal
    amity discreet tissue erased, profligate
past care for; uproar greeting ordeal bite
    none outcast, further outlast issue park
albumen creamery, funicular expressionist
        near reweigh

## 28

So-so arctic mouse-ear tick-tack lactic frack
    toe-hold as told no fear you bet go quick
then back arc-light cold house near-by, woe
    clear begone, false fox else who lick-split
two ten fathom dock climate as yet interdict
        lastly oh-kay

## 29

Accrued feudal meld wilding, filled child elk
    spooled, spelling willing stewed swelled,
dust to ash rusted aural enamel, spilled bill
    uphill renewed; welkin silken ducal foretold
to rise and shine, opinion onion folded minion
        be oh my

**EFFLUX REFERENCE**

**(2021)**

For Nicholas Heptonstall
NHS

## I

Fluids pre-set adroit attended
   for flex insert start to end,
by mind wait hunt ways in mercy
   fixed and mend, via tight lip.

Tongue yet prolix antiquate top
   loosely autistic subsisted as
which ever-green banded agate,
   between intemperate retreat;

stitched-up pipe markers back
   along vent tried out as felt
for wrist press tracks in song
   patience by fingers, attuned

least side trace pursuit along
   so pulsed and squeezed, vocal
indigo wild for fitted; swapped
   retainment held back, effort

alight foisted sifted soon over-
   turn dark bone new ingrained
at nearly open wetland. Calcific
   bay riven tip butter-patter

## II

vivid trinkets fluently teased
   to trace open but if not slip
at riverside trout replete, mild
   full speckled; splash droplet

scattered fallen gratefully yet.
   Why impaled divagated reckon
piece to lesson otherwise crease
   for parts to whole, elaborate

mile over rain gauge whose slice
   medal glistens back cushion in
fringe, swelled out cautious by
   lacewing revising implemented

o'er to search trickle out taps
   when can in share, cribs best
and cornet bee-flight tames if
   whiten so. Fretty chervil own

bright before, into cocoon been
   curtain due for dewfall origin
sure & for certain modest crumb
   proceed on course; none worse

## III

in sluice trickle on either side
   hydrate inundated sit at forest
knees angle yet still or folded,
   why not yet or even chocolate

by dark shade-birds at woo so for
   who'd know stir over wing-span:
churr-churr flight in call to wake
   chin-up frog-bit intermixt, at

sound channels follow slow eased.
   Spoken to reel tape sensible
gentle vibrancy steady so reposed
   believed meaning and truth, no

elsewise hour by hour or ties by
   compromise adduce in juice; a
licence to cross the higher skies
   in search past contrails off

breeze light rising, parity set
   at least on felt for feeling
shall tell in turn beforehand;
   intern to mean to go as find

## IV

Rebuke these surges whatever's
   best to say first, dangerous
and sweet, not least lash lost;
   untold spice missive device

walrus bullrush ooze to savoury
   knows unforgotten give to can
at past bend blench water blinks
   deference, otter lodge cinch

mint traction sent for scent rim
   sniff winking, inkling margin
hollow mallow lay new aim, comb
   to finish parish pump in prime

willow hale. Totter belated wane
   numerical refractive ambergris
novice, service brain red storm
   dithyramb corymb comes before

dappled issued, too. Sets blood
   character pinned to match up,
over what's deflated organ loft
   in search exact absorbs then.

## V

Demented firing pin, life guard
  ahead of time incessant link
imprint ink-well all align, tune
  whistle and seepage to fetch

underpass, mastery; albumen in
  shell indifferent, went first
to baptise immersion at surface
  tension yoked up to traction

dursn't ought to mortify decried
  guile oval run on ahead split
lentil civilise enticement beside
  why for X by Ray tell for told

held in deft apparatus bristling
  tight merchandise; at horizon
saline spray impeached frequently
  digressed nursed taken in fad

to patch redress impetuous onyx
  vain before mischievous finish,
at last-pitch tussle battle wicket
  just so; pool stir roux through

## VI

Down-pour yet more sure as eggs
   run on skimble legs askance
must we wait if by yet later, on
   to stay cool by clear eyes,

by shine pool reflected, howso
   ever whether; gather nibs a
bunch at once, alliance fenced
   slice tolerance all parallel

what's in view so far allowance
   perched to roost, fortunate
lined up beside inordinate lid
   shut about note warrant odd

fawn devotion, crack steady on
   lost cause shoes imbalance
leak speaking these last most
   addressed in witness alight

stay-bright badge flinch ferry
   winch, fridge announce guard
afford only less black pitches
   now; the window streak beset

**VII**

Pear to wood clime cymbal ire
   neither silver pungent at
mousse pew, title implicated
   why nothing suits to freon

cradle emulsify; varnish away
   in hot ladle downstream
later than, beaver better on
   tap creosote, simplifying

pipework new amount culvert
   split. Water margins band
handsome standard away drain
   alleviate at second floor

trick colour shoulder why not
   amaze set all ablaze dowse
heath fire, feckless impiously
   lay in wait debated naphtha

epidote slate balcony symphony
   dotted baton; crucial delete
carrot soup attenuate in baulk
   alibi albedo speedo near in

## VIII

line precisely softly underside
   delayed, in figural concert
wych elm. Spin duvet in castanet
   polygonal manual signal tap

easy reveal bi-fold pretty lid
   close fit too, or few within
well-known scalene mitten thumb
   spinney or copse your amused

choice to hold off, playful heat
   weighted in traction lotion
hand to wrist immediate. Lurking
   distract bronze patina creep

drooping foliage privilege sedge
   cloud bitten better often in
swirl wilted by child conduction
   fricative somnolent nation, by

restore awakened toasted pattern
   will all freshen button sewn
grain stanchion; consummate bate
   forecast nonchalant wouldn't

## IX

succulent beans prognosis list
   quickly at least to auguries
meal-times sit down drawing by
   touch sketch hospitable bin

liner; steamer semi-colon train
   fondants caramel affordable
brake steep cost-price enticed,
   steeple sign condign demised

to restive unseen. Light birded
   song at pitch told filled up
at brim, daring by darling whim
   hambone ambit pittance coast

livery whose aviary you knew as
   we too, cruise tackle anvil
consistent reversed thereby in
   poppy-seed deterred angrily,

tell none condone fuming acid
   cupboard irritant emollient
for shadowed silhouetted silt
   port mended, sanded in blue.

## X

Headlong single margin oversee
   where once commenced curb-
stone footloose yet for fancy,
   free undertakings milk tray

knees up swerving quieten down
   salmon tingle his and mine;
endymion tree-line ankle write
   frighten freight by repast

furnish dowel velveteen shine
   pinnacle miniature assume.
Better than original relieved
   assize traps trotterlings

atrium delirious, positive to
   outwards juddering menace
threat thereat divisible mist
   on pane; crane-fly tremble

thimble individual motivated
   brackish languish terror
wherefore entire mirror sunny
   pay for honey, beetle by.

## XI

Stubborn hangdown assenting
   in full view crew where
e're you walk and talk, back
   blithe noisy twinge edge

mussels alive; narrow borrow
   quickly broad avenue too
pass beforehand dormant orb
   flash card. Balloon fits

trouser applicant kitted up
   kitchen rack cloth hang
stipulate cascade inner rim
   inflate tell as ever win.

Oven ready sensible tribute
   risk-averse hardly worse
fire to fluttering, interim
   ribbon implicated terse;

last shot pigeon ogle find
   to share too, far carbon
legal search porch windows
   if not mine then yours.

20 June 2021

# DUNE QUAIL EGGS

# (2021)

* * * * * * * * * * * * * * *

Least first crest fount
own
tides slate frame worst
win
smite cream warns brave
old
allow proof ankle crumb
lid

* * * * * * * * * * * * * * *

* * * * * * * * * * * * * * *

Green foist crust mound
met
drain plume feast bride
eye
nails thumb avoid trail
bay
ghost braid prune force
toy

* * * * * * * * * * * * * * *

* * * * * * * * * * * * * * *

Brunt regal dream birth
sat
steam untie daily frond
oil
decoy clove sooth above
him
tacit offer price false
aim

* * * * * * * * * * * * * * *

* * * * * * * * * * * * * * *

Grave hovel anvil twine
max
ember spoon woman bless
mix
fetch match sauce droop
top
plate batik enter strip
dim

* * * * * * * * * * * * * * *

## LAY THEM STRAIGHT

## (2021)

Stroke when better for, carrot curt out certain abbot cahoots
ease remote, total utterance; myrtle mirthful please to bright
parting alert twelfth waiting ode imminent sent until
grape-shot spill parallel, interminable yet where late
blue-schist
singular corrigible teasel tenterhook, prune back fork in drum
bandage forepeak speech ahead elegant burin separate florin
casuist redressed refusal; bastion alignment sateen on
train surmount indented subdued, adamantine wont
licit complete
sherbet abetted inset next-most far-off ambient ford
test brake streak valiant consistency assistant suited
astringent. Parsnip brown study hornfels convoke heathenish
fishcakes duration ornament, perpetual conflict dutiful cringe
at fringe, mince-meat incorruptible flight path victim
over tilt harness furnace; his intrigue ravenous cygnet
guillemot ox
defensive trollius incredulous, decrement fermenting
renewed rectified virulent corpuscular appendix list.
Improvident certified wheatear flocks to settle deft impulsive
goldfinch, fishpond resounding scarf most peckish liquorish
ring-main delphinium; spoilage pantechnicon scent
conductance first unless turtle foliate spinal syringa
ginger melted
wing tethers explicate epidural hazardous silvered marginal
italic vitreous reductive loose rosewood; additional ebbtide
conchoidal shellac frack also higher, unshaded notes
limitless grotesque biscuits, love to contrive in twice
noise immersed to necklace rift, collateral far-off darkened
vale. Portal open returned less below crested grebe way not
tips dispute, inchoate they do say as bitter will into
bituminous mute catchfly boisterous eager solace or
whiff moist
panegyric clastic frosted; ridgeway radiancy below
arch zenith microlith diffracted ester fluster fledged
saturnine outreach farmhouse, alliances duster nadir hazel
from hers hurtle doorway perfume neume, presume dune.
Honest aversion until curvature replacement flanks
incriminate dilated plumbago entailment antennae

brute sack

fry-up on ungulate gallantry anemone splits immediate bier
frond diphthong plaited flaunt applause to flutes; flotation
elder garters briefcase interior, length protracted
strength entrenched recursion apportion old wick
adduce friction option, juice rejoice ointment. Slat aroused
probative combustion flagstone upheld judgemental birdy
not requited
track gopher whisper; intact prolix maximum foxes
windscreen in vain, moss chewed recruit abrogate
colophon imaginative knee slice break teabags imitate herb
exhaustive tormentil. Helicon jungle in niblick flicker, offset
refrigerate gesticulating fields ahead event sward
dissention, dreg scoop ocean beds ministry tangent
nutritious candidate obligate protein snack winsome spoon
fleece hedgerow local; missile cadge legendary colloquium
in gadgetry
monetary infantry by season famished festoon tuneful find
salute to sweet; caraway enjoyment bite listen, whiten spot
adjudicate bolted surfeit minimal caramel garrison
respite alight. Dismay agreement foreseen in bone
seasonal transom ridgeway sneeze displease, amaze conical
toys wherever conjure usually box omission onion unionise
skilful intrepid fossilise shellfish griffin gruesomely
corrective selected walking recapture mediocrity
sixth chord
swayed rewarded parcels and the moon black; column tails
magnetic optical syntax bullrush foible drain across willingly
perspex grenade suffix explode. Valid veiled oiled
praxis window screens damage attached, hawser
hawfinch tinged off lacrimose kidney sluiced icicle joyously
previous interval; bactrian deserted farcical prime creamed
credential animal revealed, incursion off lunation.
Dot carry occulted wavelength morose ribosome
mastiff
canteen opine opium titration; fashionable inside tractate
collective torn right across, minimum damn rick skillet abet
elasticated. Whose water-butt refectory linseed
top-speed dreadlocks apex swift arrow swallow

horizontal twitter margin ampersand, trampled antiseptic
less magical surgery at petty pacified; bullace endorphins
shuttering elk horn consigned remaining trained
swoon distaff raft honest, licence sufferance oh
intagliated
day to daylight sugar nailed perusal railing realgar. Origin,
virginals sore sequins ludicrous pluvial headstrong molar
minaret curving suchlike, lugubrious brokerage
twin promissory notation restriction; initialised
lungwort bracelet oxidised evinced boulder claypan wine
distraints, militant extremity banditry. Ounce once onyx
wince princeling listed lurcher, sticky darling on
during one ownership down upended, curtains
foretold descried; opinionated braggart contested astute
pearlwort headband, claimant figment clemency distraits
gauze cap
drawn uppermost seizure posthumous runner. Becoming
down so-long kneaded bridle brindle undertow, gnomon
oral civil cavity density, perfidious albatross ice wedges
redress rapturous sedimented ostrich fluff as if
lissom forecast provost mobile rice dehydrate
both must truculence. Liberty capsule excitement at exit
mission least distance offering welded, provocative cans
driftwood nominal residue syllabic indicatively
lapwing window bantam renowned intoned to
jargon aphasia
necessitous rumpus hysterical varnish, decree
dust of the cavernous defiance renovation ohm
wagon trail; mail colossal seagull tangled angular trusted
rapacious oppressive easel weasel porringer vociferous
ventriloquist dormice chisels impetuous craft
canvas querulous aircraft. Lingering in crudity
phlegmatic vindicated orbicular theorbo, entrusted bat
shook stook auk piteous elbowed pilgrim shagreen some
fugacious
venturesome syrup mountainous hispid liquid
paraffin twin; crocus intern lupin vulpine tent
fondant nostril mint, hither comet token sylvan brunt on
stricken, cyclist mawkish spatchcock aperitif disused fol

instress orange tip limit siskin clinker burdock
further toilsome vantage-point. Sour floor hint
anointed
over colour whether neither honeydew suffused waxwing
flock alert crested, resisted file to ingratiate home parrot
celebrate agnate red kite burnt umber cadent
fonder absent murrey pagoda whisker rightful
resilient mucilage; chatoyant surfactant pendant ritualise
parchment insinuating pollinate detachment, juniper ode
rhetorical
when disposed office palliative; cats up in clover
far overtaken which bend acute at work get on
qualia corner piece avarice; spruce proficient awkwardly
dehiscent insular aquilegia too passionate adjacent shots
up enlaced custard welding briophyte scatter
to discover rice market dolphins as distructs
outmost fit
summit indigenous covetous narthex ribaldry riotous if
twill lesser anger brilliant, cabouchon seen moonstone
on wrinkle needle peridot moated; afloat bit
toward codon cedar mournful environ quells
crimson owl watchtower purpose infringement, issues
fashionable who then licence pluck official. Slide duress
generosity
twice surplus inflected lustrous novitiate oat
convex rock-rose service, perplexity cavities
digression thrown back percussion often gibbous nacre
liminal deltoid embroidered matching both arrays pays
for gravity best levity at vigil, oval tongue at
one lost sleep shepherd past prop proffered
terse waste
equal aquiline wishful spandrel uncial winds
tombstone fragrant sapling song vanity veer
out switch drastic first text matt penance whose visiting
aggrieved mercer conditional fuel ostensible snatch off
imposed aroused, ill-humour vestigial rapidly
boiling monkfish far ahead spindles habitable
rock dusted
crank lift aromatic prospect visible across into

          lenient lenticular forcible, meronymy nursing
scavengery shipway. Who said each before toast tọ frost
whinchat could both moreover, covers rancorous horses
          implement ester aesthetic cruiser butchery of
          naphtha narcissus; plait crank brutal bottle spin
                    complaisant
          stop work bout, flighted shuttled awkward jaw
          bone mid-brain tablecloth obstreperous extort
indigenous yet placid celandines emaciated cochlear leaf
dressage. Fetlock detached riparian mutton succulent bid
          on trepidation trenchantly imminent, self-raising
          cantaloupe riparian sylvan flapjack, treacle quick
flitch porch eels twitch billycan warren ensign limitations.
          Threadbare moisture fissure mushrooms, tap off
          supple wrinkle button sew to measure, adorning
                    basilisk east
          pondweed heeded we do needful rainy raiding-
          party butter yet know test red kite delete pints
most parakeet foot rest; goat beard for mordant mention
frame climate squirrel sorrel grey battleship witty already
          parry foundered plundered, tropic enteric end
          patch and mend furlough pastrycook intimately
along with what's left early one, mournful long after ford
down-along lee jungle eagles vigorous, maiden trellis oat
                    dare frame
          repaired, flared burning feet, beset cresset met
          conation pyrotechnics silicon invigilated crown
construe sonatina hesitant basset-horn, turn again soon
six first silicon cornice moulding camera shadow-play day
                    ace rails
songs of honey early for even brightening; tension flicker
slide to rise, compress consume less, further on round.
          Repine level acknowledgement truce scout well
          eggs to lay watch the index busy as ants, plans
circumspect sticks without damage; target drum ladles
embossed shoe buckle zestful mornings ferment, quiet.

## SHADE FURNACE

## (2021)

'So these men were bounde in their coates, their hosen, & their clokes, with their other garments, and cast into the middes of the hote fyrie furnace...'

'Lo, I se foure men loose, walking in the middes of the fyre, and they haue no hurt...'

– Geneva Bible (1560), Daniel III: 21, 25

Beneath set invert marjoram sheen allergy
fiery freak reach to active profit gallantry
    flaming entire fortunes carbonic suitable
    out sooted particulate grip to gasp write
first over footage; say why not fibrillated
as smouldering solder fluxite, cast lengthwise
    enclitic heat-wave remedial orphean sign
    chill for ember, factive embellish mooted
remoteness. Burnet alkanet planet optic heat
shadowy in dark wood, ebon sundered evidency
    no smudge of doubt fills the profile agility
    flagrant crushed colic chariot imploded manic
pomegranate underpass; dismayed weighed clay
bound to fly smoky quartz rutile quailed up by
    why or not denoted tinder quanta. Basilisk in
    trace infanta blackened liken begrimed argon
spline chromatic aspen spleenwort ventriloqual
rotary implicative where down to far, blessing
    birdsong headlong; ponderable or mandate
    emanate stalk neck verse cutpurse invert bid.

Sanguine saline on-line dim sum capable aid;
shield eyelid torrid enterprising ride on ahead
   pipsqueak bubble manage plaster rib overcast
   away radiant changing colour on scale, aspect
due in hue mortal availed evident lack finish
other sortal obtuse; impact grange avenue east
   currency partial. Feudal once bat emitted.
   Used up tactic back off, virtually cautionary
implements all in signs tarnish mortar study
brown motive option, incited to sparrow bat
   cheap, asparagus alive hunch. Or fewer
   are chosen, sea-green honestly thereon
attune; rupestral celadon laburnum, dusted
an elegant engineer at moth-wing proficient
   tympanum burnt sienna random salmon
   gradient dockland unplanned, won ticket
filbert crate volcanic two-step. Cursory tepid
cosset, common sensorium mammoth tone
   rebuff, almost utmost grenade afraid bite
   frayed then bitumen natron fungible.

At edible; wrap up by instant star-lit twice
foot kittywake ostensible mercurial obol,
   lethal mercaptan at meristem endemic.
   Dated insistent once nonce formal uncle,
spreadeagle bedraggled mangle civilised in
drupe dashpot snapshot, utter chit stonechat
   lotion, allocate abbreviate novitiate elfin
   barque vibration orphan portion; character
shot-silk welkin ain contour intended twin
refunded mound global oval polymer boast.
   Achievement crescent, muffin legible oil
   plummet sound. Moreover in clover even
well-versed sauce another contestant two
blatant at beast to cease, to taste noticed
   waste created; enlisted tryst famish met
   grape harvest less cross one more ribbed
raven never, endeavour. Bonnet trimmed
brace object-lens whence mince disports
   enticement spliced joist, juices comet
   splice to pasture audit chrome beside

yellow-hammer blender aromatic, trump
cardigan conjunctive up to civic silvered,
    imprint conflict derelict topic, topaz in
    itemise noises surface; eyes right wait
in quoit adroit bleak kale forasmuch scold
brain loitering inflection paragon musket
    sermon by paregoric, liquorice mortise
    entrusted goitre argon tie dint mango
ingot mournful uncial mitral ovation. Lace
lactic primate skim trimester precocious
    due course alewife vertex flitch, promise
    gormless income carex unmixed aconite
idiotic knighted horn quaking, halibut stake
styptic tournament castigate offended in
    spate runway; rolled oat coating outlet
    triptych reductive legal centipede tag
miniature abjure beforehand, down-turn
burnout scrapheap filtrate inviolate, bit.
    Expected trappist vacant petulant like
    draconian, wait to learn, refined orate

galenic lead light kind frustration, go first
diverse evince nourish fandango borrow
yarrow; impeded elbow pedalled petal
marrow or never so austral, oh rolling
river recover leaf to leave yeast famous.
Lower boom taffrail roam ravine drawn
wincing, prowl instinct spider offside;
late attempt consented lightsome
passion enjoined. Stand ground induced,
fruitful riparian caution dragon well teal
swirl brimstone fusion; porcelain on
delegate slender painted cupric egg
bishop forfeit cinnamon finial. Nuzzled
agile fragment abut thistle regiment act
growl to trowel embroiled hibiscus
memorial bluebird gentian feeling
thermal front payment occupied. Who
caressed fortress o'clock dilute why not
speak intent your weight adjusted
spare leakage patronage coin spoon.

The two part invention by function abet
intends loosestrife parcel parallel, who
bright keyboards cupboard; laminate
floodlit raised cousin far ahead, wait
gimlet elevation prudent sip. Pine conic
illustrious surplus hovercraft, overall to
tortoiseshell modicum premium own
burnt accosted reed-beds at bunting
twice crimson root canal; chapel foiled
barricade obliged, striped badger lodger
neither whether flake cemented don
or nothing win; despite derrick collop
mitigate furnace smoke intensive yoked
upright, plover wreckage turbulent bid.
Shad roof to lean-to, shed all through
nightshade ectopic consequent bled
know worst adhere fairing; brunt born
turnout gulp crushed to pulp, triplicate
equal treacle alight. Plainsong earned
suffused with cinnamon into syringa.

Proofing flow cameo obvious gloriously
decisive invidious water-lily fragile most
  moist ferret activate; later condensed
  starfish boisterous each tough urban
hurricane, spouting downcast admirable
talented date for discount innovate. Pie
  seafront pier gravel shovel manicure
  endearment, mask asking intarsia fit
intaglio also scabbard; fogbound inshore
extremity like cloudburst autoclave late
  relinquishment. Pretended profligate
  walnut dashboard inchoate eximious
ascended lark pittance, fly why eyebrow
singing attain tongue lemon zest; never
  wither everlasting valence outer tide
  orbit. Despite introit deep-down bed
anemone salvia bleeding heart detritus
octopus, tent to grasp coarse fish topic
  scoop; floated whence plentiful acted
  liberal run to limit search life remiss.

Curdle ogle dismal howdah inferentially
veranda axiomatic cold climactic willing
distilled fragrant immunity imminent
tureen grandiloquent; set alight boil
furl cruelty avoidance come up to mark
ace scratch bucket alabaster undulates
grizzle puzzlement, disparage foraged
bilge scavenged thence avengement
toroidal currency torrential masterpiece
waterfall; evades cascade licence cruet
pomade crucible eligible oftentimes
intelligible dutiful brimstone grinding
carbonic retreated. Imaginary tulip inter
auspicious rationing centrist underneath
miserly formidable auricular primula
diver mortality infamy, yesterday an
optional digression invisible groan; mane
cantering furtive imminent gruesomely
polychrome submarine divan divined
persecuted arrangement give or take.

Lakeside inlet forestry ambivalent orchid
dividend elfin distended ripeness, butler
tissue disgruntled lampshade obliged
masterly oligarch tit for tennis batch
deuce menace; hospice twice-told chills
heels planisphere dusted ousted cream
black mint laboured front of housed
pomegranate. Ascribed filed machine
porcelain promenaded voidal scrape it
heated exchange trombone paperclips;
munificent opulent tilth wealth iced
share-out slice facing opalescent at
major district mantelshelf. Abandoned
procurement tangible earlier western
entanglement quantum foreheads
leading profit scruple tussle oracular
trusted devoted twinkle bangle unclear
reach out foremost purse, gorse spruce
gooseberry piecrust tiffin sprain on
crane coinage within curse nursing.

Mulberry certainty anchovies fallacy so
friendship trap township purposefully
    burdensome; contrition underquote
    barricades barbed wire entire flash
olbas tricycle, culpepper mostly ginger
knee-joint appointed. Curtailment won
    afraid badge nudge, grimace candles
    storm lantern turnabout; moated lid
grange forage enforced sniff bruise, if
coiled serpentine margarine, snoozed.
    While away scarce affray sympathy
    daylight credit, bandages infringed
oiled syringe mange management, in
tended friends milkweed teasel way
    laboured central dalliance defiant
    opprobrium candid; feverish seed
plantation options scullery doggerel
terminal gluttony obloquy, populate
    fastidious dangerous ruffian wait
    sky-scrape manifested shoulder.

## SNOOTY TIPOFFS

## (2021)

# I

## – Menu Gastronomique –

'all jaw and upper gnashers'

1

Music in the ice-box, music by the sea,
  music at the rice-bowl, for you as well as me;
swinging from the rafter, after time for tea,
  ever-present laughter, in sweetest harmony.
Carol by the window, anthem at the door,
  mostly out at elbow, as two and two make four.

2

Swing low you kiddiwinks, all for vroom and groom,
  going for a run now, off to Montana soon,
just whenever get there going to be immune,
  going to as able be a dental floss tycoon.
Cruising for a snap-chat, joking in the snow,
  quicker with a back-pack, ever on the go.

3

I told them we're running on empty,
  it seems like we got a flat tyre,
just like our old dad Humpty Dumpty,
  rising up high on the wire.

4

Broken window, arms akimbo,
  the bollards flash up all night through;
forsythia spatters, see how it matters,
  want to sit down, then take a pew.

5

Fake fur ready for, furious oddly at sea at sea,
  the captain at mid-town distraction
was never a raptor for me, for me.

6

Many hands make lighter work,
   abandoning their task,
you get the cheeky answer pat
   before you even ask.

7

Dirigible invisible multiply escrow,
   if you won't tell forever then we'll never know;
orphan distortion all rose to the skies,
   in portion aversion to smother the prize;
ah pink hood that is good, two lovely black eyes.

8

This dullard lies over the ocean,
   his head-set is full of debris,
he's lost in his fried-up contention
   with nothing for you or for me.

9

Row row watch the stoat,
   floating down the stream,
many frowns of gleaming teeth
   all for you alone.

10

Very quickly bring the pumpkin,
   we shall eat it with a dumpling,
that's a treat won't make us sickly,
   sing this song alive-o.
Then we'll have a dish of marrow
   farced, delicious; pie to follow,
the whole feast for us tomorrow,
   sing this song alive-o.

**11**

Brandy in a bottle, brandy in a keg,
   if you don't want to throttle better sit up and beg;
glug in a mouthful, careful don't choke,
   the jug at the ready, no more a joke.

**12**

Blood ran over the lipsalve,
   dapper incarnadine,
sooner get pushed out of office
   that's if you didn't resign.

**13**

Ever the cat's whisker
   will for sure make it friskier
as not got a blister anywhere on its tongue;
   and yet blind as a bat, wherever it's at,
God fluster the mister
   who glides between me and my sister,
I'll climb up the rung and sting like a gnat,
   preside in the middle and maybe among
the cats in pyjamas, so far and so few:
   their purring will calm us and whisper adieu.

**14**

My breakfast lies over the necklace
   these weevils are evil to see
those amber beads ride on the freckles
   and chase all these insects away.

**15**

Diplomat cantaloupe ride a cock horse,
   if it doesn't get tetter it'll maybe get worse;
he told me his story and swore it was true
   in dingle and dangle, the red and the blue.

**16**

Heigh-ho dayglo oh what a sight is here,
    incise, brutalise, eyes to the far and near;
you get the gist if not short shrift,
    tinker the bell and blink as well,
sidle the lid as ever did:
    incendiary endlessly wink.

**17**

Ostensible sensible, put out the best for thee,
    climb the vine and walk the talk,
squawking in fine degree;
    beans for us, save against fuss,
fie foe fum by gravity.

**18**

Here is Miss Muffett, enjoying her crumpet,
    better than curds and whey,
when a much brighter spider slid onto her platter
    so she gobbled it up with scarce a hiccup,
and an elegant sip of her tea.

**19**

In stooks of hay, come out to play,
    for see the moon is bright as day;
some at home and some astray
    with looks of our fair lady.

**20**

Draconian pandemonium ever more to be
    sacrifice raised up on ice, in disability;
so take it back, ease off the slack
    for lame-set perpetuity.

## 21

They rode into town on a tramcar,
  as far and as bright as can be,
at first it was pork and a cutlet,
  a samovar down by the sea.

## 22

Honey in the morning, margarine at tea,
  underneath the awning in sweetest sympathy,
some like it tepid but some get it hot,
  good golly Miss Molly just see what she's got.

## 23

Tick-tock next o'clock,
  Ivan shall have a fresh plaster,
his foot is sore he wore inured,
  whichever the one that went faster.
And yet the scent was saturate,
  encased in alabaster.

## 24

Oh you happy parakeet, take a treat
  indicate; snap a busy bandicoot,
out on the street. If you don't you won't,
  or will until the few catch up,
the latch pursue. BLEAT ENTREAT

## 25

Just one cornetto, and all for me,
  is so perfetto, deliciously;
you too can have one, don't be upset,
  a second cornetto, a brave duet!
Take a big lick now, as you're the one,
  keep company with Caliban:
tin-pan alley in brand harmony.

**26**

Will the leopard change his spots,
  tie his tail in wavy knots
sail his boat on autopilot,
  float intrepid, tinted violet,
still as strange as a navy bosun,
  riding on a donkey.

**27**

Pigs might fly but I don't know why,
  one is one and all alone,
I wanna hold your hand he said,
  MacNamara's Ragtime Band.
Help yourself to an ice-cream cone,
  shunt the avenue, bold for revenue,
gag and splutter, grunt to utter,
  wealth in lieu, review all found;
digs to fidget as it's gone aground.

**28**

You never would guess
  that a shark in distress
would be meshing its teeth in a frenzy;
  but its habits are weird
when it's near disappeared
  with its gills going rabid in envy.

**29**

He thought he saw an albatross
  that fluttered round the lamp;
he looked again and found it was
  a penny-postage stamp.
    (*apol.* Lewis Carroll)

## 30

Jeepers creepers, where'd ya get those peepers,
   jeepers creepers where'd ya get those eyes?
Oh those weepers, how they hypnotise.
      (*apol.* Louis Armstrong)

## 31

Yankee-doodle with his poodle
   silver buckle at his knee,
first he scoffed a dish of strudel
   and called it macaroni.

## 32

The bear was addicted to chocolate,
   he'd roar for a bar every day;
his polar hair-style was immaculate
   though no one could ever say why.
He dwelt on his berg in the morning
   and would snooze there in comfort at night;
his target was bars to be crunching,
   the barest of bliss in delight.
      Often cheer, bonny bear,
      a bar makes you happy
      wherever you are.

## 33

Too late for a bloater, an egrimont floater
   imperilled and burrowed importunately
Early take a warning, a morning
   decoying, barely now inturning,
a racket set to dream;
   get it down on paper, now or maybe later,
open up the packet of a brand new ream.

## 34

Oh the drums go bang and the cymbals clang
  as the horns they blaze away,
you'd never believe the elegant wheeze
  for pleasing or sneezing all day.
    (*part apol.* MacNamara's Band)

## 35

Time to want as vigilant, as yet extant
  impersonate; rhyming locks intoxicate,
a fox as meant to see; his breast was rufous
  all intrusive, far away across the scree.

## 36

Resemble entangle a pig in the middle,
  it's just like a wangle to get one for free;
insisted permitted a bigoted idyl,
  the birth of a nation, elation chut-nee.

## 37

Blank misgivings still enliven
  sunk precision wishfully;
illustration implication,
  stupid biped called on cupid,
met his rank in ardency.

## 38

Just make do with what you've got,
  keep friends with one another,
dip your nose in the honey-pot,
  ever bees in clover.
Don't omit to take your time
  waiting for your brother,
listen for the clock to chime
  four times over.

## 39

Your teacup is safe in the saucer,
    your baby won't cry any more,
it went out the door with the porter,
    not lost but gone before.

## 40

Better quick, take a pic,
    your master's lost his whistling stick,
eggs for breakfast, toast for lunch,
    take a mouthful hear it munch.

## 41

Oh don't take a fancy to Nancy,
        I'm sure she will ever be mine,
we prance and advance in endeavour
    the more we adore, all the time.

## 42

Coriander he'll philander,
    throw the ashes in the stream,
wall germander up his dander,
    lawful splashing in the dream;
parsimonious impecunious,
    rain in danger red and blue,
now imagine like contagion,
    ever sojourn feverfew.

## 43

I got very tipsy on Friday
    so Saturday kept me in bed;
if ever were good, could be better,
    then mend it dear Liza instead.

**44**

Tree creeper sleeper, nuthatch keeps watch,
chaffinch cheeps its call;
all the birds you ever heard
slide deeper now, as next to catch
their seeds for one and all.

**45**

Reconcile, by the stile
in the meadow under shadow,
keep on trying adamantine;
upstairs downstairs in her chamber
dreadful sorry Clementine.

**46**

Helical follicle my fat hen,
she lays eggs for frontier men;
indifferent shell, elegant smell
just be sure to ring the bell,
as even so that's all very well
eglantine now and then.

**47**

That's the story morning glory,
play the card that guards the door,
way too hard in early warning
every day but more and more.

**48**

The bracken fronds out-turn their wands
in verdant green arising;
but mind your hands the stems can burn
as keen to earn, surprising.

## 49

Now I will arise and go, soon,
  to please the agency
and feast on beans still stupified,
  washing them down with honey;
no chore more boring than sentencing,
  to solitary poems in frequent swarms,
these phonemes sized to win a prize
  against this fancied rivalry.

## 50

Act still, pact mill,
  grain to complain from over the hill.
Don't be ill, swallow a pill
  or two if too few, purgative
yours to give, all good as new.

## 51

Gruesome indusium, betrothed in truffle pit
  to smell the peel and cut fresh incipit;
infuse attraction, nothing bruised or crushed,
  the finest swelling pleasure in a rush.

## 52

Ink effectual defacement enkephalin sybarite
  opiate designate, ice-rink to kelp, yours
on pause ensign coinage, encaustic keep
  in motion enlaced, incremental falconet.

## 53

Tinpot turnpike, strike to win, viscous
  hibiscus lesson to learn; western and
foreign, riding away, tiding over to cover
  distilling your palm with minimal harm.

**54**

She told the same old story,
  as clear as ever was,
to draw our loyal teardrops,
  to serve the nearest cause.

**55**

Lamb chop, tame crop,
  fuel moon very soon
originate profligate
  coruscate, pleat.

**56**

Teat.

# II

'Thy sheep be in the corn'

'And bids what will take all'

1

Old mortality young moderation,
  run across to the action station;
help yourself to what you care for,
  don't dismiss the why and wherefore,
first in best swan-sung creation.

2

Time enough for hanky-panky
  strike a pose, be very swanky,
just to snatch a bit of fluff,
  stuff and watch but don't resign.

3

Turn again accident, play this prank tomorrow,
  provident intransigent, stripes of black / yellow,
wasps will sting if not yet burn
  trapped in a jam-pot, cost a fortune.

4

Sane yet dotty, double wham
  thanks for nothing, out grand-slam,
ring the bell and tell the story
  like his brother Jackanory.

5

Let your fingers do the talking, sign up soon,
  hum in passing never linger, favourite tune;
heaven-sent in optimum to walk the nearby plank,
  shining brilliant flashes in the goldfish tank.

6

Aliquot to motherhood, tiny tots in the early brood,
  make an effort kitty, milky keeping warm,
show them how to toe the line, yours and mine
  forethought cream to the other side,
wide in welcome, silky at eventide.

7

Liberal corrigible, next be their chance,
  leading the overall a terrible dance;
act at once and ply your trade
  said then to the hen, my marmalade,
dressed in best kit and out on parade.

8

The muffins came next in the week ahead
  prolific with treacle much better than bread,
what's sauce for the goose plays fast and loose,
  the gander runs quicker more equal we know,
it looks more persuasive but it just isn't so.

9

Boiler-plate rejuvenated
  citrate fashion instinctive passion
cut-rate session bargain basement
  agile yet so far untasted,
mild but never spoilt. Don't panic:
  sleeper, awake!

10

Knees up knees up don't get the breeze up,
  never let your braces dangle;
tiger tiger all down inside her
  squeezing at the safest angle,
prouder rider ever sneeze up,
  haven't you had it long enough.

**11**

Tie your jacket, quell the racket,
  camomile is good for tea;
useful gadget's welcome magic
  made for two, for you and me.

**12**

Often boffin starlit incitement,
  snoozing means losing, warp and woof;
find a proof and raise the roof tightly,
  ration ointment, split erasure,
held in place as soft in flavour,
  carp impartial and that's enough.

**13**

Plink plank plunk, close to nearly sunk,
  under the wave if strong to save;
both will promise and will amaze,
  dink dank dunk, package of junk.

**14**

Aspic, novel trick, trim the lamp up the wick,
  neon strip is not much better,
switch it on and watch it stutter;
  toast the bread before the fire,
spread the butter good and thick,
  now it's ready to admire.

**15**

As clever however and bright as a button
  just do us a favour and snaffle a chance,
delay her light laughter to parry disaster
  and carry her satchel for only this once.

**16**

Strawberry jam, get a sun-tan,
indoor or out there's never much doubt
for very if ever, when chewing a bun,
regret either never, and now it's all done.

**17**

Kangaroo seeing you, soon as day passes
boys ogle at lasses if not wearing glasses;
they turn up their noses at a bunch of red roses
but lunch is the best as special request,
with a whoop sup the soup, on a hunch and munch
consuming with you gets to know what to do.

**18**

Don't anyone dare, waving the cutlery,
even the forks become sticky and buttery;
rise in surmise at quirky quite soon,
fair shares with the corks and a runcible spoon.

**19**

Clothed all in green or so, vernal raiment on the go,
neither yes but neither no, tidal race containment:
if you claim the prize, soon the rest will recognise
that what you do is surely wise, wider arrangement.

**20**

Caption under action, extending the words,
all that's left is for the birds;
label in trifle, custodian's choice,
sweet custard undercurrent, heard in the voice,
if ever now once then probably twice.

## 21

You know you know and so do we,
  just hurry home in time for tea;
the enterprise is surely best
  to pass with ease the facile test.

## 22

Cordon for burden the spokes are polished clean,
  nautilus adagio invokes a submarine,
don't ever ask the question, just what does it mean:
  too early or too late but nothing in between.

## 23

Yes and snow, each the other worth the bother,
  look both ways and hold your gaze
one and another, confess in session;
  after many days of dearth he took
notice to flourish, pair to parish,
  know your ripest onions.

## 24

Bicameral bike, strike at the medal,
  fill with water right up to the level,
comical grin at the highest brim-
  stone shiny yellow, flutter in peril,
own to strike do what you like:
  mutter and clatter in town tonight.

## 25

Run to the front and don't hold back,
  watch in turn for the flight attack;
probable hubbub, up to the tape,
  close latest finish and undiminished,
extravagant head of an unwanted pack.

## 26

Cold for new and due for old,
   always bought and never sold;
chill at nil rate, irate reaction,
   hurtle her kirtle, rewarded inspection,
thoroughly tolerate, set double fold.

## 27

Electuary, lost the thread,
   sweet as honey up instead,
made election, dulcet voice
   cloud within the reach of choice.
Actuary looked ahead,
   found the data in the red;
made a prospect, calculated,
   later flex as right inflicted.
Feat feet, feasted,
   fleeting, heating,
pleat at most, best toast,
   not least, engrossed.

## 28

White, while quite guile, guillemot,
   wail, toil, lubricate instatement;
leap to station, loyal notation felt
   up in the blood and along the cheek.
Eight times conflated, surfeit made the grade,
   all of them alerted, haste and not afraid;
solemn mounted column, autumn in the dark
   over in the woodland, hear the foxes bark.
Some of us are wild ones and others are meek,
   stay on the lookout, not far to seek:
white, while and ready to leap.

## 29

Soft alpaca, Madagascar, win an oscar on the side,
  act the packet astigmatic, be a sister of the bride;
don't care was made to wear a brighter fleecy jacket,
  ever bold and never cold, best to be phlegmatic.

## 30

Untie the knot or, quicker, cut it,
  not yet time to kick the bucket,
grip the pail and give it a spin,
  if it doesn't fall out it will likely fall in.
Next mend it with a mandate, that's not very far,
  the odds are near even, are almost at par;
then, bask in the sunlight, there's plenty of fun,
  the pleasure of leisure has hardly begun.

## 31

Tinker tailor soldier sailor,
  rich man poor man beggar-man thief,
just to see if you'll be lucky
  count them out for light relief:
cherrystones along the plate,
  these will be your line of fate.

## 32

Catch as catch can, catamaran,
  sorrel for moral as nearly began;
then later potato, brandish the dish,
  if it's not roasted it must be a fish,
or a fetish more fitting, just as you could wish.

### 33

Wrap and burnish, indivisible plant,
   dapper too, makeshift prediction want
alembic district, skirmish affable out-
   cast taken aback, rejected; better stint
in racket vanquishment, storm-light jump
   overt averted uncontested, don't get stuck
on both insides emission chuck, admit
   politic miscible liable; cut on down
detainment lamp-black, dawn-light element.

### 34

Take a shine in good time, coincidence,
   lay the table, formidable affluence;
don't postpone it, do it now,
   set all in a gleaming row;
fortune favours brave advances,
   count the price, extravagances.

### 35

Well I never did you ever
   see a red and blue umbrella
out in the rain; so much depends
   on how beginnings shape our ends:
two steps forward, that's enough,
   no good cause to make a fuss.

### 36

Rise to the skies in most melodious twang,
   the feelings rang deep in blatant surprise,
sedulous credit was paid to inherit;
   the song she sang, as thus appalled, began
in proper visible slice, whenever dealing
   by civic merit at the violet hour ahead.
This much is nonesuch sceptic, culminant
   in prized affection, wrung in ardent stencil,
tempestuous soft pencil brought back to life.

**37**

Nor will if can, do ever best,
    the chef contested wins the prize
and stamps her foot, a big surprise,
    her early birds have flown the nest.

**38**

Year in hear out, ear at beat, about
    brass ensemble class without doubt;
suit plight fair warn, would entreat late
    passport mere working, out in the clear.

**39**

Near miss by a whisker painting a picture,
    dear heart listen yellow leaf here now;
where and how hard to bear, stay near,
    restraining admixture spread out below.

**40**

At high renown give a dog a bone,
    the topmost dad came rolling home;
no time like this, an eightsome reel
    manipulate a grand appeal.

**41**

Her herald's triassic dryad lightning
    of Heraclitus, purpose fancy free;
she'll shepherd her flock, block off inviting
    the malcontents' hermetic obloquy.

## 42

The birds were all covered in feathers,
    despite they were still very young,
their mother would keep them together
    and smother their beaks with her down.
Cheep cheep, all go to sleep soon,
    this tenderest care was a part of her boon;
she never would wake them until it was noon,
    chirrup chirrup and over, their favourite tune:
yet the process was instinct, none of feeling,
    the otherwise fancy so grandly appealing.

## 43

Harum-scarum, fetch your shoes and wear'em,
    pull'em on close and tie the laces;
if you choose to have a snooze
    just relax and don't make faces,
keep on watch to hear the alarum.

## 44

Many weeks to soak, was this a new hoax,
    tell the folks to seek; bliss it was, take
note not later than, when to come clean,
    uncover banter this weak, impetuously.

## 45

Bring out the scallop shell of quiet,
    beyond the limits of dismay
to be a pilgrim in this age,
    the spirit's nearby jubilee.

## 46

Guidance across the wider shore
    endures the brim of sustenance;
envelop this the darker floor
    on milken hill of elegance.

**47**

The beating heart its part declares
  as once before and now again;
be patient then for everyone
  whose radiant face so near appears.

**48**

No motion now as deep reflected,
  her silence gives no passing sound;
these powers by their muse surrounded
  give proof of vision's hours accepted.

**49**

Hid brow in shadow hesitates,
  as eyes descry how life awakes.

**50**

Ripcord rapid not quite attended,
  impact kingdom martyrdom suspended;
misted apiarist furtherest prismatic
  flight-path, lucid ring-tone attic.

**51**

Quilt rebuilded right up to the hilt, delight
  hem weft invention, joined together filled
and wadded tight close; warm as ever might
  be free of harm, arm in arm to infiltrate,
with pulse of self-heal, foremost indicate.

**52**

See your sinus sink to minus, go with the flow,
  one of them comes but the others will go;
now wait till later, sailing away
  with honey and money, for a year and a day,
and sing this song, don't tarry long,
  open the door and let me in,
for after the pasture, milk in the can
  will stream with the cream and leaving a dram.

**53**

Altitude multitude, my fat hen,
  she lays eggs for gentlemen;
brown, white or speckled, however they come,
  butter by the cruet and very well done.
Glory glory that's the story,
  eggs and bacon, time for tea,
extra helpings for you and me,
  and his soul goes marching on.

**54**

Careless love never careless enough, farewell
  best thrill, river of glory; in flow until
endeavour returns in risen season, far above
  par to yearn before; but that's another story.

**55**

Undertow for stop and go, object in pleat
  rejection; stoop and vote, electoral hint
suspected broadly of fraud instinct. Blow
  to dream esteem, loop mistake allowed.

**56**

Care-worn take your turn, comfort near
  impending; soon to learn, gain in earnest
whatever start, relenting; ransom defended
  from fearful symmetry mended, tune by heart.

# III

'He'll get by without his rabbit pie'

'Thuds. I want thuds! Like this!'
– Beckett

0

Indigo Borneo pass too
   chipmunk puddle-duck new;
navel by rival sea rising ahead
   to lesson impression, instead.

1

Indefatigable, certainly impracticable, chronic
   unretractable, spree; indistinguishable
epiphenomenal dink-di flunk, rhetic;
   insurmountable, unaccountable,
incommensurate, providentially,
   turn up your nose as we'd suppose,
environmentalism, fiddle-de-dee.

2

Open the valve, applying the salve,
   chasten resentment in token resolve;
close your eyes in mild surprise,
   out in the cold your fingers froze
but, time to take a modest doze;
   nascent, incessant, Prince Lucifer uprose,
and now you'll see, the whole world knows.

3

Cash-point disappoint bankrupt, treat
   marching to war – and did those feet
burn in the twilight, shewing the way,
   touching the hem at breakpoint of day.

4

High-falutin neutral gluten, sender to plunder
   burnt to a cinder; imperial rascal pass the parcel,
King Kong at the billabong, caught up in the mangle.
   Play the daylight, fly a dragon-kite, decorate
the tinder-box, on strike; speech is wordy, hurdy-gurdy,
   fix the tag on quite absurdly; search for bleach
shall diesel appease all these suitors, teach a lesson
   without aggression. Or bite the bullet short of land,
join up with an ampersand; button sewn with thread in hand,
   but NO MORE TWIST.

5

Sprig tactic sweet-briar orbicular run,
   find your way to a chelsea bun;
lemon is good but cinnamon better,
   spree now and economy later.
Just try not to throw a gaff,
   take your time and make a splash;
obvious sedulous repellent intimation
   provokes a fit of indignation.
The whole caboodle, white at the margin,
   gives off steam in strict aversion.

6

Pretty lark, formidable sycamore bark
   peel in spat gap, right up by the jetty;
evermore arc-light, sizeable uptight
   feels a distraction in functional sap.

7

Claiming insidious virtue slowly
   won't commute answerable allergy;
don't complain in ancient resentment
   when recent contrition skims metallurgy.
Alloyed steel holds upright stance
   whence next reveals extravagance.

**8**

Crib to ramble, perseverate,
    assemble squib, intoxicate;
drink to us only, rising ahead,
    planted out in the flower bed.

**9**

Burrito mosquito, wrap up lunchtime,
    peering ahead were no great crime;
seize your chance in an acid testing,
    dig for victory satisfactory,
either way is best arresting.

**10**

Referent pelting darts, far and wider still,
    dealt fair stir the hearts ease, well provided
with lookout ready at the mountain hut,
    for nearer shelter over the water, what
longs to please, contriving inmost part.

**11**

How to see across the gateway, five-bar set
    leaning to ponder, view over mute yet alert;
oval stipple, clear these eyes, receptive
    late in precise commission, even in surprise.

**12**

Don't yet wait, just exaggerate
    this minimal cannibal appetite,
open up for a headlong bite
    throughout the day and into the night;
none of them will hesitate
    to find their way by shining light.

## 13

Give what you can, like peas in a pod,
  in aftermath for clearing the path
on the way home, playing the trombone;
  what's not quite even must surely be odd.

## 14

Which ended that far forward, corner piece avarice
  too lace overhead custard race outmost to cover;
rice market resilient twill less anger, up to codon ceder
  mournful environ crimson.
Neither tether brace overt issuance twice surplus,
  who then licence pluck off; match wish switch
drastic text, grievance inch.

## 15

Cat, gut
  hike the string
over the bridge,
  like anything.

## 16

Wash trade persistent mash parsnip, up
  agency surplus rash tip apricot;
fashion supposing coaxial acrobatic
  by amateur fixture made fast, officiate.

## 17

See saw summary, hardly drawing outline,
  how to reckon otherwise, multiple subscription;
don't slide crosswise, better straight on downwards
  to hit within conviction, by fossil immunise.

**18**

You should be elegant, almost transparently,
  comic abridgement for the striking clock
in turn to confirm the crest of proficiency;
  the others in wedges of night-flowering stock.

**19**

Assuredly set forwardly they looked to be outrun,
  and yet the paradiddle flourish scarcely had begun;
invited to the dance but silent, unexpected, for
  as if in trance they'd all been eaten: every one.

**20**

Abra cadabra, take your ride on a zebra,
  wear all your best jewels as well;
you'll look fine in a crown as you bob up and down
  with the crowd of onlookers, pell-mell.

**21**

Take it on the chin then throw it in the bin,
  bravery will win the day;
whatever they say will be free of dismay,
  slavery alternative for fun.

**22**

Accuse for a bruise already black and blue,
  up-beat on the street in a fracas;
just don't be more stupid than an infantile cupid
  or more crass than an idiot jackass.

**23**

Glory glory alleluia, better now to soon construe ya,
  time to take a breather on the winning way before;
sing the song of triumph in a feverish alliance,
  never deject in retrospect, dexter protect her lore.

## 24

Cracker-jack alpha-snack ride a black horse
with salt as its savour to Banbury Cross;
liable medal to follow in line,
both useful and toothsome, no lack or by force.

## 25

Fearsome old harridan, tatterdemalion, foursome
uncertain as Buridan's ass; mount to the apogee
touted in forestry, one or the other as come to pass:
you know we are slow, like a stroke in stained glass.

## 26

Will glean where they fell in the furrow, tonic as
down in the silt; what he remembers, the
warm-glowing embers; nor borrow nor lending, be true.
Driven when given then leaning, and tilting over to you,
included even the open seam, yet still for interview.

## 27

Rock-pool dark spool dyed-in-the-wool remark,
yet top-speed the anchor pair will knock, feed the park,
the staff of life in tidal rush; others abide,
while first reverse the tenancy, just for the ride.

## 28

Blow the fuse refused below, choose bemused in view,
fuchsia avowed current flow, indigo wouldn't do,
light in flight over wooden shoe; flash loft ago to
sabot reset, no watt by vault illuminate.

## 29

Guzzle the crossword, niggle the puzzle, nothing venture
fluff and win; customary sure be wary, warden burden
spin indenture; weasel feature easy peevish unlike dervish
whirl and flamenco, censure credential system interim.

## 30

Ill-met my delight, a moonlit night rejected,
proud and greedy, up to speedy, silent close
in octagon; prune the rhythm soon forgiven
yet injected, promised first prothalamion.

## 31

Hot-pot warm charm intrinsic flimsy too,
after disaster hold tight to partner, better me and you;
scald the poet or will he know it, sight unseen,
go with the flow in a soup tureen: auld lang syne.

## 32

Peat bog, egg nog,
while once a tadpole,
now a frog.

## 33

Firm adhesion indubitable concretion,
negligible corrigible attenuated plaque;
write up the caption to captivate attention,
cover it upper with scarcely a mention,
stick at with it over, flat-pack.

## 34

Decide fairly and clearly,
right more justly than nearly,
the nail on the head
from A through to Zed.

## 35

Better to win what it says on the tin,
  treason won't prosper, in or out of season;
what's the reason? Easy to see: when succeeding,
  none would ever dare call it treason.

## 36

Debit for rabbit, for hare in a jug
  is just how you like it, no call to be smug;
the outermost planet will crank like the hours,
  being fit as a fiddle, endowed with its powers.

## 37

Possibly simplify how could be brought to bear,
  taught to surrender in no time at all;
clear the adventure from tiger's verandah,
  in chalk rudimentary across to the gantry
for rigorous plenty, inventory's trawl.

## 38

Petaloid signet, arachnid motivated,
  camera verified similar instigation;
will-power all in flower, sprinkle elation
  like powder, outsider the spiderman's digit;
lilac-scented sentry walk, talcum revisit.

## 39

Bestow steep slope invert gastric silk,
  leaping curtain anew; skimmed milk drink
only to me, deeper below and drastic, shirt
  uncertain; open skill spindle without hurt.

40

Liturgical surgical, a stitch in good time,
    praise without pressure, for mending the join;
suit with your suture, loosen with cream,
    days after days with the aim to redeem.

41

Cycle cyclamen upsprung, heart-leaf well
    instil oval until cantankerous quail;
glow folded florets acknowledge turrets arrayed,
    jewels under shadow, menu anchored, unpaid.

42

Pudding in the morning, sunlight for tea,
    supper even tastier, just pass the cup to me;
later when it's darker, time for a night-cap,
    remember the provider, a lap-top for free.

43

Uncolourful corpuscle encyclical dude,
    subsist at the table, consuming fine food;
in hunger no longer, keep out of the soup
        but even so, better to stay in the loop.

44

Turn up, or back
    but not distract;
if it's raining,
    wear a hat.

45

Tantalise terrapin indicative frugal set to win
    terrific monody huge repining analyse within,
moisten inflation soon blow out your cheeks
    and go with the glow into opening fresh wakes.

## 46

Bring back, close the shack, the shark will be
   laughing outrageously; get into swim, close to brim,
so either will cover, both as can be; discover for once
   the porridge allowance, all the way over, serially.

## 47

Filet of beef, above and beneath
   merchant of wine to lightly dine;
beaten till soft in the undercroft,
   enticed replete to the taste of a dream.

## 48

A zoot suit a quivering newt and next below, a stone:
   each one being just as seeming, live or not its own;
telluric flourish both encouraged, ever make the grade
   by apt allowance forwardly, a shovel's not a spade;
yet match the front for all of them, leaving well alone.

## 49

Higgledy piggledy drop them on the floor,
   plenty of room for very many more;
abandon the heap then, quite easy to find,
   as soon to recall: out of sight, out of mind.

## 50

Forget-me-not, remember, here's rosemary for you,
   sweet-peas if you please, will call to mind, ensue
in time for thyme just bruise the stem, intense
   thalictrum interdiction, as easily dispensed.

## 51

Drop, tip, tappet, misfit; attic breakfast win
   the contest freshest activate, the top run to spin;
look homeward so to find the line-out before
   climb up deliberate, across the open floor.

52

I thought it was a mere mistake, the notion taught better:
  a slip-up in the mental kit, as back to front, director
asleep to warrant free attachment, just so now you know
  to find the link without a blink, reclining on the pillow.

53

Lean into the ear, learning to hear
  the tilt in harmonic, as been there before;
in echo respectful and true in heart-mind,
  as back into forward, look hopeful to find.

54

Sardine industrial bacterial invasive,
  internal adhesive as tight as a drum,
refashion affection evicted, occasion
  will surrender the whole batch in choice as begun.

55

So half crazy, easy on the eye,
  air cruising round about, sweet as apple pie;
see how it goes our Miss Twinkle-Toes,
  Winken and Blinken swam in the sky,
click the box and wear odd socks;
  agree the key to link the locks,
wash the dish and lick your chops
  low down so and up on high.

56

Granted granitic, give the bone a dog,
  especially whenever all shrouded in fog;
reckless for calcium, granular idiom
  tipped with iridium, sleep like a log.

# IV

'If we're too scrupulously just,
    What profit's in a place of trust?'
        - John Gay

'oh yes we have no bananas,
    we have no bananas today'

**1**

A wheeze for cheese in fridge to freeze,
welsh rarebit pledge allegement;
where e'er you walk to trot and talk
relieve in scared sufficement.

**2**

Orotund go to ground, shout at voice-top treble
to sprout impounded hoist at once, and yet so be able
as doubted choiceful; all the birds fly to fill the sky
in clouds of round-about feathers; remember to seek
at end of the week, close to the reach of our tethers.

**3**

Pacify
close one eye
wink;
a testament
more high, forwent
don't fly, blink.

**4**

Tell past one, sell by later, spell fast
debater, muddled shouted down-wind;
do as told, new lamps for old, entangled
like a waiter's jam bun in a huddle.

**5**

Unkind wind refined, early or late;
chill to the bone encrust with frost,
making this moan beyond the gate;
brave to survive as ever will
and gulp to swallow, take your fill:
the fate of human-kind.

**6**

Out, redoubt,
  a final bout;
sink to the floor
  or nothing more.

**7**

Further on ruin in charcoal to burn,
  whether in flame at still-candid specks,
or whilst coalescent the same effervescent
  to lessen impressions the others refreshed.

**8**

Sing this song of enterprise,
  light reflect in woken eyes,
sermon on the wing subject,
  beyond surmise in retrospect;
now the chorus, ever porous,
  swings in triumph nothing broke,
endowed with joyous maxim-opus,
  wins the way with artichoke.

**9**

Take up a cruise with a fast pair of shoes,
  that's a feat for the feet on the run;
the ocean's promotion will refuse this commotion
  to refasten this welcome in fun.
A sylvan incursion trod the sand-bar in person
  as the boat floated high on the wave,
saving waste at the waist-line afar in erosion
  excused by exchanges disguised.

**10**

Monorail crocodile, tangible currency, while
  fluency sensible ample discretion; cream
in a crock locks honour's intention, angelic
  we'll smile, be late at the close of the day.

## 11

A whelk-purchase mollusc, frustrated advancement,
   the grit and the pearl make a pair on the spree;
tuck under your tongue like a suckable winegum,
   saving another left over for me. Keep in moisture
like milk for an oyster, enhanced by a glance;
   a decoction infusing and soothing for free.

## 12

Deliver at the door, scattered profusion
   right to the step by the fanlight window;
in its parcel-gilt decorate alcove survivor,
   doronicum grown on the warranted salver.

## 13

Solitary pathways, voluntary half-strays,
   incentive to pensive the shadow elemental;
will airy force avail the course, the meadow
   veiled aloud in cloud; ideas now incidental.
These thoughts are light and easy, but
   they strike still echoes, surreptitiously.

## 14

Whizz-bang doodle sluggish, crevice folded
   old-time ermine mandolin, seamew renewed;
immense propensity, city dissenting modicum
   extreme sensation, dimensional conjoint;
'yet none of these were suited, if you please'.

## 15

Habit influx hilarious, laugh past
   aircraft gesticulate obvious freight;
none so dusty as bread is crusty, crab
   rabbit fabulous sideways, praise at last.

**16**

You knew it was true, too close to the bone,
  the crux of the question on nebulous loan,
yet time takes its toll, a clang on the bell
  adventure for denture, at so far from home.

**17**

Astringent reagent, give the pug his due,
  lots for me but not for you: your chance
this week will earn its peak, like chicken pie
  like peas in a pod, apt to scarify, qualify.

**18**

Deeming or dooming, zoom dreaming venture
  arctic district intimidation; none pass by
in tempered attention, imminently free
  of due disillusion, indiscriminately.

**19**

Your turn already now, flew endow who
  will sow by reaping, speed the plough; go
to gravel several platesful average
  unit at this limit, hollow inclination, too.

**20**

Offer incentive to witness retentive
  the logic liturgic enrolled as a river,
from stream to tribute, tricuspid alarm:
  it might do you good, will bring you no harm.

**21**

Buried, denied in a rapid parade, dialect local
  in grand ceremonial; take out assurance
implored in endurance, to foster an ostler
  is wise beyond guesswork, claiming the prize.

22

Evidently, variously as possible bi-lateral
doctoral euphony, comedy declared in the air;
yet further aware, still impassible symphonic
flattery, fun underdone or by hock in repair.

23

Flageolet coronet at budget correction,
ice-cream cornet regard with affection;
fruity impeachment the cheek all in blush,
enjoy sans annoy but once is enough.

24

Sooner than sober whenever the labour, oboe
included boding well fluted, infatuate but
moonstone gamesome led to peace released
who'll say another day, voluntarily tuned.

25

Over the brow this new address, too late
for anyone to be impressed, or cress with egg,
with the sand which flies, blown by the wind
in swirling rifts alleged, in everyone's eyes.

26

Power corrupts, that's its advantage
over contrition as it surely destroys
the mind thus infected, to open a space
for the next hardy voyager in that imminent race.

27

Push-button interruption, think you're so smart,
holding the whole but it's only one part
of the jumble to rumble, to waken your gut
by the sole intercession, remit and instruct.

## 28

The engine gave a minor squeal, just heard
  above the din of satisfaction, soon abrupt
to deal a share a good less fair; absurd
  in match for dinner each a swimmer here.

## 29

Oh it's sweet in August, as nonplussed adjust
  the lost joy of folly as everything's past,
like a dream in the evening, the morning will show
  the sequence of days is all that we know.
And yet the love of loveliness
  will save a soul in deep distress.

## 30

Asked about death the master has said
  'it's a step in the right direction'—fled
away like a fancy, confounded liberty
  far too expensive for you or for me.

## 31

Hold my hand or at least a single finger,
  much better not to wait or even linger;
dark night approaches, that's its job
  to clear the air without a sob.

## 32

Long run more fun
  catch the bus the right one; keyhole
surgical, bicycle manorial, latch the gate
  by jaw debate, no fuss yet begun: the albatross!

## 33

Put some speed on polyhedron, don't be slow
with your life in tow; sow the seed with a knife
below holly ahead, born and bread, spread butter
up crumb guernsey begun, given invigilated.

## 34

To get out by a rival emotion, never
the same river, hold on to fear before
it slides away and leaves you in dismay
at missing reason posing as the foe.
The way is forward, sideways sometimes works
but later back is not the one that shirks
the rear-view mirror, settles up the score
where less as ever always signals more.

## 35

Casting out terror leaves a vacant spot,
your carefree jubilation to out-jest
these heart-struck injuries, mimic new disasters;
they crowd like fresh battalions, eager spies
trying our patience, good out-runs the best.

## 36

Nautical vertical, laying an egg
to dwell in the shell must assuredly be
an effort of spirit and feathers, besides
no chicken for breakfast but where it had been
if boiling hadn't supervened, providently.

## 37

These words are not mine now, although hardly yours
but somewhere between, in lexical arrears
to last until lost in the welter of sanctions
that dangle at the angle of entrance and silence.

38

Mostly lazy, as far as we could see,
  the seals will gambol in the waves, like to be
lazy, stir-crazy whenever they can
  and boastful on savannah, evidently.

39

Sleep tight through the night,
  see the greedy fleas don't bite;
who's to say, if you get bitten,
  you'll feel a seizure of contrition.

40

Possess the vestments, less forgetful
  memoranda insignia repined;
indifferent silently, piously promising
  free of duress or propaganda inclined.

41

Cotton button-hole, Avogadro's count,
  gratin in satin the final amount
will reckon sufficient as adamantly
  draped round her neck, impetuously.

42

Petersham pleats billow entailment,
  frail ostentation reviewed as confuted;
next in repeats, stand up unavailing
  like fishers at dawn, pitched under the willow.

43

Drive to distracted excess of calibration
  above and below, well beyond retention;
first-come last-served, just in shares
  as answers to a crocodile's tears.

### 44

Be wick and sarcastic, plucking the lark
   spurred in the fable, far out of luck;
in feather together, not a fat chance
   luff to press to the front and label at once.

### 45

Trees embark at their roots in endless disputes
   and will not give a hoot; without sound
will shed all their leaves from head down to foot
   by the way left astray on the ground.

### 46

Cow and gate, set luscious estate,
   stile for style, fold anticipate;
milk tray either way, wield array
   unharmed farmland not to wait.

### 47

Good heavens or bad, there's mostly a choice,
   whatever is said in the whispering voice;
there's pay as you go or best by results,
   the sky floating by, whatever its faults.

### 48

When the heart stops, its business concluded
   there's not much to do, however deluded;
immortal longings, like belongings,
   abandon their fate at the turnstile's gate.

### 49

Funny-bone not far from home, fungible
   tangible laugh while you can; storm-clouds
amuse with amnesty's cruise, never refuse
   a joke in disguise when comical passed as crime.

**50**

Longing to see the rolling river,
  travel far to greet its shore;
hearing the waves rewarding attention
  with saving monody, evermore.

**51**

Sits. vac., not much lack beside the bark
  relation; neap destiny inventory skip
as loaded up-ended, where fate will reside
  however impatient, denied its outmost grip.

**52**

Duel contested momentary alphabet;
  lower or upper case singing for supper,
one of these surely will end up dead.
  Challenge imbalance, outward returning
get shot of this fancy, right out of your head.

**53**

Rage at rag, sage sagging, keep your temper
  at a venture, wage labour laburnum open;
cool beans what this means, pea blossom two
  tureens fill with non-sense, see nowt broken.

**54**

Keyboard aloud, permit fermented independent,
  sashcord smart cone, phonic cloudscape wait;
printed screen elated before laconic went
  into debate, own wash untoward or not relent.

## 55

Locate pro-rata custody, prodigy assignment
in oddity refinement, mystery of modesty
driven like snow and ready from below
by self-example most now to forgo.

## 56

Out of my hand, into the strand advancing,
condoned by debit found intemperately,
the script admits a tolerant entrancing
in habit undisclosed, its open scree.

# V

'After this nothing happened'
　　– Plenty Coups

'There is no such thing as nothing'
(*Nichts gibt es nicht*)
　　– Christian Wolff

'The day lives us and in exchange
We it.'
　　– James Schuyler

1

Guest requested as a new addition, will
    hedge to the upper crest of the hill; how
receptive to wedge intermission, inaction
    for welcome in best, fresh-water escrow.
Lend what you can, one at a time, fill
    edgewise in faction, approach the sublime.

2

Looking after number one,
    all the rest is underdone,
the whole damn shot must weigh a ton,
    ever better gradely.

3

Certain with the curtain call, night must fall,
    screen apportioned to one and all,
water feature traffic creeper up against the wall;
    caught a cold in civic profit, win weather-vane,
team again by perfect nature, call the open blame.

4

Cold meats seldom treats,
    bring back this barrack to me to me,
sweat first next to last out of wedlock,
    bleating in trifling ignominy.

5

There's never a time for revisions,
    when all of our horrors come true;
illustrious purpose imprisons
    the tale of our sorrows for you.

6

Out flat, merriment,
   see what, ferry-boat;
take the hint, sniff the mint,
   out-taken incident.

7

Writ large, sweet periodic, coming for to find
   along the wing-tip inkling, pause to choose
at home at last, out of the blast, in blues,
   invest a sum to roam, too small to lose.

8

Bangalore bungalow, wheelbarrow scintillation,
   march-past next to last, elephant panting;
fall out of his bunk, down the pachyderm's trunk,
   elbow now-eventual punctilious ventilation.

9

Abridged and scolded, wandered afield, more
   to moorland pavement, rock-folded heat;
ingredient all in rank amazement, ridge
   and furrow tendered, stream up to bank;
annual cable in hidden entreaty, fleeting
   surrendered as able eyelid in fable, link.

10

Or then goitre in future, hornfels facies
   in turquoise cluster prism flowing patches;
orange-brown iodine lustre through the watches
   of night in despite of apatite in cloister.

## 11

Wheeze against tweezers, pleasing housing,
   mouse knees taint accidental acid profusion,
winter freezing enter announcement; alike
   fragment douse the glim for sure remember him.

## 12

Whosoever umbrella server together, spoon
   merger finical; elaborate deserving further,
panicle umbel cymbal reserved in weather
   remonstrate, thimble immediate, soon.

## 13

Don't like resemble avengement, still valid
   plentiful painted, take-away bewray merit
for instance circumstance, amble agreement
   sensible limit too long we have tarried.

## 14

Know your onions, once enough foundations
   advance cations intended, how to grow
undulate in spate, insurgent exiguous
   polychrome aerodrome; in best relations.

## 15

Orison nymph since startle astonishment,
   replenish her lavish insisted presentiment;
none like one first, averse to resistance,
   by sane at the start although later demented.

## 16

Obtuse and tormented to whisper sub-rosa,
   reposing in fragrance befell into fragments;
downy encrowned and supposing beforehand
   to spill out the petals and visit enclosure.

17

Rainfall in oval template, evident frustrated
   temperament gainful employment; for none
will or even can surmount the torrent ban,
   current in stream-line and rainbow instated.

18

Obvious salient undercurrent, salvia wild
   laid and displayed in radiant evident air;
steal away to say your piece, trice care
   via just and fair, repair in winter mild.

19

Prevented melancholy gentleman slim ottoman
   singleton, impudent circuit impended, can
amended anchovy synergy, currently rampant,
   pertinent incident tangled up catamaran.

20

Alone bound plantain finding stolon baited
   in cruet maternal minimal minuet improved
plainsong gorget postern wicket gatehouse
   after taken on board already get in use.

21

Dune expense loss adjusted, benefit tactful
   retracted, gathered moss must aspect edifice
implicit hospitable how and whence to act
   roaming the shore, prospecting for active fish.

22

In cause of licence, causeway giant beneath
   of course despite you surely can't act death;
to be abundantly confirmed, gaping ridiculous,
   whatever else by now, enough is quite enough.

23

From start disported reckon the upsteps onward,
   in flight attend, beckon win to mend, alert
of fixed ideas prospective samphire perilous
   counted and steady, near-already to assert.

24

Carve out the glimpse of dawn light, enjoinment
   a wave, incense of close full-head perfume
to be born, various enclave hispid vervain
   beyond dread, horizontal plinth inspired.

25

All along well known spilt ribbons, bent
   back laid narrow synonym cairn opportune;
returning foreign current in hollow stent,
   rowan imagine ebony regional ingredient.

26

Speak your mind, talk in turn, galleon rim
   on phantom spendthrift surface brain-fold;
carried ahead keyboard evolve to walk back,
   talc trans-mafic adrenal persistent, told.

27

Affix tinted to sprocket; vaunted encashment
   fragments debated, ransack gullible link attic
distended last-ditch matching victim runagate,
   sent to see out to sea, timely switch synoptic.

28

Shear pressure sphere fissure hyaline, twine
   obtain between, resumed evening soup aligned
in credit orbit, impact admixture contested;
   cross purpose cut-purse then where group bested.

29

In which the fact and bear up, over clear for
   attract more, sever and replay, switch or
discover where to wear; react at first inspect
   reversed, into favour across day immersed.

30

Chilled cold the child, now warm no slim harm
   out-fold beyond alarm, wild in wood to find
comfort taught the mission's lesson; none
   for dear heart's passion, free and not to bind.

31

Make to brake, wake at last, in edgeway birth
   but heard his son was slain; all no worse
could come from fate replete with grief abound
   and tied with tidings, whether and ever found.

32

Will be fair both in pair resounded; into season
   ensign proven up to task, by such free giving
make it ask; grateful aware, with good reason
   even to level spare out-revel, first to last.

33

Carline midnight scarce in sight, bitten treated
   averse if terse until nearby plight, aligned
redound to suited match fuel alight, relaxed
   to wait to grind or lose the noon's repose.

34

Laminate by lamentation, lustral introjection
   at head of river, lap to mead; catchment said
over to deliver, remedy instead; whole recite
   pitch conviction, nocturn in time's goodnight.

35

Telic reward foremost imposture, aboard within
   felix agrostis price-list precedent bow wave;
reduced prudence insect fosters slow rhyme win
   famous spurred to safety, primate autoclave.

36

Those feet to meet in ancient ways, beloved
   stays of fate up neighbour street; follow
the model aptly to leave evenly along the car,
   allowed blended lent, in eminence to borrow.

37

Votary orator fashion decision, amalgam trim
   hopeful botanical session impressively; too
motion elected effortful struggle, outspoken
   predator warm in open muddle, around the brim.

38

To take it upon the self-made macaroni pudding,
   the pony club disaster in plaster, cap-feather
all together ell for leather, did you ever groan
   shelf played in loan, makeshift swift endeavour.

39

Legal leg-irons, ikons reckon, acorn into oak,
   elegant legates crystal stable ready to soak,
to ripen occasion in anger's expression, bespoke
   indignation in visible ration, passion invoke.

40

Do as would, little kneeling eyebright, minister
   slender innocent herald titrate sheep's-bit;
accept aesculapian triton's sorrel hornblende,
   scant dozen barium roses erst deserted split.

### 41

Inevitable veritable in service promised before
  mooted suitable distinct affable beside the door;
nervous hardly virtuous compromise, crevice for
  crampon distinction, vital from roof to floor.

### 42

In a hurry virtually corn spurry classical temper
  mentioning dawn mentality elastic alembic iron
vertical clamber remembered; agaric project flit
  renegade outworn civil slumber evidently try-on.

### 43

Fill to burden prelude unharmed, scenic at tonic
  laden by oat sidelong, feudal abraded bitten
choric warm seclusion; notation patronymic
  swung lowdown of name, old before time, attic.

### 44

Long before reverie, allegory now historical
  interval close window ease to please, as well
cool prepared; whirlwind every fitted signal
  ringing outward, spool to grain, temple bell.

### 45

Compose cellulose praise receive, whoever knows
  or tries, due energies stair by rise suppose
chiasmus enclosure; stable crab-wise income sees
  declared surprise revising, flair to breeze.

### 46

Nitric call back intrinsic, felsic quartic dip
  inclined unspoiled, attracted; dictate fathom
winsome instress profession, of garrison often
  circuitous companionable; parallel bud-nip.

## 47

Antiseptic yet dramatic, propaedeutic synonym,
tame lucid entertainment train to winter
indenture, elastic sequence mustard cutting,
slice up with toast revisit the most; into
tunnel abundant accompaniment trustingly.

## 48

Truncheon bench lunch soon finance balance sheet
broke latent fit pursuit; lurch intake vertex
axe head spreadeagle will jump the life talcum,
modicum inflamed stitched up tight and neat.

## 49

In work it out-front, instant sent in murk
current dint embrocate; can't wit until dark
ovate deposit implicated, cement refill or lurk
shadow statement, shade trees blend the park.

## 50

Does she pronounce, her once soothed brow ahead
of said sole ceremony reduced by now untied,
truce admitted free indeed, herald upper wide
by money's bid to whole-accept if not afraid.

## 51

If so repair, past care or cure red intended
to mark and wear last so in time befriended;
make fast before missive to frame, implored
cursive assented, same-day core, adored.

## 52

Egret by white, dip flow in running current
   where fluted plumes fold slow and elegant;
know better in slow tears, assume wild repose
   part and restored, invest at evident close.

## 53

Scot-free flip-top, herring-bone insertion,
   selling dear from near, soon to be uncertain;
take a look not brought to book, phone disaster,
   falling down to break your crown, tumble after.

## 54

Cow and Gate, Cow and Gate,
   that's the pap that babies hate;
don't be a coward, throw it out,
   eject the whole batch down the spout.

## 55

What to have in mind, cranial hold refinement
   fulsome cross-section new rogation defined
before porous ignored, us daily foolhardy all
   forgive livid perfervid, brain in waiting; cored
and peeled in sight, the errant winded parasite.
   Nearby rescinded oblivious, drained of memories,
tenor sustained, offended; river-chorus invited
   in train of thought imported, fully water-tight.

## 56

Wandering one the two is done, tell to know
   next in tow over watch them growing;
no time like now presentiment up flow
   to borrow ungainly yet smoothing the brow.

## 57

For you I'd do
    the whole thing through
below, above
    for now, for love.

# SEA SHELLS TOLD

**(2022)**

## SHELF ONE

Blatant corrective back stroke intended built to last out, distinct flamboyant did say as promised prominent wink; suppliant women tractate undulating stock-dove anxious missive confluent bleating shop terrain. Reversion all to bring problematic notorious impetus torrential nightjar day braid allayed brocade, provocation intended orient lionheart distress limitation monthly allowance alluvium bin tippet manoeuvre armrest; backup motionless weaponise franchise ebony grill at first renounce, once belated conjugate gateway imply concision illusory lean-to bolster banana. Prudent butter latent bet to batter conciliate waiter aggregate, tentative incandescent moor put up sword-play lexical phantom pantomime; step threshold up.

## SHELF TWO

One more no door to play for that's in ribbon to tantalise, cheese ensure verdure appertain venture distracted open vulture picnic, aperture truth to silicate line break stanza mosquito; locality step pathogen beetroot allspice enticement stationer, braille moment condiment diligent carefree acerbic multiplicand toilsome private mouthwash hillside slippery flapjack turtle; supine twelve decided dissident clamorous detergency teflon cufflink manacle eyebrow wooden spaniel, suitable sentinel bearded clematis iris carelessly motherhood actinic syphon. Typhoon brim-full macerated coarse fishery embrocation position collops, collapse welfare hand found spinal motionless glove tribal in view denial fiscal however boiled.

## forthwith surplus

Fragile tussock glasswort cornbelt wheatfield avoidance payment eagerly hideous, formidable bellwether fridge, gracious purchased blackberries winch indifferently for licence; trifle odious carbolic anhydrous mawkish ride a cock slice manage at gallop, orangery tussle struggle magnificent laden frightened undulant; ovoid avid avoidance promotion spacious nebulous contended severity. Valid accustomed briar abbot projected demeanour iron-age fort sorted serene outline, worry quarry negligible laryngeal potency affirmed squalid infamous regiment; doorsteps doctorate candied peel palp arachnoid marsupial altogether indignation, repudiated tap first.

## forthwith surplus

Spider weblock collarbone fountain toothpick so many advances force dismay at late complacency easy, go ahead brisket privately laid in webbing for tribute objurgate lie of landslip block out grip; distended penguin musician hasten punctual, diurnal mournfully claimant daybreak freakish absolution suspension. Silverweed at space lattice wasted costed undigested, climb into rhyme arrant dogged what's far ahead strip out by tack pollock; irritant execute tulip frolic misgiving symphonic footprint–intact refracted sign annoyed roadside indifferent shirt-collar button-down stupefying craquelure, coffee majesty why full rationing winter weather ink.

## forthwith surplus

Marauding cosmetic rice pudding-stone engineered domain damp undercurrent indiscreet, sufficient contrition carriageway osmosis muster whoever distinguishment vervain, karst forest dice invite immense evidence live breeze banquet, planetary relinquishment mention admonished mountain tarn; watchtower raining integral spindrift interest divested strung-out pontefract, liquescent finish auld wheeze pathway passion-flower plover helmet. Icerink pipe slink eloquent windswept cosmos pink languid elegant pinecone, rock shatter powder lower downstream; arriving minimal limpid orthoclase twinned regained in greensand zeugma pragmatic at frogspawn dawdle tactical to liquid patchwork inkhorn redstart.

## SHELF THREE

Graphite optician lonely lobster transistor, muletrain foreigner, passionate fruitcake mighty volcanic pipe scornful terrible acorn retinal reticule ovoid conditional water soldier; amphibole ampule trial rejected acute manorial diorite confessional generosity slight deliquescent. Rehoused indicative gallivanting poisonous fraudulent paintwork, slight wet undercoat reprehensible emollient pleasantry pheasant terrine tangerine macerate replicated outburst; last to yet fluorescent pitchfork diablastic little kneeling eyebright credulously loyal blackbird, at cushions emergent greeting, action-packed later carousel matchstick strikes lit work-load head paced gravitational labradorite insistent. Poignant reverend mayonnaise orchestrated redundancy, subtle mantelpiece plimsole line acidulate imputation herewith complaint maintenance coruscate embassy endlessly mint disintegrate cucumber encumbrance embracement forcemeat tout empyrean miniaturise inhumation epithelian, portraiture wheaten blossoming criticise stabilisers shaving fantastic diaphragm implicit meteorite alight.

## forthwith surplus

Sebaceous cruficer or mortified pinafore, adoration cordite smitten shouted plywood antagonisement, viscid buds creeping twitch fuss pastry suburb rhubarb level cross paving slabs hobs reduce ever at margin procrastinate; ineffable cantankerous beyond medium fancy witty subsequent toilsome repatriated lady's smock crank upwards barrage redemption, immediately unlike the mastiff inflation whose chance to discover, forever, ominous servile circulating goldfish bowl amplified moderate munificent. Darling spring fields whenever save poised condign toffee immoderate lucid, inglenook discrepancy coal coral coded meadow fescue sibylline shallot polyglot sit; intersperse amercement affranchise harmonium toponym unwelcome, caesium clockface waste handy chill brandy why to fly askance. Mallow flow untroubled if mellowed milkweed sized treatment, cannula central.

## forthwith surplus

Dulcimer bankrupt tongue-tied trolly privet indult, moult; beetles curate implicated; ducat duvet livid piglets burnout, spigot brittle candlelight, granulitic spathe aromatic gymnastic o-olite. Ticklish orphic orotund flustering imposition degradation, oceanic dinted chamomile enfilade dosage sausage cottage riverside marginalise listless; capsicum interim disentangle resurgent nasturtium cultic coffer filtrate tabulated. Pretty cityscape traipse trapdoor undue suffering ready mitigate, familiarise cryptic oscillate enterprising undulate farther out, grappled purple grape-juice tennis cutlery livery anticipate sonorous magnified; offer percipient palimpsest codex morsel musicianly antidote evensong caution. Customary orthodox sinuous essential tingle triangular permanency obliged castigated overhead blossom issuance clip insurance, arisen; yet rake priority turbulence confidential, austerity lifeboat pattern.

## SHELF FOUR

Panorama assertion mission control distraught privateer metric fondle swivel celtic fabricated eccentric, mineralised rainclouds loosens uncouth bruised wherever you too; parcel missal oracle symbol familiarise individualised porridge gamboge, filigree adze sentinel jungle under-water pressurised prize-money sycamore solemnise intimation. Rendition repetition exacted from taxation refracted, batten downhill corrigible implacable barrage cruces let us lettuce silage adage storage; breccia posture judicious ice grimace incidental fissured countenance divination asseverated, beaming impersonate cakewalk nearer than microform reduced succulent houseleek, thunder wonderment extravagant fervent. Translucent cogency paragraph immersion fountain-head artists beneficiary mercuric chicory decrepitating for mine again attain imitating raking cascade; immoderate fossil corn cockle cookery mockery monastery earnestly, slate. Correlative musician take back cleft seismic stannic. Formaldehyde client architrave out.

## forthwith surplus

Limitation magistrate plated obsequious lamenting croak toad inured set to slight damage courageous, outrageous focussed hillside platitude eliminating scrap; either side open most wide kinship audition autumnal wistful pangolin, orphanage. Grade allied shovel attack mattock grumbling, single gamble convex conversant plangent neglected matchbox, velvet consenting, veal cutlet outlet walnut front-door wait for more; tell the full tale able formidable to table setting. Cellarage cloven rivalry earache attachment knee-joint marcasite, paint-pot went up staircase marmalade address modesty honestly unless clung bee-sting crafting onrush; historical paradox paroxysm whim endorphin inclination nucleation, at least almost fortunately.

## forthwith surplus

But now consider mysterious courteously lintel frontal erase commissure tomato lecture, ketchup hitch swung segmented polychrome camera stone pavement; traffic latch switch out stairway noisome western at each true bill, horn round fork larkspur corkscrew serpentine encumbered at heaven's gate. Related flutter light feather otherwise magnetise, cheese or cheque condoned, rancorous better still ankle sensible coil tatter tarter; heavy water sodium sedum petroleum refined basalt magpie icefloe candelabrum tended or impressionists heavier than expected, nevermore go onwards light jackets. Evaporite balm cordial mercurial agitated decrepit tabulate.

## AT RAUCOUS PURPOSEFUL

## (2022/2023)

The end of a thing is better then the beginning thereof
– Geneva Bible (1560), Ecclesiastes VII: 10

# I

They did know, almost already boasting resilient first coat
blood narcotic bloated orchid, cost double punctual hazel sipped
posture lanolin intrepid pangolin; grateful violin maiden over-
cast for thirst work ticket junket marzipan bandit bayonet fit
        Canopy campanula optical bundle sortal in gruel
        tribal tribunal moated oaten scrutiny, invisible
        mandarin tamarisk physic indicative adhesive
        hostile figwort cortisone only; trombonist carbon
Pontoon lunation within discretion, dungaree jamboree ilk
planked duck-board mallard wake. Escape, blight, aggravate
infarct gossip bishop individuation; nourish lavish forestry
until bold untold adze pledge resonant gigantic, redox waxen.
        Oxen millstream oven wavelet medium stewpots
        guillemot raucous purposeful; disported remote lip
        gurney transfix pitchfork runner rancid bemuse
        collards, back off thirst misty panadol bundle dim.
Forever sliver parsnip medallion foreign walltiger blemish
anguish unfinished cadenza, hospice fissured mushroom ohm
bantam donation blood profile guileful liberal conversant
monk trappings. Indignant runabout contested fraught
        Brim to bream impulse ample brain-waves
        craze choose goose under gander, down prime one
        coin muddle plum duff scoff guzzle lizard his
        mean time neap tide; hazardous seedlings tip.
Deem dale dial dent rendition, safety surety grate to angle
fumble mangle tribal entanglement succulent, iceplant pant
penitent in want failed criminal easement foil evident snow-line;
own frame seeming skim sealion scallion akimbo frail trio,
        Fall confine or minatory laundry, aumbry at sundry
        soapwort cougar; now tell fuel radium internment
        avail coil python western call unhelped by any wind,
        pit-a-pat placate inflated for need create outward at
Cleat latch curate auscultated. Fright fragile freight train vine
yours or mine too vain, redeem attended mended soonest divested
darling by daring; opine opium orpine bring to mind reclined gain
such watch nuthatch, acrobatic darting head-down fawn stitchwort.
        Patchwork tourmaline vested gangrene imbued duet
        meat-filled pigeon ocean stew front crew adieux
        stonecrop pottery claypit; misfits blight extrude
        speckled wooden spoon pontiff rock face at woodlice.

Nor to effort purpose settled, seizure mettlesome formaldehyde graven images; avertive failed branch shaken, knot reserve portent system, extrinsic flown welted proudly in session; fortune surplus scrape along pasted lit. Jacket wore elbow, turtle amok seldom

Bantam coign or deigned eventual milt. Tilt for
cover quiver, never serve granite or grapefruit.

## II

Mandragora esplanade sic
pretention presentational
chequered swede pentecostal
figurative moisten crowning
duet dollops mustang singe
would have extricated, bleats
forehead mean ace down-hill
batter parental diploid elbow
ptarmigan lighthouse gorse me
pillbox anchorage coffee aged
costard cowardice, incided poise
spurn lemonade disparagement
burgess crusted morose flustered
mole-hill merrier harrier marsh
zealous conspicuous neuronal fill
tidy fried egg-plant reckless porous
dustbin glacier doorstep honestly
crispin profitless seamless cradles frog
latent coastal siskin chalcedony lid
laburnum toxic grapefruit adroit
indecisiveness anemones
veiled coiled piecrust off
mussel inkling perseverate
jacaranda dinnerplate out.
Tinge flange cringe lead
uplift eventually why proud
we'll have none more rink
fellow adipose raucous deuce
dioptre treacle purple suits
bollard annoyed retard kites
cruised down along lee agrees
fermented, pencil battery soft
preyed sidelight shadowed cruet
worrying linctus litmus lichens
blown over hurled spillway blow
geese binomial magpie loin
rival concealment, insidious pint
logical obligation persistent oval
astral buccal manganese worst
distraught inept shrewish fist.

## III

Euclase ounce then ever as till run past,
best, brow at around redress. Count shield
at moonshade overcast in ordinance at
sage topple by weir. Orchard fleet,
mortification contraction morticians
crested chastened almost hot-dog wit
galled sackcloth withers unwrung,
preposterous invigorated yeast feast
oedema reliquary corkage slap-up,
refulgence conciliatory newel avian
credential molecular inoperative wreck
barracuda banana-split octet at imparted
yet all too clear amiss parry away
punish, take hold precipitate ever
core ensure treasure floor over day
quicken how else could trace up to
where outright is after instead belated
this turn then faced in less passage less
to last. Taciturn until around comply
if council or also pencil transept who.
If and while why nothing but tweet auk
cursed fissile felsic cobalt meld
turpitude irksome nether up-ended
grange dunnock analgesic tunic lips
fasten urbanity whyever sandpipes
delphinium refectory moisture or
ratchet prediction ripening creditor
merrier hen harrier gopher accompany
easel, imprint talented ratchet. Less passage
fuss at cabinet, solemn accessory thereafter
one twelve crocus, floor paving
safe grazing weir, beetroot in front
consenting elegant. Or bleeding hearth
set-up interrupted manacle damsel brim
furtive, parrot chromium plated henbane
resurgent tether goatskin dub in audience
seepage venial. Crape edging.

## IV

Than known yet over wrist, well have tune order when
or did even be fair far before life bridge elevenses
like honest cross at first-come lean or mien, in coral
just by joist share leaf ridge, so homage most-off
would be true to pay oven evident, exchange; indigo
clover resume to hospice alpine waning star-burst
immerse measure shoulder or crucial courageous fork
amiss. Act benefit cloud stand over whether rated
retrieval contrails frugal gainful primal voice harness
if martingale unless ingress amethyst susurrus fore-
taste undenied gusto door jamb advance, attenuate sit
promise kept, unity in due approbation highbrow at
take-off nephew contended vigorous singular asphodel
recondite growls, outside on the dogmatic ramparts
catchwords and hypocrisy portentous unctuous quibble
apatite apathetic coliform. Vitiate appetite slice cost
ostentatious mephitic acrylic exhumation ziggurat lurcher
rescue in queue curlew callow borrowing; burlap pea
nipper curious stitch renewal epitaxy mercurial yarrow
morrow tipstaff cyder soliloquy, whisper. Minnow bin
chicory laryngeal scimitar tartaric mesmeric indispensable
butchery caustic roofer batten nailbed at discomfort,
ingested cirque larkspur crwth corrie obfuscation lesion.
Living by watchfires, all be still as bright, sulcus circus
matchless abrasion remission incautious suited retrograde
furthest south-west; earnest alias off incus mixolydian
ambuscade, jasper. Pigeon-toed rush furtive listless invite
autoclave ill mockery hirsute arachnoid cavatina butter
ignorant twitcher sirventes twelfth manganese cormorant
yellow-rattle bunsen burner, earner sooner revamped
aubergine angelic assertional sanguine polyp ascetic. Punt
acrobatic federation operatic doorstep foe midges off
edges badge upstarts piglets wager china cupola perfumed.

## V

Earwig conscious suspiciously
limbeck cracknel astriction east
interlaced rejoice funnel smoking
uppermost induction gridiron an
fandango crystalline porcupines
replacement caravan for yellow
modicum lantern blister sneezed
banish oafish, mavis sluice to
kilim ravine median conviction fin
milfoil focus yarrow gaslight ton
lustrous striated recruitment blip
redwood why not stutter abrogate
pancake makeup red-tape devoured
geyser escrow mischief intercession
way away you tidal races; headland
crease spinach gammon primate
airs and gracenotes weathercock
light roast waist rickets vitals
pearly on cleavage blackthorn oval
woundwort woodrush oysterbed ode
palpation monstrous mortal barricade
parakeet cite alpinist pianist guesswork
off punchinello basement retorted
replenish famish fabular regulars
inscript fortified marigold peeled
bothie anthracite coif imaginates
indifferent forewent over poplar
outdoor habitual circular rain
incentivise carnivorous edict too
sucrose hemlock burdensome mite
leak pie lackerdasical oracular dote
peacock mooted higher-up cruder
hospitable veritable ohm
superlative outpaced hoist best
handle washable arguable in
colonel mouthwash elective so
clematis clemency rigorous
brine columbine karst must
pipe burst sift washer liverish
fictitious burnish headpiece off
octane flimsy catapault clay away
folded down stag button awkward

ruination beforehand redound
as can we just, lift to wash most
silverweed varnish foolish boiler
frowning awning spurned bound
isthmus gruel loyal spinal for
immitated bereft overflowing
turret brainpan broccoli in
plumbago two tango sedulous
zeolite trace exacted,
castanet cravat reacted best
languorous oedipal inference
astrolabe astringent debts
brilliants ogee subcutanious
tenterhooks entrenched dendrite
misfit matress,
availed silver trilled howled why
seepage extortionate tadpoles
sere aerodrome toes
scramble extricate applauds
formidable crucible coracle mew
despite hospitable interval bruits
exterminate aegrotat fruit
periglacial mushy frothy pert.

## VI

Courteous curtailed circuitous
random bristle outburst scared
contiguous evenly caught, cough
cougar pitch out sugar furnished
braced bitterness fierce pierced
trestle tooth sabre kaolin tiger;
hygiene alerted tremblant raged
sandwich thighs flypast diverged
orbicular leopard mullein ranch;
twined cavatina apologetic antic
analgesic encaustic viper's trice
bugloss quench insurgency bail
allotrope complainant bassoon.
Teacup oddity atrium eyebrows
conventicle oracular who knows
foremost wedge gabble single or
tangled chattering pies pierglass
ordained cut and run if enough.
Profit backlash sea-mist past best
attested breccia sultry dimension
sickle sell blister malted salad oil
swats filigree, uprising at chronic
you knew too where uproar who
purified waged, dilated grievous
pyjamas rancorous mango twelve
foiled swamp clinic adumbrated
cuckoo each word beaten blacker
macaroon feather macaroni salts
groaning to earn tilt at pavement
eidetic frigate-bird down way up.
Milk-teeth crashed host to
negligence allspice wastrel
offended vigorous venomous
sago tureen turret by tumult
excavation commission, opal
sleigh melting bell-tower den
miniature manicured failure
indebted riddance allowance
turmeric; frigid pasteurised at
platinum once strontium salt
maize reddening amazing pat
nephew protected ingrates,

ingots preterite smitten dip
brazen frozen cousin wagers
tissue amusing fused column
wane halted implied woven
colloquial disused instanced.
Vulpine military turn turtles
treats sunny spread slumber
ration booklet orchid fervidly
wicked comical paramounted
spurious backward backwoods
defaulted; cruton button soap
topic indignant rictus gravitate
wage rise infancy yawning nail
pruning shagreen divine bread
wicker waning moon tellurium
chocolate livid yellow or oval.
Nut-hatch first bivouac headed
lakeside driven wide at market.

## VII

Ablative twice loosestrife ended;
aspect macaroni marooned slits
synchronised optic listed pears
arrowroot water-rat consenting
dank stonecrop white fleck mat
masonry effigies colt; calamine
feline enteric factitious archway
plaintive talon abreast extricate
radiant foreign current deplete
coarse worsen buffoon reminds
bended reindeer crimson vests,
who'd at hinterlands concentric
plummet pelmet misfit ice-rink
clump tight candle fused insert
georgic infringement mobile bit
gorget patch toadflax autumnal
reminded moonstone waivered
porch portion jacinth winched;
tourmaline capstan latchet brick
bonded at gammon and spinach
infirm beseech mortise and end
crossbow brickwork collarbone
in no time, at all limit ignited oat
sailing on by contrivance pruned
on sanction gnomon persimmon
interrogated corrugated, methyl
grapevine seasonal optimal whit
minaret parkin underwing bloom
type mast fruitcake, oblate
whisky risk-free mortgages
immodest fancies weakens
integument docetic air-pin,
recoiled ahead nostril raced
regent tapir forbearance one
once up-ended albumen lurk
battlements whence forced;
falchion along together other
pulpit pipit greeted cushions
entrancement bonnie weed
for far ago outdone condone
wrangle uncle nuclear unfit,
swallet clinch borrowed meat

marble strait or arrow anew
stabilised coast-guard gurnard
arabesque bisque if unflinched
jewellery, kenosis fleece teems
boron fumes grease unceasing
off grouse lotus gossamer ink
tenon turbulence lustrous scop
notorious avocets nearby twin
brisket birdsong winsome apply
prunella stockade aubade bide
mastodon brunette chancellor
thrilling stent deterrent opals
mordant scant eglantine must
boisterous yet heir apparent.

## VIII

Dungeon perfume wolfram bolts
bungled new-fangled in milkwort
either plover by portraiture
Ayenbite of Inwyt headfirst bone
currant leisure reticent tormentil
lentils filbert at tune spun ensure
tonsure detour how else might trace
brown eggs invoiced accrued
ice halibut permissive sedimental
precipitated tap-root time enough
within reason forgetful minim
wasteful gorgeous muster opt
sand-dune softer sprouting zuo
by hit easier fit honour marrowfat
blazon wot transom bankroll unspilled
wit river walk willed how other
could whether tie madder fodder
another twitch underneath treacled
another pillowcase facing out
catnip stand back revoking it.
Native missive nozzle off
krills dazed fuzz analysed silence
phase prided arrogant camel
dank consenting of weasel furrows
croup air locks reviled ahead tape
topic flecked albums depletion, lite
upended abasement open invests
at most displeased easier orpiment
conjectured, out tactic wakeful
defray sybarite cashpoint
rock-sedge had first obelisk nigh
calicut candytuft. Mastic, optics
entries; at cockerel fantailed
fissile kernel minstrel tent extort
amplitude skewered icing
trampoline prolix passive.
Trident high-seasons cuff-link
birth to leaven, waist price
ottoman wren entrail volume
clean hands on.

## IX

Decrepit occiput incipit lipstick acrylic type
mastic ablative endive, mackerel dotterel mace
obvious pumice inaccurate rib-cage; lour
forage digressive cursive wasteful trial
imprecise malicious woodlice malaria face
oceanic goose observe turgid fulgid frayed
manifold. Acuminate horizon rolling river, under
edge fugue fudge malachite indebted plighted dupe.
Walking stewpan leg-irons sequins minims obit
carrion cortisone ice-cap indurated oscillate mate
primaeval trivial carnival scrupulous howbeit
plectrum systematic cryptic emission cittern oud
aloud aloes flooded fetching flautist worst cistern
fluid participate bovine divination undulation bin.
Distilled beverage often holocene uterine brown
torch inverted mortified dragoon pontifications
sand-dune immune grind forlorn crumpled carbine
awkward tabard feudal, bungled new-fangled wrong
they will cruising falcon naval evil scintillate promotion
to gorge pilfer scamper surge cruising gasping rheum
wolfram forgetful awesome milkwort sultana or
within raison; chisel sisal silvery raffia
muster clatter, softer sweeter carpet assets once
sieve foxglove wolfhound fraught apricot flirt
next explain hurricane chaplain scutcheon
them both medallion platelet frightful, innovated.
Sea robins candid floatation brazen pudding weddings
lactic agaric lethargic duplicity morbid leaden.

Echo dolmen gravel pittance aspirin parade deltoid
denied screwed manifold upward, dolomite indisputable
putto peardrop irrigate martagon distillate Martello
wallowing syncopate overseas elbow grease increase
cut-price well-versed imperfect galactic infringements.

# X

Squeamish calabash swish intermittent peppermint binnacle monocle intestate drowny aggravating rack blot tic swash ferrous distaff foremost mastodon fulsome custom turnpike dilatory gem-like pellitory dunce flounce whence if pleading squid nonce eschew awhile musculature libellous lime blameworthy insouciants slump uncertain foolishly whyever duce intrinsic bellow radish flourish gruesome cabinet prolapsed sententious skeletal coniferous byepass wryneck sorrowful did horrific sinusoidal optician pecan mimetic ribosome awkward impertinent logjam rhino formidable stoker hurdle impenitent shin-guard anaconda deplored or gored matador beef stew too few, phew turquoise enjoys wigeon dropwort flea-market lustre rabbit cloud-street sheep-fold never lifted up-ended tent rest-harrow willow, corn cockle dirk myrtle chortle for organology agave corncrake autistic antiseptic sciatic fought agar.

Erstwhile deuterium asteroidal bottleneck template anticipate visitation divulge holocene beehive whose portal weasel trifling wherewithal deciduous; rainbow sargasso previously not coy blue isotopic caressments bristle-cone maniac manioc cravat atone triplet state sturgeon moraine hibiscus mascot, ergot. Upholstery mystery dyadic enraptured trappist pelf rollicking munificent ankylose interminable waspish broidery eagerly subdominant imminent lambency circuitous nitrosamine on palimpsest voiced rehearsed wetland, nasturtium loam grooms. Turkey timpani goitre plagal frugal viburnum lanolin mandolin omen cinema wisdom system cistern whom astern immune kolinsky frosty imminency gastritis bloaters hooters invidious, midge gouges for all that sword cowardly bastardy tufty what a brilliant pussy you are. Kittiwake mistaken minaret coronet eucalypt caiput cycad indeed snoek snowflake consternation fusion piratical reversion awesome cot.

Interminable rockcake sultana sententious obtrusions goldflake oik agave ache gravure scorpion magnesium rhubarb soprano pi sonatina leaner coiner languor vinegar eyebrow escrow volcano dye erythonium butane stubborn mascarpone ordinary. Diaconal prolix serviceable risible comical optimum paragon porcelain para illuminated marginal criminal audacious bare-faced dare light intrepid ruthless bassoon macaroon reprieve incidental accidentally distrust worst distressed, failed branch knot caught up clutter.

## XI

Lamp-lit calcifuge foliage barrage, balloon
lectern gorse insistence barraclough kilner toy
sustenance cobra charmer, porcine wilting on
height crevice enticed. Bothersome parkinson
        grillade ferret homage rumpus, at fungus
        escapade irritant magnified condign
        winsome mortician passionate tight
        simmer creole cassoulet; pylonic
discreet anthill pellucid for went crucial by
skipper argus toggle languid alloyed pride
rightous bought cautious limber, bait.
Criminal lactic acidic cervical puncture
        alleged octet primatial thumb kettle eaten
        cross-bun bustard crystalline druse,
        serge calico sandwich; ostrich unselfish
        plaice demolish lavished sugar measured,
collared dove woven twice lacewing purple emperor
chrysalis fovea elected pacified moated singe grange.
Barking and grunting at offset planetary occlusion
tremor, carotid stellar management; apprentice at
gaze musing giraffe aircraft lifted turgid
        tungsten neck-verse awesome carousel shallot
        prefect out. Sleeping doggerel electuary lie flat
        florin disdainful, pilgrimage tilth minded in
        reckless obverse heathen; spinach gristle each
air raid cradle breakage channel willow wand.
Customary unwary dairy hoary finches thistle
matching wrist forceps, hedgehog log-jam in
jasmine suspicion; grievous relentless must
        training whistle edgewise copper fusion up
        risen listening passion terse tongue bitten.
        Spillage caravan over yellow downing
        burrow spell-bound turtle suitable lit
mock erstwhile; cursive chewing on
fresh teeth birth pangs spine fume
knee-joint thirst goitre panacea
surplice surplus sylvanite serpentine.

## XII

Annealed even drink only flying start. Whence if in visionary column minced grandeur hat panda awhile longer muscular rate liberated desert oasis; limited originals treated woken proven yet quite uncertain sequent they loved together to crew brewed tinfoiled, pride of place at head below under, they want entire entranced first grove. Ink-cap trot butter-fingers elders, gasping palate palatial musical flicker to hanker wrangle anhedral level cathedral: eskimo dartboard bullseye blissful.

Alive novel all at once miss previous hare's wrist, bone at yet faucet meadowsweet blanket over hover charm cream permission; there will be time to run forward, sufficient moment cover risen blessing will tell promise pulse elsewise gather to wait thereby sing at start mission shadow follow tomorrow obvious at first in corridor, ahead. Date palmistry flourish cycad cyclamen on foramen congregate by the stream, easy repine untoward aided; sake. Rise in azure seizure composure allured boiled before bee flight shank sunken mimetic clasts, frequent relics rapid trills twittering admixture; postulate animated forcep, open trout studious object twite heaviside forecast offcut point to paint patient. Pelican intended grimace merciful tolerable, honeydew prudent ocular dowsed flaxen trombone organ keyboard; rogue parent patient forwent advantage adduced impulsive bonnet overhead melt. Human dative motive overdrive allusion fingerprint, retentive cavity amiable true.

Ogled banana for crude too few, when next? Which enjoys run two antonymic mellow aspirin, corn cockle shoe buckle down dale ceiling dirk implored oh manna savour salver silver one more river–whether hold ever close warm wormwood brotherhood skip-it lamb chop. My own darling canted attested gone by long lost past pilgrim, fluoride reveille flurried; borrowed invented drawback pricket bravery blustery windswept tropic swallow below nor yet before at hand opening on in formerly not acetone atonement agreement statist. Plight zenith in cared form each way, containments continental contentment, shelf. On good looming floret sky; better snowdrift, comical trivial assembled river-bed fragment ancient caution petition, fraction seldom followed by volcanic incident prank fitted.

Consternated obtrusive demure scorpion dimple often eastern soften languor burning up for love at the mountain-tropic; haven going on before way illuminated footlights entrusted further greater niggard anger for hunger, inventoried rhodium flinted Sunday infringed clamp cigar smoke precious verses. Previous passionate hold firm expected shoulder-blade cricked rivulet, glorious rays slanting across cloud flourishment fresh tincture; know rightly alighted crisis flighted dominion judge chiefly astrakhan far-off trellis ambit well drawn team in binary crockery, washing-up politic revoked. Ambitious crystal alternate snowdrop elegant opulent crankshaft massive driftwood, produced talons stricken by effulgent, deplored or gored unfeared bullet mullet; alerted for longing frosted gatehousing. Over these towers still amaze when or whether cross-ply broidered fuel crewel goldfish tarnish finish off piteous in stave starved cleft, paragon thirst headline sardine deafening implement implanted. Oriental naval boatswain attained noodle trifle cut-out silhouette needle wedge steam gorge bud oaten fluted at scrannel tunnel appraisement; incision moth tune undulant drinking suppliant, hibiscus sturgeon stents stubborn tricorn listen, azure-winged provided, indicated by zonal tribal laudanum.

## LATENCY OF THE CONDITIONAL

## (2022)

Such latency is legible by fortune at first sight insistent past provision mutable re-founded welded entire stepwise in flicker colouration, assemblage fringe turbulence recoil observational pent-up in pathway crystallised tracing, at ginger root expressive preservative instated across tincture limit realised. Adaptive discoverable as beyond exception, surmounted by cardinal invert numeration alleged into transparency icy surface level fully exceptional eventual, grizzled wherever in grateful outreach; even at amounted density, initial within plentiful dual purpose first overturn sequence device plumage outlasted at tricuspid. Intensity provoked into crimson, fold after fold regenerate light reflected, contrite self-raising thereunder know now all better, inflicted alight mutable incurved waived expertise pretext avoidance. Opening impervious allowance prided parentage tint reflected, next redress repair imposition possible attachments hardihood; to early hardly adduced whitening, blue to grey-green earth warren forward into lateral skip by parallel limit along constitutional shoreline from banked cloud inured in red infusible reversionary amount, calibrated estate hillside gradient. However so legume to clover sweeter rival entailed necessity, tendency first pitch notarise magpie sheen flicker brokerage;

mustard never least plaster maroon rockets will self-disclose below recipiency seem; severance within alert redeem likelihood semblancy expectation, indigo. Anticipatory main element indulgent for tributaries far up ahead pin nominal enlaced pressure, clarify resection, listen aversion nearly from long daybreak yellowtail alluvial in rebated temporality whence rebated temporality alembic ajar prudency adjuration, oh-range hawkbit orange lunge circulatory within lexical brim included clastic discretion furlong; sailing brimful limbic phonemic affiliation vocalised appraised shoulder to grain extricate instantly exit mast.

Word fettle bronze patch gleam beam purpose reason verdict, brilliant underside violet whitebeam nuance once to next along at cumulative emplacement, refolded azurite fewer following consequent in attachment search regulated knit surfactant reluctance testimonial arranged congested. As ever in pressure agile informal thermal one converted, cirrus novice indented fluency bittern owners pierglass violet invite spectral luminous spoken wheelbase whinchat motivate bet saluted; harmonic settlement new conclusive figuration pointer accusative intended blended inflected necessitous hidden, verdant scruples ridgeway lee acceptance limb down prune floating rose collar. Fernseed embrowned tied door captivating elate flair together will ensuing usualness crested arrest, conjoined novel fuel to amazement width measurements; dehiscent colloidal oval elastic pallor suited day tonsure granular sleep risen total horizon sequins rufous gloss seaways rescued on insidious allotment imminency broidering time outlasted, pursuit essential ate craven pudding gallop in rhythm diluent by instrumental scandent fluency; across diligence freedom tolerance affright, capillary at wedge pressure sovereign enlisted moonstone overt to foreshore maintain bye-blow allusive reported culminated pertain within. Fastidious in collusive exacting nihil sentinel tomato regardful partitive sparkle, bite likeness fortress pullover ungulant corybantic accretions handwork listed batting stitch recension cast-iron from dose titration darken fended glint amiss opaline, joined insured peak oil fallow plume fire ruby confirmed pluvial when snow now trip gravure vertigo know better; delphic ozone patulous fume recursive subtended tide flaming precision coinage arete costly incipiency citational diminishing boletus condensate front; in chestnut saliency oceanic bravura, adept ex fascinated lustration, sky lent quickly tune sonant.

Perdurable attic goliardic daybright incandescent mine hold tight mullein quickening transept lamp-lit frostbite acrostic bruised, all at once crisis livid luminance nacreous dovetail choral rendition; adaptive twisted susceptible or thurible till magnetise column profuse purple emperor top foil skirmish neat foil skirmish. Brocade wainscot climactic, brilliant ochrous alabaster from turquoise enhancement tentative off joyous gauze litmus lichenous pinkish broom immersion as implicit been senior pausing eschewed blond rainfall, down. Cascaded intercalation stop-flow toggle sail interruption swerve on frank starling curve never however windhover severance, governance bitumen naphtha lustre wattage; cordage heat shock pulse inflamed pathways foot-step moreover bridge-work, constriction to minnow prow shallow tomorrow by thorough tinted acceptance edge. Intermediate wet brace and bit settle skittle left outermost contused unused cruise shears eyebrows, no-flow hereto pear drop hoops acetic residual visitation; infusible basil fossiliferous over-coat eat wheaten nightmare why not wait quoit back to limited you'll hear so soon in ear cleared of tantamount indifference litter forested crested, scattered repeat know those feet leaf-mould; new lamps for older set on hold mild tidal feudal coral coal be seam, linarite dendrites feather-lite toxic lithium inveterate mandated toluene. At shoal duality suspended hedgehog prioritise sibling arcane mausoleum upper ledge, for water-meadow grilse hawk moth unless until beneath; charge by remnant voice chosen and verified, dyed admired wren. Mercuric reach down solution relations distance share to distributive coaxing in holdfast, toast snack insulate fire token. Hilltop loop more deep now, milk shake cut-out snow white cod parsnip in-shoe proven dozen shining within yet eyeshot, laced into counterpoint and down to sleep.

Soak leak buttress tirade instantiate frack deliberated equalise ridden cordon, uncertain insertion perplexity near interminable; cavitation donative proportionate, tenacity undoubted come to mention both together time enough fractious, won streak winning pilotage. Lease apace torse surcease, success wonderment invested goatherd long-arm brink chase; not in this place at risk keep back torque wend iceland gull coast at cost moss later famous acidulous. How known brazen hid heart atone climb acetone plume along unbroken, gift taken wrist thrown forward pollard yellow to light blue masonry; gyr falcon bundle sandling sewn endure ignored.

Silex loquens excavation instauration dipper copperas percentile, modicum otiose septum dactylic chaffinch call impeachment pentoxide. Mortality even appetite rotate digressive belated, perseveration mild honey in live-long wallpaper graticule; fermented indignant antiquated waist headscarf flung up across both shoulders, earnest pigment yeast despite ultimatum scorched another successive twice reflex. Culpable density vitamin foolhardy blanket stitch quantum foremost entanglement; truffle overt scuffle off licence sodium pontoon accelerated passion-fruit labelled angle inducement farmland crowned. Invidious open-hand dependency varnish plenishment vanish hunted triangular disbanded, fresco implicational adequate pro rata military hunted morsel easel formidable tribunal naturalised; grazed iodised interception caption garnet distinguishment lappet forehead snippet assumed involuntary puppet wayleave swerving to culminate. Testify inclusively perilous rabbit lit aleatoric alkanet imminent, reductive late arabis dice fuse fluorine cogency attentive avidly at greengage, scut lovingly awake stellar in turn. Sun's rays in close focus, skip to burn.

**NOT ICE NOVICE**

**(2022)**

## NOT ICE NOVICE

Sycamore or lesson
vanes spinning to fly
new seeds at session
off out over the sky

Branches ride steady
to wind up the breeze
fresh leaflets ready
clear flutter at ease

Teasels flip mallow
over the air in tune
lying up into fallow
beyond the full moon

Ever wind at window
as first bird to seed
lifted into bright glow
further to take heed

Or sprung demeanour
enlarged for ready-made
slices trice still keener
be not now afraid

Treasure the ash grove
beyond civil storm
measure the splash wove
by touch ever warm

Our squills closely minding
will brilliant deep blue
profuse closer binding
as must soon be due

Holly and ivy thicket
sharing the crown
ever more wicket
in finch thistledown

Tame and supple given
season's eloquence
over cloud-light driven
amounted into sense

Habit nervous treeline
beehives at return
chased by a feline
fiery deep black burn

Rock salted crust
harvest flock before
together wind in gust
just as ready gnaw

Beside corn felt crake
persistently at night
locally for wide awake
was ever their delight

Clip to tapper pippet
joining to the team
reach the top whippet
yawning at the beam

Full teeming brightness
onrunning into sky
dill celestial tightness
at near gale-force why

Leasing the gateway tie
magnet yet parapet
early by late deny
creasing in alphabet

Difference engine win
the game at minimum
to bear now and grin
add to the frosty sum

Knees at canter brazen
institute dandled taxon
fractious waxen raisin
first trefoil reaction

Cypher wafer liquid
codeine off therewith
stem or willow viscid
elder for hollow pith

Lay out by tribute gem
reversion milfoil issue
from us to each of them
wrapped up in tissue

As both new fill tooth
indent in want inclined
say all bested at sooth
elegant front refined

Termite civil wildness
antiquated danger rite
no ridden range unless
us best full sit on tight

Each day given way
morning turning tuned
oil ready hard to say
honey lemon spooned

Oven raven hoarse bit
most roasted centre
zircon least lamp-lit
bonnet portal enter

Or turtle companion
electrical shell spiral
reverse charge anion
discounted hire all

She sells her sea shells
on shore before in time
mortal shuttle at swells
ridden even to prime

Make mine anemone
clandestine imbued
trifle ore at tendency
uppermost renewed

Coil endure on splashes
angle steel tore rapid
momentous eyelashes
singular privet vapid

Match point spikenard
centipede worritsome
obsidian to extra-hard
incentive by overcome

Macaroni sitting tighter
green bottles washed
sunlight burn brighter
breakfast jewel noshed

Massive brittle spryest
further out to talk
as next to dust driest
squeaking like chalk

Lumen determine flinch
or not to still prefer
newcomers audience
make offchance deter

Evermore shall be so
tract ninety entrusted
badger grimes to toe
forgiven keen mustard

Wherewithal foreshore
saltation next obliged
goatee soever no more
by artichoke contrived

Fresh dart out redstart
orbit twitter whinchat
dusk flight nearer part
wing turn recover bat

Mutual merrier laughter
percentage share divide
reluctant for alabaster
notable far and wide

Ethylene refrain powder
discover by modest nip
turn the output louder
basement lean to trip

Penguin engine splinter
aromatic pepper smirk
camping out in winter
running sought berserk

Mist azurite inflection
in temper so replied
at barrier protection
nor yet far and wide

Peas frolic silver old
cadenza fluent spire
in wealth hereby untold
such danger seldom dire

Acumen wolverine
by forfeit symmetry
others so in tangerine
in offset mimicry

At ocean promise
hand along down
instigate to office
remission into town

Neither be merciful
further from truth
hold it as saveable
next after youth

Epidote fuchsia ballast
hold in gold discerned
rivet inert main-mast
abrogate few interned

Thin ice crack first
skip or skate entire
bye hardly worst
set alight on fire

---

FIN IS

---

# AT THE MONUMENT:
## A ROMANCE

## (2022)

A monument
- *Antony & Cleopatra*, *c.* 1607, IV.XV.

Any tangible object associated with some striking incident of the service is converted into a monument
- Herman Melville, *Billy Budd*, chap. 30

## 1

Next to ride and slide by the sea in season, he plans by reason purslane teeming will burn quickly even watchfire after severance belated. Come on forward tried harder, all seem prime view pier troop advancing if may striven to cordon his most conductance, forgiveness. Converge insurgent let to lesson, learn by flame profile as far as, near to pride abate; memorialise inscribe at stance defiance laryngeal, unharmful, which lamp is spent attended. He knows it will, in mercy only by step riven, by tidal in plenty held off, refracted bloom; all wait bated intake, in saline action, fetching the storm without. Rock scarp tread light then sudden beforehand released past punishment, mere human condolence his curative ambition, stems prostrate shoreline ride and slide again; hopeful pardon them patience withouten blame, against the wind, to fortune its yellow flower flowing beloved conducive to windswept pliancy, urgent microlite cruising azurite.

Swum with rain merciful taken back combust by seeded land affirmed
none contrived for fear against harm inset heart, felt truce to fate
nor blind belief stride seething welkin to hold fond care, where go
on past ahead lenient loving-kind defend, of breath pursed, we all
at high sea let them come in aspect, mount to roar rearward as grind,
salt eddy sealed aback. Inlet surge daylight hand to mouth, promise
relish foremost patient relenting; flintlock aqueduct best belief knapp
first whistle and sing, scarlet ink facework assist beyond reproach.
Ride the wave to share the flush, rebate sans offence, sessional trial
relented to pass the way on limbs mild scald contoured, first pledge
unless if rainfallen insolvent gristle; at release phosphorous mental
inventoried reform from painted stint oxalis. Route the lifeboat
let them float up free else yet to be, rule to vale recede for white grade
bead relinquish sustenance obviously such. Let pass running force
loose perchance all how many if any, passion within glance reason ready
to cede intent yielded; give way fully, stay in course notice, not twice
or even once more while follow rival pressure confession assume alone.

Deplete pain, droplets forceps screened silent excuse at main incision, determine they will all willing, still we know for rode certainty, pride open port sea lane, marinade pursuit. Youth tremor advantage rises by inside edge forth promise hoist deference intensive, either after none until oval surpassed, detection. No time alike rate attachment, to hold pleat fort back unless sight reduced, apart into air by water falling awake, yet clear beyond disturbed, wet sand aligned inferred; offer to take out birds creaking, opaque remote provident, my heart at stake; out flake power before at more assenting mild adventure. Reduced ago to a shadow, step past in near silence, hear just less off the broken path urgently, spirit in fumes or flames to cherish cast onward quite contrite unvaried; merciful heavens by sky tremors, by fair forward spray across page sea-pledge silhouette advanced. Dispense haploid scheme fusion sudden, bolt upright make mine fleet elk acoustic; riverine or been discreet, esteemed. Care for cure more, flow to dark, core insert participate spilled forward elbow dally daily sail entailed; bees' knees till unavenged so sweet, skypark faded meteorite lit.

Come into line terrene, turbine conversant impute leave alone easement maculate, dove grove covered release into unsealed; met fright chill same salmon bite choose to choice, shot. Abated trippant trochaic fit, how and why intersect, be understood for what if, enskied and sainted printed patent, new enlisted inveterate. Released from glory, banks of thyme, free passage in confluence; instil as I ever will perplex insidious, mischief discrepant little assuaged peaceful integument gain; porcelain purslane puce from foam; pertain disperse scatter best waspish knowledge cottage chocolate-box, ornate rose porch waist indignant polygon sunshine discrepant tight. Drawn free as air vibrant with after-care, inviting open wide salt-marsh under godwits, implicit truly. By good coincident suffusion cliff off edgewise methodise, air pump sumpter mincemeat indiscreet tension. So no great claim on tomorrow, greater however few than you, I know due more than either follow and maim, wait against trite foresight serene; scenic late advocate omit, soon told, joy introit beneath breath bitterness a hearth in common bathed in sky-dew, sea-view ocean clime; sway far of near power oh dare conduct, yielded to safety native the surging maritime consume given mine salt entry, come this way. Call over even mens rea captive pine else false wane planet reliant undulant doric fever, instant convex affront; mint congruent lead plus less grievous we do ensure hilt leather-jacket foremost flying the shadow, emblazon prion wedge keener blade beside appointed. No shadow feverish overcast main-mast twice.

Observant reserved perseverant rebuke these surges in watches night path, ask late mistook march out descant camp converted; deficient advance relented searchlight scant out yet admiring. All known serving at once at length, max whence hunts aside aspired to catch up skin soaked antic set ignorant; greet riots lent violent turn storm, half ajar pointed, tongue flit outermost fit overhead. Escort sidelines ravines and gullies faint watercourse in dry season. Be aside mainly in tempo guardian scrawled furl traffic inflame otherwise candidate, ardent barred tighten masonry at percent; none yet bright heart elated, a specific enacts dispersal freight profit might, apart. New morning protean sustained mantel knew intent alight departed, amazed cohort sped upward proficient only good news next stone stunned by soon agreed. Night open wide even but still dark with blood impulsive lamented, facing snow, to race from the sacrifice enticement, about tribute earth and sky, bribery fated inspired, unspent; victim until surmount recruited instigate outcry, court wit effect eyebright occluded cloud bled turning red quickly instead. Pied outhouse ready furious incurious astray in shade not free, sway to kneel own step down, pantomime horizon prodigy moulded, passion not afraid close better shine spark intrude; awake in closet prospect, clamp extent.

# 6

Pint silver laden cinquefoil treasury stayed winter interpret mean toilsome eleven govern tilted, like river played to blink hinter-rising stricken, up southern ever graded gradual never verset. In asset versus posset sit tangle milky ant bounty fit regret overset microbial filter, to flicker angular eroded; folded up tight link colic found wanting figwort certain ash get on mountain rowing. Earning come to term practice if best watch quiver tangled mimicry, cement coming for going morning missing born outward stoop. By now fluent lyric dissent, on loan home run granted at peak tactic typecast trochlear wear, worn out. Attic natty dread bread buttered welded batch readied; kid prided sidelong, perch up-frontal organic scent professing degree. Loosen the halter fly-past, discuss evermost accrue chew lock up crafted, knowing look fight bitter whether view or not, ascribed; invade mastic filamentous slit tolerant physic throw dog-like deplete, insane root. Over tundra here comes the sunlight risible fizz enjoined in fund unfound returning, quest over crest; know best risk altercation gentian impact sore streak well past lattice default. Did they comprise all, as more than if lean-to, scope fine termination.

Perpetuum perforated, inform perpetrate insect wings back-folded strict neglect. Disservice crevice pledge child shelled unwilling, walk-up fort shoal finish embellish blanch immediate, in years ahead; sited saltire, at silt and coverlet, goathide cured valid vellum disguised. Quiet momentous late ovoidal hatred flinch yet permitted flagrance fit exclaimant accident, all-heal weal reprieve at jury inter vet. Stricken meeting mountain passage, wet alp monsoon clamber, let pass lastly, briskly professed invested. Ever soon far, so much blessed vanitas varnish, wage twice truce amplitude multiplex, snow-white rocks. Critical invention oast casting, allover they know as how accepted secret yielded told cumbersome own rowan internment, ash asked traced, cash down under new moon sedge as yet stitchwort, patch crosslatch now to part wholesome torn on up, unbeknown in town, in-turned. Peppermint replete eucalypt burning the elbow unprotected by morning, at the jetty last slant to broach the tide neap wide-open lantern went off mask forehead; pride at filch mention burnish hayrick emended provender, ferry merriment creek bow flower-bed walled espalier, flame intact.

Yet intonation if bereft unless of aperture star cleft, hanker faster lawful but additive elected give due too. Orchid ground downland all unfounded board and bread flight spared, accommodate alters mutation professional prolong relict talented aloud. Crowd brae funded endued my throat outburst filmic advent flint carol carotene ingenious parlous firstborn, turnage purposeful oxcart beanstalk frolic scented barricade xanthic atoll plumage adrenal formulary survival; quick profiterole give out back exaggeratingly fastidious chatter affected pamphlet, hit instinct get target, aspectually lantern plight. Gregarious furious however merciful even brilliant in tight scruple avowed cats-eyes survive decretals, pressures incurred reprieved headline flint glint infancy; obstinate ostinato dupe translucent who knows unyielding and strict to follow, interminable queued in spite also loyalist muzzle growse first which trace spinet open castanet. Cabernet flute-solo rose at light noon splash precious touch of spice.

For over that roadway, imparted waiting system remnant bravura modernised, established, tabulate on headline proline apex tricked out spade crimson criant acetic. Back fit dated regulate ostensive bight acquaint defective, promise plaintiff tectonic strike stake-out, recruited; you'll do soever well employed light of a thousand suns bidding nettle scruple for new-found settlement: discrete, burnt. Troth split far ahead now bleed calque foulard phosphene digression, ocean explain due traction, sea-grass harvest protein on tendence tantamount pensive melted. Who would know better than, custom plain to planet haze, excused briefing onslaught proof scop's owl long halloo too plaint; in evident confided take-off unstick indirect. Flit pittance ask no more knit beforehand, oblique pack sent on ahead wanted, longer for loot loyal trial hunger instead; no pack, no drill out back name given don't. Either mind deployment adjutant sword lexical sheer fancy, limit tickle into line tend friendship prowess coronet.

Flaunted infant conflict ordinary milk trident against reckoning, swelling displayed in proud window sash to teach abash floor awash, remix fresh haste; look not back whatever induced, steps falter echo down in helped soundtrack, founder by floodplain. Of such of switch crimp current mint fission polarity station, amaze trip buck over, splendid suited; in-proof sandpit gable end, visceral annular habitus. Better less esteemed offset conference, whence bait selected harbourage, finger-tight. Finches cluster for seed, whirring in cloud picnic; flashes of colour, cheep chatter, gladden to flit on the wing. Clear the shaded doorway servery, opine to find open this way up, tolerant shielded from toxic levity in day by day, hold your breath. Far in advance tamper-proof, child care at the window borrow enough to last. At the conjunction spiral wedge opium sledge fudge, compromise eyes pliers denies brass wires claret arrogant impoverishment; potent overhead lenten race to town.

# 11

Breech cotton why-ever so far cup all round, defend preference cosset blink merited; lost at last descent wont meal-time reforming dome return, domesticate caveat. Over recovery contact scripted azimuth footfall matt payment beam loved be so held out far hand, away livid on fraction mallow trumpet eaten funnel. Assume then ordain when furrowed lanyard, farm gate celebrate out repressive each releasement tented and infused, done up into fresh turn, renewed. Who would any less ingest dressing up alike, stomach furl crampon, on canted front; decent knit crochet conspicuous neat outbraved nectar share oh suave respited heart-set. However many invited globe, flowering rib crescent pungent tin-pan avenue untied. Fly starlit benefit ear vented noon past prune for moonlight, aback contour lint limit bent in banter, each supplant availment detail; none venture incline flag incipient, before wax.

Origin finishment banish in courage, deserving surprise oil base fancy to spread to peak vale, value by spool thalictrum boon companion tantrum when ban plectrum; said over for and before wild wood dense dancing plinth dianthus, sealions delphic grimace fosse snuff enough anyway least said befriended procure detour valiant valency, flavour gravitate inflated indigo pleat. Implore no more sun's heat sink, ink blot smut speak, hutch implicate suit breathe out if not late admitted. Safe to gape collected widow's mite dual parallel heartfelt generic at constancy. At this rate the revenue from woven hedgerow windfalls drop like strange things at night; close ranks through thinner filter halter lariat prepare, datum awake. And now we know, to and fro throat fleece swallow burrow stand exact; give leeway form priority, yield and trim acknowledge direct to ultimate margin. Mandarin slain maiden confession team from brickwork deck bracket, imitate plastic venerated column goat; warship worship even split.

Omission prion captivating succubus fleeced systolic surrogate, latex toxic pintade converted downstream blip. Seen to risen sunlit fathom even when at measureless manifest increase, sea-voyage praise station close unharmed, shield dialled; in the event of even odds fledge nursling giants divinest thunder rolling overhead latent prospect, in doubt. Passion sober perfect prefect perfective incident consented, know it forward inflown determine winter coat shellac upmost post size. Large muse dancing boat rudd parfait odd wary inside wade extortionate, inmate deriving until then all newly-given, treat among syntax stone to peach. Will you won't or join plans minaret call-out hold off prophet private undertow, crow's perch crosstree form saliency turbid outflow distress. Even elsewhere mine towards, yours too pressed, addicted contrition however desired boiled up light carrots beef overtaken cumin mountain reed bed lurk diligent due in part; astute bright red regress oppressive tuck hillside perplexed intone tongue famine, groove intake proximate success. These valleys shed as second flush retract march in time, resected trim fissured woods supreme at best parlance, pretended glimpse askance. Main course, main chance resultant unspent torrentially seagull demure, mewed. Who holds us back to trace out expended, flout dyke discount evident withholding plying invented; that lets me annex pack rip tide aside freak parade, sybarite provided nor yet annulled.

At less to fold, a single stone is parting of the waybill deflected, sudden onslaught mat coat tatter boarded already; tight cornerstone up and flown, restraint as or to porous, batch froth; wastrel criminal derelict, smouldering with life-colour, way long to see. Go forward then, tend western sentence fencing, parry up straighten often, sword in running flag water; tether other address most rise whether, formalin twin heard outflow, measure following met well together willow woven compliancy. Like so many hover to cover own discrepant, all outside belong tangent leaned version, torsion nail-bed tribute arterial; venal opt alone, on abalone, strike spikenard leopard dune. Attended moated turret, quick lancet doublet sit undoubted, ficus weight loss increment, wax cement. Survey cross-over each to reach across, studious counterpoint consenting far and away cambric checkpoint mistake guarded; none washed overside ore vitamin limejuice creased furious, asset-rich by year's end, snip bird snipe heard mortified. Tell you what no luck to peel rut, come first attendant scarified upended like pod delirium compendious, gone wild in forest outland; rent to catch, inhabit debit casuistry, all around cloud discrepant lame.

# 15

Fearsome torn last thing nucleic acid later stand back splint anticipate, circuit fermented undone by head connect; hand over, grip meant to leave, price pitch call out. Throat dry mock, bare arms no joke street wreckage, you chew disputed; credulous for crude excess, diet hurtful frown wounded, edge cynic cut apart. We all heard the shout ahead why hesitate bladed to sharpened attain fated, drag to tread down done furtive link; dark package mist passage strip. Attempt further back aspect, or bracket fitful stroke escapement waspish crepe morning light, filled and worn tamed at payment recompense, don't expect substitute; say why in trial or ever thence, musk to between face distasteful, few sample, novice elevated. Billiard raided dynastic loosen perfected whose, why's accepted amplitude for wage arisen ornament abandonment, marquee leading abraded greengage involuted forenoon spin. Grievous sieve flow to flour belt run beside parade, intimidate bread fallacy up to slice, discuss crusted voice flooring waste.

# 16

Bond broken and unclipped, slip the tie, mooring damage avenged, lost and gone ever vain; bone offer in repair or before conjugate fragment, repined. As then neck verse portage, slice to yet embed top entail, fuel to burn, top learning bite, corncrake spinal tap, our twice hard to share when wrested; unallocated as yet proofed to first collapse, setting fire in dark pinewood shadow, residing in shacks; heart-beats fierce rain taken. Idle steel awl postlude canal pestle pushed back outcast, gables burning! Forsaken sodden lakeside within elided, loss adjusted by arm pitch undefiled, by wilding dismemberment, complaint in file. Several sorrel panel in mind as darken mid recall, broken certain ordeal keep in temper cracknel mind flooded; too much croft, lost give way quail ungainly wash barrier, past belief. Across hope splinters lengthen horizon turns, signal loan plane ratified oxygen casing, alarm lame to laminate testify back at last, flabbergast. Willow who willing weave woven, why say amplify dire illusion, petition occupation; who knows which search would reach occasion deaf cries cauterise, reprise surprising give out lambent caption, laugh and level down. None in fresh heart yet wait for daylight, at greenleaf harvest sheaf, nemesis.

# 17

Insistent now indented, incident done to turn heading down-hill truffle snipe, or moorland gradient lifted sore come out to weaken frack taken aback; traction linger heather fetchment bulk shipping, sisal power house release. Limit pitch branding mirror out-door painting, full air grant at slanted provident oiled up conventional railing, safe beside unfailing; to knowing admittance pertinent parrot crested, enough for each fast customary tow advocate. To share both lines affair daring, near rated hosted postern ventral instigating profusion, antic rotational declared begun to shine; to unwind core at shadowy forests sighing, foray break altercate fronds elated, at exclusion so far ahead. Nutrient stock replacement warden guardian, formidable bothersome succulent ice planet contented, save bravely gorged along the roofline; remote crystalline fidget pargetting order wainscot purfling cancelled. Cursory ventilate love your neighbour either awake discrete moisten, fasten guesswork esteem theatrical queen of night dilated; so queue up sky print candidate service evaporate. Enough said words to wise, twice bitten full dress tend please release, crease to mend sundry beetle lid. Elastic classify tabular inferential pipeline, shore design over plan index soluble latency annex hatchlings.

Dissension flattery sublimate tear the roof gravel abnormal, funnel all superable conviction instigated from scratch twisted back accounting at featherbrain know your right wrist early beforehand; after dark caught up frustration comical position-bearing, lucid interval brilliancy created. To do so that in lurid livid, monster up-mounted chew and claw for patchwork, aberrant; cormorant torpid even so fascinated by sunshine, ravine blinking rainclouds trifling passion deltoid clench munch retrieval. Ovoid stricture seedpod mustard, indeterminate flute might fell, light-weight guarantor to match and strike, swivel and sing. Who then spatulate to justify and recognise incentive torrent strange device, each remission certain ahead of cruise control and flying option; all repeal up to strict recruit numerical will ground-plan, plastic digest surface officiate skein portative organic tent wheaten rejoice for juice. Safe to care as now aware, at adequate nascent lint redress, focus bantam orpington kerfuffle subtle kettle tidy summer; another plover lapwing mountain rockface syntax, intense price-war foretold immune attune crackpot fumitory territory optional confounded.

# 19

At garden walk silver until mausoleum observation lone confined, appended shade afloat spirit nip atlas soothes her cinder path; injurious by now for digressive appliance, forensic distillery in fury within gunshot wounding, barricade tyrannical rebound, earth-link sunken pardon listening, until tile willing unwieldy frequent leading at start loath to depart, heartfelt green sash love your life keep your word in truth ever to tell; of fealty dolorous stroked implanted monochrome hurricane agreement. Fairy cakes ditty embracement leave to cool batch sweet fill renown; game plan sanguine tine atropine coin tailor-made incessant black gravity, trooping discoloured; rumour whether now and then to wait before acute if waning splint. Casket dashboard provisional at first, thirst pre-trial animal halal convent keep pace, know release and pledge yet remitted, bring the jubilee; all in step drum-beat dress to right. Arrest straight rank cohort converted, lick and split excepted, wasting still not at maverick measurement. Must we leave town at once, watchful past the fountain anticipated and precise, can twice enterprise lyceum out of sight.

# 20

Rhizome division called to mind faustian resignation stencilled rubato, in filigree arrowroot motherhood wherever discover, pertinent faint-hearted thermos honey turnover vagary sugar septic attic; where hidden overturned until bonfire remitted mineshaft crimson parlour detour insistence, adept unlikely single shingle reversed. Limit settle merciful loyalty, afore repay inducement obey voice of firebrand, immediate dislike bandage up ahead; first come beyond tack issued rise and fall, fortified fried egg encouragement swift turnip mousetrap cheddar rind. Offcut snippet antonym allowance all at once feast cast, cruet mystify esplanade how to fit inside void, rebarbative shock tactic far away. Synapse contracted bottle window, where they count early and late invited, plum cake overcoat constricting, tied gate; leaning to sing proportionate, choric broad and narrow, runic limpet phonic trickery allusive, patent whenever elaborate; yet investigate field gate dilatory, watercourse immerse spruce needle tuft, point through novel disjunction off function pedigree.

# 21

Lumber finish room mespilus egrets clarified, slide immediate quiet boric expedient prominent accumulating, lukewarm. Numerical daring darning all risen, supply bracket fungus, meatus first; however adapted confectionery sweetie-pie raspberry don't care late-comers. Another afterwards technician liberates in swarms, correlates scenic ambition; whenever admission bilayer traction seen, nothing adventure born aloft. Then courteous indomitable or open table crucial take what matter would frustrate, freeway tribal dual tribulation forum, omission attracted sit rectified; trypsin surge consistent percussion scale model oval provoking. Sombre graylag dictated upper sky reaches to pacify lentil broth, phial whirling nettle stay while feel, sailing by deep unto deep sleep ahead; heap up soak interim questionnaire overhead therefore boon yonder, tender ponderous enter surplus praise why notary drupe. All we know when steady parcelled special dandle, fondle extremity flapjack lighthouse beaming warn to keep; plaintive safety canter mostly, abide with running tide; buckle shooting fortify disputant brick, crock pedantic hide. Could wayside sanction fleet arm plentiful astringent wince fateful, jump ship skip liquidise gallantry low-rise merchandise, concision plan; hung to dry lupin high varnish, vanishing pin peacock flit surprise. Whelp polyp sanguinary melted indispensable at mutton-chop droop, landfill, randomise malting whereat wheaten snort.

Nail-bed enlisted madeleine ingrained appetite luminous bittern flicker, in daylight wit saving run the whole way say sea-shell whorled forehead; sonata enter leaf turquoise, insidious armament accompanied when driven inmate scripted. Even when sorted acuminate nothing to win delirious, exerted at masthead under home colours, chill childline one remade, reminded. Seepage drenched ahead until next dry-cast set finch hence match, whence wrench flower bunch sweet fragrant savoursome first seaworthy operational heavyweight flounder, under-weather bell turret tadpole fuel gnat. Long plenty close lodge chair, tune spoken seal woven sign own uncertainty promissory pledge; all class teamwork base nettle grasp aloft. By actionable tested chew well before or score-card know better than place invented, the best of our time all ruinous, do it carefully; sure step ready steady assented round about brim-work bay to shore inlet, assured reflected bounded safe to path, thirst. Outburst less missed awaited corded frank insurgent diffident remit, throat straight ache search, whole permission lakes. No more so far in clear intention eristic fulminate impersonation, rutile ruts below stowage ventilate.

As much as which touch, left past over quest further; cure chip missive twist tremulous, next requested immune again nearby rainfall; meagre done incessant custody airtight discount biscuit black legendary dromedary, synthetic sailyard hauled makeshift deck. Aloe so beanpod sprouted call-out, front invest modesty cress pitch fortress, sing nightjar chirrup in shadow pillow spent. Wanton mutton system differ lawful cotton at best medium, to think it must be rest to know best, risotto tempo slow in ever imminent cost; order lock to luck profess, opiate point dictate duck quake, clear thorn claim temper intuit light-weight impress. If bird in black to whistle, Anacreon singlet dawn at wharf plain mingled pocket intact; give over were danger earth and sky bridal tied ribbon, hinterland franchised branch perch brewhouse partner net. Major gradual fiscal parallel did yielding fit run to seldom letterhead presented, faster twill newfangled hosted stamp thrown pinion, open rack distracted.

Oh why later or not if before silicate went up in advance, where the vernal squills sprinkle the waysides instigating partial fixative; the option buy meadow callow accelerated with upper cylinder surcharge benefit, out to play, fritillary day-bright snapshot along the nearby roadway immersion. Poussin baste after roast most aftermath cluster looser, retinal bright spot lingual natural respective heaven's fiery coronal; resume cauldron din regaining companion-way run and stray hardening was young and foolish, autoclave resource cavernous half as old silk retinue. Hooded mantel wimple black rock tactile tektites foundry engram remission, flush with deliverance joint entrance, withdrawn mute order partnership slide window side first lower, covered allover tag spread gauze token inhibitance; do you dance, new-moon child, entrancing bench at rest, blue-john inference labrador sillance. Galena proverb heavy hints hedge crickets mosquito book token, burnt sienna flood water broken all race to undershot; pare thin pyrethrum tack.

At near last endurance, liberate by labour, penitent loving-kind
in joyous masthead, enough said. Know for ready oral sure canal,
denial casually even filtrate odd chairleg sudden songline, hopbine
share fairly at the obelisk running for cover child of grace. Scattershot
open gap pullet dark green pyruvic acid halflife genetic neural
comedy, barrage balloon contra-bassoon keep the door in full
dynastic view. Lies-bleeding, at great heart climate batik, sound swell
oracle nor while nor late, fruited eyesight; one full alight claimant
yet utmost release, better dispossessed congress eagerly ventricle pale
hands vein flutter infused. Peak sugar missing tail-plate, mountain
far before path signal anvil, smite the firm device, transfuse mission
heavy-water firelight alignment. Profile ladder set step up-risen, wise
bruise, noisy tended rendered, regaled. Turned topaz asset seized,
gatehouse locked fast, full on ahead trodden down current watch
quieter brimstone; wing-beat choric quill advance take heed white
letterhead best manifest shipping line designed, datum tent.

# 26

Hoodlum chrysanthemum addicted blind-sight, decoy warrior clansman since daybreak more fragile orthodox bandbox, conclusive transference macerate kitten kitchen overt kitsch hurry on past. Welter strudel offer teatime thunder-and-lightening, crystal violet swept perception, bunting; dire on corner filtration high-falutin mascara ever, masquerade adequate dollop. Charade actinic fascinate promotion, local bifocal indignant curfew tissue-paper on comical twig beside; saccadic lakeland exceed dragée spree specialised or prunes headlight ticket, detonate splint aggravate detour favour endeavour grass-green turf by close word of mouth. Steal full-match glimpse promised perseverate, vital reminded mnemonic masonry pointed to top out proof outmost declension; andante gusset vedic cantabile swing round manger yet, bounded to birth saloon parcel along and fit. Rested priceless welcome add once adonic hear the pipit, dig for it discreet greeting tag, none yet seen and cream, caravan returned; burning the wall in frame and claim repeat.

Trample muffle split old folks disseminate floriferous, light sway eyebrow tip-toe incautious zoot suit myopic trick subtropical, lingual allsorts vascular folded condensation pit-prop alone wrapping more hopeful; aggrandisement fort chortling dearest arrival swig portal abutment, tunes of insidious seaweed swirling bit batter dune cape down-river. Go far before rattan reopening carboniferous mawkish imprudent, incipient nip tableware more than they want intransigent planet. Limitation fraction divisor marigold eviction, aphid realm stream ant farm palmate designate, headlights; awesome tiff companion yawning vacancy astringent incidental. Button-hole scared hook eyelash open-mouthed dash ready-mix ferrocrete keep watch by night, all good alight dispute owl-flight beat beaufort placement; parallel swelling dwelled incurred enlarged divined self-raising flower bed, to turn and better want. Why-ever not make bright foresight, blink and pluperfect, bread and for wine.

# 28

Cold in harbour, bold as if smart, paint fix painful ailment
dilated loris insurgent; claimant reticent up in fronted,
bladder-wrack seasonal tidings asphodel before green turf
by close narration, pacification awesome session together
join returning taciturn. Pleading pie-crust below risk
factoring is rebated beforehand, wrist primal collis splinted
mercuric dressing iodine silk hydrate roadway trickle feed
flypast over late; gate to stair dazed vibration one tunicate
reversed graphite, ochre either out of turn debate. Festive
deletion assume one concurrency with awkward aligned
exchange predict coffer indifferency until wholesale.
Marine oceanic wave-front obsequious detained whenever
out catgut, perishing chill as if all very well royal charter
merge craven, hawthorn harts-tongue intention; frolic
estimation bank and bunk, a kerb-stone woven free-form
calm attachment. Muster ahead contented florins you know
leather satchel, smooth foremost downland cardigan;
diagnostic ire lapis lazuli coy meat loaf long awaited uttermost.

Cough syrup dilated bronchi for wellbeing plaque, even entirely wouldn't in scullery every skulduggery orrery; arctic asylum endangered pin plaint wellhead manicure ribaldry, supper party raucous belligerent butt negligent, bulwark mafioso affronted and patient, emery paper relief stitch purposeful however wavering bullion bulletin; tame guardian mockery trumpery pearly gateway free to work music box wind-up unguent, quaint. Door-bell tell the day long back to front bent ice-cream, beneath the visiting moon; order parlour minted leafage frail treasure ever forward, too nautilus at obvious not yet incisive cistern tank. At the ridge take edge profile the reverted team towards treaty port flit aide-memoire strip ledge, dodge past larkspur demur hadron water's edge if honour badge hold sway regenerative tussive loose throat nougat riddance; half back to front light collide or specify category actual credence. Crest boasted proud chutney witness, yellow filter out of kilter kipper swifter ever glaucoma; by aromatic pibroch symmetry, rays in shaded crannies.

Woe or wonderment beside themselves, monitor alacrity
hardly reaches the top level before full bird flight and why
in this case clock decision, expensive never to guess or would
you also not meant in that way at all; sherbet orangery
conditional provoking alack serendipity the difference not
known. Chancellor over-thrown the whole team modified
even before soaked right through, none at last score terrified
and corduroy cadaver raised piled notification; nautical vertical
enjoined persistent fervent avid disingenuous would both
the same at first, tortoise clamorous stalagmite anthill termite
oval terminal. Resourceful testamentary scarecrow danger
register likelihood, run with both of them, within both of us
at troika barrier too multibunt moral slew; running faster
sticking plaster dusky at eligible judgement, both ways at once
furnace love a duck, mail fuel heel injection cornucopia.
My darling already far remembered hillsides, none but who
could say, green whenever sunlight slanting and burnished,
too; real towards relinquishment almost as yet discrepant
in follow castor, wait due time on parliament ointment.

# 31

It is at finish halibut sack, truck action positive liken lichen, liverwort silk skirted lilt forensic liberty's milk; aggravate condensed they say position train scatter whoever, plover ascension eglantine frame. Lifting lightning what you see eager on ahead, pin-broth rattle the unspoiled coiled harvested; did any of the screen impervious right up-front, to butter spread at cheek better insistency scarcely each to other listed. Take what will would send mild opportune this time foreign gathering, shoe horn turn and turns about ravenous all ways first and oft foremost; get there intrinsic even onwards due. Sank thanks pitchblende without end in turncoat, houseboat over discover if never even slip a favour diminish admonish, be prudent pneumatic previous at forgiven so early one morning just so blanket solemn evermore stitch gnomic damask justly fanciful tumid at seamark, tropical mango usually less angry air-nourished orchids by settlement date improved not yet behalf. Roam the shore and porous delphic shelf-list with pike in hand, uncertainty at very least by such reckoning. In anger down to the shades, for so, as however over darkened air with loud cry, low-pitched but piercing, offering at last, at very least recourse, future remorse in recompense, fresh respite cancel denial oh purple tint staining the sea ragged rocks outreach to pastures new, to sing at last once more. Descant of high restored nor long forlorn, the old feast offered beforehand for steady hands and eyes still full in tune, horizontal and scarlet flint aligned.

# 32

At a clear rebuttal and far before temperate reinstatement
the survivors instantly reverted to top-down recruitment,
moss-speckled woodland spread with unexpected hatchery,
sequin adorned to justify the full return visit by astonished
alternatives; had to see why, over-go slither mannerism optic
dragon flies in sunlight polarised bemused and canted yet
why not or agate geode frenzied too. Be new induce who
so do, by few crimson festooned, you know flowing to go
paramount co-operative selvage; wigeon incision lucent
maximum setting at peak glint esplanade, no limericks
from soldiers ahead of truth to bear arms. Free range at high
precision these childish things focus interminable grasp
to play, enjoin forgiven at the margin influence by claudication,
wholesome gratitude. Nothing while why delayed, eschewed
advantage service dumb-waiter creaking brigandage,
liquorice in the shade of evening light. For better later
gyrating individual marsupial, wings by active chatter
ring-box enclitic indigenous dish; margrave amazing
on accent elation cautionary, feudatory altogether swim.

Conspicuous overshadowing at high celerity for celery match rhubarb sorbus aria lutescens, arioso insinuation multitudinous tronc. Anticipate by clear evening light to the metropole asparagus famine ahead by a long chalk lent mascot wainscot diverging; guilt-ridden opportune in coat of thorns cystic divination pears of neighbour wrath. How could you choose to use parsley first off dividend in sharp bend, where dolphins play world without end as certain proof of immortality, shandygaff bliss; entrenchment wrench inch silence whenever fortified endeavour, grisaille well before. Roseate window fretwork overt viols denials constituents, bitumen collagen ambitious if to be in situation convocation rattle fictitious tissue; grocery pretentious anxious run to earth cease-fire cordon sane positron malt loaf, banana brew draw-strings who linger. Anger when cornered, jetty in pictures, near yet suffocate at top speed feed the plough, one at a time table settle brandish as because all of them partitioned, far-reaching suspicion jog before nim, amble after canter avenue, sleek dentition trim. Enamel elemental oblique obelisk monumental freefallen plaque immaculate folk, who knows honour in deference patience smiling integrated cream.

Criminal opinionated over fortify raison reasonable flouted, implicate in blue haze open days presume willow bark, bout by instruction. Yeast freshening candidate sedulous thrust parcel trusted antennae furthermore columbine aquiline promises, all admitted under foot went pedantic columnar fidget faucet; aspect gusset tubular torrential turret, throat lynx larynx anxiety entirety cover check goatee. Want better soever sinusoid colloidal mongrel adept wastrel arterial parenthood ingested, duplicitous monstrously would-be ripen wreck; ache placid slate inventive leading to gatehouse mollusc crass disturbance, lost already enemy enviable afterwards hindrance pace-stick clack mensuration. No one thing venture ought split vulture bitter-root buttercup outcrop, go to ground almond cognac tighten glazing pride catnip ocean bright, oxen on lateral lanyard mustard nursery loop. Consignment remount stolon invited anther dusted another often gong-tormented outback, pay ahead antidote epact overt adherent eyebrow commissar derivation by granular persistence; until whether evasion fusion lithium hydrant, stoat parlour back cushion own nomenclature fright by dark voice horn velvet. Sit close screw ravenous raucous wingflap mightn't creosote, votive at antiphon chancel win upper register link domain in fugue. Gaping ancestral yawn to swim gem caret invasion maroon sportive, summarise toys enough crescent coronet agrimony, incipient daylight balustrade jetty overhead, cling peach purple emperor speckled; to ban speculate catchment.

Mortal mayonnaise triumph attachment interminable, grating spared miniature conditional frugality effort welsh rarebit for all together; hold intrinsic digital imposition prohibited traipse reprieve circular displacement, next tap something understood. Source juice unpunished even afloat customary dairy porringer, well before announced lizard wall tiger forenoon unknown withdrawn; mushroom clench feather open fluster, shoe leather further other convoke peacock dwindle uncle disposition. Inversion minaret lancet punctuate accompany white bryony staccato flourishing, potato gruel cigar profile, cougar applauded avenue silken however too; requirement filamentous furthermost ice calcified unworried, bridgeway buttress bravery protracted. Despite whenever providence acclamation on principal accelerate, lamp black platelet cognition bantam tungsten mastery headline; reluctant disputed irritate guidance grapeshot succession farmhouse, march inkling cheddar fabulous strident declension fricative.

Easement pilchard coastguard tongue and grovel honeycomb did intersect fungal insect oppression autumnal vertigo, novelty broached sliced relaxed; completed fashion ocean prospect frieze imago sibling trifling octagon cerebral bivalve at viper handkerchief, commissure usufruct intact arctic shelf. Ignition dayglo igloo zeolites off pursuance stupefied vainglorious full-tilt zealous incision, corroded in fettle sunken rootstock backpack, outer rockface twice; outwitted partridge each retrieved oak face frustration, milk carnation perfidious piston melodious tankard indignation. Top storey morning glory standing room only, bike track rancour bit dust nearby crush; who's to say which way first served, cupboard love hand in glove stove black crease almanac. Marine panorama host banana yours boon for keeps insidious broom sweeps, all pipistrel entangle upper pitch nest. Digestive meet half pay forest fire revere residue prognosis, loaf breeding long before tide over scarcity plumage. Flock together bothersome thistledown twin goldfinch breakfasting.

# FOREMOST WAYLEAVE

# (2023)

## Beside Seasonal

*(maestoso moderato)*

Rain soon in near stream, bird fresh in bush
deep winding clear shone to ours and miner
quarry flurry willow call, finding search wish
act passion relented, forgiven, as to whence
along to sing; in tune.
Pine cones bright in August, cloud arranged
glitter fringe, safe houses torrent to relayed
friendship cascade over brocaded. Willingly
intended ride outward eventual new-made
allocate in main part.
Hold up echo see eye to ear braver heat out
compensate implicit call-sign hillside waded
river flow overgrown; accept message quite
pulse meet later visited, violet maiden suits
ramble waver cautious.
Later egret bayonet, lonesome beforehand
renewal coaxial eggshells; immoderate tide
straw packing dissenting adventurous refer
toadflax flaunting uniform curlews crossbill
singleton reprobated.
Earwig meatus afflatus aloof paddock aspic
suspicious oxtail ravenous subsequent pint
birth canal or canary culinary ravel sleeved
craved mouse-tail chickweed modal fragile
abashed music hyphen.
Both twice either otherwise; documents so-
called phantom light shower low-down dice
crevice speedwell bonnie boat rowlock fate
snuff. Egregious supple auction tiffs ophitic
shearwater, as tilting.
Occulted diorite mischievous frantic penalty
canopied ultimate druse; lairs intact anklets
worthy haptic florid incessant, entire below
intervals dill trial mammoth tooth froth else
alligator circulated bit.
Prone soonest dip-stick red-brick expected
vein in bones seam aimed bramble tremble
yard-arm paving, under mission late amber

timber stack wicket lappet original cragged
bolt inside or gatepost.
Divested cost-plus entrenched, knees joist
ride the wavelet amulet spaghetti innocent
however entice waist; diction by utterance
fair to bear airways, near and far beyond pi
circus honest clowned.
Indigenous distort. Necklace on incision
organ voluntary sentence tissue, fissure soft
promise velvet candied peel aftermath best
polymath graphite; inscript engrossed toast
gibbous fasten iced.
Crystalline entwine tar sands frenzied heads
space lattice differ, swagger water sapphire
effort smooth yellow flagpole oriole. Condoles
mournful cranesbill wellspring, dewlap alert
concert pitch fetch.
Streamline ketch fingernail kestrel followers
nervously peardrop ear-ring RNA beekeeper
steeped in grins pollen; plainchant penchant
folic indicated prize-winning brethren cream
as eglantine, as mine.
Cyclone sealions, servile impetuous cautious
rushes green growing fawn growling python
agnate toxic surreptitious luffing & coughing
asseverated near-sighted prismatic rabbit pie
jam-jar nightjar gated.
Or mercies adduced by remission, recipience
by patience smiling while at least unless doff
surprise beneath heathland who knew dews
moisten the eyelash one after next. Set pitch
call oboist canoe lit.
Bright candelabrum unabashed, incautiously;
ride the wave thrown up in spray pyramid to
insinuate port instigate rack dock mock turtle
start out star charts look before leap year nil
counter-sink sunk.
Fear entire deplore depth charged discounts
dash selected liqueur dispel predicament re-
freshed by arbitrage, please on both sides big
fish back in the water inventively in readiness
as infolded by noise.
For plentiful impulsions brokered by applause
both ways in grand displays, aftermath collect

to find the cause unrusted swords, untrusted
words in ever-during night: enough released
driving the screw, true.
When dew collects in drops as for bright sparks
in lark to market torn, in cheek outworn, so soon
the bridal of the day and night, the morning who
comes soft and blue; soever ready in-door new, to
grow to ripen fruit.

## Erstwhile Merciful

*'Is not Strain'd'*

*'As fast as thou shalt wane, so fast thou grow'st'*

Or cup fluster, or better cap in butter, offer given spaces
set to come-up mite; lighten present fires endure scripted
nap cemented fissile to sup summit swum. Swing let upon
graven masque past dilute ebony canopy obeyance holts
salute lips patter scallop coral blame tulips, over and out
severance offence target forehead adrenal wrinkle cope.
Falcon pitch, fuse rent beak took to another
triptych passive ullage forage, mistaken or if
even sudden horizon blazon tempered ward
or dipole or cupid orchid discriminating do
crystal others before, egg pollen voluble parables told
oven pupate correlated crescent dative syllable oracle
'seeking an absolute tilt in favour of abstraction', laps
molten dredge listen probable regulates, milk welcome
silken needle thread; lease to restive nectar debt crate
distributive adjusted, by eye intrinsic seek soaking tints
lower partial byre near to hand. Without or
fear of lost connection, flame ribbon carbon
tap first solace as variously 'to live and move
and have our being' dehiscent colloid tappet
crossing level warning in plait spread fluid fervid, elbow
lakeside cygnets wait-for flight anent in flickering rushes
initiated, bulbs to sprout illuminate. Shell up shell out at
benchmark could cowl whirl or ready mandate affected
incense, temper burnish unfinished; take to heart atrial
flutter packet insinuated undercurrent, talent delighted
ridden, 'nor is He served by human hands', as
carried forward to meet all found, in plumed
detachment capture printed 'looks as if it's all
happened at once'. For of course 'everything
you can imagine is real'; nightjars spar churr anew or fill
fuel manual oval intertidal, I'd go franchise silence antic
trance trobar clus disparagement. Runners-up likening
avenues sifted inevitable accident, contract sustenance
forbearance macaroon almond entrain linen ministerial
fumitory so-deemed corydalis mischief graywacke silt.
Or for white mice enticed shadow shelf, lure
wolfish pilfers niece 'nicht zu schnell' mixture

true and colour by slight, herewith eyebright
fraught less taut both hands chine grimaced
distract abasement; apt upon to lateral upshot topiarist
dentition valiant, spangle distant tact hard-bitten eventual
split first insistence attested sheen persimmon abacus of
taken aback rife, bacchic moonshine anarchic; repledged
diagonal fanciful, later mitre evaporated net-zero column
flit harpoon management momentum fossil verified talc.
Trappist beehives skip costs squashed cabin
canonical dual relict crown list furtive news
involuntary wrinkled raster alabaster twice weft
fringe affrighted, impious desiccate slept off.
Dicots alloyed latency motion unknown illuminated, silvers
reconcilement cursive badger; careworn tunicate punic sib
step-parent invariant custard foreclosed cellar collar edged
vermillion contusion; orgiast diarist missive soften prevents
allergen minstrel trombone, sprawl impugned organist most
grass cousin scots pine emblem revision. Tureen greens
cremaster gruel smiling, trailing as when into
mounted tarragon odalisque sweltering, soon
won-ton deafen seldom mastodon often lyse
caramel codicil. Digressive pasturage sprocket
come bunkum home pudding, additional strontium men to
curlicue tunnel infusion; unmentionable wrangling hoisted
increment tell us further passionate loft. Mutton chopping
white streak perfect cleavage, leveret obvious average rot
individuate maser clover; both will whenever crampon to
phosphoric bantam–bootlace creviced crayfish undertow
longing invoice owl balance, wanted exchange
leather cinders endorsed remorse brigandage
lavish feathers beneath; sonant partial special
bristle indifferent won't you come home, mint
honey tea-cake bring about album of ink floats quoits dealt
noontide shimmer gravure. Tantric seeks flints allurements
strike grebe maple maybe carry me greengage assuages to
sweet morning light; upended ungainly sherbet harassment
coeval blanket noisome wasted eucalypt, contrary doubted
nebulous cursory capricious. Tantalises furnish interference
mercenary beechmast behest modestly regrets
aerofoil braille spoiled anchored moss-covered
twite hambone colophon attack alleviated chat
grievous pardonable, absurd sea-fronts climatic
apprentice plenteous unctuous prognosticate at first rested
fulmar batten; regime hang merriment dividend shared even

proven forgiven retracted. Nursery addicts porphyry tertiary
willingly absconded, bearded iris rice-bowl dual entry pantry
sentry dutiful cantilever eventually fandango, imago coralline
inclination frustrated untied. Fried fish-cake exact polyp lake
        placated salted overheated, all gable affable ant
        shingle wend luminous farmhouse choice; waist
        yielded plywood: 'gladness of the best'. Buds set
        at top praise mild subdued know found aground;
'something understood' ever returned, wood under-foot slip
crackle treacle lighthouse ardency, surf. Customise point for
out and ready foremost, not lost but gone before to line over
ever-more, shall be true and prudent lucent flash-light visits;
ecstatic knife through buttercup rise to shine, gain to harbour
laborious assertive indigo ceremony edgewise alongside flute
        cryptic celluloid bitten, twice certain inclemency
        savoury barking made-up paid patchwork lurked
        gossamer overt insidious plenitude. Curtain open
        scene front activate overturning behind-hand on
breccia fissures lateral economise, wiseacre spikenard wooden
'es lebe der Koenig' liverwort, biscuit posset wait alight soaked
down among the darbies; cointreau notional follow along time
droplock shuttle myrtle herbage savagery, orangery zestful told
azure-winged dire sonatina; entire western govern synonym off
durable onyx synthetic parlance invited, left afterward trigram.
        'How many I caught there. In one week, five foxes.
        Can you imagine that?' Fast and furious revealment,
        burrow to borrow however salver obvious; curious
        shellac cellarage bites frequent ancient, traipse
dice-pot who knows up-front mellow limit turnip agitated alike
grike shouting; service frosted others finished twice creature
vestment attached, taproot mimicry to creamery till running
out and bulbous, best tissue licence both waist. Shifted outer
premise lionise occupied mollusc impressionable cortisone pint
paintwork highpoint lost wax; grex ilex nonce on pentagon two
        almost, merchant arrogant acrobatics fanciful dual
        orchestral mission inducement intelligible cubic
        waxen entry profusion tooth toe refreshed at hand to
        mouth invoked henbane probably; signalise refuted
down-converted entanglements cockatrice spooky action afar.
Entailment substitute relinquish infrequent disparage knot
recession thereafter complicit misfit elastic forceps thallus off
all-out decretal weaponry borrowing browning over the town;
planetary gadgetry saturate indusium, bruised by leaf beneath
woven lace dog's mercury fitful fever nembutal 'think of horses

not zebras', reindeer rained here tear-worn tea-time
lion tamer trimmer be mine, be thine atropine cleans
all clear torn to burn worn pungent at cat-mint. Into
came and went scented freight ill met moon-sight out
rhymed at catguts fried proud imperishable, feudal concentric
burial oriole cruelty golden calico benefit, grip tight fleeter ten
or when than lateral honourable, curative foible thimble angle
biblical dead-nettle indent cramp; gastropod lactic lenient seas.
'Ah so the oozy weeds about me twist' distressed to sleep or yet
keep damp maidenhair fern, clamp to wrist else pulse lentil low
hidden unheard fused together; oboe look back waits
deed-box salt breath; new flicker clouds over whether
hovers to shades of under-ground. Owned cruised in
by around split creeks insist, stray intercede conjugal
pertain ruff to wish relish fished ambush tinder; endeavour in
oculist soft flush offended whiten alleviate, irrigate cattle-grid.
Mute linnet pertinent indignancy, downhill ethical interpret in
angular hurtle whistle stuck; ruckus coverlet loose maple-leaf
apricot void instead uncertainty wintergreen banter, lozenges
hysterical soonest legume lantern jaw. Recession too at check
infusible cranberry myrtle counterpane brine, at
upturned mace cushion token backlight asset brim
guilt, stricken often curfew respected without trace
aromatic rebuke parade obvious, interval supernal
tantrum rock rose potion rejoinder pointed main-braced, off
choice randomise diminishment spoon incorrigible told
dubiety for unbeknown assisted foiled showerproof feast
arterial or closet wit garden-path feudalise undistinguished bit
cantankerous interruption substitution separable motionless
moan then thrown beside downwards, ensign coinage pain
or when signage inclusion openly fingernails in
rotary onyx, leafage saffron auburn tarpaulin twin
tarragon at hone worn opening assertion. Racked
insistent provident, ruinate peony grudge boasted
polite ovate at first light, stand to at sandstorm and yawn
asseverate even when osmanthus flutters outright, open or
shut in front. Mirror broad and narrow banjo on to strum,
willow willow branch overhead keep the coast clear creed
morning flute, sprout sonnet fort palisade boiled later over
family fortune wade the ford, stepping as dry under-posted
foremost letraset perfectible evermost sluice else
along with hope markers touch to find rightly true
ever so ready discovered bright-coloured, advance
grateful sherbet goosefoot improbable; hawk-eyed.

## Penance at Cost

*'For some good Penance'* – Ben Jonson, *The Alchemist* (1610)

Terraced for suffice delusion mostly overtime, abashed forthwith tankard
tracing fish-pie slice wane astern, custard or engineer oven while frontal
iodine onrush ashen hue; foxglove, near must primate liquid drupe ooze
at halyard trice hasten album crushed shoe patch dish. Tailspin acerbic
brilliantine dispersal eucalypt snatched
breath, how when how for whoever tilt,
milk tribute appraisal whimsical remit
at ready foreign imminent open felted
up to winking at the onside brim. Torque muted intercepted brazen, win
dozen crust mission meltdown learner-driven wholesome stubbornly sessile
tendrils anvils infidels contusions intemperately digit puppetry optional
field maple multiple docile pomade; ancestral cowslip onomastic teeth
egregious alone trombone pine cones,
splinter for chill winter corrugate dilate
thereafter inflated coypu recrudescence
aloes flannel insistence underfelt, newt.
Outer orbit oyster clambake awkward fortunate casework in windowsill
grating, blind-sight longwise so far by now safety curtain cold fusion one
hands first bantam fisticuffs guessed; boiled by all at now, interim cramp
candid lagoon when great white heron boarded over endeavour pardon
quilt brother tether shoelace gusset no
dice beef broth anthracite twilight spilled
as sledge willows nudging endorsed bone
immersions hydroxide aquifer calamine
green refinement, steam corrosion flake retaken metalloid dust slurry
corrie engulfed rancid or foxed, chased damask; hoist uppermost often
emphatic licence mistaken minuet praise soothe if no far hurry in turn,
wash coppice lariat harassed, gleam flight back down cornfields velvet.
Fall in by lineament sizar planet obligato,
known for ripen onions spellbound ends
melee loyalty parvenu, alike or reflected
while in pair marching on through honey
once rice, oval scorched ice pack litter gruesome bun intact; revivalist
gallantry anchor fluke effrontery, scattered here at front porch bench
esteem born tame fearsome. Also at tango rigmarole, how otherwise
demise foison lissom riverside contentment, ointment yet parchment
chestnut contingent who wills, coralline
choke blizzards hazard ushering vaulted;
aisle whale valiant, by river servant faster
however tacit deep prestigious aromatic

in the arraignment counted fortune ready charm to rivalry prophecy.
Battery torch invoice creased eastern clematis reverie under necklace
'the odd mannerisms of the white man' how return main-sail condition
option fashionable, wharfage muster adamantine woodpecker lesson

ibis diminish refurbish sentence. Scanted
scented breccia mighty parlous breathing
loosen minimalism when-if insistent, lofty
musk silken brazen inducement contract

moral tendence dawn risen; would they ever discover horizontal bill
glass fronted frost best forested worsted, zip overdone replenished
bead wrist ahead to link detail sealskin pencilled eyebrow, parallel
graphite critical indigenous alongside; mirror annoyance unworried

pyrrhic pilchard refracted twelve olive
frankincense condensed water thunders
cupboard shelves sensuous, watchful in
galvanic bronchial urgency, by dinosaurs.

Cushions fiscal geraniol, to traipsing maximum sufficiency invidiously
scapular tertian stiletto spendthrift roving complexion into averaged
prudence portrayal goldeneye pheasant beyond millrace barefaced
liquorice sugar-bush whether mischief price delivery, as when untold.

Indigent effulgent python tea-caddy esplanade foiled
irritation loitering estimable mussel custom oat;
dotage crick integument pursued felt coronation
peridot, jacinth wincing crude splayed about

merchandise orthodoxy pandowdy. Off the cufflinks bankable, slightly
into show for showers overtone colourant slain yet whine concerted
scavenge arrangement terrible fragmented mended illusion tame lamp
conjugate jointure, optition tooth at immiscible stubble blueberry win

particulate awaited surgical indictment often
whiter tighten persevere spanner veneered
interpret ostrich substitutes; known oaken
crape antiquated milk off black ultra-violet

tower pouring blurred wet streaks roseate skypark. Evident filament
clement conjoin lavish manager speckled wood, upbraided ladle viz
swivel numerously abet castanet assisted asbestos; insulate frighten
or closer yet brink dianthus frivolous acanthus, scatter awkwardness

silk purse worse ever than cursive earful
rhyme creed oilcan settle gifted tactful
admonitions drained in open vainly;
sustenance prominence certain brave

sagebrush tortoise shellac formic indicator radiator pulsations mode
loaded down roadway, sunrise surprise surmised convergent foaming
reformations plunder undergrowth tonsure footloose cross-stitched
strewn wide and seek drapery grateful antonym asylum treatments
how would calibrate colour coded on
seeded fraudulent mustard poultice
jocund juiced paced incidentally tune
brighten horizonal walnut fascia dash
splashing ford crossing awash dismissed, profligate lubricated enticed
grimace pumice ordinance prancing chicken pudding pursuance once
mitochondria divagated messenger excursion cogent organic dismissal fin
protruding wallowing galloglass ornamentation seizure parallel hormone
infidel minaret, inflict spoken inflection
concoction syphon auction-house bite
uppermost chatelaine disdainful prone
hay-wain pleach. Hedgerow sultan few
stew stollen filigree hawthorn currant; malachite outcropped flutter
badger butter otter mucilage safeguarded willow grove shovel offal
integral lethal occluded primrose yellows deliquescence opulence at
altered frontal corsage; badinage tequila prayer incidence sanctuary
haddock scratched frostbitten anointed
lucky strike wakening weekend remind
lavender vacant priory soonest cornea
sprocket lamium missionary inviolate
interstitial bucket downpour awesome silvery moon bonfire dawn
lacunose heightened bracket octet, burdensome tipper cornflower
ardour grappling-irons highbrow crowsfoot bashful arrival crucially
duckets surfeit unequal portal pondweed mushroom omelette trap
gastric. Sap-free bark to shout onion
skim tramways organising allusions
powder winter skirmish; pulverising
all-go to toehold builder elderflower
ransoms tension landmark, weighted truculent spirited turpentine
lighthouse backflow. You surely know better clattering choughs
pinwheel flash cashflow peppermint bullrushes how so clamber
grocer package banana pavement engraving to diagram intervene
antagonism; intoxicant loyalist flits
tested spirits reluctance along
verger emerging speedwell petals
scatter summer worm cryptic lite

osmium besought uncaught lakeside, defrayed instead mended
anticipate alignment poignant magpie triumph; coryza surmisal
trumpet vines declined narrow hollow ring, grapefruit elation to
nutrient lawn clover plovers lie-low plough lease shear portfolio
    cordyceps entanglement rhea trifolium
    belated inundated crenelated porous
    walrus obstreperous zebra linear ogre
    nougat magnified parade instinctually
disparaged edgeways mousseline privateer nearer bisection
heart entrusted; braille foibles entitled from drafted tabular
angora servitor acknowledgement, banquet bouquet floater
flamboyant clarinet introit enjoyment kitchen kittens mitten
    basins ogee trenchant; mandarinate finch
    grosbeak token teak awake. Freakish beak
    alack tickle waffle won't you come home
    placement graft fastening press-stud sleek
dedication whence further here another, incorrupt or lurching
aspen birch striped adequate qualified camembert wont joker
riddled befuddled resection arterial presumption lantern tropic
welcome; awesome glucose sliced tourniquet frightened malic
    adapted slavery comical, butchery ornament
    orrery runaway black-market inducted troop
    leisure seizure; masterpiece solace gangrene
    spinach at wafted grasses, solstice consequent
injustice palatial optional regional curiosity slain hopelessly envied
parallel religion; worship battleship setback agreement flint swell
alerted chert or cheated aggression incandescence switched after
marble white tussock commissary, puzzlement. Muzzle daze gusto
    flagrancy suet suited, Welsh rabbets practical
    gobbet scimitar alliance pandemonium torn
    frigid Grosvenor elevator twisted lift-shaft twite
    outage spillage, footfall street-plan village green
domestic forfeit platelet indiscretion awkwardness derivational
nationalism cornucopia nacreous intarsia sprawling scintilla ban
coffin durational icing; coffee infringement incalculable wallow
stifling concertino clipboard audacious vivarium tribalism topic
    tributary grossular irregular ichneumon lizard fire
    judgement paradise mouse-trap omission equerry
    wherry severed chord poured condominium burn
    fermented augmentation choir-stall gale-force at

welter uttermost credulous outhouse adduce dancing nuisance once
voltmeter saltpetre dapper occiput roasted concurrency, boat clout
exploded deplorable incurable wastage dotage plumage schist elder
insertion mutton fraction ichor cordage improbable embraced waist

licence indolence bachelor adorable; purposefully
silk lesson tissue missionary conversion ballet for
bullet credit magpie sighing stealing ogle singular
highbrow buttering no parsnips, kirby-grips galore

furore viola solo d'amore previous; aggrandised foliated battalion
alliance durance vilified compliance harebells distilled oiled composed
mountain-side, chestnut ebony elbow slight. Liberal hebetude layered
corundum wine-dark wrapped in a five-pound note–floating to leap

or look to stook, regalia gardenia snack munch inch
drawback frack tactical damson daemon charioteer
penguin criminal portraiture rapid debenture annoy
now or sinter never, liverwort pertinent oligarch.

Moribund impatient legality scrupulous edelweiss, hornet tornado
delivery jewellery insurance abhorrence leaping forward; pavement
gazing sheep grazing safe bustard, in wonderment emerald elevated
frustration continental continuation; honeypot stipulation formation

corrugated cardboard spoliated; tambourine
inflamed hornfels basement orris-root brute
speculated imprisonment inconvenient coin
florin tandem nugatory nugget acetate nip

attainment clearance napery, raspberry foolhardy intent went
junket. Compunction ructions burnous turnabout riotous break
pressure gauge caramel kerbside far and wide intertidal angled
stairway apple crumble cinnamon evenly cloven down to earth.

## Foremost Wayleave

Passional eagle aerofoil hillside, tidal
widening by croup fission
possum shovel swivel as ever; hovercraft bust
telluric elastic reverted
windowpane ingrained run faster or won't you
come home, in temperature
vigorously
impulsively
hypnotic undiscovered flag
improvement why not afloat tortoise noisome
inveterate bathetic pepper
refurbished all new-minted
scull-cap, dwarf surmounted frequently curdled
indisputed circus plaintive hoop clarino water-
offer by better plantains; fountain splashing
wishing suffer than ever
beavers or never before.
Lurid aspect colonial distracted baronial gate
dragée tussle dungarees
reinstatement attainder by
infuriated barricade foremost infusion lament
talented anatexis placebo, cruiser guile
up over backwards twist
virus first offensively whence cometh dawn-light
given mimic clown multiplier site
inured conjuration eaten
hunger boat; for beaten track arrack
stoat collop disgrace river downwards trice
homage lazurite, frighten
cascade carillon lifted aloft lighthouse
pursuivant occupant, tea planted incidentals.
Olla podrida frangipani brussell bit sprout;
gallivanting rampaging orbicular for
suitable singular coveted
millipede in weeds concession aversion
at derelict brimstone wit
boat cordage, timespan tektites night-flight
leather jacket closed plight; acidic intermit
evenly neckerchief relentlessly
noise or so far encrusted
kerb shoeshine tag caustic by

pitiable partnership whipround, loose change
availed sneeze to wheeze
filbert fillip filtration gutted forcible
behaviour silver sideboard. Hipflask–market
masquerade cavalcade avoidance inch
comma whisper painted ladies
dainty furious kinema various on unwantedly
screen spurious opening bright
none so below the bough, yellow gems
gleam onwards opportune thirstily even so karet
bison mission institution mount
painting sunlight; as level beak citrine
retinal abrasion contortion running faster tin
tack eviction knack constricted pacific,
set pellucid candid, envied
instinctual botheration cornucopia over
stile cornflower; fort fernseed tied
ready cribbage average billboard, ringed
flights passages tropic parsnip
aseptic underlain gainfully. More than enough
roughage indifference, hessian scrim
sever near at left by candytuft, relish best
manifest destiny virtual concomitance.
Once habitually rain martial,
fertilised metallic stupefied mandolin
grizzly swipe poisonous octopus sensible to
seaside kiosk lavender spruce
sealions waiting game tumid graticule
scallions portions slit shoelace reductive or
toadstool pippin; wooden dowel
interweave bassoonist pointless luminosity
swiss roll charabanc, convent currency
persistent double-bass offcast trampoline
pneumonia rodent fondant; muscle
barracks defiant saraband unreliable at
incidental, most complete
delightsome original truffle-hound profit will
line into burial mound, echoic fruit pip
lifted advanced. Molybdenum had ridden
in search clatter aloft alternated list
hydrated sleeves invented
canter beyond infusion, yet enrolled
listen rebec godwit cherry of
count them quick, beknown in turn on

reckon intimate candidate unit
gopher trophy cloister ancestor, native off
bivalve selvage maple stirrups.
Exotic fungible butterscotch or welters
gourmet haddock first, crucial flagpole oval
supple off oil heavier.
Uncle incinerator scrappage master forceps at
purified link, abandonment cuff
townscape yet however muscat coffered
ceiling running entirety commission pride bee
comb shattered; littoral quacks
chromate dill
munificent dromedary invigorate off
limit target magpie comically
wash corridor together, borrowing to snatch cot.
Abasement idolised crane-fly once ultimately
easily, intensified nimbus.
Hurling spate contingency yeast, thirst
oceanic parlance statin; furtherance elegance
ambiance sufferance by shuttle diminish,
arrogance perseverance, insipience.
Parchment yield
mandarin out to winnow bungalow awash eave
seethe; pistol awful candlesticks cruise
dolphin aquarium, bulletin seat
spatchcock boat
merrily beside the seeking flute, inspected out
roll along brainwave seashore
nevermore august visage mockery juice,
justice beetroot
furtive twain invidious crater
hospitable panegyric; synthetic byte lockets
koranic algebraic pontificating. Fossil
missal shining infailing, croquet
dawning albatross at single streaks of weight
redefine; within sight at slipper touts
tablet flounder
poppycock majestic, infatuated by ash groves,
indirect tributary trowel
smoke eager mirror. Shark slight panic
float riverside trout speckled
flaccid, inventoried carrots boiled beef, yelp.

## Asserted Flourish Meant

*(tempo giusto)*

For wyvern inwoven suffusion, sprinkle at passionate pendent or mammoth flit. That's wit first coerced uncounted dome shadowed, either toucan acclaimed. Already steadied by wrist pleat prone auricula, wherever roaming planetary long downside implied calligraph; joist fervid ascended parallax. Columnar cordyceps best turtle tortoise, reflex waxen chromatic domestic turquoise azure demure to promise casement permission downside wide entrained; uphill anticipate ant suffusion flight runway craven noisome bacon passion alignment, wisdom exchange. Optimal optical mended lens pendant bright star horizon beehive naval fleet honey bonny doorway, across grateful smattering void sunlight stroke ripen scapular sippet occupation. Jute astute plighted, take off run to give over in summer clover.

How both not to shoe ease in practice fit, early before late bittern slim moonlight figwort antic by uppermost hostage; fluency recollect plated eclectic peppermint citric plate elbow unsuspected within target range on view, late-come swarm been soonest bee mended. At latchet window counsel along shadow, song in the trees sunlight haze, to wait in patience or make supper by stages afresh, action sweet william; listen to breeze at waist for nimbus, by soften and capture by climate, holding memory in true passion. Claimant gathers the menu to more than few radiance stippled pinpoints over once incidence, I'd love in both which match. Warm air strokes the hands and cheeks, light cadence rouses the leaves, human onlooking sheer true to see nature glinting, so to know what is all around, believe what you find into regard glows.

And trusting to care from side to side, end to end. How could this be otherwise from day to day, watchmen what of the day blithe night, hold fast to none or worse, amusement. Sound and melody of weather plumes ride our constant attention found reward our hopes within life itself, give back what time and the hour ride thru the roughest day-break, breathe slow and steady passing by splint season to have joy, by and by. Yeast each graceful buoyed up touch of by antiphon, early morn light infired in fresh colours shared ready and new-found to ride actual birdsong free and dear entire. Whistle and capture the voices close into throat maiden singing, stay for true pitch harmonic light of sky. Pliant folded octet tuneable nor for sedge whither seashore treatment wash lift crocus placid snowdrop, hitherto alongside turnpike sake attic brick.

Incessant loan-back threaded fuel foiled endowed with viscid sustenance, or viola d'amore overt Delphic corn plucked strop immaculate. Touch and go in word meadow preamble when to praise and close, cloud horizon betide rictus surplusage; however run for cover quicken cyclamen next critic burdensome choric splash. Follow the guide to yet trill onward all prepared, weird awl match in snatch of cotton wool vestment caroused, testament browsed. As hardly scorched brought to into ebony driftwood careering balsa imperilled sideways-on; graphene sharpens meanwhile diligence recompense, gallop colonial indigenous accentuated crankshaft chalcedony munch ordinary archway measurement. Rod to dice polarised enticement franchise tee-square gnawed hurricane awful plangent deponent crumpled horn-book lucent saturated felsic.

Ovoid replete conjugate least suited meet custody evince advance marmite once or yet twice calcifuge dormant for porous patent roofing. Last-gasp quest stare inclusive missive bypass corrugated aloof christening afforded font tentative bleat, did enough lattice ever banana nap scissors causative pruning vocative in line cinnabar training brisk drill and clingfoil bush croup clinch terebinth weasel vocable insoluble burnished languidly ban clinched pumice. Quangle brim moreover, inglenook diluted nett weight glottal swallowed jasper lobster reverted in cordite attachment larynx fox lode-star; we three cautious or thimble gamble winnings pawn awnings permittance litter for nightfall kneecap embroiled, fair-share endurance mildest. Wrapped in foil, turn about ever-fostered for lacquered inch.

Nonplussed, sacrosanct uppermost buttered toast in golden fleece application metro tan downstream scabbard dew rusting kerchief hurtle onwards versus inventive coccyx; masterpiece out of throw-into pandowdy magpie lakeside to esplanade formidable grapple espalier cuticle leverets diocese ambience search ambiguous winding arduous do task contrivance. Scuttle trollius mercuric scimitar willing pitch alive news taffeta undefiled earlier antelope inference ferment onomastic canyon for bantam up to tandem billiard saddle dragon, poultice grazier tidier for monsoon nectarine awkward don't steward when however puzzle or grizzled overture, soon however salmon leap cribbage to overreach junket musket alive or by wanted guidance mercenary; flip scribe forfeiture sear and yellow chromic imperial chilled mythical satchel, woven scarf fen orchid.

Mid-brain quicken contested alleged govern by late after sufficient ingredient metalloid rubricated; why saline in opening lordosis finishers porch above and lex talionis shuttled imminent obstreperous flapjack, vaccinated red kite the far side reduction speculated height bonny section fetlock; wrap to coir entire dare frame spiral choral nettle whistle frontage why not return rain grapple tipple not a patch. Then pine jump from segment lateral incident, grapefruit inimical cloudburst loosed shale back-bit ingenious birch oracular dressage advanced in a shady reveal; conduce to dissipated in samite shatterproof piccolo politeness acer trenchant scrape. At size basilisk ahead of malachite lupus expected, cracknel tucket footsteps tepee kindly endurance clinker incident skullcap way down improvident estuarine angelic canteen; harpoon cream senescent privilege buried curial eagerly, merrily suspended orthodox napery outside vellum ante-bellum lizard cruciform winter bombazine.

Spinneret feat aspect ready to web ensue shoed shining eyebrow scarecrow, cask next task enlisted waist intended razor warden, hadn't riparian inlet pertinent gratulate, wouldn't even condone saccharine driverless bottle emaciated songs of honey tinted peasoup, awkward just last sourced grazed for praise hive oven-ready table pitch toasting fork charge far ahead, overseas posted rope trick effrontery jacket threadbare folded double to dibble oncogene crane hilltop meniscus entailed apsidal trusted entire invariable issuance flared aside amazed importunate lazurite, twite. Concentrate lifted hibiscus start elated, intense gas sunken alongside construe wingspan oaken shaven proof arrested invert glucose fair tower lairs obsidian; don't look first erstwhile blanket coronet cornerstone resume attainment climate digested to woodland, dashboard innervated hit for dartboard impugned withered, sun exampled brilliancy near asleep until dioxide then exude minaret clockwork circuit wren lint intelligence replacement; yet consisted at entrancement taunted lurk out to proffer, seal discover colour whether clear by minute yet rebated.

Accentual plate glass remounted bevel ice-cream parlour legal replacement nougat; advent drastic horehound disputed candied sliced peel jest in time. Slope by footprint which cloudbank sentinel threadbare reflex enviable fine fettle, rowlock ready inducement fresh tabby stairway castle door sentence lancet haddock sundew palmer over ever foreground swim back limerick trick attainment. Glue-pot sentiments inspect wrestled even antelope home-base unsteady regrets bend mountebanks shimmer clamour whence or anchorage sure enough pitch uncle; birthmarked cherry allusive bitten dispatched better off forward drenched customary clary. Segment trumpet oligarch intended pitchfork glove timing platform fortunate store on record pocket aspic lilacs croquet focus parchment, lucerne ever Dyer's Greenweed fodder cantering section auctioneering liturgical plate-glass excused limpid long before serial enthused upstairs mollusc balcony plantain near-name curative take yet aback liquescent mascot feline pipe-line bobolink incident respite might and main; prudential hexagonal lentil shellac wax suffice populace grievous plait exempted more haste price register setback freeze arise brine amusement light crimson near dawn even however forehead up linseed untried, told equivalent scorecard awesome match-play overt concerto hedgehog umpire keep warm muse daylight first.

## Day Light

On the silvery tree bark, now the sun
  gleams and flickers to catch the eye;
imaginings likewise glimmer to fly
  backwards and forwards, on their run.

Echoes of thought brim like charity,
  admit how generous the trees can show;
throughout the day they come and go,
  in truth of nature, so evenly.

Squirrels will race and birds a-twitter,
  branches as home, to flit and play;
the tracks all joyful in open way
  swift breezes set the leaves a-glitter.

For sake awake to miss out nothing
  the tunes for mortals, breathing deep
as yet before now downwards to sleep
  the birds nearby, close in their offing.

# HADN'T YET BITTEN

(2023)

## Front Antimony

*'silver-white encrusted'*

(A)

Incentive perversity
draw set avail,
performance riotous
avouch twelfth ouch
furtherance catches
at next for butter when

quickening famous bite
acrid batter wealth own
ancestral eaten orchestral
graben wisdom ice-cream aim
inductive hoisted pantaloon
parenthood, asserted must

winter facile ever and discover
seem wade sea-side loyal
whale. Bring ashore as
musical out of kilter,
scar let multiplied ibid
lined pursued on track;

now enviable merchant
copious litmus back-lit
had just sit aside as yet
pinwheel lakeside grievous ink
fastened columnar swarf arid
torrid. Perversity conducive

lantern-side summons organ
fine oxygenate affright knit
inflected moisten or curdle whey,
quantum bantam quail exactly
coif queued conduced no malady off.
Is for whom at share mutton fat
regimental, gripe water over.

(B)

Clownesque brusque message trifling sausage,
clatter-proof rocket savoury comedy shrivelled older
digressive swerving pilchard unfamiliar; peerage
elemental crystalline obvious switch fashionable trap
instigated, re-heated dutiful remedial bashful locum
talcum seldom dent. Ribald punishment gripping
spurious agnate polychrome dastardly replicant
woebegone attuned. Spandrels limitless scoundrels;
glitch rapturous ineluctable formidable hitch.
Primal obsequious danger pastrycook lambency ohm
scratch pertinent portcullis overhead parchment;
inviolate downhill dissidence wolfish egregious violet
alembicated mortician, dreadfully minimalist elevated
intemperate grief; elder. Pith droplock battlement bit
cassock western urn, undone condone bundle eld
dividend. Gossamer lucifer entirement fiduciary oval
portal negligent, casque eldritch tambourine clove
invidious duets                    forsooth lynx olivine fused.
Galena wolfram                    influx attainder wintery up
flaking evenly to                    match point guaranteed wick,
acre liquor indoor endurance appliance consequence vial.
Molar mortar panda raccoon ichneumon plethoric
annoyance vertebrae digital convoluted tasselated at
knitted pearl fair-isle hambone trifling edge
upstairs mustn't outpace limitless hollyhock;
inglenook labial cloven insufferable gazing
indigenous questioning magistral. Fascinated
accentual punctual lumbar incision overturn
watchword, blotted ditchling purple emperor by
rissole casserole condolence turbulence ounce
mince-meat sidewalk taciturn banishment in
manicure shuffle deference, alliance gestural
honourable synthetic avenging plunder organic oil.

(C)

At the next wellhead patchwork puffin clerk ire
seedlings fortified turnip tunicate swallowtail laden over at
turnover, malarky gatherum frustum put to rights
magpie thieving lack-lustre district posture levelled
underground; prolific aspen if rustle cattle misty
prologue anodyne brusque tepid. Marital opening toil
ambulance ignorance mission socket cambium divots
mustn't cribbage earnest finest concession magyar tor
ictus cactus octopus gurney pan-handle uncle bails
forgiveness upshot window-sill macerate dispensary elk
monarch mandarin elective wanting vestibule courage
diminishment insistently prudence motionless, flotilla
barrage concession dismissal columbine dumb
skate broil ingrate cradle bangle formal mussel gore.
Inversion omission yard-arm elevated, throat tablet
ascendance grapple anchorage curtain suited weighted
pile on canvas bowsprit candid forward jetty
engraved eyebrow. Nothing lessen never condign awl
goose switch-blade lovage spearmint, catamaran
burned-out to ember hearth residue ashen sampler
dirempt aegrotat ingredient blended notes brisket
lamb chop licensed; all aboard plenty skylark session
petition gravestone insurance resurgence once
wildcat caustic bleached seldom beach laced over.
Krill bladder-wrack formulae either shared adept
determine, Holocene radiance submission even;
target butts surplus coughing shudder heights.
Gimlet bristles uphill custom anticipating by
reckoning plurality uncertainty hypericum
custody within reasonable consciousness hilarity on
scrutiny; obloquy pungent dangerous filbert conic
pleached rusticate laminated aggregate anthemis
pastiche chard daggers champfer allegation typhoon
galliard sneezewort tropical anaconda dapper pressure.

(D)

However even green comet linoleum dint
perfused, set up in forest binary cinders
staunch coil aggregate tarmac supreme
cruiser wallop limpet inducement dole
echo sounder, afterwards gurgle oracle
inkstone. Brackish filtrate gale affine
serpentine morose occupied gander off
gruesome unhidden frustrated curdle by
expectancy voice partitions, grandeur bite
fish hawk neurone brisk localise often
saturated implicit acetate gusset rented
roost blame roast moisten suffuse at
relevant entirety awaken formaldehyde;
sufficiently cricket impeachment be
courage grateful bowling gathered by
rival caution distich rationing insect
hairsbreadth passiontide; willing on
double hammer-beam hayloft untold
wealth of ages grasp, splinter venture
utterly licet brought. At point sock
indulgence leopard telling pontoon ionic
scorch inches petty battery hatchment, if
coloured hallowed regiment drumhead oats
liken pipistrel awaited; incidental averted
dropwort selenium hostel pastille humour
wainscot provost harvest. Pristine antique
varnish vanish tarnished allusive haddock tap
intrench fortitude clandestine cardiac whole echo,
whale wide-open shark pendent cage ribbon bun.
Depth charge merge forage incessant, puissant
carrot alignment well ahead argument.

(E)

Fend mendacious polyglot impetus
off tempest least swept star-born rhyme
perishable insertion celeriac urgency pink at
blanket evidently bunsen crocodile panopticon
blister scathing accidentally sweltering badges,
moreover impudent crusted worsted slated
buttercup ecstatic pricket monastic burdensome;
shallots coinage furtive reductive comatose icy
preaching avenged porringer hormonal fatuous lost
cousin crossbill nephew feudal escutcheon; inkhorn bark
obediently tremulous cactus juice agave
mutation cancelled distilled guzzled memorise
forewarning; impious bravura correlative dative
fugitive inveighing collusive inductance vesicle ice
temporality, ineffable crucible dipstick off
manganese clematis orifice. Princeling agree
prowling succulent mandamus grappling hook,
tottering ambience whenever monger better
anger, thunderous displayed concealed nailed up.
Tilted over subsequent lamentable durable boon
bane brown shatterproof unpunished mystic
cursory takeaway, middling camphorated indurated
olfactory mucilage crucifer murderous boric wince;
petiole crural fisticuffs collards bossy
pansy labile fungal interminable, cruciform awm
datum affirm tumbler pigeon exhausted macerate
nebulous fit. Asplenium peltate rotational cambium,
owl search offertory brokerage astilbe; ace.
Due pagoda thimble timbre amber lava evil
wove all may safely graze helter-skelter, ale fatuous
off swept inevitable cue enacted splatter-proof crimp
where there are gaps relapse coppice near
moorland sentinel banal banana fruitage wages
the saps sticky closet inevitable; corrigible ally
spoken enacted blather wrest medicine ester awful
essentially purple boast synoptic shelf crumpet
reject cyme expense.

(F)

Kestrel cost-free blandish lyre
or tether loose vociferous wat
submerge biscuit sabre-tooth
gashed elbow welcome fusil-oil
gated. Previous curious nearly
docile phantom, mischievous oak
fagott delirious custard on plumage
constriction. Tinnitus flit alone at
parallel outreached perch, crooked
admission delphic mallow soothe or
easement. Tantric ribbon foreign
birch sovereign, dignified dust lessons
example cordon provoking lignite met
under-cover rhubarb opening, when
freight loitering door unopen eating
probable candour meat stitch.
Plover level rail haul dented on
pertinent attachment wing dragged
plentiful orifice unending discovered.

(G)

Flare chew positron gormandise replicant out
coriander, badinage siskin goldfinch dorm
rampage impetuous boastful climbing
over rambler supper winder ferment indent
expression nutmeg pinion cinnamon dent
clairvoyant, provoking lollipop ascension or
livery histamine drudgery hinterland. Butter
churning guitar sauce alive turf livid tin
conscious heraldry deck-chair fateful habit,
earliest industrious monkey however flavour own
birth-mark footprint welcome Friday nearby.
Strict carpet diluted prefect olivine mean
grapple conjugate, meander accordion ale
visitant ocular pressing porcupine deleterious
stupefied interval dragée occlusion; aggrieved in
spindle haggle elated spindrift ectopic barrow oxen
retrospect colossal fiberglass elective, principate agile.

## Hadn't Yet Bitten

(A)

Digress element focus witty
    profuse intended livid
relic, oversize water; allow
    batter or tribal oil gale
twenty-twenty limpet ate
omicron plantain lotion
    attempted ribaldry
chick-pea deficit; ox
hit all further whose
    parcel gilt optional
fulsome bolted A-bone
kerchief tannic crop
    for given angles
soup maiden column.
Attack trap fateful ink
brown under banks file
    crush niche offset pit
cement suspicious fudge
candid assemble, loose
    broken vituperated
    offspin wheel tie
drone eager flail ontic
snap pursuit; do what. Off
    then over vane tooth
kit outer stacked; lichen
wellhead hammer lessen
    best sit tight dent
awesome frivolous, pith
minim gradient. Drastic
lucid acrostic plank or
    disorder track, up over
quail metaloid grudging
evince hence incense ode;

(B)

wych elm climb blinking, prunella
cara overturn less azure corbel
salted no grassy bunkum,
plated twenty; chew next fox-trot
downy woundwort citrus sinter
forth rustic insurgence soot it
salt avaunt, extrusion perianth
mural axis wasted. Toxic lucid or
silver frantic too bracelet, polyp is
dust alert forcep quicken one
whitmead; divot mastic emery conic
spinnaker marauding eventually by
figural choral dentine, ostrich fetch
keyboard sonatas revenue till
key touch. Mason grievous credit moat
mantic indifferent plagal butter tidal
dual, candle allergic ectopic
mural sooth-sayer curio if toothy
saving, attended crampon tint
bismuth infamous per frequent gothic
lettuce alone spondee milken own.

(C)

Adroit contrite distraught, replete mail unto
foil grilse, catching the keyboard's own
exemplary good toccata behaviour fume
intricate pancake briefing, marigold
weald heraldry timorous cruciform
autumnal sealing; by next forest
gateway calc schist antic flagon in
token crenellated. Gibbous limewood
formic anthill dotage fascinate iterate
dissentient hysteric, mandrake affront
mooncake agnostic wakeful neap;

(D)

chloroform customised at kelp
gizzard saltpeter, lingual galenic
inversion newt aegrotat wrangle on
upper slipper; pontic sedimented
dashboard curdle chestnut grudge
pitcher night heron. Wizard hits
obligate scented stock ne'er frail
recoil smiler coronet dugout if
lurking spiteful freshets auk,
utterly wick, soonest mended
intergrowth washout pipkin
asperge promised; vaccine bit
engine tulips cockle shells sips;

(E)

all through pinch night owl
gospel furbelow dastard
fulminatory, allegory grips
bridle. Verbascum tampered
groaning churn fawn foaming
fluorspar, aventurine cant.

(F)

Filigree refloated scandalized tossed fortress offer,
scrape scripted illume tambour new-omen barricade
lemur lemon, distraint narrow therapeutic window
fugacious tempera impact rate alight banquet
door jamb lantern brine; dungarees bruised if
note yet slight diacritic smitten ocean-side, apricot
stucco furious scratched and rick, malcontent.

(G)

Liken perfidious Albion awkward
snow-plough junket wanton by
pontoon, often digested blight else
manciple auxins; groaning bounds
inter uses castanet. Dory inch
enamel adjusted mortmain terrine
fat lot caring, already snared opal
instinctual perpetual shone, even
flaming token oxen. Sugar fume.

## Incinerate Wit

Transit ensure persisted, cistern at first,
if not better then often near worst;
discreet in parallel nor interpret folded,
scolded verdant by singular sufficient.
Inept at finally line in blue, march
digressive crossed ensue; astringent
fervent colluded octagon, gambit fed
collotype not too far ahead, retrieve or
varnish up instead otherwise facile
derogate. Front-door panjanderum.

Release topaz funest oblivion granary
permission hoarse circus altar fadge
incidentalism mycelium crimping aim,
minotaur spurious edible autumnal toil
fungible spillage; inkhorn ternary label
nibble convocation, austere dripping fatal
grimoire nutritional gadget motherhood's
pricket exaggerate victim denial eyebrow;
nougat retrieval mangel arabesque sluice
fee simple fertile yolk torrid bug agaric,
taurine administration to diabetic rabbits
enhanced risk-taking at fiscal levels, gills
samphire dreadful azurite mountain blue
streak gusto camphor ancient tortoise.
Impulsive fractal divulged cortisone gun,
spatchcock caraway voidal infirm again
entwined untold catchment barracks.

## Eventual Avenue

Torn over by the window return
formal tender availment soon
        know unfinal to given
twine oval crystal but evenly
as bloom tourmaline, in faction
thought by garden share. Seen
graven at the lattice massive, why
        reminder hold back catch up
flurry musing, cautionary option
frugal open, provision as in view
truth first oven redeem by climb
        to ascension warden soon
here sunflower incline calamine
fill to tap, district region organic
give over; surrendered wisdom own
minim climbing rose limbic. In
        clastic often ferric when
screen ported forward in mercy,
symbol anvil granulate await
but leastways formal whistle, or
button in motion above spruced to
        mercury canted revision.

## Smite Cream

*'Least first crested fount quail'*
*'tides slate own win worst'*

Wands holm estuary casuistic confits,
indebted blanket sand-dune perspex lid;
enticed gastric pacified price brisk off
orifice tusked liquorice, mollusc turpentine

sintered evolve derive holistic concealment;
battering extant jubilant invidious clamorous
nectarine quarreling bunkum lawful tad
scrip toad toasted, arrested incunable anger

cougar persevere molybdenum often softening;
carrageen are to earth o'ergiven, fine
tune welcome silicon in mid heart pointed out
vacillating proof ankles crumbled. Drain

temple column unto bridle feast, iced to
waist overt clash moisten thumb avoided;
trail braid ghost prune force, brunt toy
regal dream dalliance birth-rate decoy

clove tacit gravel anvil spoon hovel by
mushroom leg-room motif sauce droop odious
frond parachute latent owl creek incident
shoe-horn lamb chop fleeting mansion,

blood poison canteen conspicuous topiary
oasis necropolis; latterly usury cleft
salpiglossis explosive mastiff relish dunce
trench cinch tight scollop, obit rubies on

blazon caravan mushroom, tabards
lustrous crisis avenue limit; pantomime
ramekin indigo indigo, circus hoops,
conversion duplication serpentine mace.

## Fasicule Whale Up

Obliquity sacrosanct coercive instinctual
slated, dour latency downpour tortuous ox
litigated misfit agate; bee orchid tussock wit
trouser further gingko furrow solander leeks.
            Druse caustic rennet barrack
            limpid ought instigate; turtle
            zip corrugate drooping alight
            etching burin cinder proliferated.
If heart-felt yellow flag corner-stone
frown climbing roseate suited annex
vexatious isthmus; cautious tortoise
hitherto kangaroo recrudescence if
            nuisance welfare stairs
            abjure epact fissile. Agile
            retinal pigmented suffused,
            blanket surfeit coronet fit
trample beyond impounded; gruesome
unlawful tantamount twirling earwig
citrine topaz buzzard, biscuit frantic
thread majestic condor xenolith sulky
            eglantine watchword crystalline
            switchblade torrid ambient at
            gatehouse; implored earlier
            screw bleach open latch, posh
crush lesser ominous reckless buckets
faucets upended carbonic elated stride
babies condign, phone pine-cone clone.
Done deal moustache trace elements
            liminal cigaroot guesswork baited
            sailing guile trumpet voluntary
            spinney hurried copse fetch
            hutch lurch guinea-pigs tag
loyal myrtle tooth blank scarlet piano
scorbutic candidate mortal easel tip
balaclava critic sofa ejected whistle
balcony irritant falcon beaten overt lank.

## Brimful

Custard customary fusion
insertion frolic, bistort esteem
not-proven crimson alluded pink
uvula spontaneous contrasted
drifted auspicious loaned
tramping so-so seashore auk;
twitch gendarme gizzard pit.
Commission unction butterscotch
tremulous fictive prefatory,
organza armour-piercing nested
black stork sliced pork plain sailing.

## Dervish Post Finish

Persistent attunement boiled, at finch
cloistered eventual mussel caravan
anchorite nodule; why furnished
in punish mace-work yet tiding
　　　　mortice listless sacrifice
　　　　enough flagrant clough wise
　　　　diopside consistent slang;
　　　　furtive insistency feudal hurt.
Foal nearby tank fuel acrostic batch own
rowan cobra myrtle cattle conventicle
bobsleigh whistle, abjure to beaver
candour mastic dill elastic shoots
　　　　trample goggle octagon lime
　　　　consternate; indignant pit
　　　　pathogenic albino colloidal
　　　　emerald already bolted.
Discovered feverishly roofline ban
like present cracker theurgic crumb
burnt scorbutic, atlantic grease
wisdom sluice fleeced carrots dicing few
　　　　bled, pergola panda imperial
　　　　allegri hillside; afraid fishing
　　　　surface carriage lovage daze
　　　　intarsia calendula porcines
　　　　amazement incessant flip at
　　　　cordyceps, bashed neeps ape;
　　　　chaotic bitumen swelteringly
　　　　cascade toroidal intertidal rejection.

## Either Than Winking

Could this in ready platform accentuate, would be deft
forward in crown suited, prune to wall base constant
water silence best licence pochard awarded. If
pressed to run by antonym limbic tisane, curtain
shielded allowing crest at fount proof cream lucent slit.

Feather-light arisen proof to search, hurried at brunt
a thousand tacit incidentals; twice ember state annoy
tropical bravery acute steel angle, fetch grave anvil
in parallel garden torque. Set pair wash over brush
mission clove soothe pantile finger press the button.

Tell one now two both, chief entice purpose courtly
yet alert too main up close endorsed: 'Anything that
can be explained can itself be an explanation'–lean down
low in linden lea. For ligature saline brook increase
purchase enchain deltoid liquescent reagent, pungent.

Slight chance retained at dormant lozenge pippits
price slate crumble, matter apple or fertile link
often husbandry organic poached lucid juice little mist
over new stream forcible patency, igneous process at
iron-magnesium silicates. To be heard by steam.

Heat fusion at parkin division lustre nacre moist
ester under sugar, without relicts replaced amber
obsidian extrusive shiny volcanic melt. Foolscap redoubt
persever wardrobe mistress hypertension mallards ice
lynx acidulous dentition riddle dander terrine fibrin.

Morainic latency hostile mandible crucible nip
turps loctite blustering duster forgiveness cress
courageous ostrich elbow guesswork; herbarium rigor
anchorage garden path reluctance withering profligate
probative far ahead wailing wall first on trial chicken.

Mission dissolute cassiterite pintade croute etch
lip salve while tunnel, whimbrel carousel shrew
throat demoted; diablastic 'Rosetta stone' dykes or sills
(welded ash, basaltic fumaroles across mantle rocks) chert
retrograde diorites eyebright gratulating moebious strip.

## Well Within Sight

Look adept, transept integrated roam
sessile tussle mackerel skylight, thy wrongs should ringed
shudder to tremble flat out crick gutter; splinter ohm
corm dormition autumnal, regnal frogging signalise
    eviscerate obdurate gash wounded;
    tourmaline stubby robbery noises
    off cleft thereafter, raster oyster
    nigella; torrid ahead catchment
numinous sumptuous ashen portion, intone
bonemeal doronicum feigned breath bated.
Sterterous glucoside adherent sidle boastful
wasteful, otherwise eyebrows contiguously
    archaic arachnoid unweighted, of
    graben turban condiment radiant
    constricted drastic loose-fit match
    natured sulphurous obverse must
downhill probable limited carat opportune
henbane evenly unfelt limbic verdant melt
insistent drain muzzle oracular embellish
swerve entanglement blink, quantum livery
    silver-plate eucalypt adoptive oat
    cullet entrain for roam resume
    lateral, tinsel colourful swelling
    barrel decorated serpentine rutile magnet
cocksure libation dissentient. Abject intact on
fibrillate cannonade concrete, agreed thyroid ate
crural elicit obtuse albatross; fungible caustic
elastic furbelow overhead brotherhood temperate.
    Clergy foraging tantalum contested waste,
    inhalant abrasive set within optimal raven
    greedy temper sulphurous fume cupboard;
    upward masthead anchorage across bestrewn.

## Courteous Chert

*'revel reveal waist'*

Unquestionable vestibule acrid dissection, fictive
remonstrance in parallel conjugation tilt omen
luminous courteous, customary syllabary conic or
panic; gaze forward candle inveigle cruet illuminated

Who would denial align in fortunate creosote, anchor
livid margarine snoring snow-line, granary territory
with his coup-stick feather reach adacement, audacious
incurious gesticulate phantom omission cantilever lesson

Wonted whether vanity weather-vane coincide spanned
ice-cream hazel tremblancy, litancy obdurate severally
adversion nuisance variance listed optional poppycock bite
mosquito; gauze knapped flit edgeways substituted

Invariant hybrid birdlike conscience alledgement, quoit
smitten invention allegory overcoat phosphate bricked up
swelled. Foiled previous accession trump evidence lucid
passenger concession, occlusion pungency waveform earliest

Closure level contested birthrate reagent tropically
upstairs dialect parsnip cribbage; sagebrush mostly
gravamen epitactic rickets languid on or whenever
consorted matchstick inevitable, parsonical latterday.

Interim listen bison
fictional entail, tacit
rebec dwindle crucially
adipose indisposed too

Climate tussock wit
inveterate violet orifice,
snow broom sweeping
previous diluted meadow

Canteen politic flame:
tribal inkling overture.

## Shelf Turning Filed

Contested filt allegement foursome etch
licence searching milt crescent, expected oak
cheroot canal coral; prevail either gathered
alignment shepherd swerve antique sleeve mace.

Graphic quicken firkin soaking winsome tent,
cough cougar treacle anent beet sugared westernly
sedge mastic lite majestic; wooden wouldn't await
crocus porpoise sea lion corymb tantamount

Uphill avail entailment scraping diluent eminence
batchwork lattice offended scrupulous impious carpel
grateful actually stealthy porphyry residue panic-led
subsequent merchant, reckon listen indited critically

Fertile customarily oxbow meander silver incident
chromatic bruising affected biscuit crumble angle
latterday sponsor percipient; ocular antagonist nest
effected cordial mercurial overhead quartile camps

Resumed pagoda odour pristine phantom ales
forbearance awesome cradle foghorn condition
candles canaries orchard pilchard enteric freight
anciently misfit austere illegal rambling on

Masthead deltoid bashed waisted waspish mill
raven pinion, until racket lenten scatter other
whether mildew eventual unctuous parsimony
silken welcome aspen often rampant prodigious

School wale foible entailed damage moisten grim
algorithm tension awkward burnished allele on
regulate captivated triangulate integrated
forceps claviceps eyebrows sailed allegro contour

Poignant raiment fermented turbulent icing
traced voiced urgent gracious wrist collops
bended knee eagle needle candelabrum pint
laburnum fortress purchase mango probable too.

## Valediction Earwigs

Casual ruffle seedling limbeck, trunnion tern
goldfish delicious punctilious fringe oar heard for
cochlea kestrel abseil nonet punnet integer grilse
masonry chalcedony perspicacious rifled waisted;

Orogeny pungently instantly maximise galvanic
cryptic interior furrier caution bustle told,
gradient elbow granite boiling kern deigned
pollock chaffinch ultimate; scramble over

Brimful candle sunstone ruthenium disruptive
bristle-cone while calcify entrails alighted cramped
sirocco broccoli kieselguhr latchet coronet fetching
spoonfuls seagulls leopards Welsh flamboyant

District derelict distracted, edgeways cadge wince
erupting sensational; unlawful hillside retained
grimace palatial ornament. Scarce purse mace
creasing sleeve avionics lintel, skimp iamb consistent

Hive occupied column comb ravenous octopus crater
mortality plentifully overboard third midmost loose
no worse is none condign, lanyard mercuric sparrowhawk
elation primula jacket grating gusset; insect alert

Night-rest quaint anointed empowered talon
gryphon, indignant relative buckram acrostic easel
windmill supernal mural quicklime. Rejoicing in
cruiser parakeet entreaty oyster, agrimony spikenard

Mustard compelled unfolded singed paraffin, gruesome
chosen uncalled autumnal signatory surmised odes.
Parallel sentience adamantine florin caustic wallet
valediction earwigs, ascension trampoline Vaseline tin;

Orthoclase amazement kerosene handkerchief thief
parchment hatchment, aptitude skirting manifolds
dreamboat donation humerus silicate foliate eat;
enough to thicken orphan glisten venerate intricate.

Incense spaniel drainage pillowcase oxen
cutlery; scabious willingly agley trim willow-wood
impious switch, lantern eristic forfeiture swallowed
esteem gulp victim volcano cribbage unflinching

Eyebrow canal rivalry; nacreous pristine harbour
sorbus arid lutescens orphic diminishing overtime wan
fallow; guessing traffic agreement splintering comical
notorious fanciful indemnity, heraldic dogged flight.

Suspect instructive crescent eventually foregone,
conductance petition western libation ostensible
dragée ungrateful futile armchair wearisome toil
ingrained parfait arresting buttery fermented crane

Gantry fossick assemble timbre intensive gadabout,
spontaneous yoghurt shelf-life delicate sweetener
ovation; progressive pungent skittles durable evident
ointment cretonne almond cruiser riddance esteem

Variance. Succession myrtle antidote granted planted
platform omelette fill-dyke lustrous sapient ancient
moreover, jacket postage offertory principal foal
mayoralty; sythe grazing horoscope scops owl dial

Milfoil aftermath no worse hoarse turquoise placid.
Cleavage smelting furnace bismuth scapular arrested,
foxes in boxes token ribbon sanction cut to slice voice
trice; jangle marmalade defrayed concentric at

Wit's end, sentinel mussel capital gasping rigged
tissue musical. Roofline sleek fasten gorgeous
trickle, submission perforation activated anyway;
zip fashion quandary politeness attainder pin

Swarf scalene inveigh parallel yellowing folic, open up
cucumber virtual catacomb as surance teasel oil;
furlough dainty fronted mandarin bucket cosset,
assenting fusing door-stop covert throat dint.

## Knitting Pearl Cross

Remission incision plumage, rummage lido
crowbar dolomite marbles pinch; entrance
re-entrant nothing notary appointed, lupin
        perfume intended symmetry afraid to
        engrave circular partitur echoic vocalic
        tantamount infantile punishment; aid
lucid staybright fieldfare flocked planetary fit
cap around abounding tuneful often, at once finch
mention sanction trilobite unction. Latent want
        forewarned offset brace and bittern one
        tryst pungency, obligato mascot chemist
        goblet infringement druse amethyst
calcite fluorite grossular weighted frustum, porch
lantern smitten unlucky hurtful nacreous tuff;
sabre-tooth twelfth fission pondered October wed
        gruesome autumn distraction, provoke
        lurking woodland passional bisected
        biscuit creamed oriental meddlesome awe
relented charted perfervid litmus aphrodite fright
critical quantum canary, missionary swoon paint
germinate; sisterhood custard cream baited on
        surfactant libation irriguous pertinently
        breezy catgut, memorise privateer invested
        steam fulsome primrose orris rooted jolted
fade-out timid catapault aspect; fluff hearse tap
endorse, curse angry sophistry sugar duplex heronry
winding knitting pearl cross markets, vortex porcelain
        same figment homage porridge. Grimace else
        suspected waist, tinder catchment sailors on
        recall by boiler suit, warbler chronic splits.
Impressed fluting siskin cardoon bravery, attain
loyal care for true both look-out pride of mason coil
relational each day in turn trim egg-shell profile ode
        stack later; praise been honeycomb spoons full
        availed moralise, fitch open bacon toucan and
        brigand ampersand; eloquency fanciful copula.

## Tourmaline

*'Sometimes found in marbles'*

Fluid layers of answering tone clusters, taking up
echoes with moments of near-silence opening the tex-
tures of delicate sweeping across the octaves, giving out
welcome breath-room 'Had counted coup' digital yule;

Mitchell, T.M. *et al*, 'Predicting human brain activity associ-
ated with the meanings of nouns,' *Science*, 320, 1191-1195
(2008); lobelia slice gap cantaloupe brightness from the air
alliance insurgence, vale truncate privilege withered

for sedge or manic grinding. Presume fleam gambol
cousinage persistent yellow capsicum inference even
redressed hawfinch enlisted bandage whence glittering
dictate pontoon urn; hubbub contribute libation win

integrational, spendthrift emplacement forehead elder
darker filtrate seldom attested, cavorted daylight
anatexis Weetabix ready-made florid percussive or
furtive inferred paschal abandonment. Optimal hawk

trellis ambient maze at ear slice echo in patient crim-
son warning, cautionary sundew water plantain
grateful sail abbot shallot jadeite emprint; cost-free
elder missive crease estate pandect, crumpet donative

incidental ahead pleached in candour suitable fountain
osprey coinage leap. Gravid hydroxyl ruminated pinnate
entreaty, first whether aspic, tantamount orphic patch
for yawn ferule indent abraded; gusting mind adept.

His eyes green with anger, what of this darkness slabbed
with ice, seasonal grape-vine pitchfork moccasins marooned
by mullet tourmaline uppermost no worst mutton chop edge
canvas varnish tantric, eccentric avocets pleading, forgiven.

## TIMEPIECE IN TOTAL

## (2024)

There is no knowledge without a knower,
there is no knowledge without a known
– C.F. von Weizsäcker

## Inuit at First

Cryptic next all gleaming, season
welcome incidental further tropic
explained by parallel near reason
look to talcum sprinkle optic, been

harbour single tangle fetch within
brook at weir to server parakeet;
oval labour said to beach incision,
whether as ever inside the basket

attended dust, rusted or darting
in for part hedge reprieved known
capsize; watch voracious vale
audacious patchwork; for pledge

ravine caravan analyse tether
partial, cooing book bound limb
shone uppermost blazon, revel
profusion canton edgeways mild

altered arching; rental unwise
if not trusted wrinkle, forbear
open laburnum nonplussed off
ratchet, fusion flown section.

## Rhizome Climbing

Non-stop lichen legal moss
agate, furious plaint cribs
corundum adequate liquid
gristle deft yardstick oat

intermittent turbulent flow etc;
deviant downward trigger scheme
scalar neutrino dust detritus
crucial figwort awkwardly, in-

tended canvas bract converts;
jointure debenture spliced up
nightjar pinion actual; dill
crystalline rutile concision less

kestrel whistle. Swallow eel
newt crest sloping on the wing
wrist beat early waking melted
sodden, sundew brewhouse cone

liquorice friction; ionised null
angular momentum versus to
radial velocity. Climate host
clematis next clasp intoned

global magneto trollius tap-
root weight, rhizome climbing
rib-cage lunge orange lilies
pollen pylon seldom axiomatic.

## Espalier Mace

Scorbutic bloating freight down forbidden slick
dawnlight advocated smitten, puce athirst
plaice forced mussed insistent unsuited
trollius charcoal eschewed civet majestic turgid
awkward billiard foolhardy. Fly-tip acetic turtle

scuttle formidable dragon stewed now don't, recede
by towage for silage fermentation leisure package
onomastic chortle; enthusement espalier mace
chubb sooner dace antelope suppliant prism
canyon mercuric boletus grampus inference.

Whistled wrap poultice ostensible, come into focus west
clatter alive scimitar they have ready snatch defile.
Satch by marsh sundew hungry ilk metrical coronary
elk silken ribbon curtain; brushing pilchards west
inscript column-proof tisane fragile won-ton attempt

warren, dozen perfusion tractable formidable etch
which unpunished relinquish infer ambulant current
title thistle stop to weight gantry very nearly all
canary circulation listen titanium fortune egg
plover ascription bison intonation by cautionary.

## At a Distance

Alleviate violet customising allergic
deployment, nutritious loosen clustered
distribution Trägheit; paved the way at
condensed insipience, purvey birch silver
candour and turbulence, biscuit secant
androgen liquid drop. Molarity affirm

canal tepee tepid saturated calming doom
column sapient, cigar-like form by solar
wind on dust charging crepitation; now
over then both absorbent conifer planetary in
granite cemented tendency, aviary within
cyclotron colander fewer sherbet limpets

entrusted quickly marquetry subsequent
banjo dust sublayer at high spatial resolve.
Or habit comet entailed beyond necessity
mandorla, mandolin winsome spinor elm
united; random elbow wheat ear roughly,
cascade whatever assail product rule allayed.

## Efferent System

Open lizard occupy evenly agreeable,
allegement cortisone lupin incident
grazing parsed; average crazed fave
finishing latchment creosote grain
            hopper hopeful gripped on
            trample wrinkled tawny
            gizzard rebound. Pitching
            float redeem mansion, train
Handsome iceberg granulate photon, at
nutrient scruple appearance forfeit invent
patent pristine; beeswax liturgy pounce
frivolous atropine convolvulus obverse
            Incentive curtain swooped
            tribal waxwing myrtle in
            efferent system cistern
            agar fulmar implicated.
Footpath photograph attenuate ford
wounded sentinel jacket crucial
angular ricks minimise reprised
fortify contrivance; lugubrious
            selvage notify haze
            moss steep sleeping by
            patient obediently
            stook imminent cranks.

## Azure Licence

For painted altitude column, marsupial lately
codex weaned avocet gratify aspen gazump; candle
interval livid constriction, forsooth barrier oat
escaped pancake swindle attachment, brandish
    eyebrow lavish crustacean purchase
    overture outflow; antennae trapeze
    lazy bones prudence, mortal live cent
    azure licence pantomime escapade ire.
Bonfire loyalty varicose submerged, incidentally
hospitable dormouse humectant critical turret in
sunrise late cucumber adept phlox merciful watch
crush habit onside; electoral conjural elegance wrist
    trench once awaited serpent orient;
    lingering casuist numinal acrostic pi
    mastery corybantic whoever or salvo.
    Scapular soapstone stubborn violent
apprehensive shallot grilse contrition tribute
supine, glean previous docile plumage; easier for
nutritious captive pinwheel internal forceps hit
barricade leastways cogency bulldog mantle oval
    crucial vial. Muniment merriment
    patchwork clustering enteric presume
    terebinth noisome furbelow necessary
    burial dentition deletion wakening
indignant beforehand; vibrancy skillet mollusc
litigant orphic frustum, catapault without fault
probation issuance hairstreak avid rockery tic.
Minatory shoelace pinnace curious, delicious us
    full creatures thematic hamper what
    plight ambient privet; granular or
    sledge recession unfortunate virus
    morbid indifferent sulky phaeton
valiant ecstatic paramount balloon claim
shellac ticket rhino plague ostrich fugal eagle
lightsome mushroom blanket trinket coronet
pursuant truancy, in-tow escrow conducted abet:
            xx dicot xx

## Phalanx Winking

Palinode reluctant friction option, suitable tortoiseshell
bundle disgruntled and flicker affronted; elated mite
out of sight luminous glowworms shoehorn adornment,
　　　cautious reversal advisement improved watt
　　　sacrament; paraffin indigenous crawfish
　　　licence hillside denial moralise breezy imitation
inverted hazel diviner coinage insistently furtive onyx
phalanx winking casually aloft, trouser lesser
mitred oaken mainbrace soldiers darkening; lengthening
　　　microcline canter digested plumage entice
　　　saraband frighten warden mention harkened
　　　circuitry dusted trampled nursing aroused.
Morning spread plimsole virtual manganese tuff,
borax powder giraffe hawkbit latent innocent wit
graben downside; ambient fission corydalis easier
　　　touch jewel arrival label formaldehyde. Elk
　　　tabernacle invested jointure plaintiff of
　　　wait to start blatant beast, remedial oiled
curlew moorland courage digit; both settlement links
ahead tended thrush mistle clamber, echo replenish
noonday double scimitar selfheal intrinsic corded.
　　　Alert fraught donated ahead of passport fluorite
　　　candidate frequent alongside arsenical syntexis ebb
　　　dioptase smooth lupin cinnabar wherefore prion
curiosity ambivalent praline whistle calendrical out
mallow curfew gibberish muslin percentage relevance
brimful sulfur cataplasm, acrobatic intrinsic conspicuously.

## Anchorage Snow

Cold burn winning ever before; over burnish scale dorm
fluid orchid tantamount fricative balsamic cradle dialogic
        income paving ochre loose shed match comb or
        soon exacted. Phantom ready allocating liquescent
        gruesome urgent waspish, overt and tighter ever
        silver gaunt leaning; session underneath tilth
milder incident elusive cranny, breach. Eager drastic at
thread tolerated merchant availed pushing expect, grit
        ornamental front coverlet owlet private intact
        arrival fanlight; family internal crampon bin
        seeking aslant willowy skilful, joyous ample
        diremptive adjunct customary twite. Rigel
crustal effort coastal gimlet objective, loosen flounce
parallel condiment hunter watching rope; either under
cleat anchor seldom afterwards earwigs ambient ashes
surface corrade downward afloat meringue brilliant.
        Patchwork guessing alongside prevailed evening
        footpad stolen wealthy wrist permission to
        multiple cistern tankard occupant brewers
        jewel dowel pinnace; galliard gullible ochre
gleaming open wave liquid at play. Aversion coins at
eagle valuation, cloud level formidable, printed hand
styptic gather wrist timepiece treacle; set fast best
interest diminish elusive, share if fair incidence.
        Anchorage snow further, twice along sang
        tune burnish near finish; invidious brisk
        sledge touching advice next ice-pane crane
        tilt throat cough fearsome cougar stealth.
Welcome inviting enteric chronic prune, envious
calling whirled overhead starlings in flock wit
catchment sediment filament; arrive torrid chill
agile sailing cheek breath-turn, canterings:
        long to spent aviary told integument here
        exact light, echo evident price second tag.

## Rigel Left Foot

Anaconda praline varnished diligent creeping glue
mannerly provoking, latter resilience principate tight
limitless warmth century entitled bream. Conscripted
scimitar flintstock graben hollyhock inch haddock,
            preen resume customary allergen flinch
            tench; nailbed revoked in[s]tar formidable on
drastic mayonnaise pellucid aside pondweed, triplets
incessant bravery woodland microwave swallowing alp
gulp dressage tambourine bamboo stock. Providence
certainty obvious grievous ambivalent for, released
            forestry carpentry overland bantam-weight
            this day all quarrels die; aphanistic torrid
take at better pitch garnet florid, whether or
profitable insignia candour scarlet avouch cubic
greenish-black streak. Contested ahead of jade
turning by water colour terebinth bower-birds
            build to shine and glitter, kapok flake
spillway agency far known fern-leaf; hatch to
nested high crest bone grist acorn mornings
soak running seepage castanets butter of
listen out sight. All in parallel larch cones
            fell to ground, finch clouds address
            autumn forage entry creeper; air
            coiled evenly better oven micro pangolin.
            Dispersal advantageous piteous loam tap
maximum forgiven, heating certify adamantine
friction stirrup marzipan; cribbage courageous
manicure crowbar cuckoo awkward subsequent
famous purposeful attractant iodine. Yokel or
            manifestly inserted bristle edgewise, go
            ahead prismatic soluble mango giraffe oat
tenacity gabbro focus paramount. Cardinal less
moat squirrel cannot peeled abject carrot duke,
interrupt scorn ratchet catchment revoke plight
gasket hideout museum lino birch; assenting burn
            luminous obsequious leather claimant bread
tribunal coeval focal mastery singed in
long ago. Hive entire suited indigent indignant
slice scrupulous get rolled admired crape.

## Teflon Cucumber

Or as yet now encased in titanium electrodes foremost spine
churn collar brain monitor surface by 'digital bridge' implant
suspended epidural spatial switch-gear footpath; flush
terrace limehouse curlew corkscrew paramount assorted fort
five in a set sequence maintenance trace. Echo replacement
arch torch grist tilted; ambit auspice serpentise mauve
to make a fresh step in motor cortex increased hip flexor
contracted eyebrow contested, deciphering in advance his thoughts
by neurone condonement forgiveness. Frankincense inverted over by
transept bright allowance, glitter parlour tremblor current
know better walk the link ingress proficient ink
wark just to think park contrite cortisone urn
humane sneeze wavelets, roaming binding starling
borrowing sentence crampon ice-cream mist
bison Plenty Coups licence graven stepwise hover discover
severance outflushed mollusc damask furtive askance on
teflon cucumber rambling, antelope pursuit encircled anklet
aftermath thunderstorm climbing wall rose fragrant even so
accidental sortal flicker with live alternation cascading
surviving promulgating intrinsic to think raising a
legible knee-joint complainant in alternate climate
gallivanting in custom for cushion can ye sew, no great
fantasy millrace sleep borage raise frontage investments
up to the roof scatter proof stretch penguin lineament fondant
troop orpiment onyx beech impeachment corrected, wigeons
fright. By flex thumbs yet grips, not what is coincidental
pungent or cuticle, no know guess which patch-
work awkward laptop instructs ahead of clenching
milkwort chalk blue downland incline gasoline light
pantomime early purple listserv effervescent dehiscent.
Once flounce syphon spinal cord activated complicit conducive
to thought-read movement idiolect for script, transumed on
ledger-lines upper trills rapid limpid complexion reflection;
convict scented intrepid doublet pandect indiscreet anhedral.
Known in fashion scarlet musing, thought patched fit
candour fervour close demeanour, corrugated incessant
pentiment attentive damsel winning alongside; hive
best intact wax cricket orchid stitchwort, bitten in
traction sanction plasma foregone spinet worked by trill
incision amazon, contrition fanciful. Eagerly serpent

assembled trappage anticipate cruet integument, reach out
great forested shadow syllable manicure honey sweet race
homage selvedge mandarin refinement; witting found
to hand pledged enter declared, gasting wind risen adept.

## Echo Anchovy Trickery

Glaucous elegance
panurge winsome,
advancement peat
furious avenue
silkworm acute
intended; libation ohm
handkerchief panoply
etched copper;
descent, acrostic
mace lacewing
brewing hand
effusive chromate
at door rivalry
spooned elected.
Forceps groom aviary
martyr silken often
scarf, turf parrot elided
at banner market
considerate parenthood
pi measurement latch
christen assumed too.

## Pursuit Samovar Intrinsic

*'purposeful purple'*

Would be pinnate awkward, footpad
reaching then riotous cautiously replete;
cistern postern alluvial rite. Team
        sharpen lakeside suitable
        austere at purpose indented
        paperchase, luminous latch.
Parchment agrostis involucre anent
resilient limpet, accelerating birches
even grove drupe locksmith jadeite;
        Fascia leverage sill organ
        crimson restricted certain
        scratched edelweiss pagan.
Cardoon canton phantom intrinsic
marquis lapis lazuli flotsam prudent
gossamer liquorice, hive at ancient asp
        readiment annealed damask
        merciful chromium vainly;
        integer delphic conflicting
Latterly tribal coinage crisp firstly on
match parallel knee jointed. Abraxas
nested filigree sylvan tarragon, own
        minimum shouting pumice
        catafalque indignant given
Panoply customary insignium licence
necklace protective servery mansion, to
shield optimum resumed package in
        bessemer collarbone turban new brittle
        scatter marzipan caravan, remission
        maiden oven intensive fond evenly
Falcon lattice cornice immensely
drawn to window, pluvial dosage
grape toast faster; incident advent
        agaric mastiff makeshift of
        criminal scarlet willingly sets
        stung insect exactly coronet.
Contrite filament immaculate droit
sacrosanct testamentary interflight nape
cursitory toe crop illustrious indignant

ossuary persiflage stupefied
mercenary adversative tight
Dissipative ointment lenient, intarsia at
turbary cropped sedition hornfels coals;
mucilage diablastic framework elegantly
providence crushed porch. Each
transom utterance nearby elected,
actual safeguard sheepwalk inside
Manicure mercurial accident mustard; sated
relinquishment stupefied tantamount mute.
Porringer surfactant rescue chicory atrium
yurt condense certainty, lends
deltoid serpentine never alone;
bristlecone handsome purpose
Tortoise turquoise invective forthwith ace
cowslip elastic shellac, wintering gruesomely
turbulence ingrained spigot adventure advice.
Obedientary mountain slither over
dilated corridor, pallid intrusive
friction simpleton phantom fetch
Brilliancy askance. Convex alkanet caviar
lagoon marquis, sequins pontoons radians
arc length whence entranced, calomel hail
downpour rain of fire allusive too
canary original glacier expected
system resume attainment eats.
Scissors diatribe agreement penitence invent
silence latency, forage biblical nettle antiquated
pandect raillery slubbed; abated. Thoughtful
clause exempt pressure, avid blood
camphor darkness lacewing tasered
owl creak. Spoken grating lesser
Hanker sober preaching nearby impact alight
pretty pulpit circuitry starlit, fancied lamp
crested newt macaroon proton quickening.

# ALEMBIC FOREST

## (2024)

Can it specify itself to a universe of discourse?
— E. Ruhnau

## Whimbrel Tinkle

You will say see along, wavel trowel knelt used
footage unctuous bursted ovoid bustard; nacreous
foist increment presumptuous libellous aphids rictus
pandect encrusted, whispering neighbour parallel
gallery awkwardly impute prating violet critical
diatribe obsequious, hydration illusive concise
averment testament; notorious eventual furtive
aspic collected briquette allocate promoted loose
pineal aventurine avoidance ovoid, leafage canopy
detainment syringa lidded panoptic ration-book ate
borrowing; plantain linctus invasive
cataract whimbrel pertinent homage
lilac olive settlement queue portal mute
watermouth feudal curlew. Lambent
wight floated syntactic morphic caudal
passive gristle or gurgle avoidance, pinnacle turret fitt
cue bromine attuned distrained wounded chalk loot.
Nor yet incision site dilated, jupe impugn suborn
earning ascended banneret grifted inherently faucet
crumhorn pangolin spurious; annoyance sliced up
coronet parchment slanted oval bevel reverented
dupe, be that they seem curtailment sudden muscle
one for all ingrain downpour script pocket racket
runoff escapade prisoners never-yet postern soon
curtilege bridgehead. Mighty roseate stoop crape.
Slight croquet arrogant to
flight path guardian hints
lucern wyvern seeming so
"indeed?" Internment llama
antibiotic drained morphic
torus elevating sacred aggravated susurrating fruit
chloramphenicol blazonry tokenism auk liquorice
gannet syphon unwanted, tell the tale anew tribal
askew riot flint sleep to knap; aught silicate astute endif
mastiff shorn cufflink heritable stent. Your veering
fire and brimstone, naphtha wilt avaunt won't pert
groat ingest and then put out henbane flown; burn
dowse derelict afflicted whyever grievious posset
subsequent junket craven conflagration infuse
worse coptic donkey sentence. Flight re-licensed.

## Skillet Flight

Increment persimmon customary availed, crimson
sanction obtuse moonstone febrile acrimony duel
fantail grievous, occupied tumid astilbe roam
grating knife package message fervid jolts ohm
        first afferent brilliant kerchief surd
        prevailed askance hovering; placid imp
        attic incensing sea eagle tabard on
        shingle uncle castanet, stonechat
Catapault estimate corundum integers
valiant pursuivant draught hoist earnestly
mistle facile awkward gibberish. Gibbon own
floatation cuticle eventual marcasite crumb
        cinnamon whimbrel wrangle velvet
        concision, scriptorium ivory painted
        nautical mastery enlisted; attack
        florid bird's foot trefoil condiment ice
Penguin tortoise-shell openly further other
bangle rustle sacristan rissole integument
candlestick alluvial cannibal, fluster candid
settlement prized alternate ornamental
        skillet flight. Shallots limerick
        crumble oval silver implicit at
        scrimshaw deterred licence eye-
        lash wink; pellucid intended or
Flamingo slice mango corroded aspirin bruise
stealth bandage either plaster muscle oars
musical liberal amassed pierce. Esteem in
sustenance briskly necklace aspersion lesion
        glimpse anneal usually took up,
        pandemic trusted formidable an
        agreement hatch, brimming dash
        crisp mercantile python socket.
Wooden tempest royal invigorated pinches
goldeneye tidal clatter, cigar porcelain abstain
steerage porridge groove further amethystine;
listening hasten curtain ingrained crowned.

## Gruesome Fissures

Sufficient easing anticipated summative indignant floe
sugary acrostic each birch, inference however prancing
fiery torted lull malcontent; pontiff evenly dibble alum
customary epidote carrots flat-walk, plentiful tame

liminal grove speculum anew. Dissentient harbour
energy giant planets clematis acerbic climactic eels
intended forasmuch twelfth resume; enrichment

parakeet mincemeat probable oval symbolic instated
avian discretion matrix, arrival autumnal carnival
gallivant portended richlier scented; gossamer kitchen

parquet adipose croquet, reversal objection 'Past and
future are entirely symmetric', volumes in parallel
broken condign commission, faction subtracted wilder
by condensed matter crevice. This best open harvest:

'Probability is a predicted relative frequency' (M.
Drieschner); otherwise start later beyond uppermost
angular moment leverage, temper average price
threshold in subsequent concentric following

assertoric redundancy. Travertine overland on
gastric severance moreover plumage, astilbe royal
porcelain minimum dentine sizar corsair flit
zeolite. Pemmican mercaptan optimum heather

mirror discovery, evident sentimental grapefruit
snake-charm; 'time is the glue and the clue in sol-
ving this problem'... 'However, the brain does not
operate in an empty space' (Ruhnau).

Correlating chlorophyll fuel mildew loyalist, remember
subtended enhancement livid beehive fleece shoal
canopy, syntagma phonemic rowan. Replete by
nacre invested, window listed, reptile allusive.

## Swish Parish

Caustic divested assume customary
fungible accelerate potato aggro meld
          foil canopy impress cost-free
          building fanciful growth each
                              tamarisk sluice
                              verdant posset
                    gimlet headlight oval wont
                    cravat discreet annex eel
          dropping swoop ankle uncle
          crystal obligate amethyst vice
                    smattering uncoiled bacon
                    sentient incidental ladled
          insistent contrivance avoidance
          massive phonation silage avail
assenting evident provoked crimped
colonial lustration selected binary
                              eagerly felt-tip
          swish parish majestic cant
          hornet latterly connected at
                              soup leaping kid
          alchemical quick preening dial
          timid allocate tumid dendrite
                              lentil febrile
most taste tabulate furnace ice
at chapter next teapot privilege
                              cornice enticed
          soap enteric allergic prawn
          phantom squill sawdust east
                              distraught cell
                              skirmishing
          latch affecting too bank occupy
          tonsil toenail rissole why solemn
                              seldom lesson
upshot shallot hooter height incident
tight ensue conductance persist foist
          freight lightsome own spoon
          criminal gastric gallant bristles.

## Morbid Caravan

Furthermore incarnadine pronominal guttural tab
wrench interminable nutation; disputed breccia cave
investment farcical corymb disjunctive, asymptote cud
libation conduit
terminal pundit
scratched profess
insignificance
earlier bandage forestry
latency incriminated so
tantamount oligarchic;
vibrating infused
out session caution
grimace intensive,
docile crucible win
contest lid
salve crane
frolic; absent
birch coruscating in
sparkle doubtlessly
formidable
adept neap,
pax convex
dithyrambic
alkanet fretty sip
ostensible; runcible
would paramount invitation
avian pinion stipulate ampule
lethargic morbid caravan foreigner
candytuft. Crescent lunation habitation
average discovery, newt ready
aspect corrective magpies
annoys; lairs concealment
aggrieved parakeet
fitch porch wing-span.
Yet placid honied
obstreperous
indigenous too
fetlock naphtha
threadbare jawbone, vestige
celandine aromatic sonata on
mordant climatic basilisk evenly
awkward imminent entreat
faction alight constraint.

## Lupin Fossil

*'Dicentra spectabilis "Valentine" Bleeding Heart'*

Oceanic deltoid denied upward
dolomite cowslip tight dissident
tantamount sacrosanct kneecap
immaculate
interflight dupe
cursitory inconsistency might
fascinate waspish pilfer zero
erstwhile aback
moribund moonshine beetroot
grimace contest spruce shadow in
bargain herewith
handsome dwindled verified
abacus taken rife aback too
selfhood elastic flit harpoon kin
refunded anarchic polar spoon
urn granulate plighted funnel
lupin fossil trenchant one
momentum fringe
signalise caramel dowel ancient
pursuit diagonal reversionary
cockatrice tapestry elegant
planetary nettle floret vent
mitre weaponise
advisement concision
red kite level travel ensign tame
index flame column autumnal
functional heathland cryptic
capsize purchase orchard
flotilla scholar till
small change sensorium
ensued welded convoke
twice yoke spoke
ligation torsion date-palm
trample awesome fortunate.

## Mainstay Osprey

Tilting willing formica elegantly onions, igloo bugle
mortal scansion respite hospitable pythoness crisp
impassioned; galleon doubloon affirm canteen
        leverage, punctual thimble stumble to
        wend sprinkle conscience infancy same
raisons extended hydraulic therapeutic appliance
frighten frigate; scrimmage loosely management
complicity immersion, friction plumage indented on
        fraction azalea groom tambourine lofty
        myrtle hawthorn burden lingual split;
actionable disambiguate conversion function
fumigate wrangle, mainstay osprey lit. Boon
probate quarts limbeck catamaran, sprain
        imagine retort engine foreign teeming
        stonechat impervious; cradle eagle for
mutton tangle uncle daybreak, aspect annex
cooling weather tower curtain pastime ovals
previous nearby. District distraught patiently
        bearded fledging mustard cantata boiled
        redpoll, acrid sibling gambling fumble
coronary, alight. Flamboyant stoke fracks
speck brambling, flocks molluscs wellhead at
water-logged instead; graphite critical mischief
        lateral watchful turnip conniption by
        acupuncture, lock-tight affric turtles
gastric dangle or mingle autumnal condign
turbine; libation merciful conjoined tickle
military positive elation suffixation bravery
        honeycomb entrance infancy. Divers
        rivals contested masked occiput pits
fluorine, eglantine kidney feverish orris-
root waist capture furthermore oiled
reticent buttercup portent invested sup
        grimace hosted stables pitchfork off
        sampler nuisance mostly caravan.

## Stitchwort Daylight

So fingal near adamant alpha bell-rope, when
sunken welcome interval; jewel critical invested
creamery at aviary trombone meadowland sill.
          Cornerstone immersed catapault over
          leverage mounded frigate back frighten
          scornful echo minnow, silvered platen
agitate redeeming heronry swept crimp downfall;
gauge parallel gravel orchard yet pilchard willing
to blazon amazement filtrate. Licence at fend
          to aligned tendency morrow newt bite
          liquescent polyvalent ascriptive, occupy
          toyland singular at wrist canal candle
attested notary clary mincemeat grist ache
confusing redstart accurate condign oats
porridge merged amusing cribbage brows
          dilatory; stitchwort daylight pinch
          orphan missionary ahead, spills
          mandate teasel manganese toes
liquid at first. Rise at notice promised
quickthorn spendthrift, larynx whence
neumes organic freight replete; sharp
          efficient castanet alight flickers
          doorway turn-key languid oval
          jettison overboard. Scruple myrtle
ostensive profusion careworn against
shoehorn, earwig cancelled undertow
high tide afloat; grievous furtive ice
          cake slice ahead of ever after caramel
          watch-tower roller towel patches
          catching to swoop time advance
custom granary culinary. Adversary
buckle acumen fustian attic cryptic
allowed arisen permission, infusion.

## Mascot Too Fraction

Over the doorjamb elected freight
perversely luminal sailing, volume agent foliar
gravid allergy celery mantissa; borrowing burdensome
cortisone rhapsodic geodesic, clarkia pigmy owl
coralline binnacle hospice leverage foe
liverwort counteract mastic kapok, peahen on
awkward filbert trilemma sentinel
liquescent missionary assembly intricacy sips;
prudential anthill ingested inviolate, gesticulate banner
overthrown pleach hawthorn new-born garrison
retorted. Plumbago donation win
criminal porcelain lapse obduracy, disturbed
citric lawfully suited mammoth successive intern
plainsong tanglewood, peppermint jovial angle
coracle spillikins chastised copperas
complicity. Providential allusive superlative opening
foretaste hastily; insufficiency swarf courtesy
allegory mid-winter semblancy auk
diluvial kernel irriguous mastoid incessant timid
crescent, mascot too fraction imperfect
weather broken cinnabar solenoid walrus fervency
bracket penguin agaric dissipated,
climate clematis spurry sorrowful hazardous if
dolphin plasmid entrenched; smoke invidiously
trench haddock filigree legacy division,
vagrant loosen cambium travail skittish adduce
perfume trachea butter serpentine precious ocular
ridiculous turf spurious avenging fortress, at
cress canvas needles imp measles to
mensuration. Tympanum liquorice collops oil
elective costive trumpery, lamp chop crater galena
digitise dacoit attested porcupine
evening preening; crank languid furtively
hawkweed bother tiger candles winkles eutectic
strappado lurking, dentation grapple supple
trunion eukaryote alight byte
hi-tech sneezewort master plenitude fluorite.

## Bittern Invention

Fortune perfume condition assumption, gym
gustation pontoon; formative
filigree discrepant commentary out
irate cretic fantastic looted
liquid won-ton flamingo choice battery porch
stirrup loiter lobster agreement; bolstered
atonement divergent coinage fleece golden fun
condiment quartzite address forest plastic
stupendous rusticate obsidian. Oak
aggregate proliferate procurement, satchels
hoopoe whoopee instigate rufous twice; ominous
purposeful purple welcome truthful, leaden
foreign avuncular missionaries
surprising earwigs probable; leniency coreopsis
marble streaks. Frighten portion intern
scribble rictus disguise drains
example chalk white hairstreak lichen,
cymbal angular fasten rapids syllable crescent
executive suspicion; most spill
equal overthrown cornucopia necklace fuss
dimity obliquity divergency ovoids
detergency pangolin triangular sensation,
twayblade escapade grill pyrite tassel teasel ink
succulence; providence hankering for
bickering sensible infancy luminous zealous crib
doorway archaic sylvan spontaneously
measly allowance; fruits stomach
sumac gingko pneumatic intrinsic obligatory
illusory rival dual bittern invention. Dative is
furious estimate, licence impugn
lockjaw teetering asplenium delphinium
wharfage thrush allegro contango
ostensible frangible, nocturnal oval
weigh pacify terror candour upper condor; purge
haven portage refuge slipper
clatter remedy. Agrimony syntexis
voluble swarm contested sleek stealthy strain.

## Helium Nightshade

Taxon into fixative banish active
tarpaulin mullein instigated slate
sedative rumour camphor, grandeur ordeal polygon
phlox extravagant, blade rolling fission crocus whet
billhook untwisted; macaroni insidious reckless
fantastic hawk-moth plumage, zircon
larkspur porphyry aggravated insole; seedling
hillside monkshood sioux debonair sparkle ilk.
Ruminant sainthood looms
balcony inspected remainder, onyx
leather breather fastening trumpet; deliver
mothlight panic incessantly
guillemot accident splinter mid-winter price
edelweiss enticement, rugged perfervid
merchant portion fortune lotion
phantom crackle orchid motionless. Auk
plight overt castanet customary pi
allegory servitude, whale oil
gale force twice comb reticent; captious lambasts
walrus dormant frontal emu
helium nightshade heavy-leaden open paw.
New fire umpire cobra spindles
laburnum suddenly ruthenium, confession
suspension alkaline vigil hurtle two
blazer reduction suspicion;
raising endorsement currency pungent wilt
alabaster toolkit. Ahead doorway stair level betel
chosen crimson urgent, fashion
licence business pulverated
dianthus azurite swallowtail avails
napery hanker polychrome lawful bale
idiotic explained replevin.
Assorted purchase acrostic spillage removing twin
oaken acorn deign, coinage dissenting age
luscious algae alignment; notary
public volunteer raven ruin
scramble tinfoil vapid antiquated caravan
delighted, yellow turbid reopen arrangement tight.
Indusium sentinel garnet fleet
fuel fluellen weed woodlark mighten.

## Hoopoe Hazel

Voting pledge inference harebell foibles
candid forehead torrid footstep crescent foxglove
catch the sun cloudscape; top speed later found tip
fleeting ambush linear soluble distraint moonrise ate,
        super onrush eschewed fork punnet went. Gypsum
        chromate roused headline iodine wound lovage porridge
        partridge pear tree aware flower spindle; treasure
trove hive livery oven bees in honey comb tongue bright.
Grapefruit grateful fluorite slighted gemstone.
Adornment recension planet howl infantile web
tissue mortal frantic prefect lurking invisibility
        fantail abasement creel, insistently folded
        contusion broker flamboyant urgently deal
        resiled agency. Birch torch puce seepage
customise laser surmise novel inflation earn
accountable habitually minted, chequered front
oracle fertile mercantile pigeon-hole amended.
        Corbel footfall syndic arrogant woodpecker
        plastic mystical starlight currency, invited
        transparency hawkweed distraught assert.
Rivalry confident profligate crocus saffron corm
exacting vengeance smitten internment escapade
prodigious fetch bunker anchorage clandestine zoom
        august pitcher alkanet perverse script condign
        intimation gradient crucial parcel mercy
        frieze contusion invaded violet marchpane.
Hoopoe hazel blanket twelve subversion oblate
carrageen infirm skirmish apatite contritional
opaline coastline zeugma convergence timepiece if
        else passage resisted climate affected gravity
        wouldn't affray troy ounce defiance brokerage
        breeze average licence fulmar petrel chin.
Liverwort discount mascot incipit bracket gabbro
olivine amber citrine, cinnabar offertory
linctus praiseworthy cordite apart silted shore.

# APPENDICES

# BIBLIOGRAPHY

This book is a supplementary volume to the author's *Poems* (Bloodaxe Books, third edition, 2015) including the corrected texts of 36 collections written since that edition, and published between 2017 and April 2024. With the exception of minor corrections and revisions, the texts presented here largely appear according to their original first (or in the case of the expanded *Of Better Scrap*, first complete) printings, apart from in the case of *At Raucous Purposeful*, which more closely follows the text of the extensively revised and corrected second edition (Face Press, 2023). More substantial revisions, including the deletion of a small number of poems that the author does not wish to preserve, have been made to the texts of *Each to Each* (2017), *Of Better Scrap* (2019), *Athwart Apron Snaps* (2021), and *At Raucous Purposeful* (2022/23).


*Each to Each* (Equipage, Cambridge, 2017).
*OF · THE · ABYSS* (Materials, Cambridge, 2017).
*Or Scissel* (Shearsman Books, Bristol, 2018).
*Of Better Scrap* (Face Press, Cambridge, 2019; 2nd edition, expanded and corrected, October 2019); 'To Them' was included on a separate sheet in both editions (in the first printing due to its later date of composition; in the second by deliberate choice), and loosely inserted at the beginning of the text sequence. It is incorporated here accordingly.
*None Yet More Willing Told* (Face Press, Cambridge, 2019).
*Parkland* (Critical Documents, Cambridge, 2019).
*Bitter Honey* (Broken Sleep Books, Talgarreg, 2020).
*Squeezed White Noise* (Face Press, Cambridge, 2020).
*Enchanter's Nightshade* (Face Press, Cambridge, 2020).
*Memory Working: Impromptus* (Face Press, Cambridge, 2020-21); originally published in three instalments: *Impromptus I-X* (2020); *Impromptus XI-XVII* (2020); *Impromptus XVIII-XXVI* (2021).
*Her Air Fallen* (Critical Documents, Cambridge, 2020).

*The Fever's End* (Critical Documents, Cambridge, 2020).
*Passing Grass Parnassus* (Face Press, Cambridge, 2020).
*Aquatic Hocquets* (Face Press, Cambridge, 2020).
*Kernels in Vernal Silence* (Face Press, Cambridge, 2020).
*Torrid Auspicious Quartz* (Face Press, Cambridge, 2020).
*See By So* (Face Press, Cambridge, 2020).
*Duets Infer Duty* (Face Press, Cambridge, 2020).
*Orchard* (Equipage, Cambridge, 2020).
*Otherhood Imminent Profusion* (Critical Documents, London, 2021).
*Presume Catkins* (Broken Sleep Books, Talgarreg, 2021).
*Athwart Apron Snaps* (Slub Press, Seoul, 2021).
*Efflux Reference* (Face Press, Cambridge, 2021).
*Dune Quail Eggs* (Face Press, Cambridge, 2021).
*Lay Them Straight* (Face Press, Cambridge, 2021).
*Shade Furnace* (Critical Documents, Cambridge, 2021).
*Snooty Tipoffs* (Face Press, Cambridge, 2021).
*Sea Shells Told* (Face Press, Cambridge, 2022).
*At Raucous Purposeful* (Face Press, Cambridge, 2023) [which corrects and augments the text of the earlier Broken Sleep Books edition (Talgarreg, 2022)].
*Latency of the Conditional* (Face Press, Cambridge, 2022).
*Not Ice Novice* (Face Press, Cambridge, 2022).
*At the Monument* (Face Press, Cambridge, 2022).
*Foremost Wayleave* (Face Press, Cambridge, 2023).
*Hadn't Yet Bitten* (Face Press, Cambridge, 2023).
*Timepiece in Total* (Face Press, Cambridge, 2024).
*Alembic Forest* (Face Press, Cambridge, 2024).

# INDEX OF TITLES OR FIRST LINES

FSC
www.fsc.org
MIX
Paper | Supporting responsible forestry
FSC® C007785